D0604484

Inquiry:
The Key to
Exemplary Science

507.1
Y10

Inquiry:
The Key to
Exemplary Science

Edited by Robert E. Yager

LIBRARY ST. MARY'S COLLEGE

press
National Science Teachers Association
Arlington, Virginia

WITHDRAWN
ST. MARYS COLLEGE LIBRARY

National Science Teachers Association

Claire Reinburg, Director
Jennifer Horak, Managing Editor
Judy Cusick, Senior Editor
J. Andrew Cocke, Associate Editor
Betty Smith, Associate Editor

ART AND DESIGN, Will Thomas, Jr., Director

PRINTING AND PRODUCTION, Catherine Lorrain, Director

NATIONAL SCIENCE TEACHERS ASSOCIATION
Francis Q. Eberle, PhD, Executive Director
David Beacom, Publisher

Copyright © 2009 by the National Science Teachers Association.
All rights reserved. Printed in the United States of America.
11 10 09   4 3 2 1

LIBRARY OF CONGRESS CATALOGING-IN-PUBLICATION DATA
Inquiry : the key to exemplary science / edited by Robert Yager.
     p. cm.
  Includes index.
  ISBN 978-1-935155-04-1
  1. Science—Study and teaching—United States. 2. Science teachers—Training of. 3. Inquiry-based learning. I.
Yager, Robert Eugene, 1930-
  Q183.3.A1I586 2009
  507.1--dc22
                          2008052430

NSTA is committed to publishing quality materials that promote the best in inquiry-based science education. However, conditions of actual use may vary and the safety procedures and practices described in this book are intended to serve only as a guide. Additional precautionary measures may be required. NSTA and the author(s) do not warrant or represent that the procedure and practices in this book meet any safety code or standard or federal, state, or local regulations. NSTA and the author(s) disclaim any liability for personal injury or damage to property arising out of or relating to the use of this book including any recommendations, instructions, or materials contained therein.

PERMISSIONS

You may photocopy, print, or e-mail up to five copies of an NSTA book chapter for personal use only; this does not include display or promotional use. Elementary, middle, and high school teachers *only* may reproduce a single NSTA book chapter for classroom- or noncommercial, professional-development use only. For permission to photocopy or use material electronically from this NSTA Press book, please contact the Copyright Clearance Center (CCC) (*www.copyright.com*; 978-750-8400). Please access *www.nsta.org/permissions* for further information about NSTA's rights and permissions policies.

Contents

The Centrality of Inquiry for Teaching and Learning Science

Robert E. Yager
University of Iowa

*I*nquiry has become a revered term in science education. It is central to the National Science Education Standards (NSES) as a form of content as well as a way to teach (i.e., having a curriculum component as well as describing more desirable teaching strategies). Further, the term *inquiry* is something nearly all persons accept—perhaps blindly or without careful thought. Desirability and lack of fault may make it important and attainable; unfortunately though, it is often accomplished by mere proclamation. Most textbooks, curriculum frameworks, teaching activities, and government agencies (local, state, and national) claim to provide avenues for achieving and experiencing inquiry. Perhaps clarification of the term is needed; perhaps the term has too many forms, too many levels, too many uses, and too many different functions to be meaningful as reforms are sought in science education.

The NSES refer to inquiry throughout the 262-page document (NRC 1996). In addition, a supplementary monograph was published four years after the release of the Standards (NRC 2000). The 202-page companion to the NSES illustrates the deemed importance assigned to the term. Bruce Alberts, President of the National Academy of Science, offered analyses that indicated a needed elaboration of inquiry; in the foreword of the new inquiry monograph he says:

Inquiry is in part a state of mind—that of inquisitiveness. Most young children are naturally curious. They care enough to ask "why" and "how" questions. But if adults dismiss their incessant questions as silly and uninteresting, students can lose this gift of curiosity. Visit any second-grade classroom and you will generally find a class bursting with energy and excitement, where children are eager to make new observations and try to figure things out. What a contrast with many eighth-grade classes, where the students so often seem bored and disengaged from learning and from school! (NRC 2000, p. xii)

The challenge for all who want to improve education is to create an educational system that exploits the natural curiosity of children so that they maintain their motivation for learning not only during their school years but throughout life. Alberts asserted further that we need to convince teachers and parents of the importance of children's "why" questions. He was reminded of the profound effect that Richard Feynman's father had on his development as a scientist. One summer, in the Catskill Mountains of New York when Feynman was a boy, another boy asked him, "See that bird. What kind of bird is that?" Feynman, answered "I haven't the slightest idea." The other boy replied, "Your father doesn't teach you anything!" But his father had taught Feynman about the bird—though in his own way. As Feynman recalls his father's words:

"See that bird? It's a Spencer's warbler." (I knew he didn't know the real name.)

"You can know the name of that bird in all the languages of the world, but when you're finished, you'll know absolutely nothing whatever about the bird. You'll only know about humans in different places and what they call the bird. So let's look at the bird and see what it's doing—that's what counts." (NRC 2000, p. xiv)

Alberts argues that the inquiry process must begin in kindergarten and continue, with age-appropriate challenges, at each grade level. He writes, "Students must be challenged but also rewarded with the joy of solving a problem with which they have struggled. In this way, students recognize that they are capable of tackling harder and harder problems. As they acquire the tools and habits of inquiry, they see themselves learn. There can be nothing more gratifying, or more important, in science education." (NRC 2000, p. xiv)

Inquiry was chosen as the theme for the sixth Exemplary Science Program (ESP) monograph because of its centrality to how science is defined and to illustrate various ways inquiry can be approached. It is not another textbook, a platform for teaching at all K–12 levels, a set of clever activities, or a new kit full of explicit and precise directions for teachers who may be willing to try them. Many nominations for inclusion in this monograph centered on materials and use of prepared lessons. Many provided no evidence of program impacts and successes. The various chapters *do* include ideas, show relationships to the NSES goals, and illustrate the *More Emphasis* situations that summarize each chapter concerning the acts of teaching, the nature of needed professional development of teachers, the elaboration of the essential features of inquiry, the nature of the total curriculum framework, and the systems of needed support and structure. All of these can be used to illustrate the centrality of the learner for understanding and using inquiry.

The table "Essential Features of Classroom Inquiry" (NRC 2000, p. 29) was shared with all persons and programs nominated for inclusion in this monograph. This table indicates levels of variations of use of inquiry in indicating degree of self-direction for students and the quantity of directions from teachers and/or provided by the instructional materials used. Although these five "essential features" are included in several chapters, they appear below to illustrate the framework we used in our search for exemplary programs that illustrate these features, and the degree in which each is teacher- or student-centered:

- Learner engages in scientifically oriented questions.
- Learner gives priority to evidence in responding to questions.
- Learner formulates explanations from evidence.

- Learner connects explanations to scientific knowledge.
- Learner communicates and justifies explanations.

The National Advisory Board for the Exemplary Science series pushed for as much student-centeredness and use of inquiry in every aspect of the program outlines as possible. This included all the organizational frameworks for the NSES, focus on the four goals for teaching science, the nine ways science teaching should be defined, the need for continuing teacher education, the nature of appropriate assessments, and the specific content exemplifying inquiry. Many nominations and initial outlines were rejected and others withdrawn when authors reflected on the features indicated as essential.

Each facet of the NSES begins with an elaboration of the eight features of science content that are recognized and advocated. The first of these eight was discussed as a general preamble to each facet—but there was fear that too many would merely look at the listed features and not even consider the one that was offered as most important. It remains the one left out of most attempts or Pathways to NSES, to current lives, to activities, to assessments. In another sense this first one is designed to illustrate all features of inquiry. This first form of content is the "unification of science concepts and processes." It is recommended that this must be done in context—not allowing individual content to deal exclusively with important concepts of science or a focus on process skills. Such a program was first developed as *Science: A Process Approach* (SAPA) (American Association for the Advancement of Science [AAAS] 1968) and recommended for K–8 schools in the late 1960s. Traditionally such a two-pronged view of science consisting of concepts and processes does not help with science learning or the meeting of any of the student goals. Concepts taught merely as definitions and processes taught as isolated skills are rarely successful for anything other than for students to remember as prescribed and used as assessments of their "learning." But, such tests rarely are accurate measures of real learning.

The first of the four goals also is another way of looking at an inquiry focus. For some this first goal is the one that should be given the most effort and attention; it is argued by some that it should represent 50% of the focus for a given K–12 science course. This goal calls for every student (every year) to experience the richness and excitement of knowing about and understanding the natural world. This experience and excitement comes from students who are involved with the five essential features of inquiry. The first and most important of these is starting with student questions, which serve to indicate their curiosities. Curiosity is something all humans have. Unfortunately it tends to disappear the longer students study science in school. Albert's opening statement that "Inquiry is in part a state of mind" illustrates well this first aspect of experiencing inquiry phenomena.

The NSES goals also call for science for meeting daily and personal challenges—again focusing on student-centered instruction that can be used in and outside of school. A third goal calls for students working on school, community, state, national, and/or world problems (e.g., environment, energy, weather, or health hazards). The fourth and last goal focuses on awareness and understanding of possible careers in science and/or technology. Inquiry can be a focus for meeting all four goals.

This look at inquiry also assumes a common view of both science and technology, in terms of the exemplars and those who will learn from them. Several exciting new programs, as well as several reform efforts undertaken over the past half century, have considered the history and philosophy of science. These considerations are again included as one of the eight facets of science content included in the NSES. None of the best efforts at meeting this goal have resulted in many changes, other than defining a desired curriculum and then expecting teachers to use it. Such efforts to deal with the meaning and history of science are often portrayed as exhibiting inquiry.

At times, scientists and science educators have tried to standardize and outline in general terms a definition for the human activity called science. One of the most influential scientists in the United States was G. G. Simpson, who proclaimed science to be "the exploration of the material universe with attempts to explain the objects and events encountered—keeping in mind that the explanations offered must be testable" (1963, p. 81). Many use these attributes to identify the precise aspects of the activities characterizing the explanations proposed and the evidence produced and/or available to support the possible explanations offered. This sequence is sometimes characterized with the following five steps:

- formulating questions about the objects and events found/observed in the natural world;
- offering explanations for the objects and events encountered (hypotheses formation);
- testing for the validity of explanations offered;
- communicating the results to others; and
- confirming that the results are compatible with "established" views or that they represent new understandings and theories not previously known, proposed, nor accepted.

These features of science also define the major aspects of inquiry. Some argue that the results are more important and better indicators of learning if the results can be used in new contexts and by other people. But, too often students are never expected to propose such uses; some teachers spend much time suggesting other contexts in test items, which represent possible contexts the teachers identify, not something students are expected to do.

There have been attempts to move school science beyond science known and practiced by scientists. There have been attempts to unite science with the field of technology—unlike the efforts in the late 1950s and early 1960s, which sought to remove technology from science and relegate it to "the shop" and designate it as appropriate for non–college bound students. But newer programs have tried to reverse this and recognize that technology—that is, focus on the design world—is seen by most people as more interesting, useful, and product-oriented than pure science. The major difference between science and technology is that one has to accept the natural world as it is found in science endeavors. When it comes to technology, though, the answer is always known, as we use phenomena and explanations from the natural world (science) to develop devices seen as useful to human existence. The differences remain, but the domains and activities characterizing both are intertwined. In some ways schools do a disservice to treat them as separate.

Many attempt to explain inquiry, often varying views of it, to develop inquiry activities, and/or to specify Scientific inquiry (always with a capitol "S") all for intended use in casting science as inquiry—but accomplished and directed by teachers. These are teacher-driven efforts to encourage greater learning for understanding especially for the most "gifted." Others (e.g., Eastwell 2007) try to define types of inquiry as confirmational, structured, guided, and/or open.

Others have proposed adjectives like "coupled" or "full." All of these raise questions about the real need for modifiers before using the term *inquiry*. Such attempts to specify differences raise issues about grade levels, past experiences, interests, choices for use, relative importance, and specific procedures for meeting any of the four NSES goals offered for teaching science.

Paul Hurd (1978), one of the most prolific and informed science educators in the United States, caused quite a stir when he offered the following statement about inquiry:

> *The development of inquiry skills as a major goal of instruction in science appears to have had only a minimal effect on secondary school teaching. The rhetoric about inquiry and process teaching greatly exceeds both the research on the subject and the classroom practice. The validity of the inquiry goal itself could profit from more scholarly interchange and confrontation even if it is simply to recognize that science is not totally confined to logical processes and data-gathering. (p. 62)*

Perhaps this monograph will serve to illustrate various forms of inquiry while also beginning the effort to back up such impressive examples in terms of planning and execution—with actual assessment of the effectiveness of the programs in terms of student learning, development of more positive attitudes, and actual abilities of students to use concepts and skills in completely new situations.

Carl Sagan (1998) has written that everyone starts out as scientists; i.e., full of questions about the objects and events around them. A uniqueness of humans is not only curiosity, but the desire to satisfy it. All humans do it; e.g., poets, musicians, artists, and religious leaders. And, of course, scientists do it too! But the uniqueness is that in science the proposed answers/explanations must be accompanied by evidence concerning their validity. The evidence must be used to convince others (the science establishment) that the explanations are accurate ones. When this is accomplished, the information can be used and becomes a part of the framework for the inquirer. It is interesting to note the changes in perceptions and understandings over time. Studying the history of science can be a fine way to understand science as well as inquiry.

All students come to places called schools with many experiences. Perhaps too many are willing to believe teachers, parents, grandparents, or friends for satisfying their curiosities too quickly, or without questioning and the actual gathering of evidence for the answers they offer. In schools, teachers are always right! But, why do schools not take advantage of curiosities, personal explanations, and use them to illustrate science itself? Instead, we tend to give our students the explanations and language used by professionals. If they know terms, do they know science? Many students only know definitions with no real context or meaning or potential use. This is related to the Feynman point about naming birds, included earlier in this introduction. We are trapped into being transmitters of the known and fail to approach dealing with the unknown. We tend to short-cut the process of science itself. We are poor at collecting our own evidences for the validity of personally offered ideas.

Do we really need to expand on the simple definition for inquiry? Do we need to do more than to encourage our students to question, to explore, and to provide evidence for the validity of the explanations offered, and to share the evidence and thinking with others? Do we all understand science as a form of personal inquiry? Do the Exemplars described in the following chapters provide platforms for raising more questions? I hope so!

Feynman (1985) has written that science consists of persons called scientists who deal with three foci that define science in other ways. These include persons who (1) deal with the things that they know they don't know (this is where most practicing scientists work), (2) deal with the things they "know" that are not so (often very difficult to identify), and (3) deal with the things that they do not even know that they don't know (an impossibility). Perhaps this is a view of science that science educators should consider more. Instead, we want to teach students to follow directions (directly or guided) or to "confirm" what they are told or read about to be true. We do not question textbooks, kits, labs, or curricula that are labeled as "inquiries." Are we good models of inquiry in our own views of teaching? Should we profess less and participate more in questioning, explaining, and testing explanations for validity? Why do we leave our students with fewer questions after our instruction than before real science experiences begin? Why do we not care more about the fact that students are less curious after instruction than before and have more negative views of science, science careers, and science teachers? Let's continue to listen, to encourage, and to support thinking and curiosity that characterize inquiry and science itself. Perhaps one of the problems is that too few science teachers have even had a full experience with science themselves! How many view science teaching as a form of science?

In one sense, inquiry can be used as a synonym for science. Both include starting with questions, collecting evidence concerning the explanations offered, and arguing with others about the validity of the explanations. Science is a continuing quest for better understanding of the natural universe. This quest is inquiry! This quest for exemplars has led to this sixth Exemplary Science Program Monograph in the NSTA series. Those of us involved with reviewing submissions have been impressed—but still full of questions and anxious to learn of the next iterations. We will also be interested in the reactions of the authors as they continue to share their experiences at NSTA conferences. We expect all to continue to grow, to change, and to enjoy inquiry teaching more each year. We encourage teachers of every school grade level as well as those at colleges to continue to improve and make the process a basic ingredient of teaching and to recognize teaching a part of what defines science itself.

References

American Association for the Advancement of Science (AAAS). 1968. *Science: A process approach.* Washington, DC: Author.

Eastwell, P. 2007. More on inquiry. *The Science Education Review* 6 (4): 139–142.

Feynman, R. P. 1985. *Surely you're joking, Mr. Feynman.* New York: Bantam.

Hurd, P. DeH. 1978. The golden age of biological education 1960–1975. In *BSCS biology teacher's handbook, 3rd edition,* ed. W. V. Mayer, 28–96. New York: John Wiley & Sons.

National Research Council (NRC). 1996. *National science education standards.* Washington, DC: National Academy Press.

National Research Council (NRC). 2000. *Inquiry and the national science education standards: A guide for teaching and learning.* Washington, DC: National Academy Press.

Sagan, C. 1998. *Every child a scientist: Achieving scientific literacy for all.* Washington, DC: National Academy Press.

Simpson, G. G. 1963. Biology and the nature of science. *Science* 139 (3550): 81–88.

Acknowledgments

Members of the National Advisory Board for the Exemplary Science Series

Lloyd H. Barrow
Professor
University of Missouri
Columbia, MO 65211

Bonnie Brunkhorst
Past President of NSTA
Professor
California State University—
San Bernardino
San Bernardino, CA 92506

John Falk
Professor
Oregon State University
Corvallis, OR 97331

Linda Froschauer
Retiring NSTA President
K–5 Math/Science Curriculum
Instructional Leader
Weston Public Schools
Weston, CT 06883

Steve Henderson
Professor
University of Kentucky
Lexington, KY 40506

Bobby Jeanpierre
Associate Professor
University of Central Florida
Orlando, FL 32816

Janice Koch
Professor
Hofstra University
Hempstead, NY 11549

LeRoy R. Lee
Executive Director
Wisconsin Science Network
4420 Gray Road
De Forest, WI 52532-2506

Shelley A. Lee
Science Education Consultant
WI Dept. of Public Instruction
PO Box 7842
Madison, WI 53707-7841

Donald McCurdy
Professor Emeritus
University of Nebraska-Lincoln
Lincoln, NE 68588-0355

Edward P. Ortleb
Science Consultant/Author
5663 Pernod Avenue
St. Louis, MO 63139

Michael Padilla
Associate Dean and Director
Eugene T. Moore School of
Education
Clemson University
Clemson, SC 29634-0702

Carolyn Randolph
The South Carolina Education
Association
412 Zimalcrest Drive
Columbia, SC 29210

Barbara W. Saigo
President
Saiwood Publications
23051 County Road 75
St. Cloud, MN 56301

Jon Schwartz
General Manager
Wyoming Public Radio
University of Wyoming
Laramie, WY 82071

Patricia Simmons
Professor
University of Missouri-St. Louis
One University Boulevard
St. Louis, MO 63121

Gerald Skoog
Professor
Texas Tech University
College of Education
15th and Boston
Lubbock, TX 79409-1071

Sandra West
Professor
Texas State University—San Marcos
San Marcos, TX 78666

Vanessa Westbrook
Director, District XIII
Senior Science Specialist
Charles A. Dana Center
University of Texas at Austin
Austin, TX 78722

Mary Ann Mullinnix
Assistant Editor
University of Iowa
Iowa City, Iowa 52242

About the Editor

Robert E. Yager

Robert E. Yager—an active contributor to the development of the National Science Education Standards—has devoted his life to teaching, writing, and advocating on behalf of science education worldwide. Having started his career as a high school science teacher, he has been a professor of science education at the University of Iowa since 1956. He has also served as president of seven national organizations, including NSTA, and has been involved in teacher education in Japan, Korea, Taiwan, and Europe. Among his many publications are several NSTA books, including *Focus on Excellence* and *What Research Says to the Science Teacher*. Yager earned a bachelor's degree in biology from the University of Northern Iowa and master's and doctoral degrees in plant physiology from the University of Iowa.

Inquiry at the Ocean Research College Academy (ORCA)

Ardi Kveven
ORCA at Everett Community College

Introduction

The Ocean Research College Academy (ORCA) is a full-time, dual credit, early college program designed exclusively for Washington State Running Start (juniors and seniors in high school) students. Students in ORCA are together as a cohort for two years, at the end of which they will earn an Associate's Degree in Arts and Sciences from Everett Community College and a high school diploma from their sponsoring high school. In just four years of operation, ORCA at Everett Community College has become a model of success in educational reform, particularly in the use of real-world science as the platform for inquiry-based learning. As the early college initiative garners national attention (Hoffman and Vargas 2007), ORCA's powerful teaching and learning serves as a replicable model for both community colleges and high schools, as any regional focus can provide opportunities for in-depth study and community engagement.

ORCA was initially funded with a three-year grant from the Bill and Melinda Gates Foundation. Just as inquiry is learning in context, the development of ORCA continues to be an inquiry experience for its faculty. The administrators at Everett Community College (EvCC) were willing to take a chance on a school designed from the ground up, adapting the key principles from the National Research Council's essential components of teaching and learning: active inquiry, in-depth learning, and performance assessment (NRC 2006).

ORCA is a program sought after by students and fully funded by EvCC. ORCA students choose to attend this interdisciplinary program in lieu of their high school. The ORCA early college model utilizes the Running Start funding framework. Running Start is a Washington State initiative that allows high school students to earn free community college credits. Only ORCA and one other program in Washington State use the Running Start model of dual credit leading to dual degrees to support early college initiatives. Because ORCA is not part of a school district, it has had a tremendous amount of freedom to use science as the interdisciplinary platform. The application of inquiry-based science methods of asking questions and supporting ideas with evidence permeates all ORCA classes. Critical thinking forms the basis for all coursework, challenging the students to support their ideas, make connections, and conduct extensive research in all academic disciplines.

During the planning of ORCA, founding faculty members strove for integration between non-traditionally integrated subject matter (e.g., math, English, history, and science). The faculty did not want the integration to feel contrived or forced. We struck upon quarter-long projects as the vehicle for the integration. This chapter highlights our latest work on an overarching project that students work on during their two years of ORCA: The State of Possession Sound (SOPS).

The essential features of science inquiry are the unifying theme for the learning community at ORCA. Active inquiry and place-based learning are the foundations and fulfill the key principles in the ORCA vision: a community of active, responsible, inquisitive learners who grow through rigorous and integrated studies grounded in the marine environment. At ORCA, students are continually asked to think critically, ask questions, and make connections. Courses such as college algebra, statistics, U.S. history, English composition and literature, oceanography, biology, and political science are linked whenever possible for students to connect information in one discipline with information in another discipline. By the end of their experience, all ORCA students will have earned more than 30 transferable college credits in science and math, regardless of the major they choose.

The Ocean Research College Academy (ORCA) is the school I dreamed of creating as a science educator. After 14 years of teaching five periods a day, the traditional classroom setting of 55-minute periods became stifling as I strove to implement true scientific inquiry. I took a leave of absence to write proposals to initiate this innovative early college program founded on the principle of students asking and answering their own questions in the local marine environment. As I have learned through collaboration in the development of this program, the questioning stance that I place at the heart of scientific inquiry actually permeates all disciplinary studies (e.g., mathematics, history, and literature). Now in year five of the program, ORCA is a fully funded magnet program at Everett Community College experiencing tremendous success in student learning in all content areas by applying the essential features of inquiry in all disciplines.

My desire to create a new approach to teaching science was first grounded in my own experience. In many undergraduate science courses, teaching had been telling students about science. This is how I was trained in science, but my most powerful learning opportunities stemmed from field research courses. My science teaching preparation introduced discrepant events as a way to start classes, but inquiry was not discussed. Labs were a recipe students followed. I continued this traditional "cookbook" science teaching approach, giving students a step-by-step procedure to follow with a predetermined result in mind. I found that when student experiments did not produce the expected results, they felt frustrated.

In my continued professional development and master's degree coursework, I participated in many science research experiences in the summer. The most powerful event came as a REVEL (Research, Education, Volcanoes, Exploration, Life) teacher, spending three weeks at sea as part of a research cruise to the Juan de Fuca Ridge to study hydrothermal vents. At sea, there were no step-by-step procedures to follow, the science was groundbreaking, and no one had answers, only more questions. Whatever data were gathered were the data; they were neither right nor wrong—and how data were interpreted led to further probing questions, potentially to be tested the following year.

This transformative event changed my teaching. I no longer gave students experiments with the procedure spelled out; instead, I asked them to design the procedure after making observations and inferences. My science teaching became about the processes of science, not the answers. Additionally, I discovered that it was important to support the students through a relationship-rich environment. The students would take risks and forget about what they thought was the "right" answer if they felt safe to explore, test, and deal with unexpected results in the classroom. My metamorphosis from content-driven teaching to inquiry-based teaching paralleled the development and first product published as the *National Science Education Standards*. The Bill and Melinda Gates Foundation's (BMGF) new "3 Rs" of education reform (rigor, relevance, and relationships) proved remarkably consistent with my new experiences in the classroom. Thus, a targeted grant opportunity through the BMGF provided me with the impetus to design a new school based on the data I was gathering in the classroom.

The use of real-world science and the application of student research to the local community represent well the application of the targeted *More Emphasis* features in the National Science Education Standards.

Built on a Foundation of Inquiry

According to the National Research Council (NRC), the essential features of classroom inquiry are:

1. Learners are engaged in scientifically oriented questions.

2. Learners give priority to evidence, which allows them to develop and evaluate explanations that address scientifically oriented questions.

3. Learners formulate explanations from evidence to address scientifically oriented questions.

4. Learners evaluate their explanations in light of alternative explanations, particularly those reflecting scientific knowledge.

5. Learners communicate and justify their proposed explanations. (2000, p. 25)

The State of Possession Sound (SOPS) project is deliberately scaffolded to incorporate these features. During a faculty planning retreat, we were brainstorming suggestions for interdisciplinary projects. One of the suggestions was to have the students develop a mock environmental impact statement (EIS) for the wetland near our campus. This did not integrate the oceanography course taught at ORCA in the fall and my bias for students as active learners, so I suggested boat-based work and a modified EIS. Thus, SOPS evolved. SOPS emphasizes student participation in real-world scientific monitoring. Students strive to answer the question, "What is the state of Possession Sound?" Over the course of a year, they use evidence from their research to support their ideas. The articulation of scientific knowledge by student presentations is amazing to lay and scientific audiences alike. At the end of the year, students have compiled an impressive document, justifying their explanations, which are presented to local stakeholders in the community every quarter.

In order for this project to be replicated or modified by other educators, it is important to understand the sequence of events and how the purposefulness of pushing students to ask scientific questions and then attempt to answer them (or asking more questions) unfolds.

The rigor, relevance, and relationship platform is the cornerstone of this early college program. At ORCA, students stay as a cohort working with the same core faculty and students for two years. The deliberate building of trust and pushing students to ask questions starts at the beginning of the year. In their first two days at ORCA, students attend a retreat in the field (a Puget Sound shoreline). One of their first tasks is a walkabout, during which they make and record observations about all aspects of the natural environment. At this overnight retreat there are three goals: (1) to get to know the students and for the students to get to know each other and the faculty; (2) to explore the dynamic marine environment; and (3) to introduce students to the questioning mantra at ORCA. Beginning the school year outside the classroom sets a different, more personal tone among students and teachers. It also reinforces a key goal at ORCA: Learning happens everywhere when learning is relevant and students are empowered to ask real questions (Kveven et al. 2007).

Over the course of two days, we encourage students to ask questions and take risks. There are no grades, so the stakes are not high at the retreat. During this observational period, students generate questions such as "Why is the kelp all oriented in the same direction?" "The sizes of the rocks on the beach get smaller as I walk across them . . . Why?"

Teachers model the transition from an observation such as "the anemones are in crevices in the rocks," to wondering why the anemones are in crevices and not in more open spaces, to constructing a testable research question. At this point the focus is on helping students understand the process of moving from observation to testable question and hypothesis rather than jumping to what they can or cannot actually do in the way of data measurement caused by constraints of equipment or background knowledge. Later they can look back and reflect on what makes a good testable question.

The retreat lays the foundation for the inquiry work for the rest of the year. By setting the stage for student-driven questions the first two days, we sequence and scaffold the curriculum to help students continue to explore the power of asking questions. Though we use the local marine environment as our interdisciplinary focus, really our common focus revolves around applying scientific methodology to all the disciplines (even in looking at historical documents and literature): What do you notice? What do you wonder? What's the evidence? What does it mean?

Active inquiry and place-based interdisciplinary learning are the cornerstones to the educational experience at ORCA. Consistent with the educational reform recommendations of the National Science Education Standards, students at ORCA learn through investigation in collaborative settings that emphasize field work; debate approaches and findings; investigate over extended time periods; use evidence for revising an explanation; and communicate science explanations. This is done primarily through the grassroots student-driven monitoring project called the State of Possession Sound (SOPS).

The State of Possession Sound Project

Possession Sound is an estuary located in Puget Sound, 30 miles north of Seattle in Snohomish County. Possession Sound is a highly productive and fragile ecosystem, providing habitat for extensive waterfowl, salmon, orcas, and gray whales. Home to the largest marina on the west coast, Kimberly Clark Paper Mill, and Naval Station Everett, this local watershed hosts one of the fastest growing populations in Washington State. Possession Sound currently lacks significant or consistent ecological monitoring, as there is no single government agency charged with monitoring the ecosystem health. ORCA has been ground-truthing the State of Possession Sound (SOPS) project for three years.

ORCA students study Possession Sound by boat-based research. Once a month, they spend six hours on a boat and three days in class preparing to identify problems, refine research questions, develop the methodology, and interpret the results to share with a broader audience. Initially designed as a project to blend the Oceanography 101 student-learning outcomes with active inquiry, the SOPS project has changed dramatically since its inception. This project was originally designed around the key tenets of the State of the Sound report, a document authored and published by the Puget Sound Partnership (PSP 2007). We continue to experiment with the design to ensure that all students are active participants in their own learning, constructing research ideas, evaluating data, and striving to make connections to the various intricacies that make up an estuary. Students share their results with local stakeholders and decision makers. ORCA students collect and critically analyze long-term temperature, conductivity, dissolved oxygen, nitrates, phosphates, pH, sediment distribution, turbidity, plankton presence and abundance, marine bird and marine mammal presence and abundance, and tide and current data. Research supports deeper student understanding, retention, and subsequent action when coursework is applied to genuine—rather than classroom-contrived—situations (Meyers and Jones 1993). Additionally, we strive to help students make connections that cross discipline boundaries by integrating writing as part of the SOPS project. Students also apply the skills used in mathematics (graphing, linear regression, and statistics) to their data sets.

The SOPS project is deliberately structured to quickly hone the students' newly developed questioning and science skills. Four weeks of instruction blends core course content with inquiry before students go on their first research cruise. Lab work focuses on student development of the big picture ideas surrounding oceanography: physical oceanography (waves, tides and currents), chemical oceanography (dissolved solids and gases), and biological oceanography (plankton productivity and life cycles).

An example of a lab revolving around currents starts with questions: "What is a current?" "What causes a current?" "How could we model it?" "How could we measure it?" After each question, students hypothesize and then conduct a quick think-pair-share in their lab group. The instructor focuses the discussion on density and the variables that affect density. Then, students are able to construct a mini ocean in order to experiment with making pycnoclines in a five-gallon aquarium. From the introduction in lab, students are ready to go out and test for currents on the boat.

This transition from lab to field is key to student development of the five essential features of active inquiry. The following example from one of our students highlights her transformation from a passive learner to an active learner. When on her first SOPS cruise, she found an incongruity with what she had learned. From laboratory experiments she had conducted, she understood that colder water is denser than warmer water. The ocean normally has warmer water at the surface and colder water at depth. However, at this sample station in Puget Sound, her collected samples from various depths showed the colder water layered on top of the warmer water. She was forced to grapple with this incongruity. Her data were her data—they were neither right nor wrong—but what was she to do with the information? She questioned what she knew, reflected on it, and finally was able to explain this unexpected result: Colder freshwater had flowed in from a river and layered on top of the slightly warmer and salty ocean water. Discovering this explanation on her own empowered her to continue to question, evaluate, and explain what she saw in the world around her.

One student's comments regarding the SOPS project illustrate student responses to newfound independence: "The thing I liked the most was the responsibility given to us for the State of Possession Sound Project. I enjoyed the fact that ORCA students can be given the responsibility for things like driving/navigating the vessel. It was awesome how none of the faculty took charge of where they wanted to go, but left it all for the students to work that out." Obviously, students like this one received instruction in bathymetry and rudimentary navigation, but the information did not become real until he felt the burden of responsibility for applying his new knowledge in the actual environment.

On SOPS cruises, students work in groups of five, collecting data on the boat and then synthesizing data back in the computer lab. SOPS groups discuss, "What did we get for salinity at station 1? What does it mean?" Students use a spreadsheet program to set up tables and generate graphs. All ORCA faculty participate in SOPS cruises. The mathematics instructor works collaboratively with the science instructor to help students build and analyze their graphs. As they enter numbers, they begin to look for how the measured values change in relationship to a given variable, such as depth. They have five sample locations, so there is an opportunity to compare and contrast the data trends. The graphs allow them to look for trends. Students can choose to analyze the data spatially or temporally.

These are complex data sets and can overwhelm students. However, first-year students are mentored by second-year students, who have been through the data collection and analysis previously. The second-year students teach the first-year students how to use the equipment (when to deploy, when to bring up). Also, the second-year students present their SOPS findings to first-year students prior to the first cruise in the fall. This gives first-year (11th grade) students a vision of what data collection methods look like, what data sets look like, and what an analysis of data sounds like. The English instructor blends English composition with the written component of the SOPS research as the students develop their writing styles and analytical essays and submit their best works in their English 101 portfolio.

Students Learn by Doing

The organic nature of SOPS permeates all the students do in science for the rest of the year. The skills and strategies developed over time cross traditional content boundaries and contribute to the development of the whole student. To prepare for six hours of boat-based research, each group serves like a PI on a research cruise. They nominate a group leader who is ultimately responsible for management and organization of the data and methods, putting the electronic data on the shared computer drive for all to access. Students decide what data to collect in areas of biological, physical, chemical, and geological oceanography. They design or refine protocols for data collection—what to collect, how to collect it, and how to interpret it. From this process, students learn the real world is messy and things do not always go as planned. On board the boat, students need to think on their feet and solve problems immediately. Students are in charge of the learning, such as when they forget to turn off the probe and collect tons of data and figure out what data tells about deployment. These are important unscripted events. The lesson that data are your data and what you do with them and how you interpret them is powerful. This all comes back to my experience on shipboard research and the power of using real-world science as the interdisciplinary lens at our school.

Reflection as Part of the Learning Process

The development of the skills to be part of a group is an additional outcome of this project. Students work as a collaborative group to develop a plan for the equipment needed and the data to be collected (each group determines what data they will collect). All this preparation drives toward the overarching questions, "What is the state of Possession Sound? What body of evidence can we collect to determine the oceanographic processes at work to explain what is happening in Possession Sound?" Though we have developed a long-term data set that we share with local agencies, this project tries to balance the data and inquiry, with the emphasis on the students learning about the processes of scientific inquiry. We strive to maintain the integrity of the data set, but the fact that students learn by engaging, responding, and explaining is the most important aspect. It is paramount that we ask students to think about what they are learning, how they are learning, and how we can continue to help them learn. This metacognition component is a powerful strategy adapted from NRC's *How Students Learn: History, Mathematics and Science* (2006). The power of the program is evident from the student narratives provided at the end of this chapter.

Every practitioner of inquiry has experienced moments when students think of ways to do things that we did not consider. Providing the freedom to try different experiments is imbedded in the SOPS work. For example, students have changed the plankton sampling protocol every year. The first year, organisms were counted on the boat by one individual resistant to motion sickness; she was able to count hundreds of individual plankton through a microscope on a rocking boat. This year, students developed a protocol that preserved the sample and brought it back to the lab to count, justifying their change to the previous protocol to reduce statistical bias (applying their learning of mathematics to their science).

As the students hone their questioning skills and research methodologies, the evidence they collect in the field becomes more systematic. The ability to collect, represent, analyze, and interpret data becomes the emphasis in the second and third quarters of the SOPS research. Students are using new tools, reflecting on previous strategies, and applying that conceptual understanding from the lab to field research.

Public Communication of Ideas

The collaboration through dialogue and activity among teachers and students encourages and supports the risk-taking and confidence to publicly state ideas. Students are better able to construct understanding as they socially negotiate ideas among themselves, stimulated to do so by real-world questions, and as they check their ideas with a knowledgeable instructor who provides feedback through targeted questioning. As an extra benefit, a classroom or community that values the contributions of all students is more likely to retain and attract women and minorities (Seymour and Hewitt 1997). Collaboration, not competition, fosters deep learning for all. It is not a fluke that over 70% of the students enrolled at ORCA are female. The safe environment, where everyone is a valued member of the community and contributes to and collaborates on the body of work, is a deliberately scaffolded component of ORCA.

To disseminate the research to not only students but also the local community, students prepare a poster of the quarterly SOPS research and present it initially to their first-year colleagues. Students are encouraged to give critical feedback, and because of the relationship component, students do not take it personally. This happens every Friday after a SOPS research cruise. At the end of each quarter, students then present to a community audience. The importance of a capstone event legitimizes the process, creates ownership of the data, and helps meet one of the core outcomes at ORCA: Students communicate to a variety of audiences in multiple contexts using diverse approaches.

Applying the Results of Experiments to Scientific Arguments and Explanations

We have struggled the last two years with helping students digest and analyze the data and relate it back to the holistic understanding. The two days after the cruise are dedicated to entering and analyzing data. Then, students share their findings and look for connections to other SOPS parameters. For example, is there a connection between water clarity/turbidity and substrate? Is water clarity affected by location? (One station is near the mouth of a river.) Students put up their graphs and say, "Here is what we think is going on, here is what we saw, and why we think we saw this." Then they open the floor to other groups who then draw from their data. We typically spend three hours having the students look at each other's data and make connections to their own data. Through this data debriefing, students feel a sense of ownership of the SOPS work; the students participate actively because it is their data, they generated it, it is their project, they own it. The role of the teacher is as a facilitator who pushes students to ask probing questions such as, "Why do you think there is that salinity gradient at station 5?" (Students have not mentioned the fact that the station is at the mouth of the river, so the teacher's question encourages them to analyze what affects salinity) and "Our deepest sample site is 500 feet deep (charts are in feet). No birds were seen at this site, nor mammals. Why do you think there are no birds or mammals at this site?" The instructor as facilitator helps students connect primary productivity to upwelling.

Faculty Metacognition

Each quarter, students provide anonymous written feedback on the SOPS project (see Table 1, p. 10). Our internal review of the SOPS project over the last two years revealed that students tended to be too specialized. They stayed in their group, sampling one parameter the whole year (e.g., water chemistry). Students struggled to make deeper connections with respect to the entire Possession Sound ecosystem rather than just one component of the system. This year, students will rotate and sample a different parameter each cruise. It is our hope that students will make connections across the parameters rather than just focusing on the one they studied. We are striving to push them to apply knowledge from one parameter to understanding interconnections in the system. Probing questions such as, "What conditions contribute to fine sediments occurring only in the deepest part of the Sound?" helps them address questions of connecting substrate to current rather than just connecting substrate to location. The move from description of a site (what sediments or substrate exist here) to looking for interconnections across parameters (what conditions contribute to this substrate existing here) contributes to a more complex understanding.

We also learned more about student analysis and struggles by listening to the plankton group present its findings. Though able to recognize the plankton bloom in spring and attribute it to more sunlight, students did not connect it to the material learned in cellular biology and relate it to cell division triggering population increase. This gap required us to look at instruction and be metacognitive about our own work, realizing the teacher needs to make connections between text content and field experiences.

As the only marine science focus offered in early college in the nation, ORCA is uniquely poised to disseminate the efficacy of inquiry-based student-driven experiences to the local early college network and interested educators. The data from three years of student surveys support the effectiveness of a school developed around rigor, relevance, and relationships (Table 2, p. 11). The first ORCA graduates are graduating from local and national universities. These students have used their place-based research at ORCA to further their education. One is in a paid summer internship with the Department of Energy conducting eelgrass research. Another is coauthoring a paper that stemmed from her research at ORCA on bioluminescent system responses in jellyfish. Another presented a talk at the international Environmental Monitoring and Assessment Network (EMAN) conference on his adaptation of EMAN sampling protocols to measure benthic macroinvertebrates in lakes. These snapshots of student work are indicative of the exemplary preparation ORCA students receive and illustrate the long-term impact of active inquiry.

Thus far, three cohorts of students have graduated, where 100% of enrolled students earned their high school diploma, 85% of enrolled students earned the AAS in two years and 95% transferred to universities, earning a combined $550,000 in scholarships to continue their studies in a variety of majors. All students are asked to fill out quarterly evaluations. We have learned a tremendous amount about the efficacy of the ORCA program and the work we do with SOPS. A snapshot of the questions we asked and the responses students provided are included in the following tables and lists.

Students responded to an attitudinal survey about the school they attended prior to participation. These are compared to their responses after one year at ORCA. For the results see Table 1.

Table 2 shows the results of the 10 questions on the State of Possession Sound (SOPS) evaluation instrument.

Tables 3, 4, and 5 (pp. 11–12) provide samples of student responses concerning what students like best about SOPS, what changes they would suggest, and what they learned about themselves.

Graph 1 is attached as a summary of "Strongly agree" responses to the 23 evaluation questions. The results provide evidence of the success of ORCA experiences when compared to students' opinions regarding their previous studies.

Table 1. Student Opinion Questionnaire Regarding ORCA Experiences

Administered on the first day of ORCA about the school they attended last year, and on the last day of ORCA year 1

Directions: Please rate these statements about the school you attended. Mark letter to the left of the number.

A Strongly Agree	B Agree	C Neutral	D Disagree	E Strongly Disagree
At the school I attended last year I...				
1. ...felt safe.				
2. ...felt like I belonged.				
3. ...felt challenged.				
4. ...felt like I was in charge of what I learned.				
5. ...felt successful.				
6. ...had opportunities to choose my own projects.				
7. ...had teachers who encouraged me to assess the quality of my own work.				
8. ...had teachers who prepared me well for what I want to do after high school.				
9. ...assessed my own work.				
10. ...enjoyed learning.				
11. ...did my best.				
12. ...was treated with respect by teachers.				
13. ...was treated with respect by other students.				
14. ...understood how to apply what I learned to real-life situations.				
15. ...think students had opportunities to learn from each other.				
16. ...think students had opportunities to learn about each other.				
17. ...think students respected other students who are different than they are.				
18. ...know a staff member I would feel comfortable going to with a problem.				
My teachers...				
19. ...knew me well.				
20. ...listened to my ideas.				
21. ...challenged me to do better.				
22. ...gave me individual attention when I needed it.				
23. ...helped me gain confidence in my ability to learn.				

Table 2. Results With the SOPS Evaluation Instrument

Directions for Part 1: Circle the number that most closely represents your thoughts.

1 strongly disagree, 2 disagree, 3 neutral, 4 agree, 5 strongly agree		Avg.
1. I liked experiencing real world science in the field.	1 2 3 4 5	4.5
2. I liked the boat trips.	1 2 3 4 5	4.8
3. The instructor provided clear expectations for grading.	1 2 3 4 5	3.7
4. We worked effectively with our partners as a SOPS group.	1 2 3 4 5	3.9
5. We had enough time to work with the instructor on SOPS.	1 2 3 4 5	4.0
6. My understanding of the complexities of interrelationships in Possession Sound has increased.	1 2 3 4 5	4.1

Rate your level of confidence for the following:

Use the scale 1 low confidence, 3 average, 5 high confidence		Avg.
7. Ability to understand the purpose of SOPS and articulate that purpose concisely in an introduction	1 2 3 4 5	4.2
8. Ability to represent data visually	1 2 3 4 5	4.1
9. Make connections to data from other SOPS groups/ stations	1 2 3 4 5	3.8
10. Construct a testable hypothesis	1 2 3 4 5	4.2

Table 3. Student responses to question, "What do you like best about SOPS?" (open-ended question #11)

- I liked that we could choose our own projects to research. It was more open ended. In high school they gave us a sheet to follow. In ORCA you may feel more attached to the subject because you chose it."
- "I like that I have begun to look at science more analytically, rather than just as facts. I think more deeply about things inside and outside of school."
- "SOPS was also an amazing experience which gave us an opportunity to see how scientists actually conduct experiments."
- "SOPS also demonstrates how fragile Possession Sound is."
- "I like that we get to see things that affect our community."
- "I like SOPS because not only did we get to expand our knowledge of the sound, but it is fun."
- "I would get very excited when my aspect would change."
- "Boat trips are fun and presentations to show off your data."
- "I like the boat trips and how oceanography is connected to SOPS."

- "Finding samples and making connections is really cool. This has really helped my critical-thinking skills as I make connections and find trends."
- "We direct our own research and have control over what we test and observe, as far as collection goes."
- "The boat trips are fun and it's interesting to see how different group's data connects."
- "What I liked best about ORCA is this quarter was Oceanography and SOPS. I liked them because I was never interested in the ocean before and now that I have done this I am much more interested."
- "I really liked doing SOPS this year. I have learned that there is more to the bottom of the ocean, and it has almost everything to do with what else we are studying."
- "I enjoyed SOPS the most because it got us out on the Sound for some hands-on testing."
- "I loved that the faculty was so personable and the SOPS cruises. I am a very hands-on learner and the cruises were extremely useful."
- "SOPS was an amazing experience, which gave us an opportunity to see how scientists actually conduct experiments. I liked the responsibility we had, which allowed us to learn things we hadn't before."

Table 4. Student responses to the question, "What suggestions, changes, or improvements to SOPS do you recommend?" (open-ended question #12)

- "I don't know how to explain this exactly, but I think the different groups need to be less separate and more interrelated. I don't know how to do this, but it would make SOPS a lot better."
- "If we could learn more about our topic and factors/effects of it with other aspects of the sound, that would be better."
- "We should be given time to make connections to other groups and their data."
- "There are too many people in some of the groups. It might be beneficial to split some groups into two and have each do a different aspect of that study or to create more groups to study a wider range of subjects."
- "It would be nice to have a way to visualize all the data at one time."
- "I think a crash course on how to effectively present a project would be most beneficial."
- "More designated work days where everyone shows up."

Table 5. Student responses to the question, "What have you learned about yourself?" (open-ended question #13)

- "That I am interested in nature and the ocean. I have learned what my views are of nature and the world. I have also learned how much a work load I can handle."
- "I have trouble making connections with data. Math can be done. I can study hard but still struggle to retain information."
- "I have learned that I can do whatever I want to do and I can reach goals I never thought I could achieve. At first ORCA was so hard and I struggled, but then I found way to deal with the work and realized I could do it."
- "I have learned to think critically and I have discovered an affinity for nature."
- "I find my educational experience really interesting—I want to know more

about my world! Choosing my projects is really helpful in creating passion for my assignments."

- "This year has been a huge process of realization for me. I know that I can be pushed to develop my ideas to an unbelievable level, and that I respond to the pushing. The only limits are self-imposed. ORCA has helped me realize that."
- "I really like the student-faculty relationships here. You truly care about our learning and our journey, and you do whatever you can to help us along the way. Faculty such as those at ORCA is perhaps what the world of education really needs."
- "ORCA has given me such an incredible thirst to learn. My adolescent mind-set of "I know it all" has changed to "I know little" but I want to learn by doing research, hearing others' perspectives, and applying my own understanding to problems or issues I face."
- "Growth really only comes when you're challenged."
- "I have learned that I can overcome and achieve anything I put my mind to. I've learned that I've grown tremendously in motivation, self-determination, and self-drive."
- "Growth is the major element in ORCA and the greatest outcome."
- "I have learned that I can no longer filter feed. I now have to attack, understand, think, question, persist, define, and assess myself as a learner."

Graph 1. Summary of Student Responses to Student Questionnaire

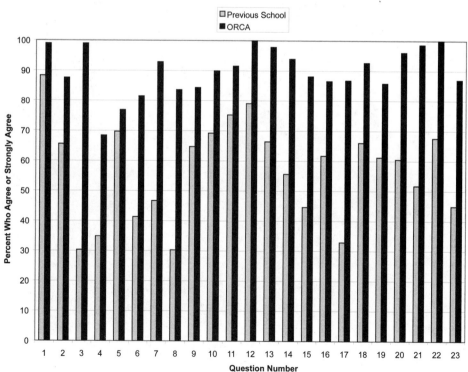

Attitudinal Survey of ORCA and previous high school—Cohorts 1, 2 and 3

References

Adelman, C. 2006. *The toolbox revisited: Paths to degree completion from high school through college.* Washington, DC: U.S. Department of Education.

Bransford, J. D., A. D. Brown, and R. R. Cocking, eds. 2000. *How people learn: Brain, mind, experience, and school.* Washington, DC: National Academy Press.

Hoffman, N., and J. Vargas. 2007. *Minding the gap: Why integrating high school with college makes sense and how to do it.* Cambridge, MA: Harvard Education Press.

Kveven, A., S. W. Last, E. M. Silva Mangiante, C. Fiducia, E. Keroack, R. Simpson, J. Richards, G. Skolits, H. Richards, and F. A. Draughon. 2007. Snapshots of science in practice. *Educational Leadership* 64 (4): 48–54.

Meyers, C., and T. B. Jones. 1993. *Promoting active learning: Strategies for the college classroom.* San Francisco: Jossey-Bass.

National Research Council (NRC). 2006. *How students learn: History, mathematics, and science in the classroom.* Washington, DC: National Academy Press.

Puget Sound Partnership (PSP). 2007. State of the sound. Available online at *www.psp.wa.gov/documents. html.*

Seymour, E., and N. M. Hewitt. 1997. *Talking about leaving: Why undergraduates leave the sciences.* Boulder, CO: Westview Press.

Natural Scientists: Children in Charge

Lauren I. Inouye and Steve Ross
Hanahau'oli School

Introduction

Hanahau'oli, which means "happy work" in the Hawaiian language, was founded by Mr. and Mrs. George Cooke in 1918, in Honolulu, Hawaii. It is a coeducational, nonsectarian, elementary day school offering an eight-year program that begins with a four-year-old junior kindergarten class, continues with multiage classes of grades K–1, grades 2–3, and grades 4–5, and culminates with a sixth-grade class. Hanahau'oli is a small school whose philosophy reflects the teachings of progressive educators, especially John Dewey. We encourage firsthand experience with the community and nature, encourage children to ask questions to guide their learning, and emphasize collaborative group projects, classroom decision making, and discipline integration to promote understandings about how the world works and the many ways to express what has been learned.

A social studies/science based curriculum has always been the foundation of the Hanahau'oli program. Because there is a clear connection between science and the nature/condition of society, it is natural to connect science with the social studies program when appropriate. The overlap between the two does not imply that one can substitute for the other; each has its own questions and approaches to answering them and, yet, each promotes similar habits of the mind. Science and technology emerge from particular historical and cultural contexts and it is only natural that the lines between the two subject areas will be blurred at times. Yet, we must not substitute one for the other nor should we assume that by teaching one we are teaching both.

Thematic units form the basis of each class offering, with skills and concepts integrated within that context. The conceptual strands build upon each other as children progress through the school. Content is selected to support the development of understandings about the world that allow students to encounter new information with a framework for comprehending it rather than accumulating information that does not connect to broader understandings. Content studied in our science program relates to the overriding themes of constancy, change, and systems. The disciplines of math and language arts are integrated through unit experiences.

This chapter reports the results of refining our practices to allow young children to begin to develop inquiry process skills. In previous years we addressed the process skills of science because we felt they were vital to all learning, not just in science. Our participation in National Science Teachers Association (NSTA) conferences, reading NSTA publications, and reflecting on how we taught science in our classroom resulted in experiences for children aligned with *Best*

Practice: New Standards for Teaching and Learning in America's Schools (Zemelman, Daniels, and Hyde 1998).

It is our belief that inquiry shapes and guides all learning experiences. As teachers we believe that children construct meaning by interacting directly with their world, develop useful skills and understandings from real-life problems and situations, demonstrate different strengths, and develop at different rates. We allow children's prior knowledge, experiences, and questions to influence the units of study and investigations.

At Hanahau`oli, we believe that children are born scientists. What motivates their learning and our thematic units is their endeavor to answer three key questions: *Who am I? How does my world work? Where do I fit in that world?* Their search for answers allows them to be in charge as they inquire about their questions, pose possible theories, plan investigations to collect data, assess results, and share them with others.

In the multiage classroom we will discuss in this chapter, there are two teachers and 26 children. The strength of the group comes from its diversity. This mixed-age group is heterogeneous, made up of an equal number of boys and girls from various ethnic and socioeconomic backgrounds and with varying abilities and talents.

Three types of opportunities for children to experience being a "scientist-in-charge" are available in our classroom:

- thematic units designed around important content that is developmentally appropriate and supports developing concepts;
- extended investigations that emphasize the scientists' extensive data collection, recording, and analyzing; and
- unplanned experiences (within units, as extensions of them, or totally serendipitous).

In our classroom of grades K–1, children are guided in active and extended scientific inquiries in all three types of experiences. We find that doing more investigations develops the understanding, ability, and values of inquiry as well as knowledge of science content. In this chapter we discuss our "Food as a Basic Need" unit. In this unit children learned about the origin of different foods, the variety of food chains in their lives, and the importance of balance in food chains. The children learned that the source of most of their food and an integral part of food chains are plants; furthermore, the animals they eat also eat plants to survive. Given the importance of plants, they were asked, "What do plants need to survive?" The children quickly responded that plants need the Sun, air, water, and soil to live and grow. We guessed this knowledge was based on previous experiences, something they had heard, read about, or seen on television. For some, the knowledge was probably from planting experiences they may have had in the past. But, when the children were asked, "How do you know that plants need the Sun, air, water, and soil?" there was silence. This was a perfect teachable moment. With varying degrees of support (depending on the needs of the groups), six groups of children, as scientists, designed six different investigations to find out if plants need air, light from the Sun, heat from the Sun, water, soil, or fertilizer to survive.

This year we have also introduced a new focused and extended exploration of weather, hoping children will begin to understand that while weather changes from day to day, even in Hawaii some months are warmer or colder than others, and some months are wetter or drier than others. During this exploration, the children also have the opportunity to practice using simple tools such as a thermometer to measure the temperature. This nine-month investigation, which includes collecting data about temperature and organizing the information into monthly charts and graphs, helps children see the patterns of average temperatures, getting cooler in the fall and winter and getting warmer as spring progressed.

Both studies allowed us to emphasize science as a social endeavor. The inquiry process provides children with opportunities for scientific debate within the classroom community with cooperation, shared responsibility, and respect. Children worked in teams as they designed and carried out their plant investigations. Children also worked in teams as they designed and tried out their wind and rainfall measuring tools. Throughout the process of "being a scientist," children were encouraged to "try out" their ideas and questions on their classmates as well as to respond to their classmates' ideas and questions. In this way children taught and learned from each other. These scientific debates and discussions were successful because they occurred in a safe environment where diverse ideas were respected. This safe environment had been established earlier in our classroom and each member of the classroom (children and adults) practiced well-defined collaborative skills.

In many aspects of the school day and our units of study, children are in charge. Children conduct our morning meetings. Social issues are brought to the group for resolution. Children feel empowered to bring to the group problems or suggestions of better ways to do something. Children's ideas and questions influence units of study. They work in teams on challenges (for example to design a wind measuring tool) and to design and carry out investigations to answer their questions. The children know that while the teachers have the final authority, there are 28 (26 children and 2 teachers) important members of our class who have input into how things are done.

Our "classroom agreements" help to establish a safe environment where all children and their ideas are valued and where all children are free to ask questions and share diverse ideas. The children practice collaborative skills including problem solving and compromise. We, as teachers, also trust the children and the process. We give up some control and trust that the direction the children lead discussions or activities is of value. We often find that the children's ideas take us to more relevant and appropriate places than what we had planned. These are the conditions that form the basis of scientific inquiry in our classroom.

Thematic Units: Shared Leadership

The inquiry process is the foundational element of all of our science studies, whether they are thematic units or extended investigations. Using the Hanahau'oli School science curriculum, *Benchmarks for Science Literacy*, and the *Atlas of Science Literacy*, we developed Intended Learning Outcomes (ILOs) for our thematic units. The ILOs for our "Food as a Basic Need" unit were: (1) Children should begin to understand where the food they eat comes from, (2) Children should begin to understand how food chains work, and (3) Children should begin to be aware of the importance of protecting/ taking care of the plants and animals in their ecosystem/environment (stewardship).

Each unit of study begins with focusing questions to determine children's ideas and perceptions. Focusing questions for this unit were "What is food?" "Where does food come from?" and "What do you want to know about food?" Children have previous experiences and knowledge about food and these questions help the teachers learn more about their perceptions and plan accordingly. All the children's responses were recorded on a chart with their initials written beside them. At this time it is not important if responses are "right" or "wrong."

Next we ask the children about questions they might have about food. Some examples were: "What is chocolate?" "What is salt?" "How is ice cream made?" "How is pizza made?" "How do we get food?" During this question asking time, we allow the children to respond to each other's questions. We do not investigate every question ("Why is the sea salty?") because some explanations are difficult to understand given the children's developmental level and lack of previous experience. Sometimes we need to just provide quick and easy answers that they can understand. Sometimes we wait for a better time to elaborate or deal with their questions.

During our "Food as a Basic Need" unit, children research the origin of chocolate, salt, and vanilla. In response to the question "What is salt?" a child brought a container of ocean water to share, which we allowed to evaporate. This unplanned learning experience demonstrated the value placed on children leading. To answer some of their other questions, children made pasta, pizza, and ice cream from scratch. We assisted them in tracing the ingredients back to their sources. For example, the children learned about the vanilla plant/bean being the source of the flavoring of the vanilla ice cream they made. Visiting a farm, a food distributor, and a grocery store allowed children to follow food from its origin to the dining table. After the visit to the grocery store, the children created a grocery store in the classroom and dramatized various roles they had observed during our visit; this is an example of the intersection of science and social studies. There were shoppers, checkers, and stockers, with the store manager role being the most coveted. At the beginning of our unit, when we informed families about the ILOs for the unit, one family offered a visit to their home to help the children learn about the food chain of Jackson Chameleons. They also learned about food chains through learning trips (Hawaii Nature Center and Lyon Arboretum), games, internet research, literature, and videos. These experiences allow children to construct meaning about food and food chains by interacting directly with their world.

During the learning experiences children were asked for their ideas and observations. Children were continually asked, "What do you think?" and "Why do you think that happened?"

For example, to understand how food chains work, we played a popcorn food chain game to demonstrate the importance of balance in a food chain. In this tag game, some children were birds and others were crickets (the birds' food). While the crickets were "eating" plants (gathering popcorn spread around on the ground in plastic baggies) the birds were hunting the crickets. When a cricket was tagged by a bird, the contents of the cricket's baggie went into the bird's baggie. We played the game several times, varying the number of birds and crickets. When we played with 10 birds and only 3 crickets, there were not enough crickets for the birds to eat so many of the birds "died" because they did not have enough food. We ended each game with questions such as, "Why do you think many of the birds died?" and "What would happen to the plants that are food for the crickets if there were no crickets left to eat them?" Similar questions were asked after games in which there were few birds and a lot of crickets and an equal number of birds and crickets.

Extended Inquiry: Following Their Lead

Scientists often carry out extended investigations. Like scientists, our students, with support, carried out a school-year-long weather investigation. We began the study by discussing, observing, and learning about different types of weather. The children brainstormed and agreed on different weather symbols to be used to record the weather on personal weather calendars as well as the classroom weather calendar that is used by our class "meteorologists." They also recorded the morning and afternoon temperatures on the classroom weather calendar.

Wind velocity and rainfall impact children's lives (e.g., clothing they wear, outdoor play-time) and are concrete and measurable forces of nature. With a partner or partners, the children invented tools to measure both wind velocity and rainfall. The wind and rain tool projects focused on both the learning process and the learning that occurs when something works or does not work as planned. The learning process was social in nature, giving children opportunities to collaborate in creating a particular item such as a tool to measure wind velocity. When the tools were completed, the children had opportunities to share their inventions with their classmates, discuss their own efforts, and respond to their classmates' questions.

The students decided that their wind tools should have a light part that moves in the wind and a heavier part that would be used to hold the tool. They also decided the wind tool should indicate various wind speeds to be effective. After some initial planning, brainstorming of ideas, and some trial and error, the student groups built wind tools that met the criteria. One was selected by the class to be used each day by the class meteorologists. Wind speed was then added to the classroom weather calendar.

After brainstorming what would make an effective rainfall measuring tool, the children, in small groups, drew up plans that included how their tools would work and wish lists for supplies. When supplies were gathered, each group constructed its rainfall tool. The completed tools were left outside for a couple of days to test their effectiveness. Two major problems arose in many of the rainfall tools: materials such as cardboard tubes and boxes and paper cups did not withstand getting wet or the tool was not stable and fell over. Groups then made adjustments to their tools, as scientists do when something they have done does not work. Some tools were redesigned using waterproof materials such as plastic cups.

When the rainfall tools were strong enough to withstand the elements, they were placed in an area on campus that allowed the tools to measure the rain (and not water from the lawn sprinklers). Daily rainfall was recorded on a cup, with a line marking the amount of rain and one of nine descriptors signifying how much rain fell. New descriptors for the amount of rainfall were decided by the children on days different amounts of rain were measured. Some descriptors included "a very lot," "a lot," "medium," "a little," "a drop," and "none." These descriptors allowed the children to compare how much rain fell from one day to another. Rainfall cups were saved each day, giving the children unplanned opportunities to explore the idea of evaporation as the rainfall collected in cups from earlier days "disappeared." As observations were made, students shared their ideas about what they "knew" about evaporation and asked questions about what they would like to know.

Over a few weeks, the children measured rain using each group's rainfall tool. Children observed that some tools captured more rain because the collection container was bigger or the container may have had a larger opening that allowed it to "catch" more rain. As scientists would do, the students decided that there should be only one rain tool for consistency and accuracy in comparing rainfall from different days.

After two and a half months of measuring rainfall, the number of cups saved and the number of rainfall descriptors made the rainfall investigation difficult to manage. The problem and the three goals of measuring rainfall (measure daily rain, measure monthly rain, and compare monthly rainfall throughout the year to see if some months are rainier than others) were brought to a classroom "community circle." The class brainstormed several ideas and discussed the pros and cons of each until they agreed that daily rainfall should be tallied on charts for each month. They also agreed on a reduced number, five instead of nine, of rainfall descriptors to use. These suggestions met all three goals and solved the problem because cups would no longer have to be saved each day. Students volunteered to help design and construct the rainfall charts to be used for both the current month (January) and for previous months, using the saved rainfall cups. At the beginning of each new month, children made a new rainfall chart.

Children also volunteered to design and construct a chart and graph to help organize daily weather reports (weather, temperature, wind speed, and rain) that would allow them to compare monthly trends in weather. Examining the charts and graphs as the months progressed helped the children understand the idea that weather changes from day to day but some months are warmer or colder than others. The students also learned the science process of collecting data over time and to draw conclusions. They learned that the average monthly morning temperature was lowest in the months of January and February; a similar pattern occurred in the average monthly afternoon temperature. The average monthly morning and afternoon rainfall graphs showed a similar pattern. Using the data, the children concluded that the months of January and February were the coolest and rainiest this school year.

Throughout the study of weather, children made suggestions and decisions about weather tools and recording weather. They were asked to work together (listening attentively, respecting different ideas, and cooperating) to problem solve and propose solutions to any problems that arose. They took ownership for their learning and the procedures used to study weather. Just as important as the content learned, the students learned and practiced a variety of social skills.

Unplanned Inquiry: Children in Charge

Sometimes unplanned opportunities extend or expand on planned inquiry. There are generally two possible starting points for these investigations: (1) an observation or experience or (2) a perception from a past experience. They can arise as extensions of units, perceptions expressed by children during units, or totally serendipitously like when a queen bee lands with her hive-mates on the metal play structure or a child brings a caterpillar to class.

After learning about the importance of food chains and the negative impact litter has on them, the children decided to do a school campus cleanup as an extension of the "Food as a Basic Need" unit. They divided into teams, gathered the necessary supplies, and set off to different parts of the campus. While on "litter patrol," one student observed that some parts of the campus had more litter than others. When his group returned to the classroom, he asked, "Which part of campus has more litter than others?" With teacher support, he designed an investigation that included dividing the campus into different areas, defining what constitutes a piece of litter (Does size matter?), and created the investigative process. He invited his classmates to join him and got five volunteers. Once a week for three weeks, these children collected and counted litter and organized their data on a chart and finally on a graph, an opportunity to develop useful skills from a real-life situation. At our weekly Friday assembly, the group shared what they had learned with the entire school community and challenged them to litter less. While the student and his group needed some support, they were independent during most parts of the process because of previous investigative experiences. The "litter" investigation, while it gave children an opportunity to answer their own question, was also an opportunity for teachers to assess their understanding of the process of investigation. This is an example of applying information learned and the process of inquiry.

Examples of investigations that come from perceptions or previous experiences are the investigations the children designed in response to their perceptions that plants need the Sun, water, soil, and air to survive. We will use these investigations to further illustrate the accompanying flowchart titled "Exploring the Process of Being a Scientist." Throughout the plant investigations, varying degrees of support and guidance were provided to the children depending on their need. Some groups were more independent with the process than others.

Both the litter and plant investigations were opportunities for scientific discussions and debate among the children in our classroom. Sharing ideas and observations, perceptions, and experiences may have helped others "see" something they had not seen before. Children asked each other questions and answered questions posed to the group by other classmates. They challenged each other's thinking as different ideas were worked through.

Children as Inquirers

In our classroom, children act like scientists to answer their own questions or scientific questions. Our flowchart, "Exploring the Process of Being a Scientist" (Figure 1, p. 22) shows the steps of the process and notes how social interaction is integral to every step. We find that we struggle with the messiness of science. While it looks like a linear process in the flowchart, in reality, any step in the process could return investigators to an earlier step.

During the first formal step of the process, an "explorable" question is asked and children make "thoughtful guesses" or hypotheses to answer the question. The question can be initiated by the students or guided by the teacher. Questions need to go through filters before they are investigated. The question needs to be explorable or doable. The question should be developmentally appropriate. The *Benchmarks for Science Literacy* (AAAS 1993) and *Atlas of Science Literacy* (AAAS 2001) are good resources to check for developmental appropriateness. It is important to remember that just because a child can repeat words does not mean a concept is understood. The question also needs to be something of importance to learn. Children are then asked for their ideas about the question and to make "thoughtful guesses." During this time the teacher's job is to "prod," to help clarify the children's thinking. This is not a time to judge ideas as right or wrong but to understand their thinking based on previous experiences, developmental level, and what they have been told.

Figure 1. Exploring the Process of Being a Scientist

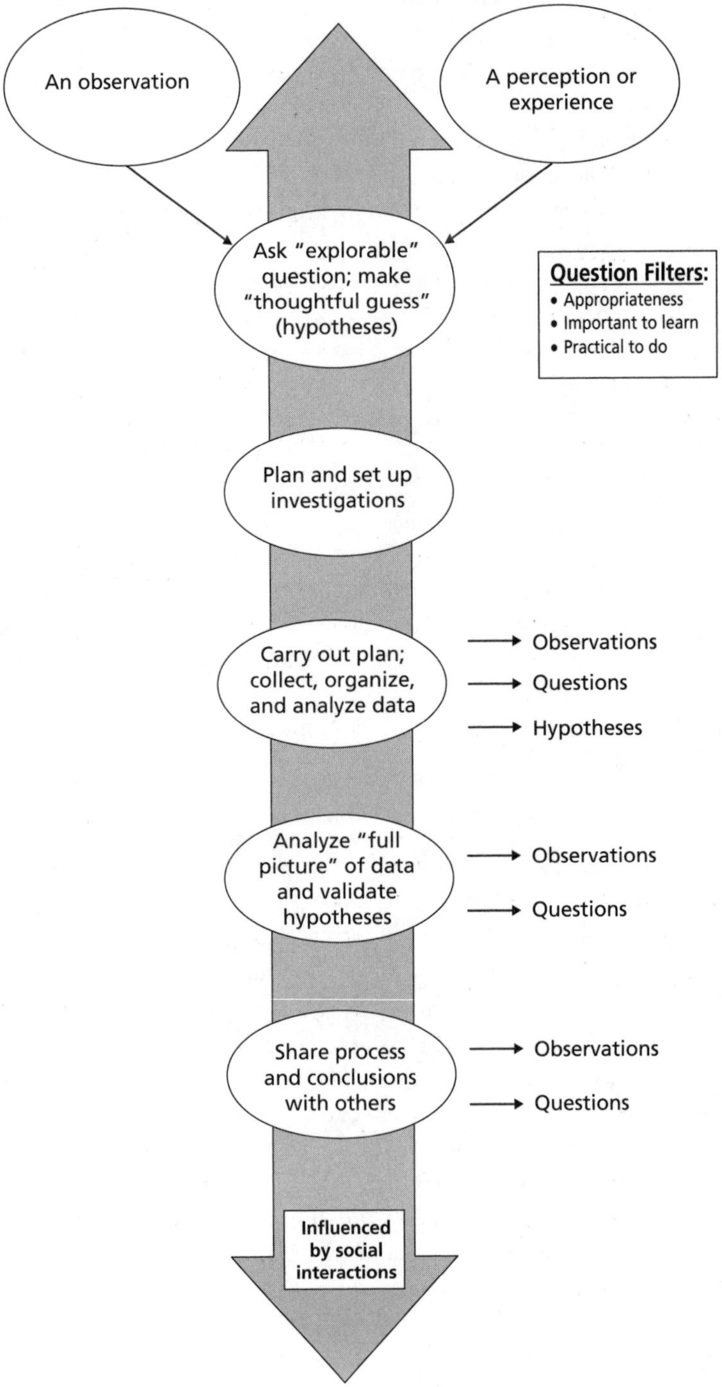

An observation

A perception or experience

Ask "explorable" question; make "thoughtful guess" (hypotheses)

Question Filters:
- Appropriateness
- Important to learn
- Practical to do

Plan and set up investigations

Carry out plan; collect, organize, and analyze data

→ Observations

→ Questions

→ Hypotheses

Analyze "full picture" of data and validate hypotheses

→ Observations

→ Questions

Share process and conclusions with others

→ Observations

→ Questions

Influenced by social interactions

Although appearing linear, the inquiry process is actually dynamic.

The larger question preceding the plant investigations was, "What do plants need to survive?" Children quickly responded that plants need air, sunlight, water, and soil. It appeared to us that the children did not truly understand the needs of plants. We asked, "How do you know?" and "How can you find out if that is true?" After some discussion, the children divided themselves into investigation groups to find out if plants need air, light from the Sun, heat from the Sun, water, soil, or fertilizer to survive. They were first asked to formulate an explorable question such as "Do plants need air to survive?" and then propose their "thoughtful guesses" about it.

Interesting scientific discussions occurred when the children shared their ideas and asked questions in their groups. As children shared "thoughtful guesses" about plants' needs, others debated those ideas based on their own understandings. A prerequisite for this step is a safe and respectful learning environment where everyone's ideas can be expressed (no right or wrong answers).

The next step in the process of being a scientist is to plan and set up the investigation. During this step, children are "in charge" (with teacher support only when necessary) and should lead the planning process. It is fine if the plan does not work out. Often the best learning occurs when something does not go according to plan. This is the reality of a scientist's work. Take, for example, the student group who planned to make their rainfall measuring tool using paper towel tubes and a paper cup to catch the rain. We knew that it would fall apart after a few rainy days, but instead of intervening, we let the children discover that themselves.

During the planning stage, children need to determine what materials are needed, what the procedure will be, who will be responsible for what tasks, and how data will be collected and organized. The teacher may have to help children with "constants" and "variables" and needs to make sure that the plan is safe, appropriate, and doable. During this stage, the children stimulate each other's thinking, which can result in even more ideas. The planning stage also provides real opportunities to practice compromising, attentive listening, and resolving any problems that might occur.

It was interesting to listen to the children brainstorm ideas as they planned for their plant investigations. Many ideas were shared and students felt safe to disagree and to point out and explain why something might not work. The process was mostly done with respect and cooperation. Because of the ages of the children, we sometimes felt it necessary to offer some guidance. The group that designed an investigation to find out if plants needed air to survive was the most interesting. First, it was suggested that they put a plant in a box so it could not get any air. A boy thought that air would still seep in. Someone else suggested that the plant be put in an airtight cardboard box. The same boy thought the plant would not get any sunlight. Then it was suggested that the plant be put it in a clear airtight container. The boy asked, "How would it be watered?" and said, "Air could get in then when the plant is watered." We knew it would be difficult to isolate the "air" variable. We had done previous research on how it could be done and finally shared with the group an idea of covering plants with Vaseline to keep out the air. This is an example of a time when teachers provided extra support so the children would be successful.

The next step in the process is to carry out the plan and collect, organize, and analyze the data. During this time the best learning occurs when something does not work, when something that the children did not expect happens, or when something interferes with the investigation. When this happens, students can make adjustments to the plan. Teachers need to be understanding with things that go wrong and support children as they analyze what went wrong and what they can do about it. If possible, teachers should let students determine if something has gone wrong with their investigations.

As investigations are carried out, data and observations are systematically recorded and organized by children, with teacher support as needed. Children begin to analyze the data, making observations and drawing conclusions about what is observed or experienced.

As the investigation is carried out, responsibilities should be divided and shared. This step in the process gives children practice working together, sharing ideas with each other, and listening to each other attentively. Students can help classmates "see" or discover something they may have otherwise missed. Children with different levels of experience or expertise can support the learning of others.

Something unexpected happened for the group who investigated the question "Do plants need heat from the Sun to survive?" They put a plant in a cooler (cooled with ice, without a lid), a plant outside in the shade, and a plant in direct sunlight. At first the plant in the cooler grew more quickly than the other two plants. The children concluded that plants do not need heat from the Sun but that they grew better in cool temperatures; they did not separate heat from light. We did not correct their ideas but did urge them to confine their thinking and interpretations. We did not, at this time, get into photosynthesis or any in-depth discussion of the negative impact of light on plant growth. The students' conclusions were logical, based on their observations up to that point. As time passed, the plant in the cooler died while the one in the sun thrived, compelling the children to rethink their conclusion to better reflect their new observations. Their new conclusion was "Plants do need heat."

When the investigation was complete, the children analyzed the full picture of the data to validate their "thoughtful guesses." Teachers support the children by asking, "Does the conclusion make sense?" "Is it logical based on your observations?" "Is there more we can do? Or, are there other sources for information?" There may be more than one way to look at the observations. There may be two or more logical conclusions. It is not always important that the children's conclusions are 100% accurate or scientifically valid. It is fine for children to have temporary information. The process is usually more important than the outcome.

The student groups made posters to share information with their classmates about their investigations and what they had learned about the needs of plants. On the posters were photographs of students and the plants they investigated, accompanied by text describing what had transpired during their investigations and what had been learned. The children came up with a variety of conclusions such as, "For plants lots of water is better; but for seeds a little water is better." "Plants do need heat." "Plants need light." An interesting conclusion one student made was "This plant needs air to survive." This student understood that only one plant was investigated and did not generalize the idea to all plants. Much is gained and learned by each member when different conclusions are discussed and debated. The focus, however, is on observations and what actually happened.

The last step in the process of being a scientist is for students to share their investigative process and conclusions with others. Children, like scientists, have the responsibility to share what they have learned with the community. There are many ways investigations and conclusions can be shared, such as in music or a song, a poster, a diorama, a book, or a dramatization. Sharing can become a discussion of ideas. Sharing is an opportunity for children to learn from one another.

Different strengths (e.g., artistic, musical, communication, building) are celebrated as projects are accomplished collaboratively and then shared with others. Deciding on and working on a final project is a great opportunity for students to work together toward a common goal.

The plant investigation process was a wonderful opportunity for students to participate in an active and extended scientific inquiry. The investigative process helped children better understand and be better able to carry out inquiry. The children also formulated a real understanding of the needs of plants, based on their own thinking, ideas, and observations.

Assessment: Children and Program

We define assessment as the process of observing and recording (i.e., documenting students' work, what they say, what they do, and how they do it) over time. Assessment in our classroom is authentic and ongoing throughout our units of study and is focused on the Intended Learning Outcomes (ILOs) of the unit. We keep records of our observations of what and how children contribute to our classroom conversations and discussions. We collect representative work of the children over time, such as journal entries and reflections. We also use photos and video-tapes to record children engaged in unit-related activities. At various points during the unit, for example, we interview children about their work. We ask questions not only about their experiences and what they have learned but also about their participation in and contributions to the group. All this information forms the basis for assessing what the students are learning. This assessment process allows us to recognize and accommodate children's individual differences concerning learning styles, rates of learning, previous knowledge, direct experiences, and cultures. It also provides students with ways to demonstrate what they are learning through their own interests and strengths. Thoughtful and ongoing assessments of this nature guides our work as teachers: Planning and instruction for individuals and groups and reflecting on our teaching to evaluate how well the unit experiences are helping children to achieve the unit goals. All the information taken together provides the basis for writing summary reports at the conclusion of each unit.

In journal entries during the "Food as a Basic Need" unit the children demonstrated what they had learned. For example, one child wrote, "Orange juice comes from oranges. Oranges come from trees. Workers pick the oranges in bags. And, then they take the oranges to the factory." To accompany detailed drawings about a food chain, another student wrote, "The Jackson Chameleon eats silkworms. The silkworms eat mulberry leaves. Mulberry leaves need the Sun and rain." In a conversation about what she thought was occurring while playing the "Popcorn Food Chain Game," one student demonstrated understanding of the importance of balance in food chains when she observed, "If there are less birds, the birds will probably live because there is a lot of food for the birds." She added, "If there are less crickets, some birds might live, but most of the birds might die because there is not enough food." After a visit to a neighborhood supermarket, the children's dramatization of various roles in a classroom super-market of their creation demonstrated their understanding of a supermarket's role in providing food for people to eat.

There are many ways the success of our program can be measured. First, our success can be measured in the love and motivation our children have for learning. Throughout the "Food as a Basic

Need" unit it was apparent that the students were excited about the unit of study and motivated by their learning experiences and their investigations. Being able to have influence and ownership over what they studied enabled children to "take charge" and to be actively engaged in their learning. The students were motivated to determine the answers to their own questions about food.

Children's interest in what they were learning was demonstrated by items they brought for sharing. Many students brought in library books and unit-related artifacts to enhance the topic of study. Children often engaged their families in researching topics of interest related to the unit. Following a discussion about whether vanilla was a plant or an animal, some children went home to use the internet to gain information about vanilla that they then shared with their classmates. One child was surprised to discover that vanilla was a plant. Another student brought a bottle of South American vanilla that we used to flavor the ice cream that we made.

Parents frequently told us of interesting conversations initiated by their children about school experiences. When we wondered about salt and its origin, one child's father took her to the beach to get a container of ocean water. Questions arose: "Does all salt come from the ocean?" "If salt is not a plant or an animal, what is it?" The children decided salt is an "other." Sometimes we would overhear and take note of children's conversations at the school that expressed their interests and engagement with specific learning experiences. After learning about food chains, children reenacted food chains in games they played at recess. After learning about the origins of their food, children role-played the "trip" food takes from the farmer to the dinner table. After making pizza, ice cream, and pasta, children replicated the experiences in the sand box and with play dough. Children often excitedly shared with us relevant information and pictures they had found in newspapers and magazines. Months after learning about the effect of litter on animals and food chains, members of an afterschool sports club continued to remind others to not litter and to pick up trash.

What is learned is often extended in other learning activities students choose. After the food chain unit, children wrote books and drew illustrations of food chains of interest to them, including those of a pet turtle and of rain forest animals. Students researched on the internet and read books about the food chains of favorite animals. Small groups of children, with some teacher support, rewrote the words of "I Know an Old Lady Who Swallowed a Fly" to match a food chain they were interested in.

Our program's success can be measured by how children apply the inquiry techniques they have learned. As anticipated, there was a wide range of proficiency in the application of inquiry skills. Because of the young age of our children, many need guidance to carry out the inquiry process. The child who developed an investigation following a litter cleanup to answer the question "What area of our school (campus) has the most litter?" followed, with minimal support, the basic inquiry process when he investigated, "Do plants need air to survive?" Many children got better at asking "explorable" questions and devising their own plans to answer their questions, whether it was to ask an expert, research the question in a book or on the internet, or to do a simple investigation. The children got better and more independent at recording and interpreting data as our weather investigations continued.

The students developed their own theories as a result of their experiences when investigating the needs of plants, as when a child wrote "This plant needs air to live," as opposed to "all plants need air to live." Another student internalized his own theory, "Paper is not strong enough to withstand water," after his rainfall measuring tool (a paper cup attached to a rock so it would not blow away) fell apart following a few days of rain. Later in the school year when the children were learning about materials used to construct shelters, the same boy reminded his classmates of his first rainfall measuring tool attempt and told them that paper and cardboard would not be good materials to use to build a shelter.

As scientists work collaboratively on their investigations, so do our students. The children got better at working collaboratively as demonstrated by their work on team projects at the end of the school year. Team members worked together to accomplish a common goal.

Our program's successes can be measured by the children's understanding of scientific content and our unit Intended Learning Outcomes. Because we focus on the process, "discovery learning" over an extended period of time, and on content that is developmentally appropriate, our children develop a real understanding of concepts. Students demonstrate this in many ways, including participation in learning experiences and discussions, journal reflections, and individual and group projects. Their understanding is demonstrated during class and whole-school presentations when they teach each other.

Data for us are not determined from rubric grading sheets. Instead data are anecdotal and provided by teachers in articulation sessions and through children's progress reports. Students' reports, after they have moved on to the grades 2–3 class, as well as interviews conducted with their teachers, show that the children's earlier experiences with the processes of inquiry have a positive influence on their approach to investigating new questions. The students demonstrate a love for science and continue to ask questions and develop investigations for answering them. It was reported that a "Science Lab" became a part of the grades 2– 3 class's Community Unit for the very first time this year. Many children chose to be a part of the "N-R-G" (energy) group based on the science that would be a part of their group's focus. One student investigated alternative forms of energy by trying several different ways to cook a hot dog. He found that using solar energy and a foil-covered pan worked best but "it took a long time and the sun had to be shining on the hot dog." Another student designed a water wheel to investigate using water to create energy. Another child explored various materials to determine the best conductor of heat. Other students investigated geothermal energy and created a poster to explain how a company is working to harness the heat from our active volcano to generate electricity. In reflecting on the various investigations, one child wrote, "All the investigations made me realize that there are so many ways to make and conserve energy."

A review of "Best Practice in Science" (Zemelman, Daniels, and Hyde 1998) indicates that we were and continue to be on the right track with current recommendations for improving science education in our classroom. Our students are guided in active and extended scientific inquiries through units of study and individual investigations; their investigations develop the skills of inquiry as well as an understanding of science content; they are immersed in an environment that allows them to "take charge" of the learning process; and the social nature of the inquiry process provides opportunities for children to develop collaborative skills as well as respect for ideas that differ from their own. We believe that learning about the world in these ways will support lifelong learning.

References

American Association for the Advancement of Science (AAAS). 2001. *Atlas of science literacy*. Washington DC: AAAS.

American Association for the Advancement of Science (AAAS). 1993. *Benchmarks for science literacy*. New York: Oxford University Press.

Gibbs, J. 2001. *Tribes: A new way of learning and being together*. Windsor, CA: Center Source Systems.

Hanahauoli School Admission Materials. 2008.

Hanahauoli School Science Curriculum Rationale Draft. 2004.

Ostlund, K., and S. Mercier. 1999. *Rising to the challenge of the national science education standards: The process of science inquiry, primary edition*. Squaw Valley, CA: S & K Associates.

Zemelman, S., H. Daniels, and A. Hyde. 1998. *Best practice: New standards for teaching and learning in America's schools*. Portsmouth, NH: Heinemann.

Science Is Not a Spectator Sport: Three Principles From 15 years of Project *Dragonfly*

Chris Myers and Lynne Born Myers
Project Dragonfly, Miami University

Richard Hudson
TPT Public Television

Project *Dragonfly* at Miami University was founded on the premise that the most powerful way to engage children in learning is to celebrate their voices, to invite them into the community of discovery, and to allow them to see themselves as agents of science. Project *Dragonfly* asks youth to share questions, test ideas, author knowledge, take action, and communicate with peers through publicly valued forums and media.

The project began in 1994 when a group of faculty, staff, and students decided to create the first national magazine to feature children's science investigations. Funded by NSF and published by NSTA, the award-winning *Dragonfly* magazine challenged long-standing assumptions about the role of children in science by publishing their research alongside the research of professional scientists. Several *Dragonfly* outcomes are described for professional audiences (Wolfe, Myers, and Cummins 2001; Myers and Haynes 2002; Myers and Ratanopojnard 2003; Wolfe, Cummins, and Myers 2005). But the best evidence for *Dragonfly's* success comes from such studies as Saunders (1999) on pair-bonding in dolphins, Schamel (1997) on nest predation by arctic foxes, and Taylor (1998) on the relationship between music and memory: all studies authored by investigators who are younger than 12 years old, whose work was published in *Dragonfly* magazine.

Project *Dragonfly* now reaches millions of people each year through print, web, and broadcast media, as well as public exhibits and graduate courses for educators. In 2000, *Dragonfly* transitioned from a magazine to the PBS children's series DragonflyTV (*www.pbskids.org/dragonflytv*), produced by Richard Hudson and his creative team at TPT public television. DragonflyTV broadcasts investigations by youth to a national audience. The Emmy award–winning show works closely with science centers, museums, zoos, and similar institutions through its GPS (Going Places in Science) episodes.

In 2004, Project *Dragonfly* initiated Earth Expeditions (*www.earthexpeditions.org*), a graduate-credit program that brings teachers, scientists, and community leaders together at conservation hotspots worldwide. The program supports a growing alliance of inquiry-driven educators who work collaboratively to improve ecological and human communities. Earth Expeditions became the basis for a major public engagement initiative (the NSF-funded Wild Research project), as well as a new master's degree program from Miami University, the Global Field Program (*www.projectdragonfly.org/gfp*).

In this chapter, we describe three principles that have served us over the years through widely different media, audiences, and geographic settings—principles we believe may be useful for those seeking to support a culture of inquiry. We chose principles that, while consistent with the NSES, are too often overlooked in the U.S. education system. The uniting theme throughout is participation: what it means to participate, and how inquiry can be used to foster genuine participation among students, teachers, and communities. Evidence for the effectiveness of participatory science approaches is explored under Principle 1.

Principle 1. Publish, Broadcast, Exhibit, or Otherwise Share Children's Investigations

The assumption that youth are mainly spectators of science remains prevalent in our society and is perhaps nowhere more evident than in our learning media. It is easily possible to imagine a student beginning in kindergarten and progressing all the way through high school without once seeing a peer represented as an investigator in his or her science texts or videos. While it is, of course, reasonable to feature the work of professional scientists in science texts, to do so to the exclusion of youth (the very people science education seeks to engage) carries the implicit message that youth are not investigators themselves, or at least they are not doing investigations worth sharing outside their classroom. From a participatory science perspective, this is a problem.

A review of learning media prepared for the *Dragonfly* magazine NSF proposal revealed a common presentation of science that consistently depicts students as recipients rather than as authors of knowledge (See Diagram 1, p. 31).

This pattern is present in informal science environments as well. A survey of the Association of Zoos and Aquariums revealed that, despite a strongly expressed desire to engage young visitors in inquiry, and some use of inquiry in facilitated programs, most AZA institutions (with notable exceptions) rarely or never feature young investigators in their learning media (Myers et. al. 2007).

NSES Goals

We contend that an overreliance on science media that excludes youth can reinforce the *Less Emphasis* elements described in the NSES, such as "Learning science through lecture and reading," and "Asking for recitation of acquired knowledge." If a more participatory approach to science education is sought, as called for in the NSES *More Emphasis* goals, such as "Guiding students in active and extended scientific inquiries" and "Communicating science explanations," then learning media should also be participatory. We define participatory media as first-person media that is authored by its audience, that serves to communicate ideas among members of a group (such as young investigators). Participatory media can serve as a forum of exchange rather

Diagram 1. Flow of Information in Traditional Science Learning Media

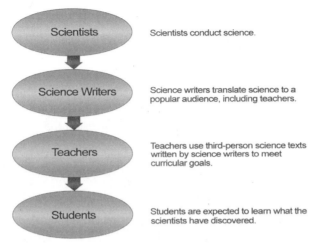

Scientists conduct science.

Science writers translate science to a popular audience, including teachers.

Teachers use third-person science texts written by science writers to meet curricular goals.

Students are expected to learn what the scientists have discovered.

Diagram 2. Flow of Information in Participatory Science Learning Media

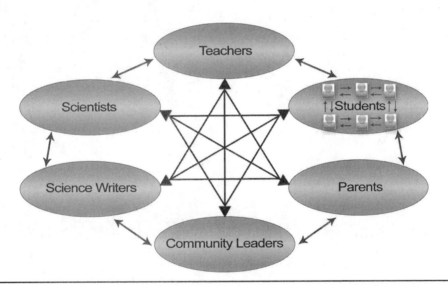

Students are seen and presented as investigators who work together to construct and share knowledge within a network of stakeholders in science and education.

than simply a source of information. At the very least, participatory media represents the voices of its audience and presents peers as agents of knowledge construction.

Inquiry is a participatory endeavor that can unite and showcase diverse voices in science. One Project *Dragonfly* example is the "Earth Sounds, Our Songs" issue of *Dragonfly* magazine, which includes an article by scientist Katy Payne about how she discovered patterns in the songs of humpback whales, an article by neurobiologist Aniruddh Patel (who studies music and the brain) that explores how and why we musically structure the "ABC song," and an article by a group of elementary students and their teacher who experimentally verified that music can improve recall on rote memorization tasks.

Diverse investigators are also showcased in DragonflyTV, such as the episode on technology that features a GEMS (Girls in Engineering, Math and Science) team designing a robot for a national competition, two friends testing their model solar car, while NASA engineer Lloyd French introduces an ice-melting Cryobot designed for the moons of Jupiter.

Figure 1. An episode of DragonflyTV was filmed during the Namibia Earth Expeditions course.

Whether youth share their investigations in a magazine, a local newsletter, a school presentation, a science fair, a national television show, or a homemade video, the act of presenting investigations is in itself a critical step in the process of science. Communities of science are fueled by and absolutely depend on the communication of science investigations. Sharing investigations allows others to reflect, challenge, and build on previous work. Including youth as authors of science has the additional advantage of helping others realize that we are all, regardless of age, keen to know more about the world, and that inquiry is a useful way of doing so.

Evidence

Several lines of evidence indicate that participatory science media improves science learning.

Experimental Results: *Dragonfly* Magazine

Dragonfly magazine promotes science inquiry and "exploratory representational play," a type of imaginative modeling prevalent in science (Wolfe, Cummins, and Myers 2005). In a nine-month study, children in classrooms using *Dragonfly* were compared with a matched set of non-*Dragonfly* classrooms on tasks designed to assess scientific reasoning, attitudes and beliefs, and science-related behaviors. The subjects were fourth-, fifth-, and sixth-grade public school students from 12 classrooms. The experiment employed a pretest-intervention-posttest design, where the primary measure of interest was the repeated measure (fall vs. spring) by condition (*Dragonfly* vs. control) interaction. The experimenters were blind to condition, and the inter-rater reliability for scoring was 96%.

Relative to non-*Dragonfly* controls, and controlling for school grade and their own previous statements, children who received *Dragonfly* (1) indicated that they made hypotheses and predictions outside of school significantly more frequently [$F(1, 83) = 3.81$, $p < 0.05$]; (2) showed a trend toward making observations outside of school more frequently [$F(1, 83) = 3.03$, $p < 0.07$]; and (3) reported using computers significantly more often for science work outside of school. Children who had worked with *Dragonfly* throughout the school year indicated that investigations played a larger role in their lives relative to controls [$F(1, 86) = 5.25$, $p < 0.02$]. When asked, "Do you think that you would be good at carrying out investigations?" *Dragonfly* subjects answered more positively in the spring than fall, while control subjects answered more negatively in the spring than fall.

A central goal of *Dragonfly* is to help children learn the methods of scientific inquiry and develop as scientific reasoners. Subjects responded to two scientific reasoning scenarios. Over the course of a school year, students receiving *Dragonfly* demonstrated significantly more improvement in their ability to evaluate the quality of a scientific explanation than the matched set of control subjects [$F(1, 86) = 3.89$, $p < 0.05$]. Among sixth-grade children, those in the *Dragonfly* condition improved their ability to ask good empirical questions relative to controls [$F(1, 86) = 4.43$, $p < 0.04$] and more improvement in their ability to develop an appropriate approach to a problem [$F(2, 86) = 3.03$, $p < 0.05$].

Experimental Results From DragonflyTV

Evidence that participatory science media motivates students and improves their scientific reasoning is also documented in evaluations over six years of DragonflyTV (see *www.tpt.org/dragonflytv/evaluations* or *www.informalscience.org* for the full reports). Building on methods developed by Barbara Flagg (2002), Rockman (2003) tasked pairs of fourth- and fifth-grade children from Boston, Chicago, and San Francisco to design an investigation. The researchers compared responses provided by youth during "prestudy" interviews (before viewing DragonflyTV) with responses provided during "poststudy" interviews (after children viewed three episodes of DragonflyTV). The pre- and poststudy youth were from the same population, but they were different subjects (so, no youth was given the same task twice). The interviews included the following research prompt:

Now I'd like you to take a few minutes to design your own science investigation/experiment. Kids drink a lot of soda (or pop), and many of these drinks contain caffeine (pause for comments). Can you help me think of an experiment that looks at one effect that caffeine has on something related to how kids do in school? There are no right or wrong answers, I'm just interested in learning more about how you would design this type of study: What specific effect you would study, what steps you'd take, and what you might expect to find. I want you to work together, and I'll give you about five minutes.

Students in the poststudy interviews answered with far more details about the process of research than the prestudy group: details such as doing preliminary research, keeping testing conditions consistent between trials, graphing the results, and sharing findings with others. In a broader survey, more than 90% of students reported that DragonflyTV helped them to understand how to do a science experiment. Apley (2007) provides a useful report on which viewing behaviors and segment features help young viewers grasp investigations on abstract or unfamiliar topics (which will be useful for an upcoming series of DragonflyTV episodes on nanotechnology).

In a 12-week study of video use in the classroom, Rockman (2006) compared teacher responses to the use of DragonflyTV with their students vs. other science programs. After analyzing interviews and logbook comments written while teachers used a broad range of science videos, the researchers found that DragonflyTV more actively involved viewers than the other programs, not only because of segments profiling the work of adult scientists, but young investigators as well. They conclude that "Our research shows that having a variety of real children featured as investigators is a powerful, motivating, and engaging feature of the DragonflyTV series. Students definitely show a preference for programs that show children like themselves or that feature people they can relate to." Rockman characterize specific responses to DragonflyTV with student quotes such as "I like how the kids do experiments in different ways than you would think because it helps me to realize that I can maybe do it someday." And, "I liked how they showed everything step by step and if I ever wanted to do one of those experiments, I could."

Principle 2. Think Outside the Classroom

Schoolyards, backyards, parks, even cafeterias and parking lots can be sites for inquiry. Location typically does not limit inquiry so much as our normal expectations of how to behave at a particular location. Here we describe some work in public spaces that seeks to change expectations to foster investigation, in this case at zoos. Zoo exhibits provide a good example because looking is the expected behavior. Many people love to watch animals at zoos, but the experience typically does not advance from merely looking to real inquiry. In a pioneering study, Dunlap and Kellert (1989) noted that many zoo exhibits actually reinforce visitor passivity. The authors discovered that zoo visitors rarely discussed animal ecology or retained even a few basic facts. "Each subject was asked, 'What did you learn at this exhibit?' Discouragingly, the most popular answer at each zoo was 'Nothing.'" Although other studies provide evidence that zoo visitors can learn and even acquire long-term gains in conservation knowledge from an exhibit (Dierking et al. 2004; Heimlich et al. 2004), no one suggests that understanding of conservation science occurs by solely looking at an animal.

But what is the next step to substantive learning? We believe the answer lies in taking casual observations one step further toward more ordered observations—ordered by a question—in a manner that makes patterns more apparent, using a process that lies at the heart of inquiry. Project *Dragonfly* is currently testing this idea through the NSF-funded project Wild Research, a partnership with the Cincinnati Zoo & Botanical Garden (CZBG) and a consortium of zoos and aquariums nationwide. Wild Research Stations are being added to popular CZBG exhibits to determine if inquiry tools can deepen visitor engagement in science and conservation. For example, the Wild Research Station at Gorilla World invites visitors to act as primatologists, observe and record data on touch screens, and compare their results with those of others, both at the exhibit and back home on the web (*www.wildresearch.org*). Gorilla Station elements include a habitat preference study, a study of gorilla social interactions, and a behavioral study. In each case, visitors make predictions, gather data, and compare results.

The idea for public inquiry on gorillas emerged during graduate-courses on inquiry for teachers on zoo grounds. For example, one teacher in a course on primates facilitated a student-led study to address the question, "Who plays more, gorillas or first-graders?" To complete the study, third-graders defined play behavior, developed a study plan, and compared time spent playing by gorillas on their play tree to time spent by first-graders playing on their jungle gym. We are now determining whether typical zoo visitors, who are not part of a class, will engage in inquiry. Other Wild Research Stations are being developed at Insect World, Lords of the Arctic, Manatee Springs, and other exhibits.

Figure 2. An Earth Expeditions teacher presents gorilla inquiry conducted at the Cincinnati Zoo and Botanical Garden.

The Institute for Learning Innovation is evaluating Wild Research. Preliminary results indicate that carefully developed site enhancements and inquiry tools can deepen public engagement in science at specific sites. We expect this is widely true, not just for sites on zoo grounds. We have witnessed inquiry sites develop in the most unlikely places, such as a forgotten corner of an Ohio schoolyard (a site that students named "Cricket Corner"), and abandoned urban lots that students transformed into community gardens.

Principle 3. Connect Inquiry to Social Change

"As I learned more about the concept of inquiry-based learning, I began to feel its potential beyond the classroom and into every area of our society."

—Emmet O., an Earth Expeditions teacher

Abundant examples from Project *Dragonfly* and from other projects (such as those featured in this book) demonstrate that inquiry, particularly of the more open variety that engages schools and communities in collaborative investigation, can be a powerful force for social transformation. In 2004, Project *Dragonfly* partnered with the Cincinnati Zoo & Botanical Garden to establish an inquiry-driven, social change program for educators called Earth Expeditions (*www.earthexpeditions.org*). Earth Expeditions (EE) offers graduate courses that bring teachers together with scientists, educators,

Figure 3. Teachers in the Mongolia Earth Expeditions course learn to radiotrack the elusive Pallas cat.

community leaders and others to engage in inquiry at conservation hotspots worldwide. In the EE Trinidad course on environmental education, U.S. educators became part of a team that reintroduced blue-and-gold macaws back to Trinidad, a species that had been driven extinct on the island decades earlier. Teachers saw firsthand why research on topics such as macaw habitat preference, reproductive biology, tropical forest structure, and community-based conservation are vital for this important effort. They conducted their own inquiries alongside scientists in Trinidad, brought research stories back to their classrooms, and developed their own inquiry action projects during the school year, supporting each other in a web-based learning community.

Advancing participatory science media (Principle 1), teachers on the EE course in Mongolia organize a conservation radio workshop every year with Mongolian youth, who interact with professionals from NPR (United States) and Mongolia National Radio. Youth are given digital recorders, solar battery chargers, and a direct channel to Mongolia National Radio, which broadcasts their inquiry reports throughout the country. Earth Expeditions teachers also create their own radio spots and incorporate this methodology back in their classrooms. Earth Expeditions teachers in the Namibia course on great cat conservation have implemented a range of successful inquiry and action projects with their students, including a long-term investigation on how cheetahs are adapted for speed, and public fundraising campaigns for cheetah conservation. Earth Expeditions courses in Belize, Kenya, Thailand and other field sites provide similar examples. Earth Expeditions teachers and their students are invited to present their research at an annual World Community Conference.

Figure 4. An Earth Expeditions teacher conducts an open inquiry in Trinidad.

A New, Inquiry-Driven Master's Degree

Based on the impact of EE, Miami University recently approved a unique master's degree program that is grounded in open inquiry, participatory education, and global understanding. Participants in the Global Field Program combine summer EE courses at field sites worldwide

Figure 5. A Mongolian teen interacts with an Earth Expeditions teacher during a participatory radio workshop.

Figure 6. In Namibia, Earth Expeditions teachers explore community-based cheetah conservation efforts.

with collaborative projects via web-based learning communities. The option of many field dates and no residency requirement means the Global Field Program can be completed from anywhere in the United States or abroad. Global Field Program graduates join a diverse and growing network of internationally proficient leaders who work collaboratively to affect change in local and global contexts (see *www.projectdragonfly.org/gfp*).

Conclusion

We have increasingly come to believe that the health of the U.S. education system may depend on how each child answers a single question: "Does my voice matter?" We should all ask ourselves if our culture of education—which sits children in chairs for much of their waking life, often with scant opportunity to engage the world beyond their classroom walls—fully gives students the confidence and skills needed to lead positive change and to address complex science and social issues.

Inquiry, in this context, is not simply a means to teach students science. It is a process of engagement and dialogue that allows participants to construct knowledge and to learn that their questions are important. This, in our view, represents the promise and potential of the NSES. Because participation is a pivotal concept in science education reform (Rutherford and Ahlgren 1989; AAAS 1993; NRC 1996), learning theory (Dewey 1916; Vygotsky 1978; Resnick, Levine, and Teasley 1991), and children's rights (Hart 1997), the implications of participatory science for schools and society are significant.

Figure 7. Teachers embark on an Earth Expedition.

References

American Association for the Advancement of Science AAAS. 1993. *Benchmarks for science literacy*. New York: Oxford University Press.

Apley, A., W. Graham, and J. Scala. 2007. *DragonflyTV: Going places in science children's viewing study*. Report from RMC Research. Available online at *www.informalscience.org*.

Dewey, J. 1916. *Democracy and education*. Reprint edition. New York: Free Press.

Dierking, L. D., L. M. Adelman, J. Ogden, K. Lehnhardt, L. Miller, and J. D. Mellen. 2004. Using a behavior change model to document the impact of visits to Disney's Animal Kingdom: A study investigating intended conservation action. *Curator* 47 (3): 322–343.

Dunlap, J. and S. R. Kellert. 1989. *Informal learning at the zoo: A study of attitude and knowledge impacts*. Philadelphia: Zoological Society of Philadelphia.

Flagg, B. 2002. *DragonflyTV. Formative evaluation of three shows*. Report by Multimedia Research available at *www.tpt.org/dragonflytv/evaluations*.

Hart, R. 1997. Children's participation: The theory and practice of involving young citizens in community development and environmental care. London: Earthscan Publications.

Heimlich, J. E., K. Bronnenkant, N. Witgert, and J. Falk. 2004. *Measuring the learning outcomes of adult visitors to zoos and aquariums: Confirmatory study*. Technical report. Bethesda, MD. American Association of Zoos and Aquariums.

Myers, C. A., D. Jenike, L. Born Myers, and D. Marsh. 2007. Wild research. *Connect* (March): 18–20.

Myers, C. A., and C. Haynes. 2002. Interdisciplinary science. In *Innovations in Interdisciplinary Teaching*, ed. C. Haynes. Westport, CT: Oryx Press.

Myers, C. A., and S. Ratanopojnard. 2003. *Community-based science in Thailand*. Bangkok: Thailand Research Fund.

National Research Council (NRC). 1996. *National science education standards*. Washington, DC: National Academy Press.

Resnick, L., J. Levine, and S. Teasley, eds. 1991. *Perspectives on socially shared cognition*. Washington, DC: American Psychological Association.

Rockman, S. 2003. *DragonflyTV evaluation report 2003*. Report available at *www.tpt.org/dragonflytv/evaluations*.

Rockman, S. 2006. *Using video in the science classroom*. Report available at *www.tpt.org/dragonflytv/evaluations*.

Rutherford, F. J., and A. Ahlgren. 1989. *Science for all Americans*. New York: Oxford University Press.

Saunders, H. 1999. Dolphin diary. *Dragonfly: A Magazine for Young Investigators* 3 (4): 4–6.

Schamel, J. 1997. Outfoxing foxes. *Dragonfly: A Magazine for Young Investigators* 2 (1): 4–7.

Taylor, J. 1998. Musical memory. *Dragonfly: A Magazine for Young Investigators* 2 (3): 26–27.

Vygotsky, L. S. 1978. *Mind in society: The development of higher psychological processes*. Cambridge, MA: Harvard University Press.

Wolfe, C. R., C. A. Myers, and R. H. Cummins. 2001. The Dragonfly web pages: Informal science education on the world wide web. *Cognitive Technology* 6, 4–13.

Wolfe, C. R., R. H. Cummins, and C. A. Myers. 2005. Scientific inquiry and exploratory representational play. In *Play from birth to twelve: Contexts, perspectives, and meanings.* 2nd ed.., eds. D.P. Fromberg and D. Bergen. New York: Routledge.

Student Inquiry and Research: Developing Students' Authentic Inquiry Skills

Judith A. Scheppler, Susan Styer, Donald Dosch,
Joseph Traina, and Christopher Kolar
Illinois Mathematics and Science Academy

Research is formalized curiosity. It is poking and prying with a purpose.
—*Zora Neale Hurston, in* Dust Tracks on a Road, 1942

Established by the state of Illinois in 1985 to develop talent and leadership in science, technology, engineering, and mathematics (STEM), the Illinois Mathematics and Science Academy (IMSA) has become an internationally recognized educational learning laboratory that inspires, challenges, and nurtures talented students. Our advanced, residential, college preparatory program prepares 650 talented Illinois students in grades 10, 11, and 12 to become scholars, researchers, and entrepreneurs. Toward this end, we find that about 80% of our graduates obtain STEM bachelor's degrees.

IMSA has a long history of supporting, nurturing, and promoting high school student participation in research through our academic curriculum and the Student Inquiry and Research (SIR) program. In 2008, we completed our 22nd year as a math and science academy; for 20 of these years we have had a student research program that now numbers approximately 3,300 cumulative student participants. The SIR program supports student research not only in science, technology, engineering, and mathematics (STEM) fields (about 75% of participants), but also in the fine arts fields (<5%) and the social, behavioral, and economic science (SBES) fields (~20%). Participation in SIR for IMSA juniors and seniors is on a voluntary basis, but in recent years, as institutional support for SIR has grown, the student participation rate has reached 67–75%.

In the 2005 NSTA monograph *Exemplary Science in Grades 9–12: Standards-Based Success Stories*, we presented and discussed student inquiry at IMSA (Scheppler et al. 2005). This monograph focused on the on-campus portion of the SIR program for STEM investigations. Evaluation and evolution of the SIR program has led us to consolidate and standardize the experiences for students pursuing work both on campus and off campus. What we have learned from having students conduct inquiry investigations and the rethinking of our science program led us to design, develop, and implement a required core science course for all of our incoming sophomore students. This course helps prepare students for their own independent investigations and supports their development with respect to various habits of mind important to science. This chapter discusses the course, Methods in Scientific Inquiry (MSI), how knowledge from this course has transferred into our science elective program, and how it has improved the quality of SIR investigations that our students conduct. Also included is a discussion of our long-term successes with IMSA graduates.

Student Inquiry and Research

The SIR program is an interactive partnership that pairs students with professionals so that they can actively pursue in-depth investigations. SIR provides a framework for students to explore compelling questions of interest; conduct original research; create and invent products and services; develop businesses; share their work through presentations and publications; and collaborate with other students, advisors, inventors, researchers, and scholars throughout the world. As their skills and understanding grow, students gain increased independence in pursuing the meticulous work of real-world research projects.

Our students follow the SIR program standards, which center on planning, investigating, analyzing, and communicating; we want students to plan experiments, make observations, use multiple data sources, and come to their own defensible research conclusions. These standards have been published (Scheppler et al. 2005) and have been used at IMSA since 2004 to guide student inquiry activity and to assess student progress. On-campus and off-campus advisors guide students in this process in a variety of ways. The students who work on-campus generate their own investigation questions, use IMSA equipment and materials, and receive feedback from IMSA staff advisors. Likewise, off-campus investigations may revolve around students' questions or students may assist an advisor on that person's research. Off-campus advisors are encouraged to provide opportunities for the student in pursuit of a question totally of the student's own interest, and many are willing to guide students in this way. Some students are able to bring work from off-site institutions back to IMSA to work on, on days other than designated Inquiry days. Each student, regardless of the origin of the investigation, must articulate a well-focused question (Marbach-Ad and Sokolove 2000).

To meet the program standards, all students must articulate their question; write an investigation proposal; demonstrate engagement, learning, and accomplishment by keeping a journal; present and defend their work through both oral and poster presentations at IMSAloquium, held each spring; and write a research paper. These requirements are available on the SIR website (*www2.imsa.edu/learning/inquiry*). We continually refine these requirements and our supporting materials, but the basic content has served us well. Each requirement is assessed, frequently in both a formative and summative way. This opportunity enables some students to present their research at local, national, and international conferences and to publish their work in professional journals.

Because students determine the topic of their inquiry and with whom they will work, the learning that occurs is very personalized. They are able to explore a specific area in depth, as well as learn skills and habits of the discipline. Occasionally, this means that the student finds that he or she really is not interested in pursuing further study in the area. Other times, and for many, these experiences solidify an interest and provide a boost to future career plans.

SIR Evolution and Demographics

Beginning in 2006, the off-campus and on-campus programs making up SIR were merged into one program, with the same standards, requirements, and assessments as described for the Student Inquiry program (Scheppler 2005). While participation for juniors and seniors is still voluntary, in 2007 SIR became a nongraduation credit-bearing course at IMSA. The participation rate for the class of 2008 was 67% (140 out of 210); participation over the past eight years has remained steady. Half the class of 2008 participants (70) participated for a second year, though not necessarily pursuing the same investigation. Of the remaining, 20 students participated during their senior year only and 50 participated only during their junior year. IMSA accepts equal numbers of females and males in each entering class.

Ethnicity data show that the SIR participation does not reflect the demographics of our student body; ethnicity of the entire class of 2008 is shown in parentheses. Class of 2008 demographics for participants in SIR: 4% African American (8%), 46% Asian/Pacific Islander (35%), 1% Latino (4%), 41% Caucasian (45%), 5% multiethnic (5%), 3% not reported (2%). These results are fairly typical of any given graduating class; we are underrepresented in African American and Latino students and overrepresented in Asian/Pacific Islander students compared to the overall demographics of the class. We are currently trying to ascertain reasons this may occur and to develop ways of encouraging more and equivalent participation from all student groups.

IMSA Science Program

In 2005 the IMSA science team redesigned its core science program for sophomores. Prior to 2005, each student took a yearlong, two-credit, core course taught by one science teacher. The course was designed to encompass the content of biology, chemistry, physics, and Earth/space science, and be taught in an integrative and inquiry-based fashion. A review of the sophomore program conducted by external experts in science education indicated that inquiry teaching in this course was deficient. Also, teachers were not necessarily comfortable enough with some content to teach in an inquiry-based way when teaching outside their discipline. Teaching inquiry skills often became a pedagogical choice, not the program initiative that it was intended to be. Additionally, given that we are a school for students interested, talented, and gifted in math and science, and that those students come from all over Illinois, these students have enormously varying backgrounds in science. With an integrative common course, we did not have a mechanism for honoring student proficiency in a specific area. More specifically, we could not exempt them from a portion of a yearlong course. While integration and inquiry were occurring, we were not satisfied with the depth and extent to which they occurred. These were significant issues that led us to conclude that we were not providing our students with the best science experiences that we could offer.

After a year of conversation and redesign, the current core sophomore program was implemented. It has four one-semester courses, each worth a half credit. Three of the four courses are discipline-specific, and are taught by an instructor with an advanced degree in that field: Scientific Inquiries—Chemistry (SIC), Scientific Inquiries—Physics (SIP), and Scientific Inquiries—Biology (SIB). The fourth course is Methods in Scientific Inquiry (MSI), described in the following section, which can be taught by anyone on the science team. Our goal is still to teach all of these core courses in an inquiry-based fashion.

Our science elective program can be likened to a small college. Juniors and seniors take electives together, with no specific sequencing. There are five biology electives five chemistry electives and seven physics electives. Students at IMSA are required to take a total of four science credits, three math credits, one additional math or science credit, three English credits, two-and-a-half history/social science credits, one wellness credit, one-half fine arts credit, and two world language credits. Most students take more credits than they need in the various areas.

Methods in Scientific Inquiry

Methods in Scientific Inquiry is a one-semester, one-half credit course that is required of all IMSA sophomores. It meets twice a week for 95 minutes each. The course explicitly addresses three broad areas encompassed by the nature of science: data acquisition and analysis, experimental design, and written and oral communication. Activities support the development of basic skills across the science disciplines and promote an understanding of scientific inquiry and the nature of research.

It is our goal that students begin to develop the skills necessary to conduct a science inquiry investigation through a variety of activities that deepen with time (Table 1). The activities support the development of skills in science, as well as demonstrate discipline-appropriate thinking. Student assignments are completed individually and in small groups. After building appropriate inquiry and research skills, students have some latitude in defining a final research investigation and report their results of that investigation in the form of a paper in scientific format and an oral presentation.

The students enrolled in MSI acquire an understanding of the generative nature of scientific practice. They gain practice in designing, conducting, and communicating the results of science inquiry projects. By doing so, students gain a better understanding of the process and nature of science, the tentative nature of science knowledge, and the falsification of hypotheses. They gain practice in written and oral communication, using the format and assessments of the SIR program. Although students encounter various concepts listed in the IMSA and National Science Education Standards, it is expected that students will leave the course with a better understanding of those concepts related to engagement in the process of science and employment of historical, personal, and social perspectives with respect to the nature of science and technology (NRC 1996; IMSA 1999; NRC 2000).

Scientific research starts with a question. During the first quarter of MSI, much of class time is spent asking and answering the types of questions listed in Table 1. The purpose of MSI is to expose students to these basic types of scientific questions, collect and analyze data, and draw conclusions from evidence. The students have much freedom in the specific questions they ask. For example, information or an assertion may be presented to them and they are then asked to investigate an aspect of that claim. The course is inquiry-based, with prompts to assist students in thinking about controls, variables, replicates, and appropriate statistical analyses. A course manual containing and describing a few basic statistical tests has been prepared and is provided to the students at the beginning of the course. They are expected to choose the appropriate statistical test, based on the type of question being asked and data being collected. While we know that we will be guiding them, they are not told any specifics at the beginning of an activity. The results obtained from these activities are communicated in writing in the form of a scientific paper or orally as a presentation. We do not begin by having them write a complete

Table 1. Methods in Scientific Inquiry

Question	Class Activity	Statistics
How can I quantitatively describe the population that I have sampled?	Student choice (for example, hair thickness, heart rate, or scores on some test)	Descriptive statistics
How does one compare the means (i.e., averages) from two populations for some variable?	Student choice (for example, temperature or rainfall in different cities, or heart rates of males and females)	t-test
How does one determine if an observed set of frequencies differs from an expected set of frequencies?	Phenotypic ratio of corn plants (for example, compare an observed phenotypic ratio to some expected Mendelian ratio).	Chi-square goodness-of-fit test
What does it mean for two variables to be dependent, and how does someone determine if one variable is dependent on another?	Student choice (for example, Is the ability to taste PTC dependent on whether someone likes a specific type of food?)	Chi square test of independence
What does it mean to be correlated and how does one determine if two variables are correlated?	Student choice (for example, Is there a correlation between population size and GDP for countries in Europe, or between the free throw and field goal percentages of basketball players?)	Correlation analysis
How does one describe the mathematical relationship between X and Y variables? Also, can one variable be used to predict or estimate the other?	Buoyancy Lab (for example, What is the relationship between the density of a canister and the percent of that canister submersed in some liquid?)	Linear regression analysis
How does one compare means (i.e., averages) from multiple populations when one or more variables are involved?	Bacteria growth (for example, students alter the conditions under which bacteria are grown and compare the growth rates under three or more different treatments)	ANOVA

Part of the curriculum of MSI incorporates statistical analyses, taught in an inquiry-based fashion. Students work through various activities while experiencing and developing inquiry skills. The activities change from year-to-year as the course is refined and modified.

paper for an activity, but focus at different times on specific sections, developing their skills and understanding of the communication style in science. Discussions of the nature of science and scientific inquiry and other topics such as content of the activity or research with human subjects are embedded throughout the course at natural times.

Student performance and learning in MSI is assessed using a variety of methods, including in-class quizzes, formative and summative written assessments, homework assignments, multimedia presentations, oral reports, and written papers.

MSI culminates with students doing their own independent research investigations that they have chosen with the help of the instructor. While students are completing the beginning activities and building basic skills and abilities, they work in parallel to choose and develop a rationale and plan for an independent research investigation that they will complete during the second quarter of the course. This includes going to the library and learning about peer-reviewed scientific literature. The students are expected to have primary science sources in their final research paper. Discussions and learning at this time also include scientific literacy, credibility of sources, and appropriate use of the Internet and web resources. As the semester progresses, the independent investigation becomes the larger course focus. Students have as much freedom to choose their independent investigation as we can offer, given that we do not have unlimited resources and time. The culmination of this final project will be a written research paper and an oral presentation. Students can work in pairs to complete data collection and analysis and the oral presentation; the research paper is written separately and independently.

Student Experiences in Science Prior to IMSA

Our teaching experiences while working with students both in the science classes and in the SIR program led us to realize that students needed specific experiences in scientific inquiry. We created MSI to give our students experience in the nature of scientific inquiry and the processes of science. A survey with questions modified from the High School Survey of Student Engagement was administered to 107 IMSA sophomores, about two weeks before the end of MSI, the first semester that it was taught. These questions and a summary of the student responses are shown in Tables 2 and 3.

Table 2 shows the data obtained when students were asked about their science class experiences prior to attending IMSA. While nearly two-thirds of them reported that they engaged in hands-on science at their home schools "often" or "very often," large percentages reported spending lots of time in science listening to the teacher and completing worksheets. Only about one-third of the students reported that they were the ones presenting and discussing the information "often" or "very often."

We probed what they experienced, prior to coming to IMSA, when they did engage in hands-on science activities (Table 3). We found that the students had little opportunity to design their own experiments, although slightly more than half reported determining experimental controls "often" or "very often." They had little instruction in and opportunity for using and performing statistical analyses. They were provided with few opportunities to communicate in a scientific fashion. Students also reported that they were not very engaged in science outside of school. The following percentages are totals of students who reported participating often or very often: Science Olympiad, 6.5%; science club, 8.4%; science fair, 22.4%; other activities, 16.8%. It is interesting that our IMSA students, who are coming to a math and science academy with a strong interest in STEM fields, report engagement in few science activities outside the classroom.

Student Perceptions of MSI

At the end of the first semester that MSI was offered, students were surveyed about their perceptions of the course (Tables 4, 5, 6, and 7, pp. 48–49). We were a bit surprised by the lower-than-expected percentages of students who answered "very often" or "often" to some of these questions. For example, students were using multiple sources of information—class discussions,

Table 2. Student Science Experiences Before Coming to IMSA

How much time in your home school science class did you spend...	Very often	Often	Sometimes	Never
... listening to a teacher lecturing/talking?	42.1%	40.2%	15.9%	1.9%
... completing worksheets concerning science?	36.4%	30.8%	29.0%	3.7%
... watching a teacher demonstration?	12.1%	31.8%	46.7%	9.3%
... presenting/reporting on science?	12.1%	19.6%	52.3%	15.9%
... conducting hands-on activities/labs?	34.6%	28.0%	35.5%	1.9%
... engaged in student discussion of science?	15.0%	24.3%	41.1%	19.6%

Sophomore students enrolled in MSI (n = 107) were surveyed with questions modified from the HSSSE.

Table 3. Student "Hands-On" Science Activities

If you engaged in hands-on activities how much time did you...	Very often	Often	Sometimes	Never
... follow a given protocol?	47.7%	31.8%	17.8%	2.8%
... determine experimental controls?	19.6%	32.7%	29.9%	17.8%
... choose the experiment?	4.7%	8.4%	27.1%	58.9%
... design the experiment?	7.5%	8.4%	29.0%	55.1%
... design an experiment you wanted to perform?	3.7%	2.8%	23.4%	70.1%
... perform statistical analysis?	7.5%	3.7%	9.3%	79.4%
... make graphs, tables, charts?	27.1%	23.4%	29.0%	20.6%
... write a lab report?	31.8%	20.6%	24.3%	23.4%
... write in the form of a scientific paper?	9.3%	15.0%	20.6%	55.1%
... give an oral presentation?	6.5%	15.0%	54.2%	24.3%
... make a poster presentation?	11.2%	12.1%	44.9%	30.8%

Sophomore students enrolled in MSI (n = 107) were surveyed with questions modified from the HSSSE.

the internet, books and published articles, and course handouts (Table 4, p. 48). When students were conducting each activity, they were required to use statistics, write about the investigation, and incorporate science content, so they were using concepts from different subject areas (Table 4). About two-thirds of the students selected the responses "very much" or "quite a bit" when asked if MSI emphasized understanding information, explaining meaning, and making judgments, as opposed to emphasizing memorization. Only about 50% of students selected the responses "very much" or "quite a bit" when asked if MSI contributed to their growth in writing, speaking, thinking critically, and learning on their own (Table 6). A slightly higher percentage (57.0%) reported that MSI contributed to their growth in using information technologies. When asked about their skills and some specific questions about what they actually got to do in MSI, responses were generally more positive; about two-thirds of the students, or more, felt that they could do what was asked of them in the MSI course, that they got to make choices, and that they could be creative. However, only about 50% "strongly agreed" or "agreed" that MSI was useful to them (Table 7). We attribute this lower-than-expected percentage to the fact that our talented sophomores are well schooled in a system that tends to value science as a collection of facts and less about generating those facts. Further, by administering the survey before the students have had other course work at IMSA, the results reflect an expectation on the part of students.

The students were not as positive about MSI as we were, but our perceptions were that MSI was making them think, it was improving their writing abilities, they were growing in information fluency and the use of technology, and they were becoming independent learners. We felt that some of these results were caused by the fact that the data were collected after the first year that MSI was taught. A new core science program had been put into place with MSI as one of the new courses. But MSI is not a typical content course, so students did not know what to expect. Also, being taught for the first time, there was no IMSA culture about MSI; no previous students could discuss what it was like, providing hints and tips, and letting the new sophomores know where they might apply the concepts elsewhere. These students were also new to IMSA,

Table 4. Student Perceptions of MSI

Thinking about MSI this year, how often have you ...	Very often	Often	Sometimes	Never
... used information from several different sources (books, interviews, internet)?	21.5%	27.1%	40.2%	10.3%
... worked with other students during class?	62.6%	22.4%	11.2%	2.8%
... worked with other students outside of class?	33.6%	30.8%	29.0%	5.6%
... put together concepts/ideas from different subjects when completing assignments?	17.8%	29.0%	32.7%	19.6%
... participated in class discussions?	25.2%	30.8%	33.6%	9.3%

Sophomore students enrolled in MSI (n = 107) were surveyed with questions modified from the HSSSE.

Table 5. Student Perceptions of Mental Activities in MSI

How much has MSI emphasized the following mental activities:	Very much	Quite a bit	Some	Very little
Memorizing facts/ideas so that you can repeat them in similar form?	13.1%	16.8%	26.2%	43.9%
Understanding information and its meaning?	30.8%	31.8%	27.1%	10.3%
Being able to explain ideas in pretty much your own words?	36.4%	30.8%	20.6%	11.2%
Make judgments about value of information/evaluate whether conclusions are sound?	30.8%	37.4%	21.5%	10.3%

Sophomore students enrolled in MSI (n = 107) were surveyed with questions modified from the HSSSE.

Table 6. Student Perceptions of MSI's Contribution to Their Growth

How much has MSI contributed to your growth in the following areas:	Very much	Quite a bit	Some	Very little
Writing effectively?	22.4%	24.3%	36.4%	16.8%
Speaking effectively?	5.6%	12.1%	43.9%	38.3%
Thinking deeply and critically?	14.0%	31.8%	32.7%	21.5%
Using computers, information, and technology?	29.9%	27.1%	22.4%	20.6%
Learning on your own?	23.4%	27.1%	34.6%	15.0%

Sophomore students enrolled in MSI (n = 107) were surveyed with questions modified from the HSSSE.

Table 7. Student Views of Themselves in MSI

How do you feel about each of the following statements?	Strongly agree	Agree	Neutral	Disagree	Strongly Disagree
I have the skills and abilities to complete my work in MSI.	45.8%	34.6%	11.2%	5.6%	1.9%
I get to make choices about my experiments.	30.8%	45.8%	12.1%	7.5%	2.8%
I have opportunities to be creative.	24.3%	39.3%	15.9%	9.3%	9.3%
I think the things I learn in MSI are useful.	15.0%	32.7%	18.7%	18.7%	14.0%

Sophomore students enrolled in MSI (n = 107) were surveyed with questions modified from the HSSSE.

thus adjusting to a residential lifestyle, living away from home, and for many of them, taking challenging courses that now required them to study more frequently and, perhaps, differently.

Faculty Perceptions of MSI

It was a consensus decision of the science team to teach MSI and to reorganize the core science program. Overall, the feeling about the MSI course is positive, but there have been some challenges to overcome. Some teachers felt that there was too much emphasis on statistics. This was coupled with comments, however, that some individuals did not feel comfortable teaching statistics. We have seen that the students are more readily incorporating statistics into their independent investigations and applying statistics more readily in other courses. There has also been more conversation and sharing between courses, especially when students are using the same skills, such as linear regression analysis, in two courses. Students' graphing habits are improving, as are their writing skills.

Initially, there was some tension between scientific writing and writing a lab report. For scientific writing, students were documenting data, but were supporting their conclusions with summary statistics and the results of statistical analyses, not listing raw data and/or showing all calculations on raw data. Some content courses wanted lab reports with raw data. Consequently, some students became confused, and a few went so far as to tell the instructor that the instructor was wrong because students were taught something different in MSI! This was easily remedied by discussing with students various types of writing, even in science, and indicating when one type may be more appropriate or useful than another.

Student Transfer of Knowledge From MSI

During the second year of MSI, we were able to compare student transfer of skills taught in MSI because we now had a population of students where the juniors had taken MSI as sophomores, but the seniors had not. These students are together in elective classes. We also looked at the sophomores' abilities to transfer knowledge from MSI taught in the first semester to SIB taught in the second semester.

We asked whether there was a difference in the ability of juniors versus seniors to write a paper in scientific format. In the Molecular and Cell Biology (MCB) elective, students crossed two strains of the fungus *Sordaria fimicola*, which each produce different colored spores, and examined the meiotic recombinant patterns. They then were told to use the class data to write a scientific paper with no other prompts. After the papers were collected, teachers made copies, removed student names, and assigned each paper a number. A teacher not associated with the class scored the papers for elements found in a scientific paper, such as embedded citations and captions on tables and figures (Table 8, p. 51). The maximum score a paper could earn was 10 points.

We found a significant difference between the number of juniors (34.7%) compared to seniors (3.0%) who scored a 10 versus a 9 or less (χ^2 =11.539; df = 1; P < 0.001). We then tallied the scores on the rubric to see if there was a difference between the juniors and seniors, and we found a significant difference in their mean rubric scores (t = *3.08*; df = *80*; P < 0.01).

We also compared juniors to seniors with respect to each rubric item (Table 9). More specifically, we compared the number of juniors to the number of seniors who scored 2 points vs. 1 point or less on the rubric. Yates's correction for continuity was applied to these analyses. Whether students had divided their paper into sections delineating different parts of a scientific paper was dependent on class, with 82% of juniors compared to 54% of seniors doing so (χ^2 = 5.74; df = 1; P < 0.05). Whether there was a table with a caption was also dependent on class. Fifteen percent of seniors included a table with a caption in their report, whereas 53% of juniors did (χ^2 = 10.49; df = 1; P < 0.01). Significantly more juniors (59%) referred to the table in the text then did seniors (18%) (χ^2 = 8.36; df = 1; P < 0.01).

Table 8. Scoring Rubric for *Sordaria* Paper

2	1	0
All sections of scientific paper present—introduction, methods and materials, results, discussion and conclusion	Some sections are present in paper	No discrete sections in paper
Literature cited section present and citations are complete	Literature cited section present but citations are incomplete	No literature cited section
References cited in text	Inconsistent citing in text	No references cited in text
Tables/figures with caption in results section	Tables/figures without caption in results section	No tables/figures present
Text in results section refers to tables/figures	Text present in results section, but does not refer to tables/figures	Only tables/figures included in the results section; no text present

Table 9. Comparison of Writing Skills of Juniors Versus Seniors

	Seniors (n = 33)			Juniors (n = 49)					
score	2	1	0	2	1	0	χ^2		
Paper had sections	54%	3%	42%	82%	6%	12%	5.74	P < 0.05	dependent
Literature cited section	82%	3%	15%	86%	0%	14%	0.03	P > 0.80	independent
References cited in text	63%	6%	30%	73%	6%	20%	0.50	P > 0.40	independent
Table present with caption	15%	57%	27%	53%	33%	14%	10.49	P < 0.01	dependent
Results text refers to table	24%	18%	57%	59%	12%	14%	8.36	P < 0.01	dependent

Scientific paper writing skills of juniors, who had taken MSI, and seniors, who had not taken MSI, in the same biology elective were assessed. The percent is of seniors and juniors scoring 2, 1, or 0 points on each rubric item for various elements found in a scientific paper. Chi-square results are for the test of independence with the variables being class (that is, juniors versus seniors) and score (2 versus 1 and lower).

Regarding a literature cited section with complete citations, there was no significant difference between juniors and seniors (χ^2 = 0.03; df = 1; P > 0.80). We also found no difference between the classes when it came to citing sources in the text (χ^2 = 0.50; df = 1; P > 0.40). These two skills are common for humanities and English papers as well as scientific papers, so there may also be transfer from other nonscience classes. Although we cannot conclude that MSI was the only factor that was responsible for the difference between juniors and seniors in their ability to write a scientific paper, we believe that it played a role in this difference.

Sophomores in SIB in their second semester who had taken MSI in the first semester were assigned to write a paper on a chromosomal abnormality. Each student was assigned a different syndrome (for example, Down syndrome, Edwards syndrome, or Patau syndrome). Besides the description of what information to include, students were only given the prompt to "use credible sources." They were not given any prompts about citing their sources in the text. All but 1 out of 71 students included a bibliography. Only 7% of the students had a mix of credible and noncredible sources, whereas 93% used only credible sources. Somewhat unsettling, however, was the fact that only 30% cited sources in the text. It appears that students are aware of what a credible source is in science, and that including a bibliography is part of writing a paper. Although all students were exposed to the idea of citing in text and were required to do so in MSI the previous semester, not all had internalized this as a habit.

Effect of MSI on SIR

Students are conducting more investigations that use human subjects. Three investigations in 2005–06, six investigations in 2006–07, and 14 investigations in 2007–08 were submitted by students to IMSA's institutional review board (IRB) for approval. These were studies where students wanted to collect data systematically using either surveys or some experimental treatment (for example, "What is the effect of music on memory?"). MSI incorporates survey design for data collection, as well as information about the use of human subjects in research and IRBs. It is possible, then, that this increase may be caused by the experiences of students in MSI. Students also understand the need for the "extra paperwork" when completing an IRB proposal because they have learned that it is a normal and required aspect of human subjects research.

We also believe that we are growing a culture of students who are more readily using statistics. These investigations, and many others in SIR, are incorporating statistical analyses of data in their final papers. Students actively seek out MSI teachers and the research office staff, for both on-campus and off-campus investigations, to determine which statistical test is most appropriate for their data.

We wanted to determine objectively the effect of MSI on SIR by examining SIR proposals or final papers for carryover of key elements of MSI such as use of statistics, embedded citations, quality of sources, and improved data presentation and writing skills. However, we feel that there are too many confounding and changing elements within SIR and our students to carry out solid analyses. The off-campus and the on-campus programs were merged together, with identical requirements and assessments for both groups of students. This has not always been the case. We have a couple of years of students where some have had MSI and participated in SIR, and others have not had MSI and participated in SIR. However, this is confounded by the fact that trying to compare juniors who have had MSI and are in the first year of SIR with seniors who have not had MSI and are in the second year of SIR is not valid.

Further, SIR became a graded course for the first time this academic year, since the on-campus and off-campus programs were merged. Students get a grade of fail, pass, or pass with distinction. The students who are enrolled may drop without penalty by the end of the first quarter. Previously, students could drop at any time without penalty. Participation in prior academic years was noted on the transcript, but completion did not carry the possibility of being noted as distinctive or extraordinary. Students who did not complete SIR successfully simply had the notation of SIR removed from their final transcript.

SIR Long-Term Outcomes

It is quite common for us to hear from previous students about the value of their IMSA research experiences and for students to tell us that they were able to obtain positions in college conducting undergraduate research, even in their freshman year. Anecdotes like the following two are quite common.

Anecdote Number 1

SIR made a huge difference for me. Mine was at Fermi National Accelerator Laboratory in 1993 at the birth of the Web, and my advisor (Matt Wicks) asked me to help him look at how to support various Web tools. This led me to learn how to program dynamic websites, which then jump-started my research career in college and graduate school because I was one of only a handful of people who had this skill. My research in graduate school ultimately turned into my company, MediaRiver. All of this would not have been possible without the opportunity offered by IMSA and the SIR program.

—Jay Budzik, IMSA class of 1995

Anecdote Number 2

I really think that my time in SIR helped me figure out what I want to do, and it is one of my most valued memories of IMSA. I wanted to let you know that I got the chance to enter an MD/PhD program, funded through the Growth and Development Training Program at the University of Chicago. I'm going to be getting a degree in cancer biology, and will be taking a leave of absence from med school to start the PhD next week! It happened really fast, but I knew it's what I wanted to do. I appreciate the opportunity to work with you at IMSA and that was a large factor in my decision to pursue a dual degree.

—Nan Sethakorn, IMSA Class of 2001

These are two very positive stories. Some students also relate that while the research experience was valuable to them, it showed them that they did not want to pursue the type of work that they had been conducting through SIR as a career. One parent related, "My daughter did an anthropology project in her junior year because she thought that was her career path. She soon changed her mind and did a botany project in her senior year and continues that work in college. We are so grateful to SIR." Even when an investigation turns out not to be as expected, most students still value the learning experience.

To address in a more objective fashion the effect of STEM research experiences on students' STEM education enrollment, we examined declared college majors and degree attainment for some of our IMSA graduates who had participated in SIR. Information on SIR participants was matched with data on student undergraduate enrollment and initial degree attainment. For the purposes of this investigation two classes were selected: the class of 2000 for initial degree attainment and the class of 2006 for initial college major. Discernable differences in both initial degree attainment and initial major in STEM versus non-STEM fields is evident when comparing graduates who engaged in STEM-based SIR experiences and those who did not.

Initial College Major for the Class of 2006

Of the 187 students in the class of 2006 for whom there was college major data available in the National Student Clearinghouse, 127 participated in SIR as juniors or seniors and 60 did not. The SIR students were further broken down by whether or not their SIR experience was in a STEM field or not. Students participating in multiple SIR experiences that did both STEM and non-STEM work are reported in the STEM group. Table 10 shows that the STEM SIR students went into initial STEM majors at a slightly higher rate than students who did not participate in SIR, and that students who had done SIR projects in the humanities or social sciences expectedly entered into a STEM major at a lower rate. This is not wholly unexpected given that early self-selection into a STEM field may be represented by student choice of SIR experience.

Table 10. Initial College Major by SIR Experience

Student Group	Initial Major					
	STEM		Undeclared		Non-STEM	
STEM SIR	74	76.3%	14	14.4%	9	9.3%
Non-STEM SIR	14	46.7%	5	16.7%	11	36.7%
No SIR	38	63.3%	8	13.3%	14	23.3%

Data on college major for the IMSA graduating class of 2006, n = 187, was obtained from the National Student Clearinghouse. STEM, non-STEM, and undeclared major data was correlated with participation in STEM or non-STEM SIR experiences.

Initial Degree Attainment of the Class of 2000

Using data from the National Student Clearinghouse, we were able to identify initial degree information for 105 members of the class of 2000, a match rate of 55%. Of those students, 54 had participated in SIR and 51 had not. Analysis of initial bachelor's degrees earned showed that students who had undertaken a STEM SIR experience were considerably more likely than non-SIR students to have persisted in attainment of a degree in a STEM field, 68% to 45%. Table 11 shows initial degree attainment by student SIR experience.

Table 11. Initial College Degree by SIR Experience

Student Group	Initial Degree			
	STEM Bachelor's Degree		Non-STEM Bachelor's Degree	
STEM SIR	30	68.2%	14	31.8%
Non-STEM SIR	5	50.0%	5	50.0%
No SIR	23	45.1%	28	54.9%

Data on college major for the IMSA graduating class of 2000, n = 105, was obtained from the National Student Clearinghouse. STEM and non-STEM Bachelor's degree attainment was correlated with participation in STEM or non-STEM SIR experiences.

While the near-term initial major data appear to show carryover from SIR experiences, the degree to which self-selection plays a role is probably strong. More interestingly, it appears that one of the residual effects of the SIR experience may be persistence in a STEM field, as is demonstrated by the data on initial degree attainment.

Discussion

The National Research Council (NRC) has emphasized the importance of teaching scientific inquiry in the National Science Education Standards (1996, 2000). According to the NRC (1996) scientific inquiry can fall into three categories. The first is the act of doing science. The second is that scientific inquiry can also refer to the way of teaching in the classroom in which students develop knowledge and understanding of scientific ideas. The third can be described as the nature of science, how scientists study the natural world. The thinking skills needed to perform inquiry are important for all students to have. The inquiry we describe in this chapter is the doing of science, often called authentic inquiry, although we do teach in an inquiry-based fashion and we do cover the nature of science.

When students do science, they take ownership of their learning and practice transfer of that learning as they solve problems that they find relevant. A National Science Foundation report (Russell 2005) assessed the value of undergraduate STEM research experiences as a positive predictor of continued career participation in STEM fields. The students surveyed indicated that the research experience helped them to plan and conduct a research project and assisted in their abilities to work both independently and collaboratively. Our data on IMSA graduates suggest that the SIR experiences that we are facilitating are supporting high school students in their STEM careers in similar ways. Our students are obtaining and continuing research experiences early in college and their high school research experiences are having an effect on their college major selection. We hope to ask similar questions of IMSA high school graduates to those that Russell did when assessing the value of undergraduate STEM research experiences.

SIR students are asked to reflect on their learning in SIR as part of their final papers. Although they encounter inquiry-based teaching in their science courses, overwhelmingly, students convey how different their learning experience is through SIR compared to their coursework. They find SIR to be more "real world" and, of course, more personalized because they have chosen the topic to explore and have gained a deep understanding of it. For a number of years, we have been providing substantial research opportunities to students, and those opportunities have been valued. However, as we have reflected on our teaching and learning and worked with our students in more personalized ways, we realized that we could improve their research experiences. To better prepare students for research, we changed our SIR program and developed MSI. Our beginning inquiry into the effects of MSI suggests that some of the objectives of the course are being transferred by the students into other courses and research experiences.

We continue to evaluate and modify our SIR program and the science courses based on our teaching experiences, perceptions of student learning, and by working in a very personalized way with our students. Our goals are to make continual improvements in students' acquisition of inquiry skills and scientific habits of mind.

References

Illinois Mathematics and Science Academy (IMSA). 1999. *IMSA's learning standards*. Aurora, IL: Illinois Mathematics and Science Academy.

Marbach-Ad, G., and P. G. Sokolove. 2000. Good science begins with good questions. *Journal of College Science Teaching* 30 (3): 192–195.

National Research Council (NRC). 1996. *National science education standards*. Washington, DC: National Academy Press.

National Research Council (NRC). 2000. *Inquiry and the national science education standards*. Washington, DC: National Academy Press.

Russell, S. H. 2005. *Evaluation of NSF support for undergraduate research opportunities survey of STEM graduates*. Menlo Park, CA: SRI International.

Scheppler, J. A., S. Rogg, S. Styer, and D. Dosch. 2005. Student inquiry at the Illinois Mathematics and Science Academy. In *Exemplary science in grades 9–12: Standards-based success stories,* ed. R. Yager, 113–124. Arlington, VA: NSTA Press.

From Wyoming to Florida, They Ask, "Why Wasn't I Taught This Way?"

Joseph I. Stepans
University of Wyoming

Diane L. Schmidt
Florida Gulf Coast University

As educators recognize the power of inquiry in the classroom, the Conceptual Change Model (CCM) is gaining popularity across the country. Those who are using CCM are reporting that students are highly engaged and excited about learning and they are gaining a deeper understanding of concepts, improving their use of process skills, and developing competency in the inquiry processes advocated in the National Science Education Standards (NSES). Directly aligned with the Essential Features of Inquiry, students involved in CCM activities use scientific processes to identify and confront their preconceptions and develop more mature and scientifically accurate understandings of the concepts they study.

The Conceptual Change Model has been used successfully for nearly 20 years by K–12 teachers and university professors to provide an environment for learning through inquiry. Although originally designed as a model for developing understanding in the physical sciences, the model is now used successfully in all areas of science, mathematics, and engineering, as well as other disciplines. CCM is now being implemented with a variety of learners at different levels and in different disciplines. This includes K–12 students, inservice teachers, undergraduate students in science and mathematics content courses, undergraduate education majors, graduate students in education, and graduate students who are preparing for postsecondary teaching positions in all fields. Significant professional development projects and preservice education activities are demonstrating changes in teaching and student learning.

More Emphasis

The following demonstrates how CCM is consistent with the *More Emphasis* conditions for inquiry defined by the NSES (NRC 1996). The use of the CCM contributes to all 14 of these recommendations, but in the interest of space, these statements are consolidated into four general categories for discussion:

- *More emphasis on understanding concepts within the context of inquiry*—CCM emphasizes in-depth understanding of concepts as learners are challenged to confront their preconceptions through active investigation.
- *More emphasis on extended investigation of fewer important scientific concepts for in depth understanding*—The nature of CCM requires "uncovering" a concept in depth, rather than "covering" many topics superficially. In CCM, pursuing a question or problem may take several sessions and some investigations may continue for weeks or months.
- *More emphasis on activities on developing process skills through real scientific investigation using the context of scientific content*—In CCM, the students pose genuine questions and learn how to analyze a problem, collect appropriate data, and analyze and communicate findings. They also raise new questions of interest to them for follow-up.
- *More emphasis on integrating and applying scientific concepts*—CCM provides a natural context and opportunity for students to make connections by generating examples and thinking of applications.

Exemplary Practices

Through workshops and classes, educators across the nation are discovering the effectiveness of inquiry by experiencing CCM lessons, observing CCM lessons conducted with K–12 students, and using professionally developed lessons themselves from CCM books for science (Stepans 2006) and mathematics (Stepans et al. 2005). Those providing instruction in the use of inquiry through CCM activities have always modeled lessons for participants by facilitating activities in which the participants act as the learners. Participants in these settings are always positive about their learning experiences, but are often skeptical about the application to their own students or future students. However, when educators witness the model's application in actual K–12 classrooms or when they teach a well-planned lesson themselves, their enthusiasm and commitment to teaching through inquiry is overwhelming. Witnessing students actively explore, discuss, and analyze data to develop and apply fundamental concepts and principles is an incredible experience. Educators repeatedly report their surprise and awe at how adept their students are. They discover that students can think critically, think deeply, and understand complex concepts and relationships.

Description of the Conceptual Change Model

The six phases of the Conceptual Change Model were designed to deliberately bring about meaningful change in learners by addressing their prior knowledge and targeting their misconceptions. The mental struggle required to bring about change is described by Piaget (1978) as accommodation, where learners must restructure their schemata. This is a facet of learning that is usually overlooked in traditional instruction. The CCM, which was formalized by Joseph Stepans at the University of Wyoming, was based on the work of Posner, Strike, Hewson, and Gertzog (1982) and others who recognized the need for conceptual change as part of the learning process. As students complete a CCM lesson, they collaborate throughout. However, each learner also has the opportunity to construct meaning in a manner that makes sense to him or her on a personal level. A typical CCM lesson has six phases:

1. *Commit to an Outcome or Position.* A CCM activity typically begins with a scientific question or a problem scenario, which may be generated by the teacher or the learners. In this phase, students respond individually by making predictions or identifying their positions on the issue presented. As they record their ideas along with their reasons, students draw from their personal experiences and knowledge that seem to apply to the situation. This short opening provides a genuine means for students to activate their prior knowledge, stimulating them to think deeply about what they know and understand and to become aware of their personal views and beliefs about the concept to be studied.

2. *Expose Beliefs.* Once students have the opportunity to think privately about the question, they share their views and reasoning with other members of the class; first in small group, then with the larger group. This verbalization helps students think more deeply about their ideas as they try to explain their reasoning to others. It also allows them to become aware of others' views. Sharing within the small-group setting provides a safe setting for this risky business of exposing one's preconceptions. When ideas are then shared with the entire class, it can be done by one member of each group without attaching names to the ideas. At this point, students recognize that there are numerous ideas about the situation or question that was posed. This generates a good deal of curiosity and a desire to explore and investigate.

3. *Confront Beliefs.* With great curiosity, students set out to test their ideas and resolve conflicting beliefs and ideas. They may do this by conducting experiments, making observations, collecting data, gathering information, and/or consulting expert resources. In some instances, students may design an experiment or determine the resources they need. In other instances, this may be determined by the teacher independently. Or, it may be a collaborative process between teacher and students. Whichever method is employed, the learning activity is purposeful and meaningful as each student uses the experience and discussions with classmates to make sense of the concept or phenomenon.

4. *Accommodate the Concept.* Based on students' observations, experiences, and discussions, each learner goes through the process of "making sense" of the topic and develops a new or more expert understanding of the concept or concepts involved. At this phase of the lesson, students are asked to develop explanations that reflect this new understanding. To do this, they analyze their data, evaluate their results, and synthesize their learning.

5. *Extend the Concept.* Unlike traditional lessons, students have the opportunity to apply their learning by extending it to other situations and identifying other examples of the concept's application. This is accomplished as students make connections to experiences and situations from their personal lives, as well as previous learning experiences and scientific knowledge.

6. *Go Beyond.* This phase of the lesson allows time for students to "go beyond" the scope of the lesson by asking new questions and posing new problems in the same manner as scientists. These new questions and problems reveal areas of uncertainty and often help the students and teacher identify the types of experiences that students need to continue their growth and understanding. Sometimes questions reveal students' need for a new experiment, controlling for other variables. Sometimes these reveal a need for reading additional scientific resources. Frequently, this time inspires students to think about how classroom work relates to the theories and research in the field.

Alignment With Essential Features of Inquiry

The Conceptual Change Model aligns with other constructivist models. However, it is also very distinct in that it is truly designed as an inquiry model. Many constructivist models are so general in nature that they are open to misuse. Educators steeped in traditional methods frequently superimpose a great deal of direct instructional practices on these models. This is not possible with the CCM. Lessons and activities are always conducted as scientific inquiry. Although developed prior to the Inquiry Standards (NRC 2000), the CCM aligns directly with Essential Features of Inquiry as Table 1 illustrates.

Table 1. Alignment of the CCM to the Essential Features of Inquiry

Essential Features of Inquiry	Conceptual Change Model
Learner engages in a scientifically oriented question.	**CCM phases 1 and 2** • *Commit to an Outcome.* Learner analyzes a scientific question or problem • *Expose Beliefs.* Learner shares his/her ideas and reasons with classmates.
Learner gives priority to evidence in responding to questions.	**CCM phase 3** • *Confront Beliefs.* Learner tests his/her ideas through experimentation or research activities; collecting data, making observations, and reviewing scientific information necessary to investigate the question or problem.
Learner formulates explanations from evidence.	**CCM phase 4** • *Accommodate the Concept.* Learner analyzes and synthesizes data and develops explanations based on results of investigation and discussion.
Learner connects information to scientific theory.	**CCM phase 5** • *Extend the Concept.* Learner makes connections to other situations, including real-life experiences, scientific literature and theories, and other disciplines.
Learner communicates and justifies explanations.	**CCM phases 4, 5, and 6** • *Accommodate the Concept.* Learner shares and justifies explanations with classmates. • *Extend the Concept.* Learner relates evidence and explanations to other situations to extend and justify reasoning. • *Go Beyond.* Learner develops new questions for investigation.

While CCM adheres to the inquiry criteria, it is highly flexible in meeting the variations of inquiry described in the Inquiry Standards (NRC 2000). Table 2, adapted from page 29 of the Inquiry Standards, describes the range of teacher directedness that can be employed during each phase of the inquiry process, and thus a CCM lesson.

Table 2. Variations in Implementing the Essential Features of Inquiry

Essential Feature	Variations			
	Least Directed			**Most Directed**
	1	**2**	**3**	**4**
1. Learner engages in scientifically oriented questions.	Learner poses questions.	Learner selects among questions, poses new questions.	Learner sharpens or clarifies question provided by teacher, materials, or other source.	Learner engages in question posed by teacher, materials, or other source.
2. Learner gives priority to evidence in responding to questions.	Learner determines what constitutes evidence and collects it.	Learner directed to collect certain data.	Learner given data and asked to analyze.	Learner given data and told how to analyze.
3. Learner formulates explanations from evidence.	Learner formulates explanation after summarizing data.	Learner guided in the process of formulating explanations from evidence.	Learner given possible ways to use evidence to formulate explanations.	Learner provided with evidence.
4. Learner connects explanations to scientific knowledge.	Learner independently examines other resources and forms the links to explanations.	Learner directed toward areas and sources of scientific knowledge.	Learner given possible connections.	Learner given connections.
5. Learner communicates and justifies explanations.	Learner forms reasonable and logical argument to communicate explanations.	Learner coached in development of communication.	Learner provided broad guidelines to sharpen communication.	Learner given steps and procedures for communication.

CCM activities may begin with teacher- or student-posed questions. Student questions are often generated in the "Go Beyond" phase of previous CCM lessons. These provide excellent starting points for new activities, as they indicate points of uncertainty or intriguing questions about applications of the content being studied. In a standards-driven environment, it is wise for the teacher to design learning experiences focused on the curricular benchmarks and expectations. Thus, the first CCM activity in a series of lessons often begins with a teacher-posed question to initiate the inquiry process. However, the remaining phases of the lesson and subsequent activities are usually far more student directed. The questions posed by learners at the conclusion of each activity are often the stimulus questions for new CCM lessons in the series.

Conceptual Change Model in Action

The following is an example of how the CCM was implemented in a ninth-grade science class and illustrates how it can be used where time and materials are limited. This example is one of a series of investigations to help students understand air pressure and specifically Bernoulli's principle. As you read the example, you might use Table 2 to assess the degree of teacher direction at each phase of the lesson.

The activity began with the teacher holding a funnel and a Ping-Pong ball and asking students to predict individually what would happen if a person blew through the upright funnel with the Ping-Pong ball resting in it. The students were encouraged to write down their predictions and the reasons for their predictions. Some of the students asked questions such as, "Who is going to blow into the funnel? Could we have Jim (the celebrated athlete of the class) do the test?" The teacher responded that if they thought that it would make a difference, they should include it in their predictions and explanations.

Once the students finished writing their predictions and explanations, they moved into groups of three and four to share their ideas. The teacher explained that they did not need to agree or come to a consensus in their group but needed to share and discuss their reasons. He reminded students that all views were valuable, and therefore should be voiced, heard, and respected. The teacher further asked them to capture all ideas on paper and choose a representative to present their collective predictions and explanations to the entire class. As groups presented their ideas, the teacher recorded their predictions and reasons on the board without judgment. The students predicted the following:

- If someone strong blows into the funnel, the ball would hit the ceiling.
- The ball will rise a few feet.
- The ball will rise a few inches.
- The ball will not move at all no matter how hard you blow.

Once predictions were listed and clarifying questions were asked and answered, the teacher asked a volunteer to conduct the test. As expected, the athlete was encouraged to step forward. Most of the students were surprised and many were not very happy when what they observed did not match their predictions. They insisted on having it done again and again. Some wanted to try it themselves or have someone "stronger" or someone with more lung capacity to give it a try. Some believed that the materials were flawed or that the teacher was playing tricks. Once they witnessed several trials, the teacher asked them to record all their observations. As students wrote descriptions of how the ball spun in the funnel but did not rise above the rim, a few students continued to voice their disbelief.

Next, the teacher asked students to return to their small groups to work on an explanation for what they observed. Some of the groups tried to craft theories using terms such as *force, energy, power,* and *pressure.* Once they had statements written out, they were asked to share their explanations with the rest of the class. Several of the ninth graders appeared to have come to a new understanding, but had difficulty verbalizing their new ideas. They talked about moving air and that somehow the power or force of the air must be wrapping the ball, holding it in place. Others surmised that blowing air into the funnel was putting pressure on the sides of the funnel and that must have something to do with the ball spinning instead of going up. As they continued to talk and discuss their ideas, they began developing the idea that the moving air was creating a kind of "dead space" or buffer around the ball. At this time, the teacher introduced "scientific" terminology such as *air pressure* and indicated that scientists such as Bernoulli contributed to our understanding of how moving air impacts air pressure.

Without providing further information on the concept, the teacher asked the students to think of examples where they had seen this phenomenon applied in real-life situations. Some students were able to connect this to kites, sports, airplanes, and the notion of "lift." Still others were able to connect it to cars passing each other at high speeds on a highway or cars "drafting" on a racetrack. One student talked about how a shower curtain moves when water is running fast, but is not touching the curtain. This brought forth an interesting discussion in which students came to the notion that air and water behave in similar ways because they are both fluid in nature.

The activity concluded with the teacher asking for questions. The students developed this list before leaving for the day:

- Does the size of the funnel matter? What if it were very large and wide?
- Does the weight, size, or shape of the object in the funnel make a difference?
- How could you measure the change in pressure?
- Why does the ball spin?

The teacher chose not to answer these questions, but thanked those who posed them. The next day, the teacher had the opportunity to review these questions with the students and to guide them in developing a new scientific question to be investigated. Students would then design their own experiments, determine what data to collect, and proceed to implement their own investigations.

If you used Table 2 to evaluate the level of teacher direction as you read the activity, you might have come to the following conclusions:

- As students made and shared predictions, they engaged in a question posed by the teacher. (This would rank as the most teacher directed.)
- As students observed the demonstration, the teacher directed them to record their observations, but did not suggest any specific criteria. (One could argue that this ranks at 1 or 2 on the variation scale, but is definitely more student directed.)
- Students worked in groups to develop their own explanations, which they proceeded to discuss, debate, and revise as a whole class. (This represents the least teacher direction on the variation continuum.)
- Students were asked to make their own connections to real-life experience, with a bit of

guidance toward the concept of air pressure and Bernoulli. (This probably represents a 2 on the scale indicating a minor amount of teacher direction.)

- In this specific example, students received little to no coaching regarding the communication of their ideas. (Again, this represents a rank of 1 or 2 on the lower end of the directedness scale.)

Although this activity involved a teacher-designed question and classroom demonstration, the level of teacher direction was minimized. Once the students went on to design and conduct their own experiments in subsequent days, the remaining activities likely fell in the category of the least amount of teacher direction.

The CCM and Abstract Concepts

There is a tendency among educators to relate hands-on experiences with inquiry. There are two flaws in this thinking. First, not all hands-on activities are implemented in an inquiry context. More often than not, hands-on activities are completed in rather traditional instructional contexts. Second, because abstract concepts cannot really be studied using concrete methods, many inquiry activities can and should be implemented without hands-on experiences. In traditional settings, students are often asked to "learn," or perhaps more accurately stated, memorize information that is abstract in nature. However, textbook definitions, teacher explanations, and models are often ineffective in helping students remember or understand this content. The CCM is highly effective for this purpose when visualization strategies such as Mental Model Building are used to develop understanding of concepts such as atomic structure, chemical reactions, day and night, mass-energy relationships, the theory of relativity, and quantum theory.

Mental Model Building activities typically begin by asking students to visualize and record their ideas about how something works or how it is structured. Rather than making a prediction, students begin the CCM activity by writing or drawing their ideas. After sharing their ideas and representations, they confront their beliefs by gathering and studying expert information from textbooks, websites, videos, data sets, or other appropriate resources. After discussion and debate with classmates, students revise their theories and drawings to reflect a more expert or mature understanding of the concept. As in all CCM activities, students continue to make connections, suggest applications, and generate new questions for study.

Implementation and Impact of the Model

As a result of using the CCM with their own students, teachers have discovered the excitement that the process generates, the high level of engagement among their students, and the impact on their learning. The following statements from teachers illustrate this impact on student learning:

- "As a result of using the Conceptual Change Model, my students started synthesizing, talking about science. They looked on their own for science materials and books outside of the classroom. They brought questions to class."
- "Through CCM, my fifth-grade students are beginning to think, to make connections,

and to ask questions. Another impact is the promotion of curiosity—They are looking for new ideas."

- "My fifth graders have started picking each other's brains. They ask, 'I wonder if…?' They are excited and enthusiastic."
- "My so called 'not book smart' students who felt ignored by others before, suddenly became very important. My other middle school students began to pay attention to and respect them."
- "I have noticed long-term learning among my middle school students, which helped them later make connections with other concepts."
- "There is a tremendous difference in the way my high school students approach learning. It is very clear that that students of teachers who embraced CCM are far more comfortable, and approach things from a learning-based perspective compared to teachers who have not [embraced CCM]."

One teacher who applied the CCM to mathematics presented her standardized test scores to demonstrate how the process impacted her students' learning (Schmidt 2004). This particular class was an inclusion class with approximately one-fourth of the students classified as "special education," referred to here as Exceptional Student Education (ESE) students. Table 3 illustrates how both her regular education and special education students performed as compared to the regular education students in the district and the state. Overall, the combined scores of the regular education and ESE students in the CCM class exceeded the district and state mean scores for regular education students. Astoundingly, the mean score for ESE students in the CCM class was higher than the district and state scores for regular education students.

Table 3. Students' Mathematics Test Scores

	CCM Class Regular Education Students	CCM Class ESE Students	CCM Class Combined Regular and ESE Students	District Regular Education Students	State Regular Education Students
Number Sense	67.5	60.9	64.8	60	56
Measurement	49.9	39.4	45.6	42	40
Geometry	63.1	62.3	62.8	60	56
Algebraic Thinking	59.3	51.0	55.9	52	48
Data Analysis	68.1	59.8	64.7	61	58
Total Math Score	324.5	309.8	318.5	309	300

Saigo (1999) compared the effectiveness of two instructional models on students in high school biology classes. Six sections of the introductory biology course were included in the study. Three sections, consisting of 42 students, experienced the traditional format, emphasizing lectures, worksheets, and confirmatory laboratory activities. Another three sections, consisting of 42 students, had CCM experiences. During the study, both groups studied the same concepts dealing with biosystematics. The participants were given a multiple-choice test covering the concept of biosystematics. The test was administered preinstruction, immediately postinstruction, and a month after instruction. Students in both groups showed significant initial gains on the first posttest, but those who experienced the conceptual change model exhibited a greater retention of those gains after one month.

Teachers have gained experience with the model through participation in professional development projects in which they experience the model firsthand and then apply it to their own classrooms. The CCM was first introduced to teachers in 1991 as a featured method in a professional development project known as WyTRIAD (Stepans, Saigo, and Ebert 1999). This project, which continues to be used throughout the nation, was named by the National Science Teachers Association as one of 15 exemplary professional development models (Yager 2005). The effects of CCM in WyTRIAD projects was studied by Cantrell (2000) and Galloway (2000). Their surveys, participants' written reflections, observations, and structured interviews provided compelling evidence that CCM had a positive impact on teachers and their students.

The CCM was also used in a large Mathematics and Science Partnership (MSP) project that was designed to enhance teachers' understanding of the science and mathematics content and to increase their use of inquiry (Henry and Schmidt 2005). Using best practices for professional development in science (Loucks-Horsley et al. 1998), university faculty from the College of Education and the College of Arts and Sciences at Florida Gulf Coast University teamed to develop and present a summer institute for 60 K–12 educators. This 2004 institute in space science was followed by a year of site-based support and workshops. This project expanded over the next two years to include more than 375 teachers in 29 school districts across Florida, and involved partnerships with four universities. Biology and Environmental science topics were added to the content options in the summers of 2005 and 2006 (Schmidt 2006).

To determine the effectiveness of the learning experiences, teachers were pretested regarding the content at the start of each institute. They were tested again at the end of the institute (posttest 1) and then again nine months later (posttest 2). Learning gains were demonstrated by both elementary and middle grade teacher participants. Increases in mathematics scores on posttest 2 were initially disturbing; however, the posttest 2 demonstrated extensive growth in mathematics understanding (see Table 4). Project coordinators believed that the institutes may have provided a conceptual basis for learning that continued throughout the academic year and strengthened as teachers applied their understanding to developing lessons for their own students (Schmidt 2006).

Table 4. Gains in Teachers' Content Knowledge

Institute Name	Space Science			Astrobiology		
	All items	**Math items**	**Science items**	**All items**	**Math items**	**Science items**
% of grades K–5 teachers improving pretest score to **posttest 1** by more than 20%	87%	48%	87%	88%	63%	88%
% of grades K–5 teachers improving pretest score to **posttest 2** by more than 20%	89%	89%	78%	(Not yet given)		
% of grades 6–8 teachers improving pretest score to **posttest 1** by more than 20%	68%	32%	68%	82%	64%	82%
% of grades 6–8 teachers improving pretest score to **posttest 2** by more than 20%	89%	73%	73%	(Not yet given)		

To determine the effectiveness of program on preparing teachers to implement inquiry learning using the CCM, teachers were surveyed on their understanding, confidence, and use of the model. Table 5 illustrates that teachers who participated in the project for a full year felt they increased their understanding of the inquiry process and the CCM. Using a rating scale of 1 to 5, the pretest survey indicated low levels of understanding about inquiry teaching. The posttest survey showed substantial increase in the percentage of teachers who rated their understanding at the highest levels.

Table 5. Understanding of Inquiry-Based Teaching

	Pretest		Posttest	
Summer Institute: Teachers will . . .	**mean**	**% rating 4 or 5**	**mean**	**% rating 4 or 5**
Understand the characteristics associated with an inquiry approach to teaching mathematics and science.	2.8	10%	4.1	90%
Understand the Conceptual Change Model and its implications for lesson design and classroom instruction.	2.7	20%	4.1	75%
Use the Conceptual Change Model and Essential Features of Inquiry for developing mathematics or science lessons.	2.3	5%	3.9	75%

Faculty at the University of Wyoming and Florida Gulf Coast University regularly use the CCM in their methods courses for preservice teachers. They use the model to demonstrate effective science and mathematics lessons so that teacher candidates have the opportunity to experience the advantages of learning in this manner. In addition, they use the CCM to structure all aspects of their classes. For example, they use the CCM to engage students in exploring topics such as learning theory, objective writing, and classroom management. Comments below are samples from course evaluations reflecting student excitement and appreciation for the experiences.

- "I have learned a lot about myself. I surely can teach a group of 30 children in an engaging way. I enjoyed your class very much, the interactions and group work was awesome!"
- "It really has been a wonderful journey. You could never truly know how you have prepared me through your constructivist methods of teaching and the reflecting we did."
- "I love the inquiry-based lessons where we were able to do experiments and ponder."
- "I really enjoyed the learning atmosphere during this class. We were always using higher-order thinking processes. It was excellent!!"

Before educators make a change in their practices, they must first believe that the proposed change is worthy. Therefore, workshops presented by the authors frequently take place in schools where they demonstrate CCM lessons in classrooms with K–12 students. Many faculty are now providing preservice teachers with preplanned CCM lessons to teach in K–12 classrooms as part of their course requirements. Upon observing these demonstrations and teaching lessons themselves, preservice and inservice teachers alike develop the enthusiasm and motivation necessary to develop skills in inquiry teaching. At the University of Wyoming, the CCM is an important component of the physical science program for prospective elementary teachers, and it is a featured instructional strategy in graduate programs there, also. In a very unique program, graduate students in the fields of science, mathematics, engineering, law, social sciences, humanities, and the arts are learning about the CCM, along with other strategies in a course designed to prepare them for postsecondary teaching. The following are representative comments about the CCM process from participants in this course:

- "This was the most enlightening strategy that we covered."
- "I was apprehensive at first, but once I was able to apply this, I think it is highly valuable."
- "Since we all have misconceptions, this is quite useful to address them.
- "Wish my instructors used this."
- "Teaching 'backward' is the paradigm shifting, but is really the way to present most topics."
- "I will definitely use this in my teaching."
- "Very powerful method. I'll use this for sure."
- "I think this strategy greatly encourages curiosity and initiates true learning."

Summary

The correlation to the NSES Inquiry Standards and alignment with NSES recommendations makes the CCM ideal for fostering scientific inquiry at all levels of education. To support teachers,

Schmidt, Saigo, and Stepans (2006) produced a handbook to help educators at all levels develop, facilitate, and assess CCM lessons and units of study. In most settings across K–12 education, preservice education, and postsecondary education, CCM has proven effective in promoting deep meaningful understanding of content and in developing positive dispositions toward the content and learning within the disciplines in which it has been employed.

References

Bransford, J. D., A. L. Brown, & R. R. Cocking, eds. 2000. *How people learn: Brain, mind, experience, and school—Expanded edition.* Washington, DC: National Academy Press.

Cantrell, P. 2000. The effects of selected components of the WyTRIAD professional development model on the teacher efficacy. Doctoral Dissertation, University of Wyoming.

Galloway, D. 2000. The impact of WyTRIAD professional development on teacher change. Doctoral Dissertation, University of Wyoming.

Henry, D. P., and D. L. Schmidt. 2005. Project LAUNCH mathematics and science partnership (MSP) program. Report to the Florida Department of Education and U.S. Department of Education.

Loucks-Horsley, S., P. W. Hewson, N. Love, and K. E. Stiles. 1998. *Designing professional development for teachers of science and mathematics.* Thousand Oaks, CA: Corwin Press.

National Research Council (NRC). 1996. *The national science education standards.* Washington, DC: National Academy Press.

National Research Council (NRC). 2000. *Inquiry and the national science standards: A guide for teaching and learning.* Washington, DC: National Academy Press.

Piaget, J. 1978. *Success and understanding.* Cambridge, MA: Harvard University Press.

Posner, G., K. Strike, P. Hewson, and W. Gertzog. 1982. Accommodation of a scientific conception: Toward a theory of conceptual change. *Science Education* 66: 211–227.

Saigo, B. W. 1999. A study to compare traditional and constructivism-based instruction of a high school biology unit on biosystematics. Doctoral Dissertation, University of Iowa.

Schmidt, D. L. 2004. *Constructivist practices in mathematics education: The effect of professional development on teachers' practices and student achievement.* Available from, School District of Lee County, *http:// accountability.leeschools.net/research-projects/pdf/DianeSchmidt.pdf.*

Schmidt D. L. 2006. Project LAUNCH II mathematics and science partnership (MSP) program, Report to the Florida Department of Education and U.S. Department of Education.

Schmidt, D. L., B. W. Saigo, and J. I. Stepans. 2006. *Conceptual change model: The CCM handbook.* St. Cloud, MN: Saiwood Publications.

Stepans, J. 2006. *Targeting students' science misconceptions: Physical science concepts using the Conceptual Change Model.* 3rd ed. Tampa, FL: Showboard.

Stepans, J. I., B. W. Saigo, and C. Ebert. 1999. *Changing the classroom from within: Partnership, collegiality, constructivism.* 2nd ed. Montgomery, AL: Saiwod Publications.

Stepans, J. I., D. L. Schmidt, K. M. Welsh, K. J. Reins, B. W. Saigo, and R. J. Kansky, eds. 2005. *Teaching for K–12 mathematical understanding using the conceptual change model.* St. Cloud, MN: Saiwood Publications.

Yager, R. E. ed. 2005. *Exemplary science: Best practices in professional development.* Arlington, VA: NSTA Press.

Student Outreach Initiative: Sowing the Seeds of Future Success

Craig Wilson and Timothy Scott
Texas A&M University's Center for Mathematics and Science Education (CMSE)
and USDA/Agricultural Research Service/Southern Plains Area (ARS/SPA)

Introduction

The Student Outreach Initiative project developed as a collaborative research community between USDA/Agricultural Research Service/Southern Plains Area (ARS/SPA) laboratories and their local communities and schools (grades 4–10). It engaged teachers and students in hands-on, inquiry-based activities linked to current USDA/ARS/SPA research and invited teachers, students, and their parents to become directly involved in the research. The laboratories extended their outreach into their local communities and the interaction with scientists and their research encouraged both teachers and students to "ask good questions." These are the questions that will lead to the next science discoveries (Karukstis and Elgren 2007).

This program targeted middle level teachers and students, as this is the age when students traditionally lose interest in science (Tai et al. 2006). The program used the National Science Education Standards (NSES) (NRC 1996a) for emphasizing cutting edge research and scientific processes, in an attempt to "create optimal collaborative learning situations, in which the best sources of expertise are linked with the experiences and current needs of the teachers" (p. 58).

For each of three years (2004–2006), 30 teachers were recruited from schools with high minority student enrollment and/or rural environments where there is a focus on agriculture. The targeted schools were within commuting distance of SPA research facilities to strengthen ties to local communities. Each year, at three different USDA/ARS/SPA laboratories, for a total of nine sites covering four states (Arkansas, New Mexico, Oklahoma, and Texas), we ran two-day summer professional development institutes to target teachers in their local communities; the teachers were supported throughout the ensuing year, and at the end of the school year, students, teachers, parents, scientists, and local dignitaries were invited to a Student Research Presentation Day. The common focus of all the laboratories was insect life cycles using the USDA/ARS/SPA research on the corn earworm (*Helicoverpa zea*) as the model around which students conducted research. One topic of research specific to each lab location was also studied.

The teachers each received a stipend for their yearlong involvement in the project and an Intel Digital Blue microscope for use in the classroom for their students. In addition, the students benefited from materials supplied at no cost to their school by the USDA/ARS laboratory plus the loan of special equipment. The contact with research scientists and involvement in genuine research practices was intended to improve the students' scientific knowledge and skills while also inspiring them to continue their studies in science (Dillon 2006).

Aspects of the NSES Visions

One goal of the Future Scientists-Student Outreach Initiative project was to create a science learning community by first linking USDA/ARS research scientists and their technicians with the teachers at a minisummer institute held at a USDA/ARS research laboratory. Then the students were engaged as they became involved and immersed in the science of the corn earworm insect, initially with guidance from their teacher and then with help from a scientist, who visited them in school, loaned equipment, and answered e-mailed questions. Parents were involved during the year and invited to attend the Student Research Presentation Day at the end of the year where student/group/class research was presented. The school principal and district science supervisors had to agree to the teacher's participation from the outset, offer necessary support during the year, and facilitate the school visits by project staff. They were also invited to the end-of-year event where posters and papers were presented. The design was an attempt to achieve one of the aspirations within the NSES where, "Teachers and students together will be members of a community focused on learning science while being nurtured by a supportive educational system" (NRC 1996a). The project also addressed each of the following goals for school science that underlie the NSES (NRC 2000):

1. Experience the richness and excitement of knowing about and understanding the natural world.

The subject chosen for study in the program was the insect *Helicoverpa zea,* more commonly known as the corn earworm, sorghum head worm, or cotton boll worm, depending on which crop it is feeding. Insects tend to instill either fear or excitement but always interest among students so it was a natural hook for their innate curiosity. Also, this insect is a major pest and causes an estimated billion dollars worth of damage annually. The students were made part of a research program and encouraged to learn about the insect's life cycle through hands-on inquiries as they were all provided with their own insects to grow through their typical life cycle. Students began by developing their observation skills, moved through data collection, and were challenged to design experiments that examined ways to reduce the tremendous damage caused to crops by the insect.

2. Use appropriate scientific processes and principles in making personal decisions.

The teachers were immersed in the research processes at the research lab closest to their school. This enabled teachers to teach their students better and to prepare them to undertake their own research concerning the corn earworm. This was a hands-on approach that had its basis in a real-world problem rather than an artificial scenario created from a textbook. Students were engaged and helped to understand that what they do and that how they conduct their research is vitally important if it is to be credible and of value. Similarly, they were expected to think about what was provided for them and were encouraged to ask questions rather than to accept something as fact. In short, it was emphasized to them that the decisions they take and the choices that they make actually matter.

3. Engage intelligently in public discourse and debate about matters of scientific and technological concern.

The obvious focus of this program was on problems related to agriculture, but it was premised on the need for scientific literacy in general and on the need to become informed on scientific matters. In order for that to happen, the teachers had to feel comfortable in the research environment. Great pains were taken to ensure that the mentor scientists could communicate well and that was one of the key features of selection criteria rather than simply identifying the scientists' willingness to participate (Pfund et al. 2006). The teachers were helped to become familiar with the research programs that were of relevance in their immediate surroundings.

The USDA/ARS is pursuing alternative courses of action to control the amount of damage by the corn earworm through Integrated Pest Management (IPM). This is a concept of preventive suppression of a mobile insect pest species throughout its geographic range, rather than reactive field-by-field control. The mission of the Areawide Pest Management Research Unit is to develop, integrate, and evaluate multiple strategies and technologies into system approaches for management of field and food crop insect pests. This was a concrete example that the teachers and students learned about in-depth and served as a model for them to see the need to become informed. Their personal decisions have to be made from a foundation of knowledge and a "broad base of scientific understanding" (Texley and Wild 1996, p. 27) before they can engage in informed debate on matters scientific and technological.

4. Increase their economic productivity through the use of the knowledge, understandings, and skills of the scientifically literate person in their careers.

The nation is falling behind in producing science graduates as evidenced in the report Rising Above the Gathering Storm (COSEPUP 2005) where one remedy suggested is the use of summer institutes "to allow teachers to keep current with recent developments in science, mathematics, and technology and allow for the exchange of best teaching practices" (p. 6). The Future Scientists program was an attempt to encourage more students to take an interest in science. The Director of the USDA/ARS Stuttgart Research Center in Arkansas pointed out that at the present time, 60% of USDA/ARS research scientists are currently eligible to retire (Freeman, personal communication, March 20, 2005) and there are insufficient American students in the educational pipeline to replace them.

Description

Inquiry-centered science is promoted by the National Research Council and was endorsed by the National Sciences Resources Center (NSRC) in 1997 so that students "learn to ask questions, experiment, develop theories and communicate their ideas" (p. 1). This was the model that was espoused in the design of the Future Scientists-Student Outreach Initiative, a professional development opportunity for science teachers.

The summer institutes were open to teachers, grades 4–10, who either taught only science or who had self-contained classes. The teachers were recommended by their district science coordinators. At each of three USDA/ARS lab sites, 10 teachers were recruited to participate in the summer institute. Half of the institute was spent helping the teachers learn about the life cycle of the corn earworm (*Helicoverpa zea*) through exposure to the research and hands-on work in the lab and field before they were shown how to grow the insect in the classroom. They then brainstormed possible classroom experiments and student research possibilities. The focus was on the life cycle of the corn earworm but the project had broader scope and appeal because it touches on the National Science Education Standards in K–4 Life Cycles of Organisms; 5–8 Structure and Function in Living Systems/Reproduction and Heredity; 9–12 Biological Evolution and Interdependence and Behavior of Organisms (NRC 1996a).

The teachers interacted with research scientists to learn about their cutting-edge research to better understand that "scientific inquiry refers to the diverse ways in which scientists study the natural world and propose explanations based on the evidence derived from their work" and that "inquiry also refers to the activities of students in which they develop knowledge and understanding of scientific ideas, as well as an understanding of how scientists study the natural world" (NRC 1996a, p. 23). Then the teachers had to decide how to apply elements of the research experience when back in their classrooms with students. This was accomplished with guidance from the project director, and in collaboration with the other teachers as recommended in the NSTA's *Pathways to the Science Standards, High School Edition* (Texley and Wild 1996) Professional Development Standard D.

The balance of the time spent at the institute was devoted to exposing the teachers to the work of some of the other research units at each laboratory to enable them to understand what research is taking place locally. This exposure to different research programs and interaction with scientists from different backgrounds allowed the teachers to break down the stereotypical picture of scientists and to share that understanding with their students. Abruscato suggests that "stereotypes of scientists may discourage children from considering careers in science or science-related fields" (2000, p. 16). Interaction with the scientists during the school year helped to further reduce if not eliminate the adverse effects of these stereotypes where a typical scientist is expected to be nerdlike and to wear a pocket protector while pouring chemicals into test tubes.

The selection of the participating scientists was a crucial component of the project (Russell, Hancock, and McCullough 2007). In a Scientific Work Experience Program for Teachers (SWEPT) that he designed and coordinated, Wilson (2001) discovered that the most effective teacher-scientist teams were those where both partners were enthusiastic and committed to their project with a lifelong "love of learning." The teacher did not necessarily have to have a strong science background.

The program was based in the Center for Mathematics and Science Education (CMSE) within the College of Science at Texas A&M University and supported by a grant from the USDA/ARS Southern Plains Area Director's office. It also had the support of the Southern Plains Agricultural Research Center (SPARC) and operated, in large part, through the efforts of the Area-wide Pest Management Unit (APMRU) at College Station. The scientists within the unit provided expertise and support in entomology and on palynology (the study of pollen) while the Research Center Director was instrumental in bringing on board a student worker with prime responsibility for distributing worms to schools.

Summer Institutes (2004–2006)

The teachers spent two days at their local USDA/ARS laboratory working with scientists and their technicians. The corn earworm was the prime area of study with the teachers handling all stages of the insect and learning how to grow it with students from egg to egg. The teachers examined field corn for worm infestation in research plots and dug beneath plants in search of pupae. At the Lubbock, Texas, lab the farm manager had taken the time to plant plots of both Bt (*Bacillus thuringiensis*) corn and regular corn, both of them late in the season, just so the teachers could actually compare differential worm infestation rates. They were able to look at student research projects, in either PowerPoint or poster format, from an earlier program before brainstorming possible future areas of research that their students might explore.

The balance of the time at the research lab was used to involve the teachers in some of the ongoing research at that facility. For example, in Beaumont, Texas, they were able to wade with an entomologist in rice fields to collect and examine aquatic pests of rice such as the rice weevil (*Sitophilus oryzae*) and in Las Cruces, New Mexico, the group went out to the Chihuahuan Desert Nature Park to study desert flora and fauna. This information was transferable to the classroom and the scientist was available to interact with the class.

Ensuing Academic Year

Without exception, the teachers considered studying the corn earworm an appropriate research project where goals were achievable within the confines and limitations of their classroom settings, with the understanding that the USDA/ARS lab resources were accessible to them. The project allowed the teacher to move away from "cookbook" labs toward activities by the students that were more reflective of what real scientists do in identifying a problem, formulating a hypothesis, designing an experiment, and drawing conclusions.

By the start of the new school year, the 30 teachers had decided if they would have their students grow and study the worms during the fall or spring semester depending on the structure of their curriculum. They kept in contact via e-mail with the scientist and personally with the project director, Dr. Wilson. He was also able to check to see how individual or group research projects were progressing and to offer constructive criticism. The whole process was geared toward introducing the students to genuine research and the understanding that science does not lend itself to 30-minute labs.

As a by-product, students often learned the valuable lesson that research does not always go as planned or produce the expected results. These results (or lack of expected results) were the culmination of the project and were presented by students at a Student Research Presentation

Day in May at the end of the school year. This was held at their local USDA/ARS research lab in front of an invited audience of scientists, teachers, parents, and educational administration staff.

Figure1. Students examine worms in an infested ear of corn, Hidalgo, Texas.

Student Research Presentation Days

For Student Research Presentation Day, each teacher selected four or five students to present their work on the project, and it was noticeable that there was an equal representation of both boys and girls (Gurian and Ballew 2003; Hyde and Linn 2006). Parents were encouraged to attend and many made the effort to accompany their child. The district educational administration staff was also represented.

The format for the day was the same at each lab site. There were two hours of student presentations, either through PowerPoint or poster presentations, with each school allocated about 12 minutes. Then there was a 30-minute "Scientist Question and Answer" panel where research scientists answered questions from the invited audience. Finally, a catered lunch preceded interactive tours of four research projects at each lab, guided by research scientists. For example, at the Stuttgart, Arkansas, lab students were able to use a radio tracking device for locating fish predators.

The Promotion and Dissemination of Project Components

Word was spread about the project as Dr. Wilson made informational presentations each year at educational and scientific conferences. A genuine attempt had been made to include underrepresented minorities in the program but this was partly governed by the location of the USDA/ARS labs that participated. However, the director was able to select the venues where he presented, and he presented at conferences like the Hispanic Engineering, Science, and Technology Week at the University of Texas Pan American in Edinburg, Texas, and also offered a hands-on, interactive display of the Future Scientists Project at the Community Day attended by thousands. Additionally, conferences like the Future Farmers of America National Convention and the National Association of Agricultural Educators Annual Conference—which had a decidedly agricultural science focus and which also allowed interactions with teachers and professionals from more rural areas—were also attended. But, it was especially gratifying for Dr. Wilson to attend and present at the National Agriculture in the Classroom Annual Conference, June 6–9, 2007 in New Orleans, where a project participant was awarded one of the prestigious AITC Teacher of the Year awards.

The Multiplier Effect

The project did not function in isolation but sought to expand its influence and impact beyond those teachers and students directly participating and is ongoing. The demand for insects has grown each year and, in addition to annual requests for insects from the teachers in home states of the project (Arkansas, New Mexico, Oklahoma, and Texas) requests for worms from teachers in 20 other states have been filled. These requests are a result of presentations delivered at conferences by the project director or because teachers can access information on the website associated with the project at *www.science.tamu.edu/usda/cornearworm*. Over 13,000 worms were shipped for the 2006–2007 year; that number has increased each year. To fulfill this demand, a student worker was hired with prime responsibility for maintaining the insect colony and shipping out supplies, at no cost, to interested teachers. A second avenue for outreach beyond Texas A&M has been for the director to work with education departments and their preservice teachers who are in Science Methods courses. Dr. Wilson has introduced the program at Texas A&M College Station, Texas; UT Pan American, Edinburg, Texas; Oklahoma State University, Stillwater, Oklahoma; and Texas A&M Corpus Christi, Corpus Christi, Texas. This past semester, preservice education majors in Rhode Island have also been involved.

Summary

Without exception, there was great cooperation and support for the summer institutes and the yearlong follow-up by all the stakeholders, culminating in the Student Research Presentation Days. The science learning community that was developed over the three years was built on genuine collaboration. The USDA/ARS/SPA research scientists who were asked to share their research with teachers gave generously of their time and were more than willing to share their expertise. The USDA/ARS administration and Center for Mathematics and Science Education (CMSE) staffs both worked to make each institute a success. This depth of implementation support, the thoroughness of the original inservice in preparing the teachers (Kyle, Bonnstetter, and Gadsden 1988) and incorporating them into the culture of the USDA/ARS research labs during the summer, and finally, the exposure to inquiry were essential to success. The project allowed the teachers to "deepen their understanding of the nature of science as a creative, knowledge-making process"

(Drayton and Falk 2006, p. 253). Importantly, the students rose to the challenge and often exceeded expectations in conducting their research.

Evidence of Impact and Success of the Program
Impact on Student Work

It was decided at the outset that the prime measure of success of the program would be the final student work that was presented at the end of the year. A yearlong working relationship was established between the scientists, teachers, and students and, as suggested by Drayton and Falk, succeeded because of the initial "scaffolding" or intense support (2006). This support carried on throughout the year and culminated in very successful Student Research Presentation Days back at the respective research facilities with a high standard of presentations, delivered by confident and poised student presenters; these provided a revelation to the research scientists. The projects varied in the length of time spent on data collection but all students were engaged for at least six weeks in the project (normal time span for the insect's life cycle). These presentations represented the full range of variations of the "Essential Features of Classroom Inquiry" (NRC, 2000, p. 29) and ranged from more teacher-directed and guided, through the teacher being responsive to student suggestions and input to the ideal where the research activities were totally student-centered and driven by their questions, interests, and enthusiasm.

Teacher guidance was often more pronounced at the lower grades where projects ranged from simple observation of the life cycle and research to determine if the insect was either a moth or butterfly to experiments to try to determine if the worms were cannibalistic. These experiments were often conducted as class or group projects but, teacher flexibility meant that individual students could pursue independent studies. For example, a third grader in Lubbock, Texas, was able to pursue an answer to his question, "Can I disguise the scent of the corn silks to deter egg-laying of the moth?" and a fifth-grade girl in Las Cruces, New Mexico, experimented to learn, "Will a thinner skinned kernel be preferred by the worms over a thicker outer skin from a different type of corn?"

Tenth-grade biology students at Valley Springs High School in Arkansas developed their project over an extended period and ordered worms over several months. Their work exemplified "open inquiry" where the students were the instigators, the ones "doing" the inquiry and, as such, included all the Essential Features of Classroom Inquiry at the most "learner self-directed" end of the scale (NRC 2000, p. 29). The students had several ongoing projects but, the initial problem investigated was, "How long is the life cycle of the corn earworm, what is the growth rate of larvae, and can we produce a second generation?" Students observed the growth of the worms while recording data on a daily basis, but they were unsuccessful in producing a second generation. They thought they had done everything correctly, so they researched factors that affect reproduction and consulted an entomologist. They knew that during the day, their classroom was kept at a constant temperature (20–22 degrees C) but found out by chance that the janitor liked to work in "arctic conditions." They now knew that the worms were subjected to cold temperatures and solved this problem by adding a warming pad at night to the worm containers. This allowed them to be successful in producing a second generation and from there they moved on to more complex investigations on the effect of temperature change on the length of the life cycle, on diapause, and on sexual dimorphism.

The scope of experiments with the insects was immense; projects ranged from looking at the egg-laying behaviors of the moth, identifying symptoms of corn earworm infestation, and calculating the percentage of infestation on sweet corn from a field to developing environmentally friendly sprays that would deter egg-laying. One enterprising sixth grader used the digital microscope to capture a movie of a moth shedding its pupa case while still other students were inspired to diverge into plant science with corn growth studies and to investigate pollen. This was in collaboration with palynologists at the USDA/ARS/SPA Area-wide Pest Management Research Unit (APMRU) in College Station.

Impact on Student Attitudes

A secondary source for measuring project impact was the qualitative data volunteered by both teachers and students in letters mailed to the project director. Invariably, teachers commented on increased student interest in science and their improved observation and research skills and were grateful for the yearlong support and links to the scientists. For example, teacher Angie Bogle wrote, "My students really enjoyed the Future Scientist Program. It did improve their interest in class and gave them an idea of what real scientists do." Teacher Patti Parks wrote, "My students not only learned from it but enjoyed it a great deal… I know that my students now understand metamorphosis that is tested on the science Texas Assessment of Knowledge and Skills (TAKS) science test. This was a great project and my students and I got a great deal from it." Perhaps the one comment that was most satisfying and reflective of the goal of the project referring to increased student interest in science, came from teacher Dennis Woodard: "As students were registering for the new school year, one bright young boy's mother told me that her son had changed his mind about future career choices, wanting now to be a scientist. The boy was one of the lucky students chosen to share his findings at the yearly Student Research Presentation Day."

Students overwhelmingly mentioned enjoying the hands-on aspect of the project. They felt that they were actually "doing" science. One student wrote, "Right now, the program is helping us to become scientists by letting us observe the growth of corn earworms." Another said, "Science used to be a bore but now I know science isn't!" Another student's words are obviously the ultimate praise for the program: "You have inspired me to want to become a scientist when I grow up." Finally, this teacher's comment sums up both student and teacher reaction to the project: "We need to push this statewide with special programs and funding. We need more hands-on, real-life experiences with more scientists visiting the classroom like your program."

National Impact

In 2006–2007, Dr. Wilson worked directly with the 30 teachers in the project and their 2,249 students (an average of roughly 80 students per teacher). He also reached an additional 295 teacher/educators through presentations made at conferences and, assuming that the average number of students taught per teacher is 80, this would mean that an additional 23,600 students were indirectly affected by the project. Then there was the director's interaction with the hundreds of visitors to the USDA/ARS/SPA exhibits at the HESTEC (Edinburg, Texas), NAAE (Atlanta, Georgia), and FFA (Indianapolis, Indiana).

Ninety science teachers participated directly in Future Scientists-Student Outreach Initiative institutes and their 9,820 students have been directly affected by the project. The ethnic makeup of participating students was largely determined by the geographic location of the collaborating USDA/ARS/SPA lab sites and when calculated over the three years of the project was 12% African American, 46% Caucasian, and 42% Hispanic. In addition, a further 710 teachers became involved indirectly in the Future Scientists project to impact a further 56,800 students over three years from 2004–2007. That meant that 66,620 students were made aware of and participated to various degrees in activities and experiments associated with USDA/ARS labs in the Southern Plains Area (AR, NM, OK, TX) and beyond (AZ, CO, GA, IN, KS, KY, LA, ME, MN, MO, NE, NJ, RI, SD, TN, WI) in the past three years.

The success and breadth of this outreach effort in reaching not only science teachers and their students but also parents, educational administrators, scientists and the general public was recognized when the Future Scientists-Student Outreach Initiative was the recipient of the USDA/ARS Outreach, Diversity, and Equal Opportunity Award in 2007 presented to Dr. Wilson at a ceremony in Washington, D.C. at the National USDA Headquarters. The project will be expanded in the coming years to include science teachers and their students in the vicinity of USDA/ARS research laboratories in Arizona, California, Colorado, Florida, Illinois, and New York.

References

Abruscato, J. 2000. *Teaching children science: Discovery methods for the elementary grades and middle grades.* Needham Heights, MA: Allyn & Bacon.

Dillon, S. 2006. Schools cut back subjects to push reading and math. *New York Times*, 26 March.

Drayton, B., and J. Falk. 2006. Dimensions that shape teacher-scientist collaborations for teacher enhancement. *Science Education* 90 (4): 734–761.

Gurian, M., and A. Ballew. 2003. *The boys and girls learn differently action guide for teachers.* San Francisco: Jossey-Bass.

Hyde, J. S., and M. C. Linn. 2006. Gender similarities in mathematics and science. *Science* 27 (314): 599–600.

Karukstis, K. K., and T. E. Elgren, eds. 2007. *Developing and sustaining a research-supportive curriculum: A compendium of successful practices.* Washington, DC: CUR Publications.

Kyle, W. C., R. J. Bonnstetter, and T. Gadsden. 1988. An implementation study: An analysis of elementary students' and teachers' attitudes towards science in process-approach vs. traditional science classes. *Journal of Research in Science Teaching* 25 (2): 103–120.

National Academies Committee on Science, Engineering, and Public Policy (COSEPUP). 2005. *Executive summary. Rising above the gathering storm: Energizing and employing America for a brighter economic future.* Washington, DC: National Academies Press.

National Research Council (NRC). 1996a. *National science education standards.* Washington, DC: National Academy Press.

National Research Council (NRC). 1996b. *The role of scientists in the professional development of science teachers.* Washington, DC: National Academy Press.

National Research Council (NRC). 2000. *Inquiry and the national science education standards.* Washington, DC: National Academy Press.

National Science Resources Center (NSRC), National Academy of Sciences (NAS), and Smithsonian Institution. 1997. *Science for all children: A guide to improving elementary science education in your school district.* Washington, DC: National Academy Press.

Pfund, C., C. M. Pribbenow, J. Branshaw, S. M. Lauffer, and J. Handelsman. 2006. The merits of training mentors. *Science* 27 (311): 473–474.

Russell, S. H., M. P. Hancock, and J. McCullough. 2007. The pipeline: Benefits of undergraduate research experiences. *Science* 27 (316): 548–549.

Tai, R. H., C. Q. Liu, A. V. Maltese, and X. Fan. 2006. Career choice enhanced: Planning early for careers in science. *Science* 26 (312): 1143–1144.

Texley, J., and A. Wild, eds. 1996. *NSTA pathways to the science standards: High school edition.* Arlington, VA: NSTA Press.

Wilson, H. C. 2001. *A multiple case study: The perceptions and experiences of four research scientist-science teacher teams in a scientific work experience program for teachers (SWEPT).* Unpublished doctoral dissertation, Texas A&M University.

Developing Inquiry Skills Along a Teacher Professional Continuum

Robert Wolffe, Kevin Finson, Kelly McConnaughay,
Michelle Edgcomb, and Shari L. Britner
Bradley University

Setting

Bradley University is a midsize, private, comprehensive university in a midwestern community of approximately a quarter million people. Of the nearly 6,000 undergraduate and graduate students attending the university, 700–800 are enrolled in professional education programs. In the past decade, new faculty members have brought philosophies of teaching that see the importance of facilitating students' involvement in their personal journeys to build expanded, connected constructs of knowledge and skills as an integral part of being a professor. The programs described are the result of a very productive collaboration between the science and teacher education faculties who view teaching through this student-centered lens. A major goal of the programs is to increase the level of inquiry-based science instruction used by teachers in local schools. Throughout this chapter, "inquiry-based instruction" is conceptualized as being student-focused activities that are within a continuum of learner responsibility and involvement in making decisions related to seeking answers to questions about the natural world. In addition to the programs described, faculty at the university are currently developing professional master's programs in elementary mathematics, science, and technology fields and in secondary environmental science efforts funded by a competitive state grant supported by federal flow-through monies. They are also working to establish a Center of Excellence in STEM Education.

Components of the Programs

The different facets of the programs described include portions for preservice teachers as well as inservice teachers. Preservice components are comprised primarily of two courses: Science for Educators (Science 101) and Methods of Teaching Elementary Science (ETE 336). Inservice components involve three variations of graduate programming: a yearlong course-based sequence (BEST), a series of independent but related one-day workshops, and a full master's degree program in STEM.

Preservice Teacher Experiences

Science for Educators (Science 101) is an interdisciplinary, inquiry-based science course for education majors that incorporates science content and science investigation skills development using research-based teaching methods (Llewellyn 2002; NRC 2000). This course was designed by a multidisciplinary, multi-institutional team, with leadership from the departments of biology and teacher education and participation by faculty in the departments of chemistry and biochemistry, physics, and mathematics, the College of Engineering and Technology, and master teachers and administrators from local school districts in the region. The goal was to develop a course that would provide preservice teachers with the background necessary to teach inquiry-based, investigative science. The course design was constructed to instruct by example, aligning the course with both the Illinois Learning Standards (ILS) and the NSES and utilizing teaching methods supported by advances in cognitive science. The interdisciplinary nature of science is emphasized by focusing on a specific theme (currently developed and used themes are energy, motion, environmental science, molecules, and evolution) and using the theme with both a life science and a physical science perspective. The scientific method and inquiry as means of understanding natural phenomena are priority foci. Students are expected to start asking questions and to develop testable hypotheses on the first day of class. Lecture and student-developed labs are fully integrated, with each portion of the course used to reinforce and expand on the ideas developed in the others.

During a typical class period, students working individually and in collaborative groups have time for open exploration of a topic with a goal of gaining a broader appreciation of the topic being considered. Afterward students share their observations, conclusions, and further questions that might be investigated. This open exploration followed by presentation has acted as an informal preassessment of student knowledge and misconceptions. A more formal process of pre/postassessment based on identifying prerequisite conceptual knowledge and desired areas of conceptual growth is currently being piloted. Student observations are used as a starting point for continued discussion and extension of the concept. These topics are then further developed through both student-designed laboratory research and the development of inquiry-oriented lesson plans. When practical, the students field-test their lesson plans with age-appropriate children.

Qualitative and quantitative data collection has been ongoing since the course was developed in 2000. Data sources include midterm evaluations, exit surveys, student journals and a Likert-scale survey concerning their confidence in their ability to teach science, their understanding of the nature of science, and gender-stereotyped beliefs about science. Relative content mastery of students taking Science 101 versus a traditional science lecture course was determined by comparing exam and quiz scores in Science 101 with comparable assessments in two traditional lecture courses with significant overlap in content.

Through Science 101, students' confidence in their ability to teach science increased significantly, as did their awareness of the nature of science and of inquiry science instruction, and their beliefs in their ability to influence their students' attitudes toward science. There was a decrease in the degree to which students expressed agreement with gender stereotypes regarding science. Student content mastery was higher for education majors taking Science 101 versus traditional lecture courses. Content mastery was greater for Science 101 students regardless of theme and topic, and content mastery in evolution, a particularly difficult content area for many students, was higher in Science 101 students. Higher content mastery scores were obtained on Science 101 content exams and quizzes despite a greater percentage of analysis and application questions than were found in assessments from the traditional lecture courses. Details of data analyses and results may be found in the *Journal of College Science Teaching* (Edgcomb et al. 2008).

Methods of Teaching Elementary Science (ETE 336) provides students with one of two opportunities: (1) reinforcing their inquiry investigative skills and experiences derived from Science 101, or (2) for those students who did not take Science 101, allowing them to learn and apply the skills requisite for successfully engaging in and completing an inquiry investigation. During ETE 336, students are given the task of identifying a science-related phenomenon of interest to them that they can investigate on their own. This task is called the independent inquiry investigation. Each student selects a science topic of personal interest, develops and conducts an experimental study to test the research question or hypothesis he or she formulates, and makes reports concerning the results and conclusions.

The intent of having students complete the inquiry investigation is multifaceted. Among those facets are:

- **Application of skills needed for inquiry.** The task provides opportunity for students to learn and apply skills through an inquiry approach. These skills can be broad-ranging, from science-process skills to specific techniques to the art of asking high-quality questions necessary to delimit and guide investigations.
- **Logistical components of inquiry.** Simply knowing what science-process skills are, or knowing some laboratory or field-based techniques, is insufficient for a thorough understanding of the inquiry process. Through the independent inquiry investigation in ETE 336, students are confronted with issues regarding not only what procedures and techniques to use, but also the manner and order in which they are to be applied. This often involves problem solving, such as that which occurs when a student realizes that the way he or she thought a variable could be measured is not workable and an alternative method must be found. Or, similarly, that there are multiple ways of measuring the variable and the student needs to determine which one (or ones) is most appropriate and useful. An example of this dilemma arises when the investigation focuses on the growth of a plant, and that growth can be assessed by plant height, number of leaves, quality of greenness, plant mass, number of fruiting bodies, and so on. Other aspects of logistics include timing and duration of the investigation; selection, acquisition, and use of materials and supplies; and suitable locations for the investigation.
- **Affective aspects of inquiry.** Along with tapping into one's knowledge base, inquiry also taps into one's affective domain. Engaging in inquiry results in emotive feelings and responses, which ultimately lead to attitude development (positive or negative) relative to doing science and to self-efficacy. Emotions commonly encountered during inquiry experiences often progress through confusion or excitement, exhilaration, frustration and/or anger, somber work, and fatigue. After completing their investigations, students reflect on the number and extent of the emotive experiences they encountered, relate

their progression to what might be expected from elementary students, and discuss ways of guiding their own students through it.

- **Increased familiarity with state and NSES standards relative to inquiry.** Having completed the inquiry investigation, students are more capable of making connections to what the state and NSES standards specify as important and necessary for effective inquiry learning and instruction. Ultimately, this leads students to a better grounding in understanding what will be asked of them as teachers relative to science instruction and standards.

After students in ETE 336 have designed and conducted their independent inquiry investigation, they are asked to adapt that investigation into an inquiry-oriented lesson with a corresponding performance assessment. The task of developing the lesson plan goes beyond simply selecting a lesson from an already-published set of materials, such as Full Option Science System (FOSS), although the use of those materials can certainly serve as a guide in the development process. Having students develop the lesson plan requires them to make applications of their own inquiry experiences in pragmatic ways for the elementary classroom setting. Ideally, the grounding students gain from having actually engaged in the inquiry investigation provides them with a foundation for the selection and/or design of lesson plans that are appropriate and effective for specifically targeted grade levels and groups of elementary students. In keeping with the idea that inquiry-learning skills must be taught to children, some aspects of guided inquiry are acceptable in the lesson planning. However, the preservice teachers are encouraged to include procedural steps in terms that are more open-ended. For example, a step may ask that the experimental procedures developed by the students be written out and submitted to the teacher. Lesson plans may also begin with a more structured whole-group activity and then asking students to identify specific factors to investigate further and to design the procedures necessary to do so.

Concluding the lesson plan is appropriate assessment. Because inquiry learning requires appropriate assessment, students in ETE 336 must also develop a performance assessment based on their inquiry lesson plans. The assessment, including a complete rubric, must address specific learning standards and objectives, and focus on the concept(s) and skills elementary students are expected to learn by completing the lesson, and to be inquiry-based. Assessments are required to have elementary students performing an act, and must lead up to having them arrive at a generalizing rule or conclusion. Although an assessment focuses on the same concepts as the lesson plan from which it was derived, the assessment cannot simply be a repeat of what was in the original lesson.

Throughout the course, to support the tasks assigned, students are involved with course instruction that focuses on particular science-process skills, techniques, and strategies necessary for successfully conducting inquiry investigations. The tenets of inquiry are discussed as the course progresses, with activities incorporated that illustrate various types and levels of inquiry. Examples are technique-dependent inquiries (such as paper chromatography), concept-dependent inquiries (such as the study of convection), the learning cycle, Suchman's inquiry training model, scientific experiment (as compared with simple hands-on activities), and so on. Students engage with Cartesian divers, pendulums, pH analysis, testing of consumer products (paper towels, for example), cratering, mealworms, and so forth. Significant effort is made to illustrate inquiry's flexible use of science-process skills in designing investigations and responding to changing needs as compared to the often more rigid use of the "scientific method" and traditional science labs in which procedural steps are laid out in advance. Attention is also given to the continuum of inquiry-oriented instruction, from structured guided inquiry to full or open inquiry. Although the inquiry project selected by each student is an open inquiry investigation, it is pointed out that elementary children need scaffolding and prior experiences to enable them to conduct open inquiry, much in the same way the course instructors provide scaffolding for them.

Throughout the semester, students are asked to reflect on and analyze their experiences in the course during small-group and whole-group discussions. These reflections include students' perceptions of their growth in learning about science and about the teaching of inquiry-oriented science. In their written reflections, they are asked to speak to their strengths and weaknesses at the beginning of the course as compared to the end, and to speak to their growth in knowledge and understanding of what the effective teaching of science entails. These reflections are included in a course portfolio submitted at the end of the semester.

Overall, the goal of this series of assignments is to provide direct experiences for future teachers in conducting inquiry projects with the goal that they will use the skills developed to guide their own future students in inquiry learning. As reported in Britner and Finson (2005), preservice teachers in this course reported increased understanding of the nature of science and inquiry-oriented pedagogy and stronger confidence in their ability to use these methods in their future classrooms. Student transference of knowledge related to inquiry-based instruction to actual teaching is assessed later in student teaching. Of 120 elementary education majors evaluated between fall 2004 and spring 2006 for their ability to utilize viewpoints, theories, and methods of inquiry, 91.7% were rated at the highest level where the student teacher

Demonstrates knowledge of viewpoints, theories, and methods of inquiry appropriate to the discipline. Consistently demonstrates viewpoints, theories and methods of inquiry appropriate to the discipline; engages students in generating and testing knowledge. (Bradley University 2007)

Ideally, the undergraduate program is designed so that students will enroll in Science 101 before they complete ETE 336. However, there are options that result in some students not taking Science 101. Consequently, the faculty was interested in determining the extent to which completing Science 101 helped students with the independent inquiry project in ETE 336. Several aspects of the 101–336 tandem were examined. Data for 229 students were used. The first question addressed was whether there was a correlation between students' Science 101 course grades and the ETE 336 grades received for the independent inquiry investigation. Pearson correlations were conducted on these data, resulting in a moderate correlation at the $p < 0.01$ level. These results can be interpreted to indicate the grade students receive in Science 101 is similar to their performance on the ETE 336 independent study investigation. This is reasonable because the major portion of Science 101 involves students with inquiry investigation and the ETE 336 investigations are also open inquiry. Students who become skilled in inquiry in Science 101 retain those skills and employ them in ETE 336. This is a good result in terms of retention of learning. The second question addressed is whether there were differences in students' performance in their ETE 336 inquiry investigations based on whether or not they had previously completed Science 101. Performance was coded on a 4-point scale (4 = A, 3 = B, etc.). The mean on the inquiry investigation (ETE 336) for students who had not taken Science 101 was 2.95 (n = 83), and the mean for those students who had taken Science 101 was 3.47 (n = 146). ANOVA procedures revealed that this was a significant difference ($p < 0.0001$) in values. As a whole, these data and results indicate there are benefits in using the Science 101–ETE 336 course tandem.

Inservice Teacher Experiences

While the evidence indicates the preservice experiences are successful, thinking that an undergraduate preparation program is sufficient would be presumptuous. An initial licensure program alone cannot produce the kinds of changes science educators desire in the teacher corps. Consequently, the second half of the plan has been to develop educational offerings for inservice teachers so they can enhance their abilities to implement inquiry-based instruction. To date, these opportunities have been in two forms: a yearlong course-based program and a program of related, yet independent, one-day workshops. A third approach is a full master's degree program in STEM education, which is being currently planned and implemented for the first time. This degree program is planned to be a good addition to the current offerings in this area and will add to the research on effective methods of professional development. Because the implementation of the first of these master's degree programs is just beginning at the time of this writing, further discussion concerning their effectiveness cannot be corroborated.

In the Building Excellent Scientists for Tomorrow (BEST) program, local K–12 inservice teachers are provided comprehensive professional development experiences that integrate science content preparation, a scientific research experience, an inquiry-based curriculum development experience, and a mentored experience in action research focusing on student learning. Twenty-two of the 25 participants in the program are educators from the high-needs public schools in the local urban school district where the university is located.

In the first half of the summer, the teachers experience inquiry instruction through the lens of a learner in a course modeled after Science 101. Next, they build their understanding of the nature of real-world science and the process of discovery by working for 150–200 hours with active research scientists on the scientists' current projects. This experience allows the teachers to connect and extend what they have learned about experimental design and conducting investigations in the content course with the longer-term projects of practicing scientists. In the following fall and spring semesters they complete their professional development in a course that combines their study of inquiry-based curriculum design and delivery with action research. The teachers either design their own units of study or modify existing curricula so that their K–12 students will be involved in a developmentally appropriate manner with designing and conducting investigations to explore real-world questions. Concurrently, the teachers identify a list of areas of professional interest based on what is going on in their classrooms. From this list they narrow their focus and develop a question to investigate through an action research project that is connected to the teaching of their inquiry-based unit. As the teachers implement their units of instruction, they collect data for their action research project. Finally, they analyze their data and report their findings in the context of research-based practices in education.

Preliminary data suggest that the comprehensive suite of professional development activities reinforces teachers' gains in each area, such that we see substantial improvements in teachers' understanding of the nature of science, concept mastery, inquiry curriculum development, classroom time spent in inquiry learning, and leadership skills. The teachers are taking their enhanced understandings and translating them into carefully designed learning opportunities for their students. Further, data analysis shows measurable gains in teachers' understanding of the nature of science and concept mastery with more targeted professional development activities, suggesting that even modest professional development can lead to some gains. These graduates are also included in the data collection on current classroom practices related to inquiry instruction.

The second prong of the professional development plan offered through the university has been an ongoing effort to conduct a series of three, one-day workshops for inservice educators. These workshops are also a part of an ongoing effort to evaluate the relative effectiveness of a variety of teacher development models. In 2007, the workshops were designed primarily to show hands-on ways of teaching concepts using inexpensive and readily available materials. Some time was spent in each workshop discussing ways of incorporating inquiry-based investigations into classroom curricula, although the time devoted to curricular suggestions varied. The investigations were deepened and made more inquiry-oriented for the last two workshops compared to the first.

The first offering in our inquiry-based workshops for STEM educators, Real Chemistry with Everyday Materials, was funded by an Innovative Programming grant through the American Chemical Society and was developed by members of the departments of biology and chemistry at Bradley University in cooperation with two local middle school science teachers. The overall purpose of the workshop was to increase comfort with chemistry education and to increase awareness of the breadth of chemistry that can be studied with household items. Among the materials provided were handouts on nine activities. The handouts included teacher pages with extensive background information, identified in Illinois Learning Standards, and safety information, as well as student pages with forms for data entry. During the workshops four of the activities were performed. While the workshop participants were given some leeway in terms of exact procedures, the inquiry aspect of the workshop was, at best, strictly guided. The workshop concluded with a chemistry demonstration show during which the principles behind the "magic" were identified and explained. All attendees were given materials to perform several of the activities with their classes. Evaluation forms were provided and completed as a basic part of the program.

The second and third workshops were developed and implemented by members of the department of biology and the Office of Sponsored Programs along with a local middle school teacher and were funded by a grant through National Science Foundation Partnership for Innovation program. These two summer workshops were more focused on a specific content area than the chemistry workshop and were specifically designed to incorporate scientific inquiry and be interdisciplinary in their approaches to the topic. At each workshop, attendees were given a GEMS teacher guide related to the appropriate topic that contained inquiry-based lesson plans appropriate for middle school students.

The second workshop, Inquiry Explorations of Solar Energy and Impact on Health, was used with local teachers and representatives from a local home school association and the education department of a local science museum. The format of the workshop began with a short introduction to electromagnetic radiation followed by a look at the health effects of ultraviolet (UV) light and the science behind sunscreen. Attendees were provided a variety of materials such as UV detectors, UV-sensitive beads, sunscreens, and clothing, and were then challenged to formulate and test a hypothesis regarding solar energy. After attendees had time to design a protocol, collect data, and draw conclusions, they presented their findings informally to the rest of the group. Presentations were followed by group discussion. Attendees were provided with a handout of background information and classroom materials.

The third workshop, Inquiry Into Weather: Your Personal Impact on Global Climate, was structured the same as the prior workshops and included participants similar to those attending the second workshop. This included a presentation used to introduce the concept of the greenhouse effect and to differentiate it from global warming. Attendees were provided with a variety of materials including plastic bottles, thermometers, soil, carbonated water, and dry ice and were challenged to formulate and test a hypothesis concerning the greenhouse effect, global warming, or other weather-related phenomena. Time was given for protocol design, data collection, and data analysis. This was again followed by group presentations and discussion. Attendees were given handouts of background information with explicit links to the Illinois Learning Standards and classroom materials.

Survey of Inservice Participants

Instrumentation: To follow up on the work with inservice educators, the research team members developed a survey to obtain information from teachers in the university's service area regarding inquiry instruction in their classrooms. A pool of survey items was drafted during the late fall semester of 2007. After the initial pool of items was developed, the research group carefully assessed the wording and ordering of the items. Some items were removed due to duplication with other items, lack of clarity (likely to elicit responses not focused on the intent of the survey question), or difficulty with formatting that could be facilitated by the size and nature of the instrument. The final survey consisted of 21 items. Content validity for the final pool of items was established through independent review by each of the researchers. The first six survey items were to obtain demographic data about the respondents. The remaining items posed open-ended questions and provided text boxes for participants to enter their responses.

Procedures and Population: The survey instrument was designed to be administered online through SurveyMonkey to teachers who had participated in a series of STEM workshops and/or the BEST program. The survey went online in February 2008. To ensure confidentiality for respondents, a graduate assistant was designated as the individual who could access the responses, keep track of respondents, and send follow-up reminders to those who had not responded. The survey was closed April 1. Information that could be used to identify specific individuals was removed by the graduate assistant from the data set, and the remaining data were then made available to the researchers.

A total of 45 teachers were contacted via e-mail requesting that they respond to the survey. Of that total, 34 responded (for a response rate of 76%). Thirty of the 34 provided their consent to use their responses (for an overall participation rate of 67%). However, response and participation rates varied greatly between BEST and workshop respondents; 17 of the 23 invited BEST teachers responded, and all agreed to participate, while 4 of the 21 invited workshop teachers responded, all of whom agreed to participate. There were 13 respondents who did not identify themselves as BEST or workshop teachers, 9 of whom agreed to participate; most of these respondents (i.e., at least 9 of the 13) had to be workshop participants, though individuals could not be reliably ascribed to either group. These differences in response rates were significantly different (74% of 19% of BEST vs. workshop participants, $X^2 = 4.94$, df = 1, p < 0.05) unless one assumes that all the nonidentified respondents were workshop participants ($X^2 = 0.14$, df = 1, p > 0.50). Participation rates were significantly higher for those respondents who identified as either BEST or workshop participants (100% participation rate for those responding) vs. those who did not identify as either (69% participation rate; $X^2 = 7.32$, df = 1, p < 0.01).

Completion rates varied among survey participants as well. Those who identified themselves as either BEST or workshop graduates and agreed to participate in the survey did so with a 68% completion rate (69% vs. 62.5% for the two groups, respectively); those who agreed to participate but did not identify themselves with a particular group had much lower (16.7%) completion rates. These differences were not statistically significant given our sample sizes ($X^2 = 2.46$, df = 1, p > 0.10). Additional follow-up to ascertain why some respondents did not answer some items did not occur, although inferences suggested some respondents did not use certain strategies and therefore did not provide responses for successive items on the survey. In other words, once a respondent indicated a "no" or "NA" response, he/she did not respond to further questions on the survey that may have related to that initial item.

Given the small sample size of workshop participants who completed the survey (n = 3, from a total possible population of 21 participants), we chose to evaluate survey responses of both BEST and workshop participants together, rather than trying to determine differences in responses between these two groups.

Demographic Information: The BEST program we described included three specific components: the inquiry-based content course (SCI 501), the 150–200 hour course in a research setting (BIO 585), and the combined inquiry curriculum and action research course (ETE 650). A teacher completing the BEST program would, therefore, complete all three courses. However, some teachers may have taken some but not all three courses. Of the respondents providing answers, 13 (61.9%) completed the entire BEST program. Three (14.3%) completed only SCI 501, two (9.5%) completed only BIO 585, and one (4.8%) completed only ETE 650. Thirteen teachers failed to provide any response to this item. Teachers were asked to identify the years in which they participated in the BEST program. Most (60%) had participated in 2007, 50% in 2005, 25% in 2006, and 20% in 2008.

The teachers were largely veterans, with 37.5% having 20 or more years of experience, and another 20.8% having between 10 and 19 years. There was a relatively large number (20.8%) who were beginners (1–3 years of experience). The majority (73.9%) taught in the Peoria school district, and the rest were evenly divided between five surrounding school districts. Grade level assignments were fairly evenly distributed, with 37.5% teaching primary (K–4) and 37.5% teaching secondary (9–12), while 25% taught at the middle grades (5–8). All responding teachers taught science. Other content areas taught included vocational studies, computers, language arts and reading, and geography. The schools' student populations were largely disadvantaged, with 77.8% of the students receiving free or reduced lunch. Ten of the schools were on the watch list for AYP. The number of years for which schools appeared on the watch list ranged from 0 to 6, with a mean of 2.5 years.

Specific Outcomes for Teachers and Students: Of interest to the researchers were questions asking about teachers' use of Nature of Science (NOS) in their classrooms, and how that was influenced by their participation in STEM workshops and the BEST program (survey items 7 and 8). Eighteen teachers provided a response to this item. Sixteen reported they made use of hands-on and inquiry activities. Several mentioned having scientists visit their classrooms, and several noted they tried to integrate science whenever possible within the curriculum. None of the teachers specifically addressed components typically associated with NOS other than engagement in hands-on and inquiry-based activities. With respect to how the STEM workshops and/or BEST program influenced their inclusion of NOS in their teaching, the most common response was that they now understood more about using hands-on activities (lessening reliance on textbooks). Four noted their professional development experiences led to little or no change in the way they approached teaching NOS. The overall picture that emerges from the data is one in which teachers have a relatively narrow conception of NOS, that that conception primarily focuses on the use of hands-on activities, and that less reliance on text sources is important.

Related to the two survey items discussed above, the researchers also inquired as to the amount of time teachers were dedicating to STEM instruction and whether this was a result of their STEM workshop/BEST program professional development (survey item 9). Nine teachers reported that they are trying to include more laboratory and investigation, but do not necessarily have more time during the week to accomplish it. Three noted they took specific steps to provide increased time, and two responded that they did not know what this type of instruction was. These results must be interpreted in context of the educational-political environment extant in the state's schools. State emphasis on annual testing and No Child Left Behind (NCLB) has focused on reading and mathematics, with little attention given to science. A consequence of this has been a steady deterioration over the last decade in schools' attention to science. In light of this environment, the results from the survey are encouraging in the sense that most of the responding teachers were undertaking the extra effort to regularly include science instruction. Such efforts largely run counter to the pressures bearing on teachers.

Building from the previous question, the researchers were also interested in how the nature of STEM instructional activities changed for the teachers who completed the STEM workshops vs. those in the BEST program (survey item 10). Ten teachers provided responses to this item. All but one noted they are using less lecture and more hands-on activity approaches in their teaching. Several spoke to being more project-oriented and focusing more on inquiry. Such results are positive from the STEM workshop/BEST program perspective because one of the major goals of that professional development was to move teachers away from didactic instruction toward more inquiry-based practice. In an attempt to better verify what instructional activities the teachers were employing in their classrooms, the survey asked them to provide the percentage of time they spend in a variety of strategies (see Table 1). For the group as a whole, inquiry-oriented instruction was utilized nearly 21% of the time. This was followed closely by lecture (18.67% of the time) and by hands-on activities that were not considered inquiry (18.2% of the time). Given the testing environment in which the teachers work, the amount of time devoted to inquiry and hands-on instruction is notable.

Table 1. Instructional Strategies of Respondents

Instructional Strategy	Percent of Time (Response Range)	Percent of Time (Response Mean)	Respondent n
Lecture	0–30	18.67	15
Demonstration	5–40	13.93	14
Textbook readings	0–20	8.85	13
Worksheets	0–20	12.67	15
Writing assignments	0–25	8.93	14
Hands-on but not inquiry	5–35	18.2	15
Inquiry-oriented instruction	2–70	20.86	14
Other	0–10	6.67	3

Survey item 12 asked teachers about how their changed use of instructional strategies has altered student engagement in their classrooms. Similar to item 12, survey item 13 asked teachers about how their instructional strategies have altered student-learning outcomes. Fourteen teachers responded to these items. Twelve noted that their students were more interested, were eager to do the work, exhibited increased initiative, and were becoming more and more able to "do" science. One mentioned how there was much more participation from marginal and moderately successful students, while another wrote about how interested students were in seeing results and trying to explain them to other students. These results are certainly reflective of the positive direction of instruction established as an outcome of the STEM workshops/BEST program, and what is promulgated in state and national standards. With regard to student learning outcomes (survey item 13), teachers reported their students showed more comprehension and understanding of concepts, increased success in assignments, and had better retention of what they learned. One teacher also mentioned students had an increased awareness of the learning process (i.e., metacognition). Ideally, if teachers are employing inquiry-oriented practices appropriately and effectively, one would expect to see student changes such as those reported through this survey.

The researchers also asked teachers if they talked with other teachers about STEM and inquiry instruction, and if so, the frequency and content of those discussions. Thirteen teachers responded to this survey item (item 14). Five reported that they had such interactions frequently. The remainder mentioned reasons why they did not, including time constraints, isolation from other teachers, and that no other teachers in the building were teaching science. Again, one needs to view these responses in light of the educational-political climate in which the teachers work. Science is not currently high on the priority list for school curricula, and a majority of teachers will focus on those subjects that are targeted on state tests.

The final survey item including usable data was item 15, which asked teachers what kind of support and limitations they encounter from administration with respect to implementing inquiry-based instruction. Thirteen teachers provided responses to this item. The responses to this item can be categorized into three basic groups: (1) teachers are on their own and have little or no administrative support; (2) administration is supportive but doesn't provide resources (i.e., does not impose limitations); and (3) administration is supportive and provides resources. Of the 13 teachers who responded to this survey item, two would be classified in the first group, six in the second group, and five in the third group. An inference from this is that 11 of the 13 are not being impeded from teaching with an inquiry approach. As noted earlier, this is positive given the climate in which the teachers are functioning.

Overall, the results of the survey indicate the professional development offered through the STEM workshops/BEST program are having the effect desired by the program designers. Although the actual number of teachers is relatively small compared to the number of teachers in the area's school districts, a core group has been established that will likely benefit other teachers and students as the focus on science increases through its overt inclusion on state-mandated testing in the immediate future. This core group has moved forward against the prevailing current.

Final Remarks

Beyond building scientific knowledge and skills, the approaches described in this chapter have provided preservice teachers with the concept of and experiences with inquiry-based instruction. Not only have the novice teachers developed their personal constructs, they have also demonstrated their ability to translate their experiences into quality learning opportunities for their students. The inservice teachers have also benefited from continuing professional development related to use inquiry-based pedagogy and are reducing their use of more traditional, teacher-directed methods of science instruction in favor of more inquiry-oriented pedagogy. Still, there are questions remaining such as:

"What are the long-term effects on science teaching of these experiences?"
"What is the comparative effect of different approaches to pre- and inservice methods?"
"How do we address the ongoing need to keep current and support lifelong learning?"

We assume that there will always be a need for multiple approaches that offer a variety of different opportunities so that the individual nature of teachers as learners can be met. Answering these questions and others should enhance the quality of that mix.

References

Bradley University, Department of Teacher Education. Form revised 2007. Student Teacher Evaluation Form. Adapted from INTASC standards and Illinois Learning Goals.

Britner, S. L., and K. D. Finson. 2005. Pre-service teachers' reflections on their growth in an inquiry-oriented science pedagogy course. *Journal of Elementary Science Education* 17: 39–54.

Edgcomb, M., S. L. Britner, K. McConnaughay, and R. Wolffe. 2008. Science 101: An integrated, inquiry-oriented science course for education majors. *Journal of College Science Teaching* 38 (1): 22–27.

Llewellyn, D. 2002. *Inquire within: Implementing inquiry-based science standards*. Thousand Oaks, CA: Sage.

National Research Council. 2000. *Inquiry and the national science education standards*. Washington, DC: National Academy Press.

Promoting Inquiry With Preservice Elementary Teachers Through a Science Content Course

Thomas R. Lord and Holly J. Travis
Indiana University of Pennsylvania

nquiry science teaching is effective at all levels, from elementary classes to higher education. It is important, therefore, that preservice education majors who will be teaching science understand the differences between inquiry instruction and instruction other than inquiry. Teacher education courses taught in the nation's colleges and universities must meet the challenge of developing this understanding for our present science teacher education majors.

Elementary and secondary science education majors have been instructed in the use of inquiry at Indiana University of Pennsylvania (IUP) for nearly a decade via faculty teaching methods and the science education curriculum. Preservice secondary science education majors at IUP complete three courses in the teaching of science: EDUC 242: Preclinical Student Teaching I; EDUC 343: Preclinical Student Teaching II; and EDUC 451: Methods of Teaching Science in the Secondary Schools. These three courses all focus on using inquiry as a means of developing lessons that emphasize critical-thinking skills.

Students interested in teaching at the elementary level complete the majority of their coursework in the College of Education and Educational Technology (COEET). The students are required to enroll in four content-based science courses, one in each of the major science discipline areas (biology, chemistry, geoscience, and physics). These courses are taught by science professors from the College of Natural Sciences and Mathematics. The program described in this chapter takes place with our preservice elementary education majors in their life science content course. The course is focused on the role humans play in the natural world; the title of the course is SCI 104: Environmental Biology.

In the initial class the students in this group were surveyed about the extent of the science they had experienced in the past and what science courses in each discipline they had actually completed prior to this class. They also completed a Views of the Nature of Science (VNOS) test (Lederman et al. 2002), utilizing their understanding of how science works. At the end of the semester, students completed a Biology Attitude Survey (Russell and Hollander 1975), which looks at positive and negative feelings about biology, and also took a second version of the VNOS test. Students completed these instruments to determine the effect of the teaching methods on developing a positive attitude and a more complete and accurate understanding of the nature of science. These tests and surveys were given at the end of two different semesters, the first with lab sections taught in a more traditional fashion as a control group, and the second taught in a constructivist manner as outlined and described in the National Science Education Standards, (NRC 1996, p. 52).

Aspects of the NSES Standards Addressed by This Program

SCI 104 is currently structured entirely around inquiry instruction and focuses on the four goals of the NSES. It is a student-centered approach designed to involve students in their environment and incorporate essential features of classroom inquiry.

Students participate in the course through two 1-hour discussion components and one 2-hour investigative component each week. During the discussion sessions, students in both the control and experimental populations worked in teams of 3 or 4 to answer questions, make predictions, and analyze graphs and charts. The sessions were structured around the 5-E system of instruction in which students explore the information in cooperative teams, then share the information they have collected with others in the class through oral responses. The instructor may elaborate on the information, or might instead initiate another explore/explain sequence. An assessment of student understanding can take place at any juncture. This system not only develops teamwork but also improves student interaction and accountability.

The investigative components of the course take place both outdoors in the field and indoors in the science laboratory. In the control population, labs involved hands-on activities, but students were given directions on how to go about performing the investigations for each activity. In the experimental population, students were not given sequential information directions to follow, as in the more traditional lab activities. Instead, they were provided with a challenge question that required them to explore through experimentation. In developing an action plan, they first discussed the challenge question as a team, then formulated a hypothesis and developed an experiment to solve the problem. This is a critical stage in the process, because teams must also consider variables that might interfere with their results. Next the students collected items they needed for their experiment from a resource table; storage shelf containing glassware, microscopes, and quantitative tools; or a neighboring supply room. Once everything was set up, the student teams conducted the experiments, making observations on the proceedings and taking careful notes on the progress of the experiment. At the completion of the investigation, teams analyzed their data and drew conclusions about their results. At this point they verified or rejected their hypothesis and decided if their experimental design needed to be improved. As mentioned earlier, the scheme incorporated all the essential components of inquiry through scientific observation, analysis, and explanation.

There are numerous NSES components built into this program. Teaching standards, professional development, assessment, content and inquiry, program standards, and system standards are all addressed through activities carried out in both the lecture and laboratory portions of the class.

To support the NSES Teaching Standards, the procedures used in this class strengthen student understanding and use of scientific knowledge, ideas, and inquiry through the designing of experiments in laboratory activities and the analysis of data in both lecture and lab. It also guides students in active scientific inquiry through the same activities and promotes shared responsibility for learning by asking students to develop questions and share results and conclusions with classmates.

Professional Development standards are addressed as the class introduces inquiry into their future role as a teacher by designing lesson plans based on class activities. These are also shared with classmates, who critique the lessons during peer review sessions. The design and execution of experiments enhances the learning of science, making the teacher a facilitator of change, rather than a director and taskmaster.

To address the Assessment Standards, the class assesses scientific understanding and reasoning through lab reports, presentations, and frequent discussion of experimental results. This is also accomplished through critical-thinking questions and analysis of research data in lecture. Students are also involved in assessment of their work and that of others through discussion of their own results and small-group critiques of both experimental designs and lesson plans throughout the semester.

Content and Inquiry Standards are covered through the integration of environmental science content in both lecture and lab. For example, students discuss topics such as toxicology and environmental pollution in lecture, and design experiments to test aspects of these topics in lab. By looking at real environmental pollutants such as salt, motor oil, and detergents, they actively investigate realistic science questions.

To meet the Program Standards, laboratory activities emphasizing inquiry and field trips to natural areas have already been noted. In addition, the format of the lecture encourages students to ask questions and predict outcomes before content is covered, and they are expected to evaluate multiple sides of environmental issues. Challenging opportunities for all students to learn science are provided in all aspects of this class.

Finally, to meet the System Standards, the course emphasizes the practical classroom use of science content by frequently having students determine ways to use the course material in classrooms, both in lecture and through the design of lesson plans based on the laboratory experiments. This course also provides a basis for developing understanding and abilities in science and science teaching by stressing the 5-E model for lesson plan design and by having instructors in both lecture and lab model an inquiry-based approach to science teaching.

Inquiry Through Modeling and Hands-On Application

Bell, Binns, and Smetana (2005) define inquiry teaching as a form of instruction in which students take an active role in learning and teachers emphasize questions, data analysis, and critical thinking. It is a form of constructivism that teaches concepts through discovery, where educators challenge students with critical-thinking questions.

Many researchers indicate that inquiry instruction results in greater student achievement and more positive attitudes toward science (Germann 1998; Travis and Lord 2004). Chang and Mao (1999) found that ninth-grade students taught with inquiry scored significantly higher than a control group on life science achievement tests. The researchers also found significant differences in biology attitudes, with the inquiry group demonstrating a more positive outlook. Inquiry has also been found to enhance learning in younger students. A study performed by Anastasiow et al. (1970) found kindergarten students taught with inquiry retained information longer and were better at mastering complex principles than students taught with noninquiry teaching techniques.

The program described here was designed to model inquiry instruction in a life science course required by elementary education majors, and to encourage these future teachers to incorporate inquiry in their own classrooms. The course was selected because it is the only content-based biology course required of the elementary education students and it contains components that permit students to use inquiry in both indoor labs and outdoor field excursions.

The course brings the entire class together in a large group theater for one hour twice a week, with the investigative portions divided into groups of 20–24 students for a two-hour lab at a different time. With this diversity in instructional settings available, the instructors are able to use multiple inquiry teaching methods. These include but are not limited to cooperative learning, jig-sawing, concept maps, student-initiated discussions, peer-review of lessons and experimental designs, student self-assessment, and student-designed investigations.

Instruction in the Large-Group Setting

In the lecture portion of the class, inquiry and critical-thinking skills were incorporated throughout the course. Major topics explored include ecosystem interactions, nutrient and energy cycling, renewable and nonrenewable energy sources, agriculture, human population growth, air pollution, and water pollution. Students were introduced to the 5-E model for lesson plan design, designed by Trowbridge and Bybee (1990), during their first meeting. Preservice elementary teachers in science content courses indicate that they are concerned about meeting standards while maintaining student interest in the lessons and encouraging critical-thinking skills. As noted by Wilder and Shuttleworth (2005), use of the 5-E model for lesson planning can make this process easier, help new teachers feel more confident about their science lessons, and improve student learning in their classrooms.

This practice was then modeled throughout the semester, with frequent explore-explain sequences used in every class meeting. Students were presented with questions prior to discussion of content, which they discussed in small groups with their classmates. Responses from the groups were shared with the class, and discussion was based on these answers. The instructor addressed misconceptions and guided students to understanding, rather than simply feeding them facts to memorize. Prior knowledge was activated and new information could be integrated through the discussion that followed. Students were able to examine this new information and compare it to their earlier conceptions, testing their own ideas against those of classmates (Volkmann and Abell 2003). More complex questions followed, with assessments occurring through tests, lesson plans, homework assignments, daily turn-in papers and presentations.

Students were also expected to develop critical-thinking skills by evaluating multiple viewpoints about various environmental issues. For example, advantages and disadvantages of various energy sources, including both nonrenewable and alternative fuels, were addressed. Students also did a small-group presentation on an environmental topic that caught their interest, with the requirement that they provide not only background information, but a balanced look at both sides of the issue for the class. They also noted how that issue related to topics discussed in class, in order to demonstrate the interrelationships of ecosystem components and the importance of being fully informed about any topic when making a decision.

In addition, graphs and real research results were incorporated into the lecture material, and students were asked to evaluate information to determine the meaning of the results. For example, graphs from research done on shorebirds were included, and students were asked to determine what the graph indicated about population changes over a period of several years. They worked through this information in small groups and their conclusions were discussed as a class. By doing this, students learned to read and evaluate information through critical thinking and assessment of the science and methods used by the researchers. They became better informed, not only to teach science, but how to make educated decisions themselves, as members of the community.

Instruction in the Investigative Setting

Science laboratories and outdoor excursions are ideal sites for inquiry instruction. The settings enable the instructor to develop unique experiments where answers are unknown and to point out natural occurrences that challenge student thinking. As early as 1957, Mead and Metraux emphasized that less repetition of experiments with known answers and more experiments where students discover something new can most easily take place in laboratory settings. As noted previously, these features form the foundation of inquiry.

The labs for the experimental population consisted of a unique challenge question that was presented in each session that class members worked on in small groups. Detailed, sequentially drawn-up instructions were not provided for this group as they were for the control population; instead student teams developed a method for addressing the challenge by performing an experiment or investigation. When consensus on an experimental design was reached, the groups collected the appropriate equipment and began their investigation, being careful to control the dependent and independent variables. They had the opportunity to collect data and look for patterns (Deming and Cracolice 2004). Results were examined and compared to the outcomes reached by a control population. Team conclusions were considered as a collective experience when the data were discussed by the entire group.

A weekly lab write-up, termed a mini–lab report, was produced by all class members. This made each student accountable for his or her separate report of the team-designed experiment (Lord 2007). The instructor used this to assess the understanding of each class member and to encourage individual consideration of the various methods utilized in science reporting. The format for the mini–lab report is found in the appendix of this chapter.

Indoor Lab Investigations

About half the lab sessions during the semester were devoted to indoor investigations. These sessions were conducted in a traditional laboratory setup with rectangular lab tables and movable swivel stools. The students worked in teams of four, which were determined by the seating arrangement at the lab tables. Together they planned and designed experiments to answer the various lab challenges posed by the instructor. They also developed a team hypothesis and performed the investigation as a group. A written report of the results, however, was done individually. Students were required to complete a one-page mini–lab report and a graph of their results each week. Several times during the semester they also prepared individual 5-E lesson plans based on their laboratory investigation.

Ice-Pop Melting Rate

The first lab of the semester was designed to introduce the scientific method by having students design a simple investigation. In this lab they were to plan an experiment that would answer the question, "Does the concentration of juice in an ice cube affect the rate at which it melts?" Groups were told they could use any material on the side counter of the lab and that frozen orange concentrate was the juice that would be utilized in the experiment. Working together, team members discussed the challenge and designed an activity that would settle the question. Teams were given six ounces of frozen juice to work with and most chose to freeze the juice in small paper cups. Teams were reminded that they had to graph their results so they should think about quantifying their data in some way. Although nothing was mentioned during the introduction of the challenge, several groups asked the professor or student assistants about establishing a control as they were designing their experiment. Some groups included ice cubes that were made entirely of water as their control, and one group included a duplicate cube for each concentration they set up. After one week, the students removed their cubes from the freezer and recorded initial observations. Two groups decided to pour off water that collected around the ice in each cup keeping track to the total amount collected every five minutes. Other groups decided to dispose of the melted water and weigh the solid (ever shrinking) cubes at regular times during the lab. Either method produced valid results and allowed the class members to generate an effective lab report and graphs.

Effect of Light on Seed Germination

In this lab, student groups were challenged to set up an activity that would answer the question, "Does the amount of sunlight that germinating seeds receive have an influence on their sprouting rate?" Students were told they could use any glassware or material on the back counter and cabinets to design their investigations. While shown plastic petri dishes used in past semesters, students were told they would have to design their own growth chambers from plastic containers of their choosing. Most of the students chose to use clean plastic water or soda bottles that could be cut down to a manageable size. Group members discussed the design of the lab, the number of experimental samples they needed, and how to include a control for their study. After the growth chambers were constructed, groups placed some type of water-holding medium, such as a piece of paper towel or some sand, in their chambers and sprinkled grass seeds in the container. Questions about their seed distribution method from the professor or student assistants helped lead the groups toward the need for consistency, and groups generally selected a specific number of seeds to place in the growth chamber. Some of the teams made holes in small boxes or teepees to regulate light levels, while others used colored paper to vary the levels of sunlight. Growth chambers were inspected daily for a week by one or more members of the team and results were recorded. During the following lab, observations were shared with team members and conclusions were drawn. Each student wrote up the results in a mini lab and constructed a diagram of results.

Salt Toxicity on Seed Germination Lab

For this lab students were challenged to "determine the salt concentration required to prevent grass seeds from sprouting." In this lab, student teams planned how to develop a series of salt solutions in decreasing concentrations that were poured on seeds placed on absorbent paper in separate growth chambers. Students took care to label the various containers containing the seeds in order to monitor the various concentrations and germination rates. As in the previous lab, students were not provided with growth chambers for this exercise. Instead, they constructed their own containers for the experiment based on their previous experiences with such design. The students discussed how they would keep records of the seed development over the week. Access to the lab was available throughout the week if teams determined that regular observations would be useful. Teams generally had someone from their group monitor the progress of their experiment and record sprouting dates and root/stem growth between the two sessions. When the groups reassembled in lab the following week, they compiled the data records, compared their results with control chambers, and discussed the outcome. The groups also decided whether they should accept or reject their original hypothesis and discussed their recommendations. They then moved to set up the lab challenge they would perform for the following week.

The Effects of a Household Product on Seed Germination

Following the salt toxicity lab, students were given the opportunity to apply their experience to a real-life application, using common household chemicals. Students were asked to "determine the concentration of their chosen environmental toxin that prevents the seeds from germinating." The teams generally set up the experiment in a similar fashion to the salt toxicity lab from the week before. Different concentrations of their selected toxins were added to absorbent paper placed in growth chambers. The chambers were checked every 48 hours and the germination rates and root/stem lengths were recorded. After one week the data were tabulated, conclusions were reached, and students constructed their lab reports and graphs. Students were further challenged to apply what they learned from the three seed germination labs to create individual 5-E lessons based on elementary science standards. They then taught a portion of the lesson to a group of their classmates during a 30-minute segment of the following week's laboratory. Peers made comments and offered suggestions about the lessons presented by classmates, in addition to hearing some creative ideas that they might use in the future.

Effects of a Household Product on Seed Germination – A Second Look

After the students checked their results from the initial environmental toxin investigation, they were asked to repeat the experiment for another week but this time they were challenged to "alter the experiment to enhance your results, using the same chemical." Teams had the opportunity to review their initial design and results, making changes that might narrow the determination of the toxic level or improve the measurement of quantifiable results. The assignment for this investigation was expanded to include the development of a team poster outlining the experimental procedure and including the hypothesis, results, conclusions, limitations, and graphs of data.

Controlling Variables in Creating an Ecosystem Model

Because elementary teachers rarely have any significant science budget, the inquiry investigations were designed to use inexpensive items easily obtained by the students. With this in mind the teams were challenged to "design an experiment to assess the effect of changing one variable on the success of an ecosystem," using 1-liter plastic bottles as the basis for the ecosystem designs. The students develop a hypothesis about which model would have the healthiest environment at the end of one week. On their own, team members proposed three or four ways to determine "healthiest environment," using variables such as the tallest grass, snail viability, or algae growth. While some of the materials for this lab, such as guppies, snails, and different soil types, were purchased ahead of time by the instructor, the majority of the items were procured by the students from outdoor environments around the university. Class members were also directed to bring several clean, 1-liter soda bottles to the lab. Teams generally determined that someone in the group must once again record data on the progress of their bottle study over the week. At the next scheduled lab session, students observed their experimental bottles, recorded their final measurements and discussed their results. Once group consensus on the results was reached, team members confirmed or refuted their hypothesis, graphed their results, and completed the lab report.

Each of the indoor investigations required that students develop scientific plans, establish reproducible experiments, collect and analyze results, and share conclusions, all important inquiry characteristics.

Planning Investigative Labs in the Field

Outdoor labs were conducted in a similar manner, with groups working to answer challenge questions dealing with field experiences. At the onset of each class, students met in the laboratory where they had access to many resource materials. The challenge question for the lab was provided at the beginning of the lab as students entered the classroom so teams could gather in their groups to discuss how they would proceed. After each group had determined their plan of action, students moved to field setting, generally off campus.

Creating and Piloting an Outdoor Scavenger Hunt

The first outdoor lab asked the teams to design and test an outdoor scavenger hunt. The assignment was accompanied by several statements that served as guidelines for the activity, including safety regulations, boundaries, and behavior. The organizing factor for each team's hunt was that the items on the list must all relate to a particular theme. Some items that have been included on lists include the following:

1. item from a human
2. item from a nonhuman mammal
3. item from a bird
4. item from a reptile
5. item from an amphibian
6. item from a fish
7. item from an insect
8. item from a noninsect arthropod
9. item from a nonlegged invertebrate (worm)
10. item from a fungal (mold) organism
11. item from a lichen
12. item from the algae
13. item from a bryophyte (moss)
14. item from a pteridophyte (fern)
15. item from a conifer
16. item from a woody angiosperm
17. item from a herbaceous angiosperm
18. item of a angiosperm fruit
19. item of an angiosperm seed
20. item of an angiosperm flower

Teams often broadened the categories; for example, one group allowed participants to find up to five representatives from each category. In addition to creating the scavenger hunt, each student was asked to develop a 5-E lesson plan based on the activity to present to a panel of classmates the following week. Once again, the lessons were peer-reviewed so students could hear new ideas and comment on things that might be confusing.

Creating and Piloting a Stream Investigation

During the next lab meeting, the teams determined how they would "design and pilot a study of biotic and abiotic features in and around a fast moving stream through a deciduous forest." Each team was told they must collect data on 10 biotic and 10 abiotic features. Students could select calf-high or hip-high waterproof boots and several varieties of nets in the lab along with an array of plastic bottles, trays, and utensils. Students also selected from a variety of indicators such as pH paper, instruments including thermometers and metersticks, and reference books on topics such as aquatic invertebrates and plants. All identifications and data were completed on-site, and after the students captured, identified, and characterized the organisms, they were returned to the environment where they had collected them. Students reported their data in their lab reports, incorporating graphs of at least three of the factors they recorded.

Creating and Piloting a Pond Investigation

The challenge for the following week was similar to the previous study, but this time they were asked to "record and evaluate 10 biotic and 10 abiotic features observed around a rural, fresh-water pond in a field setting." Building on their experiences from the previous week, groups divided the responsibilities and quickly determined what they needed to take with them. Upon arriving at the site, team members scattered to different areas around the pond, with one or two group members capturing invertebrates along the edge of the pond, another recording the vegetation along the shoreline, and someone else recording the physical features of the environment. As in the previous lab, identifications were made at the site and the invertebrates were returned to their habitat before the trip back to school.

Creating and Piloting a Study of a Terrestrial Ecosystem

The third field investigation challenges teams to "record and evaluate ten biotic and ten abiotic features in a deciduous forest." Again student teams gathered to plan their activity and to secure materials and instruments for their study. This time some thought was required as groups determined the different requirements for a terrestrial investigation. While boots were not frequently chosen by teams this time, gloves, tweezers, and large jars were often selected. One or two groups asked about using live traps, which were made available by other faculty members. Once at the site, team members separated for a portion of the lab to record various features of the environment. Reference books were utilized more frequently than in the previous pond and stream investigations as students attempted to identify things they were finding. Mammal tracks, tree branches, birds, and insects are all examples of items observed by students in the woods and identified through the use of field guides. Reports were written on this experience, once again incorporating graphs of their observations. Students were also expected to construct a 5-E lesson based on their comparisons between the stream, pond, and terrestrial environments.

Collecting, Identifying, and Constructing an Arthropod Food Web

The final field lab of the semester challenged students to "develop a standard food web based on the arthropods you observe and collect in an outdoor setting." Working in a local environmental setting such as a meadow or forest, students located and captured various arthropods. Either by hand or using nets and jars, student teams collected at least 10 different organisms, which they used to create a food web. As they observed and captured their organisms, the teams attempted to identify different arthropods that typify that particular environmental setting, for example finding crickets, butterflies, and grasshoppers in a field. Once this was accomplished, students examined and sketched the organisms and divided them so each team member had approximately the same number to identify and research. They used resources such as field guides and the internet, both in the field and back on campus, to determine the common and scientific names of the organisms and the ecological niches occupied by each. Before the next lab session, teams met to construct a food web poster for the arthropods they found. The food webs were also incorporated into a 5-E lesson plan that each student constructed and presented to a group of peers. Information from the poster was also graphed in the minilab report that each class member submitted.

Evidence of Impact of the Program

The potential impact of this course is far-reaching and significant. Although there are dozens of inquiry activities written in the science education literature, there are few tried-and-true inquiry-based science programs. There are even fewer programs specifically designed for elementary education majors. This may be a reflection on the difficulty of developing a passion for science in elementary education students because of the program demands for elementary education certification. They have limited science experience in their teacher education programs in college.

This is further exacerbated by recent state and federal demands on elementary teacher training programs to focus on methods for improving reading and mathematics scores measured by high-stakes examinations. The problem is also aggravated by the lack of understanding by parents, school board members, and politicians regarding the inadequacies of traditional teaching methods and to the value of inquiry instruction in all disciplines.

This program is particularly valuable because it has undergone intense scrutiny in its development. The program was designed with experimental and control populations of elementary education majors through biology attitude surveys and pre/post analysis of Nature of Science awareness.

Views of Nature of Science Survey Results

The inquiry activities used in this course were designed to improve the participants' understanding of the Nature of Science (NOS). This is particularly important in a course for preservice teachers, because educators with a better understanding of NOS are more likely to teach science using dynamic classroom practices that develop critical-thinking skills in their students (Brickhouse 2007). Schwartz, Lederman, and Crawford (2004) list seven aspects of NOS that define science as a discipline:

1. scientific knowledge is subject to change;

2. knowledge is empirically based;

3. it is theory laden and subjective;

4. it is the product of human imagination and creativity;

5. it involves the combination of observation and inferences;

6. laws and theories play an important role in developing new ideas; and

7. scientific ideas are validated by repetition and peer reviewing.

These seven aspects serve as the foundation for how science operates and many studies have been performed to test the understanding of these elements.

Helping students develop informed views of the nature of science has been an important goal for science education (Abd-El-Khalick, Bell, and Lederman 1998), and there have been several attempts to enhance students' NOS understanding. Academics agree that valid instruments to assess NOS understanding were not available in the initial years (Billeh and Hasan 1975). Recently, however, Lederman et al. (2002) developed an open-ended instrument called the Views of Nature of Science Questionnaire (VNOS). The test is unique in that it allows students to elucidate their own views of the target NOS aspects. It was validated by the researchers in 2002. Because of its scrutiny, VNOS was selected to verify the nature of science understanding of participants in our study. The VNOS was given at the beginning and end of both the control class and the experimental class. Results of the analysis provide some compelling support for the use of inquiry and critical thinking in teacher education content courses.

Results of the VNOS Assessment

The VNOS B and VNOS C versions of the tests were selected for pretesting and posttesting (the tests are appended to the chapter). Both tests contain open-ended questions consisting of several queries. Students are asked to write a response to each query as best they can. For example, the first question on VNOS B states, "After scientists have developed a theory (e.g., atomic theory, kinetic molecule theory, cell theory), does the theory ever change? If you believe that scientific theories do not change, explain why and defend your answer with examples. If you believe that theories do change: (a) Explain why. (b) Explain why we bother to teach and learn scientific theories. Defend your answer and give examples."

At the end of the pretest, students put their tests in a collection box and returned to their seats to continue the lab. When everyone completed the test, the box was removed from the classroom. Later that day the test scorer graded the answer sheets following a rubric established by the test authors. Except for grading the tests, the scorer was not involved in the study in any way. The scorer had been selected from a group of interested seniors from the College of Education and trained in the grading of the tests with the use of the rubric. For the question described above, the rubric used for scoring indicated that "the question aims to assess understandings of the tentative nature of scientific claims and why these claims change. It is common for respondents to attribute such change solely to the accumulation of new facts and technologies, rather than the inferential nature of scientific theories and/or paradigm shifts. The question also aims to assess respondents' understandings of the role of theories in science as well as the theory-laden nature of scientific observations." The scorer rated each question of a student's test on a scale of 1 (lowest) to 3 (highest). Final scores were calculated as a percentage of the total points available. When the tests were all scored, they were returned to the researchers.

The posttest was conducted in a similar fashion. At the conclusion of each semester, the two groups were given the VNOS C version. The developers of the test note that the B and C versions are comparable and that consequently, they could be used as pre-post testing instruments. An example of a question from VNOS C would be, "After scientists have developed a scientific theory (e.g., atomic theory, evolution theory) does the theory ever change? If you believe that scientific theories will not change, explain why and defend your answer with examples. If you believe that scientific theories do change, explain why. Also explain why we bother to learn scientific theories; defend your answer with examples." The rubric supplied by the test creator states that this question assesses respondents' understanding of the tentative nature of scientific theories and reasons why science is tentative. Respondents often attribute change solely to the accumulation of new observations or data and/or the development of new technologies, and they do not consider change that results from reinterpretation of existing data from a different perspective. Views of the theory-laden nature of scientific investigations, the notion that the prevailing theories of the time impact the direction, conduct, and interpretation of scientific investigations are assessed through the explanation of the role of theories in science. Additionally, responses often indicate views of the role of subjectivity, creativity, inference, and the sociocultural embeddedness of the scientific endeavor as well as the interdependent nature of these aspects. The posttest was evaluated by the same scorer, who had already been trained in the use of the rubric. When the tests were all scored, they were returned to the researchers; statistical comparisons were then performed on the two tests.

At the conclusion of the semester both populations were given the VNOS test, version C (Table 1). Scores of both groups were compared through an Analysis of Variance both within each group separately and between the two groups. The results reveal that there was no significant difference found between the pretest of the two groups, indicating that both groups started out with similar knowledge levels about the nature of science. There was also not a significant difference found between the pretest and posttest scores in the control population, demonstrating that the traditional step-by-step laboratory instructions did not help develop an understanding about how science is done. There was a significant difference, however, on the pretest and postest scores of the experimental population and between the posttest scores between the control and the experimental teams. The experimental group scored significantly higher on the posttest, with $p < 0.01$. The significant change at $p < 0.01$ between their pretest and posttest scores for the experimental group show that over the course of the semester, they did improve their understanding of what it means to do science. This supports the value of an inquiry-based curriculum in developing a better understanding of the nature of science.

Table 1. ANOVA Results for Pretest/Posttest VNOS Administrations for Control and Experimental Populations

Measure Source	df	SS	MS	F	P-value
Control Pretest/Posttest					
Between Groups	1	0.0189	0.0189	2.5944	0.113
Within Groups	49	0.3577	0.0073		
Total	50	0.3766			
Experimental Pretest/Posttest					
Between Groups	1	0.0337	0.0337	4.6097	0.035*
Within Groups	66	0.4826	0.0073		
Total	67	0.5163			
Control Pretest/Experimental Pretest					
Between Groups	1	7.11E-05	7.11E-05	0.0107	0.918
Within Groups	57	0.3795	0.0067		
Total	58	0.3796			
Control Posttest/Experimental Posttest					
Between Groups	1	0.0960	0.0963	12.125	0.000**
Within Groups	58	0.4607	0.0079		
Total	59	0.5570			

* Significant at $p \leq 0.05$
**Significant at $p \leq 0.001$

Results of the Biology Attitude Scale

In addition to the VNOS, the Biology Attitude Scale (Appendix C) was administered at the end of each semester to determine the students' attitude toward biology. Although not given as a pretest at the start of the semester, it was valuable as a measure of the likelihood that these students would encourage the use of science in their classrooms. Elementary teachers often come into the course with a strong dislike of science, as noted in informal surveys and conversations. By making the content accessible and enjoyable, it becomes more probable that these students will make an effort to include science in the classroom, and to take their students outside for science lessons and activities.

The results of the biology attitude survey given at the end of each semester showed generally positive attitudes for both the control and experimental populations. For 18 of the 22 questions on the survey, there were no significant differences between the two groups. It should be noted, however, that for 20 of the 22 questions on the survey, the experimental group scored higher, or more positively, than students in the control group (see Table 2). The two questions where the control group had slightly higher scores resulted in no significant differences in the responses between the two groups. One question where the experimental group scored slightly lower asked students to determine whether they agreed or disagreed that they have always enjoyed studying biology in school. On this question, both groups scored on the slightly negative side, indicating that they did not always enjoy biology. This supports the contention made earlier that these students generally come into this course with a negative bias toward biology. The other question asked students to rate whether biology on a scale of worthless to valuable, using the same Likert Scale. Both groups on this question rated biology on the high end, indicating the view that biology was valuable.

Table 2. Average Scores for the Control and Experimental Groups on the Biology Attitude Scale Questions

Question Number	Control Group Average Score	Experimental Group Average Score
1	3.57	3.79
2	3.64	3.97
3	3.71	4.00
4	3.50	3.65
5	3.00	3.18
6	3.50	3.97
7	3.36	3.71
8	3.36	3.85
9	3.36	3.50
10	3.07	3.29
11	2.93	2.85
12*	3.43	4.00
13	2.86	3.29
14	2.93	3.35
15	3.93	4.09
16	2.36	2.59
17	4.36	4.26
18	3.57	3.59
19*	3.07	3.59
20*	3.29	3.79
21**	3.07	3.71
22	3.71	3.79

* Significant at $p \leq 0.05$
**Significant at $p \leq 0.001$

Questions that did show a significant difference clearly showed the value of the inquiry method in teaching the laboratory sections. One question on the survey asked students to rate the statement, "It makes me nervous to even think about doing a biology experiment." The control group had an average score of 3.43 on a scale of 1 to 5, with 5 being the most positive and 1 being the most negative. The experimental group had an average score of 4.00 for this same question, showing that they are much more comfortable with doing science experiments. The remaining questions that had significant differences in the responses all focused on the students' feelings toward biology. The experimental group once again had more positive scores on all of these questions. The use of inquiry in the laboratory sections of this course did appear to improve attitudes toward biology among the elementary education students involved, making it more likely that they will feel comfortable using science in their classrooms.

Summary

Our course with elementary education majors is valuable because of the many National Science Teaching Standards it meets. As mentioned, there are strong indications that the preservice students who were taught using inquiry methods understand the nature of science and are comfortable developing inquiry-based 5-E lessons for their students. This is an important part of convincing students of the value of inquiry, so a substantial block of time is provided during the course for students to construct and experience inquiry lessons with groups of their peers. Class surveys, along with teaching assessments, indicate that students in the course not only understand how to construct inquiry lessons, but they understand the philosophy behind the science itself. It is our contention that the major reason for this is that students do not follow prescribed lab investigations, but instead design their own research protocols to answer the questions posed by the instructor. Encouraging inquiry by giving students the opportunity to develop and carry out laboratory experiments without being given "cookbook" directions not only improves their attitude about science, but also gives them the confidence to use science in their own classrooms. Additionally, they are able to evaluate scientific information outside the classroom in their roles as members and future leaders of our society.

References

Abd-El-Khalick, F., R. L. Bell, and N. G. Lederman. 1998. The nature of science and instructional practice: Making the unnatural natural. *Science Education* 36: 404–420.

Anastasiow, N. J., G. D. Borich, T. M. Leonhardt, and S. A. Sibley. 1970. A comparison of guided discovery, discovery, and didactic teaching of math to kindergarten poverty children. *American Educational Research Journal* 7 (4): 493–510.

Bell, R. L., I. Binns, and L. Smetana. 2005. Simplifying inquiry instruction. *The Science Teacher* 30–33.

Bell, R. L., F. Abd-El-Khalick, N. G. Lederman, and R. S. Schwartz. 2002. Views of nature of science questionnaire: Toward valid and meaningful assessment of learners' conceptions of nature of science. *Journal of Research in Science Teaching* 39 (6): 497–521.

Billeh, V. Y., and O. E. Hasan. 1975. Factors influencing teachers' gain in understanding the nature of science. *Journal of Research in Science Teaching* 12: 209–212.

Brickhouse, N. W. 2007. Teachers' beliefs about the nature of science and their relationship to classroom practice. *Journal of Teacher Education* 41 (3): 53–62.

Chang, C-Y., and S-L. Mao. 1999. Comparison of Taiwan science students' outcomes with inquiry-group versus traditional instruction. *Journal of Educational Research* 92 (6): 340–345.

Deming, J., and M. Cracolice. 2004. Learning how to think. *The Science Teacher* 71 (3): 42–47.

Germann, P. J. 1998. Directed-inquiry approach to learning science process skills: Treatment effects and aptitude-treatment interactions. *Journal of Research in Science Teaching* 26: 237–250.

Lederman, N. G., F. Abd-El-Khalick, R. L. Bell, and R. S. Schwartz. 2002. Views of nature of science questionnaire: Toward valid and meaningful assessment of learners' conceptions of nature of science. *Journal of Research in Science Teaching* 39: 497–521.

Lord, T. R. 2007. Putting inquiry teaching to the test: Enhancing learning in college botany. *Journal of College Science Teaching* 34 (7): 62–65.

Mead, M., and R. Metraux. 1957. Change science teaching. *The Science News-Letter* 72 (11): 197.

National Research Council (NRC). 1996. *National science education standards*. Washington, DC: National Academy Press.

Russell, J., and S. Hollander. 1975. A biology attitude scale. *The American Biology Teacher* 37 (5): 270–273.

Schwartz, R. S., N. G. Lederman, and B. A. Crawford. 2004. Developing views of nature of science in an authentic context: An explicit approach to bridging the gap between nature of science and scientific inquiry. *Science Education* 88: 610–645.

Travis, H. J., and T. R. Lord. 2004. Traditional and constructivist teaching techniques: Comparing two groups of undergraduate non-science majors in a biology lab. *Journal of College Science Teaching* 34 (3): 12–18.

Trowbridge, L., and R. Bybee. 1990. *Becoming a secondary school science teacher*. 5th ed. Englewood Cliffs, NJ: Merrill.

Volkmann, M., and S. Abell. 2003. Seamless assessment. *Science and Children* 40 (8): 41–45.

Wilder, M., and P. Shuttleworth. 2005. Cell inquiry: A 5E learning cycle lesson. *Science Activities* 41 (4): 36–43.

Appendix A

VNOS—Form B

1. After scientists have developed a theory (e.g., atomic theory), does the theory ever change? If you believe that theories do change, explain why we bother to teach scientific theories. Defend your answer with examples.

2. What does an atom look like? How certain are scientists about the nature of the atom? What specific evidence do you think scientists use to determine what an atom looks like?

3. Is there a difference between a scientific theory and a scientific law? Give an example to illustrate your answer.

4. How are science and art similar? How are they different?

5. Scientists perform experiments/investigations when trying to solve problems. Other than the planning and design of these experiments/investigations, do scientists use their creativity and imagination during and after data collection? Please explain your answer and provide examples if appropriate.

6. Is there a difference between scientific knowledge and opinion? Give an example to illustrate your answer.

7. Some astronomers believe that the universe is expanding while others believe that it is shrinking; still others believe that the universe is in a static state without any expansion or shrinkage. How are these different conclusions possible if all of these scientists are looking at the same experiments and data?

Appendix B

VNOS—Form C

1. What, in your view, is science? What makes science (or a scientific discipline such as physics, biology, etc.) different from other disciplines of inquiry (e.g., religion, philosophy)?
2. What is an experiment?
3. Does the development of scientific knowledge require experiments? If yes, explain why. Give an example to defend your position. If no, explain why. Give an example to defend your position.
4. After scientists have developed a scientific theory (e.g., atomic theory, evolution theory), does the theory ever change? If you believe that scientific theories do not change, explain why. Defend your answer with examples. If you believe that scientific theories do change: (a) Explain why theories change; (b) Explain why we bother to learn scientific theories. Defend your answer with examples.
5. Is there a difference between a scientific theory and a scientific law? Illustrate your answer with an example.
6. Science textbooks often represent the atom as a central nucleus composed of protons (positively charged particles) and neutrons (neutral particles) with electrons (negatively charged particles) orbiting the nucleus. How certain are scientists about the structure of the atom? What specific evidence do you think scientists used to determine what an atom looks like?
7. Science textbooks often define a species as a group of organisms that share similar characteristics and can interbreed with one another to produce fertile offspring. How certain are scientists about their characterization of what a species is? What specific evidence do you think scientists used to determine what a species is?
8. It is believed that about 65 million years ago the dinosaurs became extinct. Of the hypotheses formulated by scientists to explain the extinction, two enjoy wide support. The first, formulated by one group of scientists, suggests that a huge meteorite hit the Earth 65 million years ago and led to a series of events that caused the extinction. The second hypothesis, formulated by another group of scientists, suggests that massive and violent volcanic eruptions were responsible for the extinction. How are these different conclusions possible if scientists in both groups have access to and use the same set of data to derive their conclusions?
9. Some claim that science is infused with social and cultural values. That is, science reflects the social and political values, philosophical assumptions, and intellectual norms of the culture in which it is practiced. Others claim that science is universal. That is, science transcends national and cultural boundaries and is not affected by social, political, and philosophical values, and intellectual norms of the culture in which it is practiced. If you believe that science reflects social and cultural values, explain why. Defend your answer with examples. If you believe that science is universal, explain why. Defend your answer with examples.
10. Scientists perform experiments/investigations when trying to find answers to the questions they put forth. Do scientists use their creativity and imagination during their investigations? If yes, then at which stages of the investigations do you believe scientists use their imagination and creativity: planning and design, data collection, after data collection? Please explain why scientists use imagination and creativity. Provide examples if appropriate. If you believe that scientists do not use imagination and creativity, please explain why. Provide examples if appropriate.

Appendix C

The Biology Attitude Scale

Each of the statements below expresses a feeling toward biology. Please rate each statement on the extent to which you agree. For each, you may:

A	B	C	D	E
strongly agree	agree	be undecided	disagree	strongly disagree

1. Biology is very interesting to me.
2. I don't like biology, and it scares me to have to take it.
3. I am always under a terrible strain in a biology class.
4. Biology is fascinating and fun.
5. Biology makes me feel secure, and at the same time is stimulating.
6. Biology makes me feel uncomfortable, restless, irritable, and impatient.
7. In general, I have a good feeling toward biology.
8. When I hear the word "biology," I have a feeling of dislike.
9. I approach biology with a feeling of hesitation.
10. I really like biology.
11. I have always enjoyed studying biology in school.
12. It makes me nervous to even think about doing a biology experiment.
13. I feel at ease in biology and like it very much.
14. I feel a definite positive reaction to biology; it's enjoyable.

Semantic differential scale

Below are some scales on which we would like you to rate your feelings toward biology. On each scale, you can rate your feelings toward biology as an A, B, C, D, or E. There are no correct answers. Also, some of the scales seem to make more sense than others. Don't worry about it. Just rate your feelings toward biology on these scales as best you can. Please don't leave any scales blank.

BIOLOGY IS:

15.	Good	A	B	C	D	E	Bad
16.	Clean	A	B	C	D	E	Dirty
17.	Worthless	A	B	C	D	E	Valuable
18.	Cruel	A	B	C	D	E	Kind
19.	Pleasant	A	B	C	D	E	Unpleasant
20.	Sad	A	B	C	D	E	Happy
21.	Nice	A	B	C	D	E	Awful
22.	Fair	A	B	C	D	E	Unfair

Developing a Relationship With Science Through Authentic Inquiry

Paula A. Magee and Natalie S. Barman
Indiana University Purdue University at Indianapolis

What does scientific inquiry mean to you?" This is a question that we ask our college students, students studying to be elementary teachers. The majority of replies include phrases like "when scientists do experiments," "using the scientific method," or "doing experiments in science class."

When asked to describe their level of confidence in their ability to do scientific inquiry, there are some who feel confident in using the scientific method or in doing prepared "experiments," but the majority express a fear of science itself or a concern that they will not do it correctly or get the right answer. Their experiences are rarely congruent with the essential features of inquiry put forward by the National Science Education Standards (NSES) (NRC 1996).

Students are not describing scientific inquiry as being grounded in their own questions or as being dependent on their own ability to formulate explanations that make sense to them using evidence. Also absent is the necessity of the inquirer to use outside resources and materials in a critical way to support the development of questions and explanations. It is our conclusion that when many of our students enter our course, they are primed and ready for a teacher-driven curriculum—a curriculum that tells them what to do, and offers "right answers" and steps to follow. Even with good intentions on the part of the teacher, many students do not see themselves as capable of learning or understanding science. The clear voices of our students motivated us to consider ways to improve their experiences with scientific inquiry so that they could develop a meaningful relationship with science. We realized that it would be critical to look at the curricular decision-making process, specifically who (teacher or student) was making decisions and when. It was our goal that through this approach our students would learn about science, not only through the eyes of "able" others (teachers and texts) but also from their own thinking processes about relevant issues and questions.

As we began to think more about our own classroom curriculum and pedagogy, we were able to see our own theoretical stances emerge. For us, this meant articulating the priorities that we had for ourselves and for our students. How could we encourage students to express their own questions about the natural world? Was it possible to awaken our students' curiosities about everyday things and use them to develop curriculum? Could we help our students see themselves as learners of science? How do we help students honor their own self-developed "working explanations" when these explanations may not be fully consistent with accepted scientific theories?

In this chapter we first describe the theoretical framework that we have developed for understanding and developing our work as teachers. We start by articulating our own understanding of teaching and learning. Following this discussion we present details about the context of the course and describe four teaching strategies that we have used to move from a theoretical perspective of inquiry to a practical enactment. While we do include detailed descriptions of the strategies, it is important to realize that it is the holistic implementation of these strategies, together with our theoretical perspectives on teaching and learning, that we believe makes using the strategies meaningful for students. We will include evidence from student work that documents the impact of these innovations on students' understanding of scientific inquiry and their own development as learners of science.

Theoretical Perspective

Our understandings of teaching and learning are a synthesis of our own experiences and reflective thinking as well as the theories and ideas of educators and researchers such as Piaget, von Glaserfeld, and Tobin. Our working understanding of constructivism is built on Piaget's Theory of Cognition: that learners construct and refine their knowledge based on their physical experiences, dialogic interactions with others, and mental processing. While the statement "learners construct their own knowledge" seems so simple, the ideas behind this construction (how it happens, why it happens, etc.) are extremely complex and rarely agreed upon in all details (Matthews 1998). Like some (von Glasersfeld 1995; Tobin and Tippins 1993), we believe that the purpose of this construction is to help the learners make sense of the world (using all possible resources that include ideas of the learner, ideas of peers, ideas of experts, and print resources) and to better organize their experiences for themselves. We do not see the construction of knowledge as something that the learner does to get to a certain right answer. Creating opportunities for thinking and personal sense-making is what grounds our practice. We hope that these opportunities result in what Munby and Roberts have called "Intellectual Independence" (1998), when learners are capable of assessing the reasonableness of knowledge claims and are not dependent on experts. We have synthesized Munby's goal with the constructivist learning theory to develop a program where eventually most of the curricular decisions are made by the students based on their need to know. In order for this shift in decision making to be effective, the teacher needs to analyze his or her role reflectively. Oliver and Nichols's review in *School Science & Mathematics* (2001) highlights the importance for the teacher to change his or her role in the classroom from planner and conveyer of knowledge to listener and facilitator to support the development of intellectual independence.

Through this theoretical perspective, we provide opportunities for students to construct their ideas about science. As the students engage in inquiry, we prioritize the value of the individual student's working understanding of a scientific idea and/or concept. We also prioritize the development of the student's work to establish the *viability* of "working explanations" from his or her perspective. The student does not immediately or without question "accept" the scientifically agreed upon answer at any point in the inquiry process, but rather uses the knowledge of the scientific community as a resource.

We describe below the course that we have modified using the framework just described. Practical aspects of the course (things that we do, strategies that we use) will be detailed and we hope to show that one way to engage students in productive open inquiry (we define *productive* here as meeting the NSES standards) is through being mindful of intellectual independence, constructivist learning theory, and curricular decision making.

Background About Q200

The course we have taught for the last 10 years and revised in the last 3 years, Q200: Introduction to Scientific Inquiry, is a required course for all students who are seeking admission to the elementary teacher education program at the Indiana University School of Education (SOE) at Indiana University Purdue University Indianapolis (IUPUI). The course, offered by the SOE and taught by SOE faculty, counts for 3 of the required 12 general education science credits that students need to complete before applying to the program. Traditionally students enroll in the course when they are in their second year of college.

As a way to shift the locus of control from teacher to student, Q200 students learn how to ask questions related to the natural world, plan investigations, and formulate working explanations based on their own experiences and thinking throughout the course. Q200 emphasizes the development of critical-thinking skills, and by the end of the course students should be able to

- explain how their curiosity and ability to ask questions are important in developing their understanding of science both in and out of class;
- articulate how they make meaning through investigation, discussion, research, and reflection;
- explain the nature of science and the importance of having that understanding;
- apply critical-thinking skills to analyze and synthesize evidence and information while investigating questions and solve problems related to science;
- design, conduct, and report the findings of scientific investigations while using oral, graphic, and written communication skills effectively; and
- demonstrate an understanding of science processes and science content as well as the ability to apply them to everyday situations.

To accomplish these goals, Q200 is currently taught using an inquiry approach. As evidenced in the literature (Martin-Hansen 2002; DuVall 2001) there are many ways to understand what an "inquiry approach" means. As recently articulated by Settlage (2007) and Johnston (2007), the idea of inquiry as content *or* process is still something that is hotly debated. For us, inquiry is a way for individuals, within a group setting or learning community, to investigate and critically think about science with the goal of developing viable understandings and a positive, meaningful relationship with science. Unlike science teaching that often assumes that certain things "will be learned" if certain things are "done or taught," we have taken the approach that an individual's resultant understanding and development of intellectual independence is completely controlled by the learner. Our focus on teaching in this way has helped us to think about decision-making power issues in the classroom and the roles of teachers and students. Making the transition from teaching *about* inquiry to engaging our students in self-developed inquiries has forced us to look at the power we had as teachers and the ways in which we had removed power from the students.

We expect that students will actively inquire (ask questions and challenge understandings) at all times in the course. This inquiry is enacted in multiple ways that include teacher- and student-devised hands-on activities, reading from multiple sources, and discussing ideas with peers and instructors and critically thinking. A main goal of Q200 is the development of personal understanding through a series of long-term investigations. We believe that this personal understanding is best developed through a process that starts with "physical and mental messing around." We use physical and mental messing around (described in more detail below) to challenge the idea that science is a discrete set of facts that can be easily memorized. From the physical and mental messing around students are encouraged to develop questions and working explanations from the observations that they made. It is the *students'* constant checking and challenging of these working explanations that is the driving force for Q200.

Description of Community Learning Space

Q200 is a lab-based science course that meets in a room intentionally designed to support long-term investigations by small groups, technology integration, and whole-class discussions. The space includes a classroom large enough to house six large "lab" tables at which 4–5 students can sit and work comfortably and an open area (19' × 10') up front for whole-class discussions. Off the main classroom are several separate small rooms (~5' × 5') that contain sinks, tables (for storing student products), laboratory supplies, and secure storage space for 30+ laptop computers. Science trade books, as well as science and science education texts, are available for student use. For discussions, students sit on ottomans and cushions arranged in a circular shape and science talks are held regularly. The classroom is designed for students to have full access to the materials and equipment as needed.

Curriculum and Instruction

The Q200 curriculum is also markedly different from other science courses. We have made the decision to use the particle nature of matter as the overarching topic for Q200. Unlike science content courses where the particle nature of matter might be "covered" in a lecture, we spend the entire semester supporting students as they develop a viable understanding of the particle theory as the foundation for understanding many phenomena related to everyday experiences (e.g., phase changes, density, pressure). This iterative process of testing working explanations encourages students to develop a deeper understanding of related concepts within the context of their question. While we see Q200 as much more than a collection of strategies or instructional innovations, we start here by describing these key components: thinking starter, physically and mentally messing around, discussion circle, and weekly response.

Thinking Starter

"Thinking starters" are the vehicles that we use to engage students in articulating and questioning their present understandings about an observable event. They are purposefully open-ended, challenge conventional understandings about science, and require students to make decisions about "what to do next" (see Appendix A). Developing an awareness that observable phenomena are more complicated than what students have thought is often an outcome of using thinking starters. We prepare a few thinking starters for the first few days that stimulate the students prior knowledge of solids, liquids, and gases as well as initiate their own questions. In the beginning the instructor creates thinking starters that relate directly to ideas or questions posed by the students during class or in their weekly response (described below). As the students take more responsibility to plan their own next steps, the instructor creates thinking starters only when needed.

Messing Around

While students are working on a thinking starter, they are encouraged to ask questions, try out ideas and develop working explanations for the observations that they make. We use the term *physical messing around* to refer to the more spontaneous physical manipulation of materials that students choose to do (Hawkins 1965). It is from these experiences that students ultimately generate more scientifically orientated questions. This is an iterative process that continues throughout the course. We use the term *mental messing around* to refer to the critical thinking that students do as they develop their own viable understandings of the observable phenomena. As instructors we support the physical and mental messing around of our students by posing questions that encourage *them* to challenge their present understandings and emerging ideas. We are careful not to offer explanations, especially when students perceive the instructor as a holder and dispenser of knowledge.

Discussion Circle

Sharing ideas and listening to others effectively is a critical part of learning and an integral part of Q200. To support these goals, students are given opportunities to share their ideas in small groups and also through whole-class discussions. Many class sessions start and/or end with the whole-class discussion. One benefit of these discussions is for students to hear different ways of thinking about the science concepts they are trying to understand. Students are encouraged to hear and make sense of their peers' ideas without automatically negating their own. To facilitate these egalitarian discussions in the whole-class format, the class gathers in a designated discussion space. This space has been constructed to allow all members of the class to sit viewing each other. Instructors sit with the students but students lead and facilitate the discussions.

Weekly Response

Weekly written responses require students to communicate their ideas, questions, and thinking with their peers and instructor. This communication facilitates reflection and critical thinking by the students and helps the instructor identify ways (thinking starters, resources, specific questions, materials) to support students in their work. Sample prompts include the following:

- Describe the activities your group engaged in today.
- Describe any working explanations that you are developing at this time.
- What do you plan to do on Monday?

- How do you predict that this will help with your understanding of solids, liquids, and/ or gases?

These ideas are not presented as strategies that we expect others to replicate; however, they are representative of ways we have begun to "walk the walk."

Connecting to the NSES Essential Features of Inquiry

As a way to think about inquiry and Q200, we look to the NSES. If students are developing a deeper understanding of inquiry, one that goes beyond the process skills or doing activities, we should be able to find evidence in their class work. We have chosen to focus on one of the projects for the course to identify statements that shed light on students' thinking. In this section we will identify each standard. Following the standard we will discuss our interpretation of the standard and our analysis of student work that supports meeting the standard.

1. Learner Engages in Scientifically Oriented Questions

In Q200, students' questions about the natural world are encouraged and valued. If students are to be autonomous critical thinkers, they must possess and be able to identify their own sense of wonder about the world around them. We see this awareness as a vital first step in the inquiry process—a step that generates questions developed by the students. Students use these initial questions to begin physically and mentally messing around through which authentic scientifically oriented questions emerge.

The following is a description of one final project that was inspired, developed, and carried out by a small group of Q200 students to further their understanding of a phenomenon they had observed during the course. Midway through the course, a thinking starter was developed that encouraged students to mess around, mentally and physically, when different liquids were put together. This group observed what happened when liquid food coloring was added to different liquids in a graduated cylinder. They noticed that the food coloring behaved differently in water and oil. They were specifically intrigued by the globular appearance of the food coloring in the oil. One person in the group connected this to lava lamps and asked what would happen if the oil were heated. The students continued their inquiry by identifying the main concept as density and looked for concrete ways to continue thinking about their ideas. The group decided that creating their own lava lamp would be a good way to learn more about density and to further develop their ideas. At this point they looked on the internet for activities, found "recipes" for making lava lamps, and proceeded to follow the directions. When the recipes did not work as expected, they began to think more critically about what was going on. At this point the students started developing questions that challenged what they thought they knew and allowed them to check for the viability of their ideas. Students began to question several things regarding the workings of the lamp: How does heating affect the materials in the lamp? How does adding solid material to the bottom affect the materials? How different do the densities of the liquids need to be in order to make the lamp work? Was there some vacuum in the bottle? Did the shape of the bottle make a difference? It is important to note that the instructors did not provide any of these questions. They were generated by the students as they dove more deeply into the group-designed inquiry. While we agree that it is important to be able to develop *a* specific testable question, we have found that it is crucial for students to first develop a collection of non-contrived questions, questions that we, and the students, consider to be scientifically oriented. This allows for the development of a richer more complex understanding of a concept that has been contextualized by the students.

2. Learner Gives Priority to Evidence When Responding to Questions

In Q200, students begin to generate their own questions relatively easily once the class begins. However, using evidence (their observations) to make decisions regarding "what to do next" is a much more challenging task. This mental messing around requires an admission on the part of the students that their own ideas are worthy of investigation. As expected, students are often distrustful of their own ideas and do not feel "smart enough" to make decisions regarding their own scientific learning. Because we do not offer answers or activities with specific predetermined "answers," students must look to their own sense-making to decide what to do once they reach a pivotal point in their investigation. In this setting, where the instructor does not tell students what to do next, but rather asks questions to help them think through their options, students are supported to develop their ability to make decisions regarding their own scientific learning.

In this example, a student realized that the lava lamp was not working as she had expected, but she did not ignore this observation. Instead she used it to continue the questioning and investigation. Here she acknowledges the evidence to help her think more deeply about her questions:

Our lava lamps were only partially successful. When we placed the lamps above the heat source, a 100W bulb, we were able to get some small bubbles of mineral oil to float toward the top and then descend once again. However, after being left on the heat source for some time, the bubbles stopped cycling up and down and we began to observe convection currents in the alcohol layer. Eventually, the oil coalesced into a large blob. I think that these problems resulted from at least two, and possibly three, factors.

First, I think our heat source was too hot. Most of the lava lamp "recipes" called for 40W or 60W bulbs (Helmenstine, n.d.; Make Your Own Lava Lamp, n.d.). Debbie [another group member] examined her son's lava lamp and discovered that it had a 15W bulb. I think that our 100W bulb produced too much heat, which adversely affected the working of the lamp. In order for a lava lamp to work properly, the heat needs to be concentrated near the bottom so that the lava will heat up, while the top of the less dense substance (in our case the alcohol layer) remains cool. This allows the lava to cool off and condense once it reaches the top so that it can sink and resume the cycle. The presence of convection currents in at least two of our lamps indicates that the entire alcohol layer was heating up and the convection currents were responsible for moving the tiny drops of oil. Eventually, the oil condensed at the bottom. I wonder if this is because the alcohol eventually heated up enough that it also became less dense and so the oil, although less dense than it was at room temperature, was still denser than the alcohol layer.

From the excerpt we see the student using evidence, the observed behavior of the droplets, to respond to her own question about how the lava lamp works. She recognizes that the droplets are not behaving as she expected and she develops several "working explanations" for why this might be. In the passage above she makes a conjecture that the lamp the group used was too hot and therefore the blobs were not sufficiently cooled by moving to the top of the lamp. To support her working explanation she includes a nice description of how she is thinking about the workings of the lava lamp at this time. This description is supported by the observations she made in this activity.

3. Learner Formulates Explanations Based on Evidence

In Q200, students are asked to think about how what they are observing supports, changes, or challenges the ideas that they have. In this example a student describes her "working explanation" of how the lava lamp works. She uses the observations that she has made to decide on the viability of that explanation.

> *As the oil layer heated the molecules became active and moved around more. This caused them to expand and become less dense than the alcohol layer [explanation]. We did have success in getting a few small bubbles to rise and break through the alcohol layer [evidence]. When the bubbles reached the top of the alcohol layer [evidence], where it was cooler the molecules started to move close together and become less active [explanation]. This made the oil layer denser than the alcohol layer [explanation] and the bubbles of the oil started to sink back down [evidence]. That's how a lava lamp works.*

By the way the student intertwines her ideas with her observations, we see her explanation grounded within the evidence. Her ability to synthesize different components of the working explanation speaks to the complexity of her thinking. In Q200, we want the students to leave the course with an understanding that their "working explanations" are viable but also to be aware that those explanations should continue to evolve based on future experiences and thinking.

4. Learner Connects Explanations to Scientific Knowledge

While the working explanations of the students are grounded in their physical experiences, students are also expected to compare those explanations to reliable resources as a way to further develop their understanding. We usually wait a few weeks into the semester to promote researching outside sources so students become invested in their own questions and ideas and are less ready to abandon them. Once the students have articulated their ideas and compared them to multiple resources, our hope is that they will synthesize an understanding that is meaningful to them. We see the emergence of their own ideas as a critical beginning step in developing more complicated understandings and the development of intellectual independence. As part of Q200, students are encouraged and expected to use reliable resources (print media, web resources) to help develop their understandings. In these passages we see students Laura and Tom making these connections.

Laura: *I came to an understanding of how lava lamps work, as it relates to density, through a variety of ways. I've already mentioned a helpful website that not only provided a visual of what the molecules are doing, but also gave me information about ingredients to use, how heat was a factor, how density works, etc.*

> **Tom:** *I think that another factor influencing our results may have been the difference in densi-ties between the two layers. Most of the internet sources on lava lamps indicate that the two liquids should have very similar densities (Harris, n.d.; Helmenstine, n.d.; How is a lava lamp made? n.d.). The closer the two densities are, the less heat you will need to apply to the lower layer because it will require less energy to make it less dense than the top layer.*

In both of these examples students are using web resources to make sense of the questions that they have and/or the observations that they have made. Throughout the second half of the course this strategy is encouraged with a strong reminder to always be a "critical reader" of the infor-mation. In other words, unlike courses where students are often asked to memorize informa-tion, Q200 students are asked to think about how their reading connects with their own ideas and observations. Another important distinction to make here is that students are not using the resources to find "the" right answer. In both examples the students use the resource information in a way that supports the complexity of the science.

5. Learner Communicates and Justifies Explanations

In Q200, students are continuously prompted to express, in written and oral forms, their expla-nations for things that they observe or experience (through weekly responses, science talks and discussions with peers and instructor). As a result of this, students become more aware of justi-fying and developing their ideas and are able to communicate these ideas effectively without step-by-step directions from us. In the passage below a student describes her experience with her iterative process of making lava lamps. She develops reasonable and logical explanations for her observations of the lava lamps and communicates this to us. Unlike the other quotes, which were taken from formal papers, these quotes come from a weekly response (prompts are included).

> *Weekly Response Prompt: How are you making sense of what has been happening in the activity itself?*

> *I was able to get my home version of the lamp cycling better with less heat, and I suspect that this is because the densities of the two layers were probably more similar, although I do not know this for sure. After making this lamp and seeing how much faster it started to work and how much larger the bubbles were, I started to think about how using the same materials in a different way may have affected the working of the lamp. Using a mineral oil whose density falls between that of the two alcohols allows one to create an alcohol mixture whose density is only very slightly less than that of the oil. This means that the oil's density does not have to change as much which, in turn, means that it does not have to be heated as much. With less heat applied to the base of the lamp, the alcohol at the top remains cooler and the lamp seems to function better. It was easier to fine-tune the density of the alcohol layer by mixing the oil and 70% isopropyl first, then slowly adding 91% isopropyl until the oil began to descend. When we tried adding the 91% first in Lamp 2 [a previous attempt] (as recommended at www.oozinggoo.com/ll-form2.html), I think it was a lot more difficult to judge when the oil was ready to "jump" from the bottom.*

Conclusions

We recognize the NSES Essential Features of Classroom Inquiry and Their Variations as a beginning articulation of necessary characteristics for inquiry to take place in the classroom. In addition to the essential features, we include changes in the student–teacher relationship and types of interactions as crucial to implementing inquiry successfully. As we have worked to increase students' awareness of themselves as learners of science, we have had to challenge the role of the teacher in the classroom. First, by valuing students' own meaningful ideas, questions, and reasoning during all stages of their learning process, the curriculum becomes a flexible guide in the classroom rather than a prescribed document. Students make decisions about how to investigate and make sense of observations and experiences. They discuss their working explanations with others and research additional information as they evaluate the viability of their understanding. We believe that the viability of their understanding of related concepts is strengthened because of the personal context of the inquiry.

We close this chapter with a student explaining her thinking process which includes her initial ideas, student-to-student shared information, desire to test their statement herself, and realizing that she does not have a complete understanding at this time.

I think that dissolving is when a solid substance is introduced to a liquid and then the solid breaks down to its smallest pieces and disperses throughout the liquid. I think that to dissolve does not mean to break down completely, I believe this because group two has explained to me how the salt crystals were still in the water even though they could not be seen with the naked eye. I would really like to get the microscope out and see for myself. My understanding has clarified a lot, I have never even thought about what dissolve meant before, and when I began to think about it I realized that I really didn't know what I meant when I said dissolve. I now have a partial understanding of what dissolve means, I feel like that will clarify as we discuss this in class.

References

DuVall, R. 2001. Inquiry to science: From curiosity to understanding. *Primary K–6* 10 (1): 3–8.

Harris, T. How liquid motion lamps work. *www.howstuffworks.com/lava-lamp.htm*.

Hawkins, D. 1965. Messing about in science. *Science & Children* 2 (5): 5–9.

Helmenstine, A.M. How to make a lava lamp: Nontoxic version. *http://chemistry.about.com/cs/howtos/ht/nontoxlavalamp.htm*

Helmenstine, A.M. How to make a lava lamp: Realistic version. *http://chemistry.about.com/cs/howtos/ht/lavalampreal.htm*

Johnston, A. 2007. Demythologizing or dehumanizing? A response to Settlage and the ideals of open inquiry. *Journal of Science Teacher Education* 19 (1): 11–13.

Khishfe, R., and F. Abd-El-Khalick. 2002. Influence of explicit and reflective versus implicit inquiry-oriented instruction on sixth graders' views of the nature of science. *Journal of Research in Science Teaching* 39 (70): 551–578.

Martin-Hansen, L. 2002. Defining inquiry. *The Science Teacher* 69 (2): 34–37.

Mathews, M. 1998. *Constructivism in science education: A philosophical examination.* Boston: Kluwer Academic Publishers.

Munby, H., and D. A. Roberts. 1998. Intellectual independence: A potential link between science teaching and responsible citizenship. In *Problems of meaning in science curriculum*, eds. D. A. Roberts and L. Ostman. New York: Teacher's College Press.

National Research Council (NRC). 1996. *National science education standards.* Washington, DC: National Academy Press.

Oliver, J. S., and K. Nichols. 2001. Intellectual independence as a persistent theme in the literature of science education: 1900–1950. *School Science & Math* 101 (1): 49–56.

Settlage, J. 2007. Demythologizing science teacher education: Conquering the false idea of open inquiry. *Journal of Science Teacher Education* 18 (4): 461–468.

Tobin, K., and D. Tippins. 1993. Constructivism as a referent for science teaching and learning. In *The practice of constructivism in science education*, ed. K. Tobin, Washington, DC: AAAS Press.

von Glasersfeld, E. 1995. *Radical constructivism: A way of knowing and seeing.* Washington, DC: Falmer Press.

Appendix A – Thinking Starter

How do we describe these substances?

1. Each person documents your "Messing Around" activities, thoughts, and questions

2. Write (or read) your understanding of what the word *solid* means for #2. Talk about your understanding with the people at your table. What is similar and what is different?

3. Observe (look and feel) each "item" on the tray. Write down a few words that describe each.

4. Based on your written understanding and discussion, discuss whether you think an item is a solid or not and why. What did others in your group say? Take notes!

5. Important—Record your questions, wonderings, and thinkings you are not sure of at this time.

Materials

- wooden block
- plastic block
- cotton
- clay
- sand
- sponge
- ice cube
- aluminum foil
- Jell-O
- drinking straw

Science Projects: Successful Inquiries in Eighth-Grade Science

Pascale Creek Pinner
Hilo Intermediate School

Hilo Intermediate School is an urban school in the downtown area of Hilo, Hawaii. The school serves a racially diverse, economically disadvantaged population of 550 students in seventh and eighth grades. Six different elementary schools send students to Hilo Intermediate. Due to the No Child Left Behind Act (NCLB), three of these schools are restructured, another is in corrective action, and the last two have made adequate yearly progress in their curricular programs. This means that the majority of emphasis in the upper elementary curriculum is placed in the areas of math and language arts, with science covered only briefly, if at all.

School Science Curriculum Goals and Vision

It is the mission of the science department of Hilo Intermediate School to ensure that the Hawaii State Standards and Benchmarks are addressed through the seventh-grade life science and eighth-grade Earth and space science classes, including a focus on material that was not considered in the upper grades of the feeder elementary schools. Data from the first year of the Hawaii Statewide Assessment in science indicates that more than 56% of the students who enter seventh grade are below proficiency in the areas of inquiry and physical science. The department feels strongly about their vision that every student who exits eighth grade will be able to think critically, solve problems creatively, be self-directed learners, and develop inquiry skills that serve them through their high school years and beyond. This will be accomplished through the development of a variety of short- and long-term, research-based inquiry science projects. As stated succinctly in the *National Science Education Standards (NSES)*,

Students in all grade levels and in every domain of science should have the opportunity to use scientific inquiry and develop the ability to think and act in ways associated with inquiry, including asking questions, planning and conducting investigations, using appropriate tools and techniques to gather data, thinking critically and logically about the relationships between evidence and explanations, constructing and analyzing alternative explanations, and communicating scientific arguments. (NRC 1996, p. 105)

This statement exemplifies the vision of the school's science department and its mission to ensure that students each develop a variety of self-selected science projects through their two years at Hilo Intermediate School. The department's SMART Goals place an emphasis on scientific research and inquiry, as well as the use of formative, performance, and summative assessments that are coordinated and provide data about the attainment of the standards in science. Additionally, the department expects students to create quarterly portfolios and self-assessments of their progress in meeting the standards throughout the school year. Finally, a variety of short- and long-term science projects are incorporated in every academic quarter.

The science department provides a variety of projects in seventh-grade life science that builds the basic skills needed for inquiry (e.g., developing testable questions, identifying variables, creating and following rudimentary procedures, and analyzing experimental results). The culminating "Create an Experiment" project occurs during the last quarter of the year and asks students to develop an environmental service-learning project based on local ecology concepts. Students complete this project in groups and report on it to their peers.

When students enter the eighth grade, the first unit they complete is "Habits of Mind: Thinking and Acting Like a Scientist." Incorporated into this unit are the scientific processes learned in seventh grade and the first large inquiry project titled Mystery Substance: Robotic Rover Engineering Challenge. The next unit on atoms and electricity has students developing an understanding of the basics of electricity using a variety of experiments that ask students to build circuits and finally create a physical electricity product of their choice (like a game board or working electrical item) to illustrate what they have learned. Although implemented by each teacher, these units were created by the author and are unique to the school. Additionally, they address both "need areas" indicated on the Hawaii Statewide Science Assessment of inquiry and physical science. All these lessons lead up to the development of a self-chosen, research-based, long-term science fair project.

Physical Context of Eighth-Grade Science Classes

There are 250 students in the eighth-grade Earth and space science class. Ethnically, the students represent the school's diverse racial population. Students in these classes range in abilities from special education to above average, with the majority of the students falling in the average to below average ability areas. Many students qualify for instructional adaptations; some are mainstreamed special education students and others are students with emotional or academic needs who qualify for support services but do not have the special education designation. Culturally, there are varying attitudes toward the "value" of school. For many, school attendance does not have any priority in their lives. There is also one class designated as gifted and talented which is comprised of students who are racially diverse but academically high achieving. Although diverse in academic strengths, all students complete a team science project in seventh grade and an individual eighth-grade science fair project.

Three years ago, the school was restructured in response to the No Child Left Behind Act and the America's Choice reform model that was mandated for the school. A 90-minute block schedule was implemented, which only allowed the students to have science two times a week. This has proven very difficult for the building of concepts and processes over time. However, most students enjoy science and try hard when they receive positive feedback.

Each science classroom's environment provides a large space for students to move around freely so they can do activities, work in the team mini computer lab at the rear of the room, and store any work in progress in their class period area. This is supportive for long-term projects like the science fair project, portfolios, and many other laboratory experiments that need to remain set up from class period to class period. This set up also facilitates students doing many different things all at the same time and allows the teacher to orchestrate the learning time.

Eighth-Grade Inquiry Units

The important focus for all the introductory inquiry units is the use of science as an inquiry process. The specific standards addressed by the units are National Content Standard A: Science as Inquiry, as well as other national standards specific to each unit's content. The Hawaii state standards are Scientific Investigation, Nature of Science, Nature of Matter, and Energy and Force and Motion.

As stated in Marzano, Pickering, and Pollock's book *Classroom Instruction That Works: Research-Based Strategies for Increasing Student Achievement*, generating and testing hypotheses is one of the 10 instructional strategies that have a "high probability of enhancing student achievement for all students in all subject areas at all grade levels" (2001, p. 7). With the number of students entering Hilo Intermediate School below proficiency in both math and language arts, it seems prudent that the content area of science build strategies based in their domain that support student achievement. Thus, projects that ask students to develop and test their own hypotheses "fit the bill." In addition, asking students to generate and test hypotheses is the foundation for student inquiry.

Additionally, in the book *Inquire Within: Implementing Inquiry-Based Science Standards*, Llewellyn proposes several theoretical models that incorporate true scientific inquiry (2002). They include the Inquiry Cycle and the 5-E model, just two examples of ways that a classroom can become a place where student-centered inquiry can take place, allowing students to really learn. Additionally, the NRC document on inquiry identifies five essential features of classroom inquiry. These features include the learner (1) posing scientifically oriented questions; (2) determining what evidence will be collected and collecting it; (3) analyzing the collected evidence; (4) explaining the connections between the evidence and scientific knowledge; and (5) communicating justified results in a logical manner (2000). Overall, the inquiry process requires teachers to create an environment where students can explore, question, develop experiments to test their ideas, and evaluate and communicate their results when they are done.

In the preliminary units for eighth-grade Earth and space science, a foundation is being built to support the skills necessary to complete the longer-term science fair project. These learning experiences allow students to make observations, develop questions, and then determine if the questions are scientifically important. All these are important as students develop an experiment to answer their own questions. Students also gather results, analyze what they have learned, and make conclusions, which they communicate to their peers and others.

Mystery Substance: Robotic Rover Engineering Challenge

Students start with a simple lab experiment observing a "mystery substance" that reinforces scientific observations and data collection that is not biased with inferences. After the initial experiment, students develop questions that they would like to investigate about the physical properties of the mystery substance. They are given the scenario explaining where the substance was found and some basic background information about the environment and a problem they must solve. This leads directly to the development of "testable" versus not very testable questions to guide experiments. Students then individually choose a question they want to answer through a controlled experiment that they plan and develop (Figure 1).

Figure 1. Mystery Substance Day 2: Example of a Lab Report

MYSTERY SUBSTANCE

PURPOSE: You have just completed preliminary observations of the mystery substance that was taken from the crust of the cave on Survivor Island and submitted your conclusion describing the mystery substance. Now your company has assigned you to a group of scientists/engineers that are designing a robotic rover that will need to enter the mystery substance–coated cave, travel down into the center, and retrieve a metal box containing your prize money. Another group of chemists in your company is analyzing the mystery substance to determine what it is made of. Unfortunately, your observations have not given you enough details to finish designing your rover. What other questions do you and your fellow scientists have about the mystery substance? Which of these questions and their answers are necessary to design your company's rover so that it can successfully retrieve your prize? How are you going to find and share your results?

QUESTIONS: After the class reviews the necessary and unnecessary questions posed about the mystery substance, record below ONLY the questions whose answers will be needed to help you tackle the mystery substance–coated cave with your robotic rover.

1.   3.

2.   4.

THE QUESTION I WILL BE TESTING TO FIND AN ANSWER IS QUESTION # _____

MATERIALS: List below all the materials you used to conduct your test(s).

PROCEDURE: Record all of the steps you created to test the mystery substance below.

DATA & OBSERVATIONS: Describe what happened to the mystery substance during your test(s). Draw and label at least one picture of your test/experiment.

RESULTS: From your experimental results, formulate an answer(s) to your question.

Students are grouped according to their question choice. Together, they create a list of materials and procedures to use. The group shares this chart with the class, who may critique their work and help revise everything, resulting in a concise list of specific materials and a clear procedure that can be followed by all. This is where questions about quantity, amounts, trials, sizes, and step-by-step instructions are clarified. The teacher only needs to guide the students, as the students are very capable of pointing out items that seem unclear or are missing. Once the revisions are completed, students individually prepare a lab report form (Figure 1) in order to be prepared to conduct the experiment during the next class period. This is a perfect time to cover safety with demonstrations and regulations before they actually get to do their self-created experiment. Excitement builds as the time for the experiments arrives. The students have to follow their own materials list, work together, follow their procedures and conduct at least three trials of their experiment. The students determine what evidence they will collect and how they will represent that data on their lab report. They draw and label pictures of their experiment, collect observations, and collaborate together regarding their conclusions. The group's conclusions are then shared as a series of specific statements about the physical characteristics of the mystery substance.

Next comes the Mystery Substance convention. This is where the groups share their results. All results are linked to the original question and a class list of results is developed. Students are then given their Robotic Rover Engineering Challenge. Students individually choose the four results that they would like to use to design their robotic rover to complete the "prize" task. They must use their results as the criteria for the specific item that they design their rover to do or apply to the mystery substance. They must also be able to explain how the group worked together to complete their problem tasks. Students must either create a labeled drawing or a model of their robotic rover and a short explanation of the results chosen to enhance their design. The table of results and their application of those results to solve various aspects of their task through their design are evaluated with a checklist. The rover itself is evaluated with the student-generated "I CAN Do Quality Work in Science" rubric.

This series of lessons ensures that students use a variety of hands-on activities that are self-directed, and yet facilitated by the instructor, to experience firsthand the various aspects of inquiry: hypothesis generation and testing, analysis and application of results, and finally communication of their designs. The unit incorporates the essential features of classroom inquiry where the amount of learner self-direction is optimized and the amount of teacher direction is kept to a minimum (NRC 2000). The student-created quality rubric provides the impetus for the generation of a final product that meets or exceeds standards.

Electricity Explorations

The next unit requires students to build a repertoire of complex problem-solving skills, as well as continue to develop basic measurements and investigation processes. Students move from basic experiments about static electricity where they determine what materials to use to experiments that ask them to determine what materials are conductors and insulators. The idea of semiconductors and how various electrical fixtures work is considered. Embedded in this work is a hands-on look at the periodic table and how electricity is actually generated (i.e., the movement of electrons). These are described by their characteristics and thus placement of elements in specific series on the periodic table. Next, students move to investigations about series and parallel circuits and determine their own definition of efficiency of a circuit caused by its configuration. The final segments of the unit ask students to use switches and various circuits and power sources to create an electronic game board or other product of their choice.

This unit is unique to the district in that it addresses several standards and benchmarks for understanding chemical interactions and electrical forces. This is interesting because the elementary schools that feed into Hilo Intermediate School have no experience with this content. Therefore, it is incumbent on the science program at the school to use this less familiar content to incorporate process skills that allow students to work on scientific inquiry projects and products.

Science Fair Project

After completing the discussed units during the first quarter of the school year, the students begin the development of their individual science fair projects, which is the focus of the remaining portion of this chapter. The science fair project requires students to develop the ability to think and act in the ways associated with inquiry, including asking questions, planning and conducting experiments, collecting data, thinking and analyzing results logically, and finally communicating those results to others. Scientific inquiry methods are very important for our students because the process of inquiry will help them develop ways to solve problems logically in a step-by-step manner. This translates into usable skills students need for daily living, resolving community problems, possible careers, and their own future education. The three major goals the students will meet through completing this unit include

1. utilizing the methods of scientific inquiry to complete a self-directed science project;

2. integrating the use of scientific and technological tools throughout the project; and

3. using hands-on activities to apply the difficult concepts of experimental design.

A total of 10 weeks (the second quarter) is used to complete this project. Each phase focuses on specific processes that the student learns and eventually applies to their individual project. Assessment of each phase through various assignments builds a foundation of skills necessary for the students to complete this long-term project. These phases are invaluable in providing opportunities for revision and contribute to students successfully achieving all the learning goals stated.

Phase I: Topic Research

The first activity is the scavenger hunt on the Science Buddies website (*www.sciencebuddies.org*), which focuses on the use of technology as a tool to stimulate curiosity and provide background information about specific science concepts and topics. Students use the internet to learn about, select, and research a topic in order to record the background information for each individual project. The completion of the scavenger hunt, the notes, and finally, the research paper with references cited are the products assessed. At this point, students create a science fair folder where they place this work. This folder was not allowed out of the classroom, but students could add to it or take home copies of items that they need.

Phase II: Use of Science Inquiry Skills to Design a Science Project

In order to address the standards and benchmarks associated with scientific inquiry, every class period is central for learning and developing the various parts of the experimental design for the individual science fair project. Students structure a preliminary question, as well as a hypothesis that indicates the variables of their experiment. They conduct additional lab experiments where identification of variables and the manipulating of those variables help to clarify student experimental designs. Labs also emphasize the *doing* of science, including development of a testable problem/question, hypotheses, control/variables, materials and procedures, data table design (trials) and graphing, collection and analysis of data, and reaching sound conclusions from the data analyzed. Activities like "Come Fly With Me," "Bug-O-Copters," "How Many Drops on Top?" and "Which Is the Best Electromagnet?'" require students to use the steps of inquiry and introduce procedural variables and controls for experimental designs. A more complex lab report is used for each of these activities, which then prompts students to conduct a complete discussion, an analysis of their data, and prepare concise and clear conclusions (Figure 2 p. 134). The accompanying homework asks the students to apply what they learned and define their topic question, hypotheses, experimental variables, constants, and controls. Assessment of the skills included the lab report rubric (contact author for rubric) and completion of the homework questions for their individual projects.

The students continue the process by writing in detail about materials and procedures, which are then fine-tuned by the teacher with comments for rewriting. Finally, designing data tables to include the proper placement of variables, the placement of actual data, and the data table for each experiment completes the experimental design portion of student class work.

It is then time to take student folders home to do the experiments. A parent letter explains the expectations for completion of the project. The bottom portion is returned with a parent signature so that the teacher knows that parents are informed and aware of the processes their child is working through.

Constant feedback is also provided through the Science Fair Rubric (contact author for a copy) for each portion of the process as students revise their questions, hypotheses and variables, experimental materials, and procedures. The ability to use the feedback from the rubric, as well as from the teacher, reinforces student self-direction. As they work on each piece of their project and revise those pieces, they are really applying self-assessment techniques to a project that they are developing. The tough part for the teacher is that every day the folders need to be reviewed and comments provided. This means a total of about 60–70 folders a day. The specific criteria on the rubric helps but comments are needed as well. After these activities, the collection of data from their own experiment with scientific equipment is completed and recorded in their log.

Phase III: Final Product

After the students return with their experiment completed and their data in their science fair folder, Science Fair Rubric II is provided. The first step involves students designing a rough draft of their graphs concerning their own data. Once the drafts are approved, computer training on the use of the Excel program allows students to create final drafts of their graphs. The purpose of the project is written at this time because the students now understand the importance and value

Figure 2: Sample Lab Report Form

Title of Experiment: _____

I. PURPOSE: problem question

> A. What is the **problem or issue** to be solved? _____
> _____
>
> B. Rewrite the problem as a **question** – be sure it is a question that you can test
> and is connected to your problem/issue to be solved.

II. HYPOTHESIS: A predicted answer or educated explanation to the problem question. Be sure to use the "if…then…because…" format so that your hypothesis is specific, testable, measurable, safe, and useful.

> Hypothesis: If _____

III. EXPERIMENT: Test the hypothesis.
    A.   Variables:

> **Control** (Describe what you are **NOT** going to test in order to compare your results to it):
> **Independent Variable** (what is being changed/compared):
> **Dependent Variable** (what is being measured because of the change):

    B.   Materials: Make a complete list of what is going to be used in the experiment. Be sure to include safety, measuring items, metric units, the amount and sizes of items, and brand names (if needed).

    C.   Procedures: Step-by-step NUMBERED instructions to do the experiment that can be easily replicated (done by others).

    D.   OBSERVATIONS AND DATA: Record general observations (written) and draw at least 1–2 labeled diagrams during the experiment. Collect observations and quantitative data in a table. Organize the table for easy interpretation of results.

IV. DATA ANALYSIS: Discussion of results. Use the data to explain the results that were collected.
    A.   Analyze and explain any patterns or relationships discovered from the observations/data—including any outliers to the data.

    B.   Calculate applicable mathematical statistics (mean, median, mode, range) and explain how they relate to the results.

    C.   Explain if there were any errors with the data collection—if there were not, state as "no errors encountered."

V. CONCLUSIONS: Summarize the experiment.

    A.   State the original hypothesis and determine whether the data agrees, disagrees, or partially agrees with it.

    B.   Make recommendations (changes) on how the experiment could be improved if it were conducted again.

    C.   State how the results of this experiment could be applied in the real world.

    D.   Develop at least one related question that could be developed into a future experiment because of experiences with this experiment.

of the question they investigated. The students are very familiar with writing the data analysis and the conclusion sections because these are the same questions used on the science lab report form they used throughout both academic quarters. This class activity forces the students to look at their own data, the graphs they created, and some explanations for their initial questions. The abstract, which is a summary of the entire project, is completed last. At this point student work often shows a need for more detailed explanations for each section. With specific feedback from both the teacher and their peers, students are able to produce a final draft that is much clearer and concise.

A final rubric is given to help students focus their presentation board on a quality product. Once completed, they use the rubric to both self-evaluate and then peer-evaluate projects. Additionally, the school fair (more than 250 projects) is the place for student interviews to take place. Interview questions are developed by the students as a part of their social studies standard of informing an audience of "multiple perspectives," as well as successful interviewing and oral communication skills.

The large variety of "sense-making" activities allows students to build skills to complete their own projects successfully. Students were provided lessons in word processing, writing, and peer reviewing in class. Statistics, data table, and graph production using Excel were also taught. The skills they learned during this project emphasized how different subject area skills come together to enhance future work and life skills.

Assessing Learning Along the Way

One of the roles of assessment for this project is to provide hands-on activities to practice the scientific method with opportunities for feedback and revision to the individual project components after the other lab experiments were evaluated. Students are also taught to use the rubrics as a part of their own work to assess how they are doing on their individual projects. Some peer and self-assessments focus on individual parts of the project itself; others focus on the clarity of the experimental data analysis that has been completed. Additionally, rubrics are used to provide feedback on how effectively students use and apply scientific and technological equipment to the specific parts of their projects. Thus the learning goals for all students are completed through a variety of class assignments, homework, labs, quizzes, writing logs, the Science Fair Folder Rubrics I and II, peer/self-evaluation rubric, guided note outlines, and the final project display board and associated report. These methods are appropriate because they provide a large variety of activities and assignments to indicate student success. Because lab experiments are intuitively intriguing for kids at this age and because the project is put together in parts that are checked weekly, students have many opportunities to review and revise their work, which contributes to the development of a positive work ethic in the science classroom.

Inquiry Challenges

There are many challenges inherent in teaching a unit of this magnitude. The largest is that every student chooses his or her own topic. These topics cover a broad range of scientific areas. I assist with this challenge by providing a variety of resources to help students with the facts, definitions, and vocabulary. Another challenge is that some of the processes within the methods of inquiry (e.g., developing a specific testable question, defining variables, and making multiple trials) are hard for students to understand and apply to their projects at this age. Providing a variety of lab activities focusing on these specific areas helps students to understand *and* apply their learning to their own project. Breaking down the process into smaller parts helps the students and allows me to identify those who were still having trouble developing the various portions of the experimental design.

The last challenge is sustaining interest over an extended period of time. Providing constant, specific, positive, written feedback in the Science Fair Log is the way to motivate students and identify those who were really having difficulties or those who have not done their work. Because a project like this requires each step to be set up before the next can begin, this monitoring is paramount for successful completion of the entire project.

Being flexible with lesson plans at certain times during this unit is also very important. At the beginning, some of the lower ability students may not be able to choose an appropriate topic. Providing a variety of easy and fun science experiment books for them to browse through and on occasion selecting a specific topic for a special education student or one who is unmotivated may be necessary. Modeling additional experiments using the department's science lab report form reinforces what is needed for the completed experiment portion of the science fair project.

Building in extra class periods for rewriting parts of the experimental design, including the background information, topic question, hypotheses, materials, procedures, and variables may also be needed. It is important to talk with every student in the class as they use the feedback entered into their logs to redo their work. This is also where differentiation of scientific detail for various portions can occur through challenging feedback, requiring more specific details as well as trials and data analyses from those of higher ability. Finally, offering very specific ideas to those who need extra help allows all students to reach their best potential. Requiring quality work from everyone is paramount, but adjusting the levels of scientific details that students can produce allows all to complete a project successfully.

Schoolwide Project Analysis

Every child in eighth grade participates in the various science inquiry lessons that take place over the first and second quarters of the school year. This sets the tone for the development of individual projects and experimental methods for the rest of the school year as well as those that they will encounter in high school and beyond. Over the last two years, articulation with the high school has supported the importance of the inquiry projects because the teachers are seeing the students come prepared to conduct experiments on their own and the high school science department continues to use the lab report format developed by the author of this chapter.

Science fair projects have been in place at Hilo Intermediate School for the last 15 years. Students have competed not only in the school fair, but also successfully at the district and state levels as well. This year 21 students went to the district fair and 16 of those students went on to compete at the State Science and Engineering Fair. Over the last three years, the winner of the Junior Division at the district fair was from Hilo Intermediate and last year's entrant also won the State Science Fair. Many of the students have gone on to compete in various national competitions as well.

Not only do students do well at the school, district, and state science fairs but also an analysis of reflection essays over the last five years has shown that when students are engaged in inquiry projects, their perception of "doing science" improves. More than 85% of them state that the science fair, mystery substance, and/or electricity project was the one that assisted them the most with their learning of how to do science independently. Their positive comments range from being able to select their own topic, to having to do the experiment by themselves, to actually completing a long-term project of their own. Few had ever worked individually on such a large project before.

The assessment of this 10-week quarter works well and is fair. Throughout the project, students completed assignments that are graded and they are given multiple opportunities for completing revisions to the components of their project. This ensures that students complete each portion of the project before moving on to the next assignment, as well as giving them ideas for continued quality work. A project of this magnitude requires the teacher to look at the student population and the lessons one needs to emphasize annually. Long-term, self-directed inquiry ensures that students really use their complex thinking and problem-solving skills and apply them to a project that they feel is important and thus, something on which they are willing to concentrate for the time needed to compete in the school, District, and occasionally the State Science and Engineering Fair.

Over the years this science fair unit has undergone many transitions. During the last two years, I have had the added responsibility for instructing new department members about this unit, as they were also required to teach the unit to their seventh- and eighth-grade students. The sequence took into account the varying degrees of ability within our heterogeneous classes, including special education. The new teachers were able to implement the inquiry units successfully into their curriculum because specific lesson plans, student exemplars, a timeframe that was appropriate, and the help of the author supported them when challenges arose. Overall, each teacher has made the inquiry units their "own" through the experiences they had with the students they taught.

References

Llewellyn, D. 2002. *Inquire within: Implementing inquiry-based science standards.* Thousand Oaks, CA: Corwin Press.

Marzano, R. J., D. J. Pickering, and J. E. Pollock. 2001. *Classroom instruction that works: Research-based strategies for increasing student achievement.* Upper Saddle River, NJ: Pearson Education.

National Research Council (NRC). 1996. *National science education standards.* Washington, DC: National Academy Press.

National Research Council (NRC). 2000. *Inquiry and the national science education standards.* Washington, DC: National Academy Press.

Inquiry Is Elementary: Differing Approaches to Inquiry Within Two Elementary Schools

Patricia C. Paulson
Bethel University

Linda Williams-Tuenge and Susan Roth
Riverview Specialty School for Math and Environmental Science

Rose Wippler and Douglas Paulson
Monroe Elementary School

Scientific inquiry is practiced and celebrated at two elementary schools within a school district of 40,000 students, located within a first ring suburb of Minneapolis. Only three miles separate the two schools. While their approach to inquiry differs somewhat, the commitment to inquiry learning is central to both schools, and in each school, inquiry is viewed as developing scientific thinking, scientific understanding, and science as an ongoing process rather than as a series of one-time experiences, and both schools are committed to maintaining this focus. This chapter will compare and contrast the approaches employed within the two elementary learning communities.

Monroe Elementary was designated a magnet school in 2007, with a Science, Technology, Engineering, and Math (STEM) focus. As a part of the district racial isolation plan, Monroe was given a state grant of 1.5 million dollars over three years and is part of the Northwest Suburban Integration School District, a partnership with seven adjoining districts. Monroe, a K–5 building of 500 students, has a diversity of 45%. As a STEM Magnet school, math (specifically algebraic understanding and reasoning), science, and children's engineering are the linchpin content areas, using such resources as FOSS, Engineering Is Elementary, and ongoing opportunities from the Science Museum of Minnesota. An engineering lab, fully equipped with MacBook laptop computers, is staffed by the curriculum integration coordinator.

Riverview Math and Science Environmental Specialty School was opened in 2003. A K–5 school of 400 students, Riverview has a diversity of 33% and was the recipient of a 1-million dollar state start-up grant, as well as internal desegregation funds. Riverview Elementary is located on the Mississippi River, and students regularly conduct inquiry activities with a naturalist at the river. The school also has its own greenhouse where a master gardener meets with students, a weather station, and a science laboratory. Environmental education is the linchpin for this school, using specifically adapted lessons from FOSS, as well as active partnerships with the Science Museum of Minnesota and two local universities.

Both schools implement district curriculum, which has been designed according to the Backward Design (Wiggins and McTighe 1998) from the state standards, outlining key understandings, essential outcomes, and essential questions for each unit. Inquiry is spiraled as the students move through the grades, so that by the fifth grade, students are able to design and implement inquiry independently. The commitment to staff development is central to the successful teaching of science through inquiry, and staff takes advantage of on-site, district, community, and national opportunities for professional development.

To engage learners in scientifically oriented questions, Riverview posts "Big Ideas" at each grade level. Questions arise also from the activities at the river, such as "Who dirtied the water?" As students plan grade level gardens, they actively search seed catalogs, and have planted "Global Gardens," while actively designing inquiries as to which international plants will grow in specific areas. They have also planned "Rain and Butterfly" gardens at grades 2 and 4, and planned a "Prairie Restoration" at grade 3. Each of these activities, in addition to planned classroom lessons, is designed to assist children in forming scientifically oriented questions centered on environmental issues.

Monroe students design questions from an engineering perspective, and content is presented as a problem. Using a design developed for the curriculum Engineering Is Elementary at the Museum of Science in Boston, students undergo a circular approach of Ask, Imagine, Plan, Create, Improve, and Ask again. Students work cooperatively on projects, such as kindergarteners designing freestanding letters of the alphabet from materials of their choice, to fifth graders designing a bridge that will span three feet and support two math books. Students expand on their own prior experiences, using common vocabulary, and actively engage in Webquests to design such structures as cars, factories, cities, and tops. Emphasis is placed not on success or failure of a project, but rather on how the task could be redesigned.

Evidence is gathered throughout the investigations with examples such as Riverview students conducting water tests on dissolved oxygen, pH, temperature, clarity, and type and number of microorganisms. They measure the depth of seed and bulb plantings, the height of the plants and the germination ratios. Each following year builds on evidence from the previous year's findings.

At Monroe, the question is also posed as to what constitutes evidence. For example, kindergarteners were able to articulate the fact that the balance of the weight was more essential to their tops than the sharpness of the axis. As fifth graders compared their bridge designs, such factors as the type of support were analyzed and synthesized. As both principals articulated, children quickly learn that their answers are neither right nor wrong; whatever they discover will contribute to their understanding.

Learners formulate their explanations from evidence; Riverview students were able to explain the similarities between butterfly and rain gardens based on their research, and combined the two gardens while answering the questions, Why do we have rain and butterfly gardens? Where should they be planted? What are the advantages of each? The evidence they collected from their gardens was directly related to their initial research questions. They are also able to articulate factors contributing to water quality at the river, explain factors impacting the migration of monarch butterflies, and even at the earliest grades formulate answers using interactive reading and writing strategies.

At Monroe, students are able to explain such factors as tension and compression with bridges based on their exploration, explore force and motion with wind-powered vehicles, and present a model city based on their research. Vocabulary is used within each inquiry, rather than a memorized list, and students use the terminology naturally.

Students in both schools connect their explanations to scientific knowledge through journals and online research, as well as leveled nonfiction books designed to accompany the inquiries. At Riverview, students in grades 4 and 5 participate in the Junior Master Gardener program and most earn the certificate at the end of grade 5. At one particular open house, first graders explained hydroponics to interested observers, while at another station, a second grader kept asking the superintendent and other district office personnel if they were able to understand the scientific principles, or if they needed further explanation!

Learners communicate and justify explanations when investigations are followed by group presentations at both schools. At Monroe, students frequently use blueprints using blue paper and white crayons for planning throughout the design, then construct PowerPoint presentations upon completion within a predesigned format of the stages of an engineering design. As they describe their modifications and continued testing, they are able to communicate and justify their plans. For Riverview students, interactions with the naturalist, the master gardener, and employees of the Department of Natural Resources require clear communication and justification.

Description of Inquiry Practices

The *National Science Content Standards* (NRC 1996) for inquiry point out the importance of inquiry beginning at the elementary level, where children ask simple questions, complete an investigation, answer the question, and present their results to others. They state,

> *From the earliest grades, students should experience science in a form that engages them in the active construction of ideas and explanation and enhances their opportunities to develop the abilities of doing science. Teaching science as inquiry provides teachers with the opportunity to develop student abilities and enrich student understanding of science. (p. 121)*

Imagine a group of third graders receiving a package from the National Aeronautics and Space Association (NASA) containing basil seeds that were on the most recent space expedition. The Monroe students were asked to engineer a special lunar seed chamber to grow the seeds and record germination and growth rates. After comparing these seeds to "normal" basil seeds, NASA wants to have them report their findings. The excitement in the room is palatable, as one student exclaims, "They want to know *our* results?" Not only will students gain an understanding of germination, the needs of plants, and soil nutrients, they will also be working together to solve a problem in an authentic world context for which there are not the static answers as might be found in a confirmation lab.

Riverview students also embed inquiry throughout the content and integrate mathematics and science in all areas of the curriculum, with the overall mission "to provide students with unique learning experiences that will lead to higher levels of thinking" (Anoka-Hennepin Independent School District 2007). By the end of the fifth grade, it is expected that students will be able to

- formulate appropriate questions and use analysis skills,
- demonstrate knowledge of environmental systems,
- apply skills for understanding and addressing environmental issues, and
- recognize and communicate personal and civic responsibility.

Ongoing investigations at the river, in the greenhouse, and in the classrooms provide students the opportunity to hone these final outcomes at each grade level. Students connect with other young scientists through the Journey North, describing such factors as weather and landforms learned within social studies units. Children as early as kindergarten begin to monitor the growth of larvae, the time in the chrysalis, and the number of successful emergent monarchs. They have multiple books to assist them in developing background understanding and formulate questions for investigations. When they again monitor monarch growth at grade 5, they track the migration success rate of both birds and butterflies to determine factors impacting survival.

Monroe's goal is to provide students experiences with inquiry, critical thinking, and problem solving to

- nurture curiosity,
- develop confidence and competence,
- increase effective communication skills, and
- foster teamwork (Anoka-Hennepin Independent School District 2007).

By allowing students' curiosities to drive the questions, students are encouraged to work together to make discoveries by building on their previous learning as these goals are spiraled throughout the grades. The engineering fields of mechanical, environmental, industrial, package, aerospace, and transportation all provide robust opportunities for inquiry and problem solving.

Inquiry and the National Science Education Standards (NRC 2000) defines the five essential features of inquiry. Settiage et al. (2008) describe these features as a "skill set" where students are actively engaged in all five components. Both Monroe and Riverview use these five facets as central to inquiry, but the approach of each school often differs depending on whether the focal point is environmental science or children's engineering. Let's examine the five facets and how they are implemented at each school.

Essential Feature 1: Learner Engages in Scientifically Oriented Questions

Questions are at the heart of inquiry, and research on the brain and learning supports that the brain responds well to environments where making sense of data and then reflecting on findings are integral (Bransford, Brown, and Cocking 2000). Caine et al. (2005) speak to the importance of connecting information students already know with issues of importance to them. They believe students need to be given opportunities "to use the information to answer personally relevant questions and to act in practical ways to solve problems and make things happen in relatively realistic contexts" (p. 5). When a local television meteorologist visited Riverview, she expressed excitement with the depth of understanding students demonstrated from work with their school weather station, as well as the level of questions the students posed based on their own research.

Malley (1992) identified two different types of scientific questions: existence questions and causal/functional questions. Existence questions are typical of many of the "why" questions posed by students. Causal/functional questions are typically expressed as "how" questions. While "why" questions often cannot be easily answered within the classroom, they can often be adjusted to "how" questions and investigated. For example, at Monroe, students concerned about the 2007 I-35W Mississippi River bridge collapse began by asking "why" questions that the teacher helped them formulate into "how" questions, such as "How do the materials used affect the strength of our bridge?" or, "How can we strengthen the bridge by the way we put materials together?" Students engaged in research, designing, testing, and redesigning their own bridge construction, as Caine and Caine (1997a) suggest: processing, analyzing, and examining the experience and relating it to their own central purposes.

While there is still debate regarding the validity of claims regarding the support for brain research from the field of neuroscience, as compared to the behavioral and social sciences, the Santiago Declaration, crafted by more than 64 internationally recognized scientists in child development, puts forth several important principles supporting the inquiry process practiced at both schools:

- Children are active, not passive, learners who acquire knowledge by examining and exploring their environment.
- Children, as all humans, are fundamentally social beings who learn most effectively in socially sensitive and responsive environments via their interactions with caring adults and other children.
- Young children learn most effectively when information is embedded in meaningful contexts rather than in artificial contexts that foster rote learning (Santiago Declaration 2007).

At Riverview, each grade level is centered on essential questions such as "What can our senses tell us about the world?" and "How can we organize our observations of the world?" and "What is the relationship of the river to life in Brooklyn Park?' and "How do the behaviors and structures of organisms help them survive their environment?" From these bigger questions, students formulate their own questions to investigate. Because local water supplies come from the river, issues of water quality strongly engage learners as they investigate factors such as the effect of fertilizers and road salts on levels of dissolved oxygen or macroinvertebrates. Both the previous examples illustrate Llewellyn's (2002) premise that investigations are driven by the student's curiosity, wonder, interest or passion to understand, and the process begins by noticing something that intrigues, surprises, or stimulates a question.

Essential Feature 2: Learner Gives Priority to Evidence in Responding to Questions

Evidence is purposefully collected throughout student inquiry at each school. As the NSES (1996) convey, "Even at the earliest grade levels, students should learn what constitutes evidence and judge the merits or strength of the data and information that will be used to make explanations" (p. 122). Duschl, Schweingruber, and Shouse (2007) affirm the essential role of evidence: "If the educational goal is to help students understand not just the conclusions of science, but also *how* one knows and *why* one believes, then talk needs to focus on how evidence is used in science for the construction of explanations" (p. 188). Students planting their global gardens had to not only research the type of area where plants from other countries are grown, but also try to re-create these environments within their local schoolyard. Evidence came not only from germination rates, but also from qualitative and quantitative data as they observed growth. In a somewhat different type of investigation at Monroe, students actually designed a lunar chamber for growing seeds. Even though data collected as evidence is similar, the evidence would connect with much different background conditions. While at the upper elementary grades, the Standards point out that students are more able to describe effects and relationships based on evidence, developmentally "students tend to center on evidence that confirms their current beliefs and concepts (i.e., personal explanations), and ignore or fail to perceive evidence that does not agree with their current concepts" (p. 144). Therefore, students need developmentally appropriate guidance in determining evidence, and benefit from more guided than open laboratory investigations. As Abrams, Southerland, and Evans (2008) describe scientific literacy and inquiry, the students are "building" processes that develop along a continuum when they are enculturated in the practice of inquiry.

Children begin to understand that all evidence must address the question asked. For example, third graders at Monroe were designing "puff mobiles" using straws, paper clips, tape, and Life Saver candies. Students initially believed there was "one right answer" and began to design traditional cars with four wheels connected by straws and paper clips. One insightful group began to question the evidence of friction and asked if they could place the Life Savers flat, then later asked if they could lick them to remove any ridges. Since they were not allowed to put the candies in their mouths, they ran water over them. The data supported their design by being the fastest puff mobile! At Riverview, the muddy river is often viewed as "dirty" or "polluted" based on their own concepts and beliefs, but the naturalist guides them into evidence to support their claims. By collecting actual data of temperature, pH, dissolved oxygen, and number and types of macroinvertebrates, rather than just water clarity, students discover the multiple factors impacting water quality. The importance of uncovering students' prior knowledge was essential in both examples to assist them in determining appropriate evidence, as the NRC's (2000) publication *Inquiry and the National Science Education Standards* confirms, "The abilities and understanding of inquiry are neither developed nor used in a vacuum. Inquiry is intimately connected to scientific questions—students must inquire using what they already know and the inquiry process must add to their knowledge" (p. 13). Children often come to the classroom rich in experiential knowledge that can form strong connections to classroom experiences, as Michaels, Shouse, and Schweingruber (2008) explain:

Cognitive researchers have become much more sophisticated in probing children's capacities. In the process, they have uncovered much richer stores of knowledge and reasoning skills than they expected to find in young children. Studies show that even children in kindergarten have surprisingly sophisticated ways of thinking about the natural world based on direct experiences with the natural environment. (p. 6)

Essential Feature 3: Learner Formulates Explanations From Evidence

Explanations need to be connected to evidence, and as the Standards state, "students should check their explanations against scientific knowledge, experiences, and observations of others" (p. 122). Students engage in inquiry as a community of learners and share their findings, often questioning discrepancies in findings at both schools. While the design of their investigations or their engineering plan may be unique, they still focus on central principles, and plan modifications or questions for further study based on peer feedback. Monroe uses an adaptation of Dweck's (2000) *Self-Theories*, in which a distinction is made between a fixed theory that can trigger a helpless response and performance orientation, and an incremental theory that can foster a mastery response and learning orientation. Table 1 describes some of these triggers and strategies.

Table 1. Self-Theories: Teaching Triggers and Strategies

Fixed Theory: Triggering a Helpless Response and Performance Orientation	Incremental Theory: Fostering a Mastery Response and Learning Orientation
Triggers Helpless Response:	*Fosters Mastery Response:*
• Micromanaging, hovering	• Delegating authority, observing
• Adjusting equipment, etc., for students when they have questions on how to use it	• Keeping hands in your pockets; clarifying instructions with words
• Offering irrelevant feedback: "Good", "Nice handwriting"	• Providing substantive, specific feedback: "Conclusion well supported by data"
• Providing person-oriented feedback: "You're so smart at this."	• Providing strategy-oriented feedback: "I noticed you tried a different strategy to solve this problem."
• Emphasizing a desired outcome or result of an experiment	• Sharing and comparing results; discussing methods and conclusions

Science Museum of Minnesota: Professional Development
Adapted from the Triad/Science & Health Education Partnership (SEP) at the University of California, San Francisco (UCSF)
Key Reference: Self-Theories by Carol S. Dweck (Psychology Press 2000)
December 2007

A key component for both schools is the emphasis that whatever students discover will contribute to their understanding, but some evidence is more essential to the research question. Therefore, students maintain science journals to document findings that can be later connected to explanations. As Monroe students constructed bridges, they discovered the importance of the materials selected as well as the design. As students compared similar designs from different materials, they were able to use the evidence collected to redesign their bridge. By providing incremental theory ideas, the teacher was able to facilitate the sharing of evidence to help students help each other, as an actual scientific community might function.

Riverview students base explanations on evidence from not only their own investigations, but also findings from previous years. Changes in the river, weather data from their weather station, seed planting success, and prairie restoration success are documented and saved. As a result of earlier evidence, new investigations were designed. This year, for example, fewer pumpkin seeds were ordered from the seed catalog, because the pumpkins last year dominated their small gardens, and additional questions arose when river depth levels were compared with previous years. New evidence will be added to their expanding body of data.

Llewellyn (2002) asserts that inquiry in science education should "mirror as closely as possible the enterprise of doing real science" (p. 5). Duschl, Schweingruber, and Shouse (2007) describe the importance of reflecting and connecting evidence to explanation rather than assuming a scientific viewpoint will be achieved through a discovery process: "If the educational goal is to help students understand not just the conclusions of science, but also how one knows and why one believes, then talk needs to focus on how evidence is used in science for the construction of explanations" (p. 188). By empowering students to collect relevant data, and connect it to the data of others, students develop richer understandings of the concepts under investigation.

Essential Feature 4: Learner Connects Explanations to Scientific Knowledge

Learners further enhance their scientific understandings as they connect their findings to scientific knowledge (Moscovici and Nelson 1998). As Duschl, Schweingruber, and Shouse (2007) stress,

> *The emerging evidence suggests that learning how to design, set up, and carry out experiments and other kinds of scientific investigations can help students understand key scientific concepts, provide a context for understanding why science needs empirical evidence, and how tests can distinguish between explanations. (p. 257)*

Both schools house extensive libraries of nonfiction science books at multiple reading levels as well as readily available computer access for internet explorations. As the Standards stress, "Scientific explanations emphasize evidence, have logically consistent arguments, and use scientific principles, models, and theories" (p. 148). Sometimes basic vocabulary needs explanation prior to the design of an investigation, but most often, students seek out additional resources to help them understand the factors impacting their investigation, as Michaels, Shouse, and Schweingruber (2008) describe as "just in time" for new ideas to be applied (p. 129). For example, as students collect insects found in their Junior Gardener investigations, they are motivated to determine whether the insects found are helpful or harmful to their garden.

Interesting stories emerged from Monroe's bridge designs, as they connected their knowledge of bridge building to the I-35W bridge collapse. Parents described how children had tuned into the news and described the plates involved and the connection of the bridge to the pier; parents stated, "We learned a lot at the dinner table!"

Students at both schools frequently embed scientific explanations within their journals to later incorporate into their conclusions. Journals are maintained throughout their investigations to provide multiple opportunities to reflect on each stage of the process. Michaels, Shouse, and Schweingruber (2007) describe the value the Committee on Science Learning, K–8 places on the knowledge process:

> When students engage in scientific practice they are embedded in a social framework, they use the discourse of science, and they work with scientific representations and tools. In this way, conceptual understanding of natural systems is linked to the ability to develop or evaluate knowledge claims, carry out empirical investigations, and develop explanations. (p. 34)

Essential Feature 5: Learner Communicates and Justifies Explanations

Both schools provide opportunities for the learners to communicate and justify their explanations. The understanding of the importance of clarity to enable replication of the investigation is stressed. Findings are shared within the classroom to broaden and refine thinking, and opportunities are provided for scientific argumentation, as Duschl, Schweingruber, and Shouse (2007) suggest, "The practice of developing and defending knowledge claims involves students in participating in a scientific community as they learn from and attempt to convince their peers of scientific claims" (p. 286).

Through interactive reading and writing at the primary grades, to journaling, blueprint designs, and PowerPoint presentations at the intermediate grades, students describe their question, procedure, data, conclusions, and further questions for investigation. Often these presentations are to authentic audiences, such as NASA, the Department of Natural Resources, district school administrators, or parent engineers. By sharing their findings, students discover alternative explanations, defend procedures, and clarify the evidence and scientific knowledge.

Conclusions

The intent of this chapter is not to presume one approach is superior to the other, but rather to describe two different but effective approaches to scientific inquiry. Actual state science test results will not soon be available, because the test is still in the development stage. Whether or not standardized tests actually represent the four strands of scientific learning (understanding scientific explanations, generating scientific evidence, reflecting on scientific knowledge, and participating productively in science) described by Michaels, Shouse, and Schweingruber (2008) is subject for debate, but as those authors assert,

> Students who understand science as a process of building theories from evidence develop many of the skills and practices that scientists demonstrate. They can be taught to apply their existing knowledge to new problems or in new and different contexts. They can make connections between different representations of a concept. They can ask themselves why they believe something and how certain they are in their beliefs. They can become aware that their ideas change

over time as they confront new evidence or use new tools or models to examine data. They can learn how to ask fruitful and researchable questions, how to challenge a claim, and where to go to learn more. (p. 6)

Both schools demonstrate compelling examples of such strands of learning through unique but effective use of scientific inquiry. Both schools have a high retention rate within a structure of competing schools under the school choice laws and parents, students, teachers, and administrators describe the effective components of inquiry set forth by the National Research Council. Riverview parents who have had children at the school for the last five years describe a high level of satisfaction, as a sampling of their comments affirmed: "The whole family learns through experiences provided to the student, to families, and the community" and "The children at Riverview are different in how they talk about things; the vocabulary they use, the way they explain their learning. Our kids have helped our family to see the world in a different way and notice more." Fourth- and fifth-grade students stated, "Our teachers teach you stuff you might know but they teach you to understand and find out more information," "Teachers don't give you the answers, you try to come up with your own answers," and "We figure it out; teachers don't tell you what to do." Teacher comments were also collected, such as the third-grade teacher who stated, "I have really noticed through observation and conversations with others, how open our kids are to challenges. They are willing to take risks, do the work of digging and experimenting for answers, and generally take mistakes as a learning opportunity instead of a defeat." A fourth-grade teacher also summarized,

I would add that teaching with inquiry feels totally natural, both for the teachers and students. Since kids are naturally curious and inquisitive, inquiry can sometimes seem like the "logical" process to take to allow kids to explore, ask questions, and begin to formulate their own understandings. I feel like teachers are allowed the freedom to ask the guiding questions based on students' knowledge and misconceptions, and this increases both teacher and student understanding in science. Approaching an activity or project after your brain has already done some pre-thinking, questions, and formulating can only increase achievement and learning in the long run. Our students at Riverview not only do this in science, but in all areas. When you hear conversations like, "I wonder if it's because..." or "Why does this..." you know that they are really getting it. That's the goal!

Students at Monroe, which is only in its first year as a STEM school, voiced similar thoughts with comments such as, "It is fun and educational because the whole group got to pitch in and work with each other," "We get a lot of fun challenges," "I enjoy working and testing different materials," "We get to look at things like an engineer would," and "It is fun because you can explore designing things in different ways, we are never wrong, just need to think more sometimes." In a recent survey of 81 fourth-grade students, 96% indicated that learning had been more challenging, but fun, 94% felt they had learned more by engaging in the process, 89% felt they had been more engaged working in groups, and 99% have used engineering language (ask, imagine, plan, create, improve) while working in a different environment.

Teachers at Monroe have also been supportive, with comments such as, "The students are very excited about creating, building, and testing structures," "As a teacher, I am excited to see students solving problems and working cooperatively in teams," and "Monroe Elementary has taken pride in creating a friendly and academically challenging environment for learning while having fun."

These elementary schools believe that inquiry can empower students with the skills and knowledge to become independent problem solvers, increasing their interest in science and moving them toward becoming scientifically literate citizens. Students engage in authentic investigations, formulating questions that arise naturally from bigger linchpin questions. Riverview uses the Native American proverb, "Tell me and I'll forget; Show me and I may not remember; Involve me and I'll understand." Inquiry is conducted through the lens of an actual scientist in the field, not simply within a confirmation type of laboratory experience, as the National Research Council (2000) summarizes:

In the final analysis, review of the research on the effectiveness of inquiry-based teaching and learning leads to a discussion of one's objectives for science education. If one accepts the full sweep of content in the National Science Education Standards, including conceptual understanding of science principles, comprehension of the nature of scientific inquiry, development of the abilities for inquiry, and a grasp of applications of science knowledge to societal and personal issues, this body of research clearly suggests that teaching through inquiry is effective. (p. 125)

References

Abrams, E., S. Southerland, and P. Silva, eds. 2008. *Inquiry in the classroom.* Charlotte, NC: Information Age Publishing.

Anoka-Hennepin Independent School District #11. 2007. *Anoka-Hennepin K–12 curriculum plan.* Coon Rapids, MN.

Anoka-Hennepin Independent School District #11. 2007. *Monroe specialty school: Mathematics, science, and children's engineering.* Coon Rapids, MN.

Anoka-Hennepin Independent School District #11. 2007. *Riverview elementary: Mathematics and environmental science.* Coon Rapids, MN.

Bransford, J., A. Brown, and R. Cocking, eds. 2000. *How people learn: Brain, mind experience, and school.* Washington, DC: National Academy Press.

Bybee, R., ed. 2002. *Learning science and the science of learning.* Arlington, VA: NSTA Press.

Caine, R., G. Caine, C. McClintic, and K. Klimek. 2005. *12 brain/mind learning principles in action.* Thousand Oaks, CA: Corwin Press.

Caine, R., and G. Caine. 1997a. *Unleashing the power of perceptual change.* Alexandria, VA: ASCD.

Caine, R., and G. Caine. 1997b. *Education on the edge of possibility.* Alexandria, VA: ASCD.

Duschl, R. A., H. A. Schweingruber, and A. W. Shouse, eds. 2007. *Taking science to school: Learning and teaching science in grades K–8*. Washington, DC: National Academy Press.

Dweck, C. 2000. *Self-theories: Their role in motivation, personality, and development*. New York: Psychology Press.

Engineering is Elementary. 2008. The engineering design process. *www.mos.org/eie/engineering_design.php*.

Llewellyn, D. 2002. *Inquire within*. Thousand Oaks, CA: Corwin Press.

Malley, M. 1992. The nature and history of science. In *Teaching about the history and nature of science and technology: Background papers*, 67–80. Colorado Springs, CO: BSCS.

Michaels, S., A. Shouse, and H. Schweingruber. 2008. *Ready, set, science!* Washington, DC: National Academies Press.

Moscovici, H., and T. Nelson. 1998. Shifting from activity mania to inquiry. *Science and Children* 40 (1): 14–17.

National Research Council (NRC). 2000. *Inquiry and the national science education standards*. Washington, DC: National Academy Press.

National Research Council (NRC). 1996. *National science education standards*. Washington, DC: National Academy Press.

Santiago Declaration. 2007. Available online at *www.jsmf.org/santiagodeclaration*

Settiage, J., L. Meadows, M. Olson, and M. Blanchard. 2008. Teacher knowledge and enacting inquiry. In *Inquiry in the classroom*, eds. E. Abrams, S. Southerland, and P. Silva, 171–229. Charlotte, NC: Information Age Publishing.

Science Museum of Minnesota. 2007. *Professional development*. Adapted from the Triad/ Science & Health Education Partnership (SEP) at the University of California, San Francisco.

Wiggins, G., and J. McTighe. 1998. *Understanding by design*. Alexandria, VA: Association for Supervision and Curriculum Development.

Science as Inquiry at Sir Winston Churchill Collegiate and Vocational Institute

Doug Jones and Cynthia Kaplanis
Sir Winston Churchill Collegiate and Vocational Institute

Wayne Melville and Anthony Bartley
Lakehead University

Setting

Thunder Bay is a city of 110,000 people, located on the northern shore of Lake Superior, at the convergence of the broadleaf Laurentian forests and the coniferous Boreal forest. The economy of the city and region has traditionally relied on the forest industries and as the transport breakpoint for grain shipments eastward from the Canadian prairies. Since the early 1990s, both industries have been in decline, a trend that has accelerated in recent years. One response to this decline has been the active intervention of government in the establishment of new industries in the health and biotechnology fields. The economic situation is reflected in a slow decline in the city's population. A second significant demographic shift is the rapid growth of the Aboriginal population within the city.

Sir Winston Churchill Collegiate and Vocational Institute is one of four public secondary schools operated by the Lakehead District School Board. Situated on the banks of the Neebing River in a middle-class residential area of the city, the school has approximately 1,100 students from grades 9 to 12, and serves a wide range of socioeconomic groups. Within the student body, 7% are in the essential/workplace stream, 26% are in the applied/college level stream, and 67% are in the academic/university level stream (all 2007 figures). The level of enrollment in the applied/college stream has been steadily increasing in recent years.

School Level Leadership

The science department has always benefited from a positive relationship and strong support from the school administration. Much of this can be attributed to the leadership of the principal, Art Warwick, who retired in June 2008.

Warwick has been the principal during the entire time that Doug Jones has been the science chair at Churchill. His strong leadership was one of the reasons Jones decided to transfer to Churchill. Principal Warwick played an instrumental role in interviewing and hiring those staff who Doug felt were important pieces to the puzzle. The primary considerations for those new staff were exemplary teaching practices and an aptitude for learning scientific inquiry. Warwick was willing to support time-tabling initiatives, equipment requests, professional development needs, and exemplary student work. He always made time to visit with the various scientific and educational community researchers who spent time with the Churchill department over the years.

The school also has two vice principals: Jeff Upton and Nancy Petrick. All three administrators take advantage of any opportunity that the science department faculty gives them to interact with and recognize the efforts of the student work in science. This is important for both staff and students alike. Parents notice such behaviors. Examples include our school science fair, year-end culminating performances, science partnerships with the community, and support for the national biology competition team and the international Envirothon competition. Upton has organized and led two parent symposia on educational research and practice where the science staff led inquiry sessions.

Getting Started

The inquiry program at Churchill has been a work in progress since 2000. It arose from concerns that school science, taught from a behaviorist paradigm, was only reaching and engaging a small percentage of students. By accepting inquiry as *content* that incorporates understanding and abilities and as a *teaching strategy*, it was believed that the science department would provide students with the tools to consider, challenge, and potentially solve some of the issues that will confront them during their lives. The evidence from publications such as the American Association for the Advancement of Science's *Science for All Americans* (1993), and the National Research Council's publication of the *National Science Education Standards (NSES)* (1996) and *Inquiry and the National Science Education Standards* (2000) supported the belief that inquiry could also promote knowledge retention and transfer, rather the memorization and mediocrity that characterized so much science education. In addition, the Ontario Ministry of Education's *Curriculum Document in Science* (2000a; 2000b) states that students should be able to develop the skills, strategies, and habits of mind required for scientific inquiry in order to meet the overall aim of the curriculum and that every graduating high school student should be scientifically literate. Developing skills of inquiry and communication is an expectations strand in every science course and the units within those courses are loaded with expectations requiring just that: proficiency in the ways and understandings of scientific inquiry. The achievement charts at the ends of grades 9 and 10 and senior curriculum documents provide separate evaluation details.

Another key understanding was that, in adopting inquiry, teachers would also have to be prepared to change how they both conceptualized and taught science. Such changes are always difficult, as science teachers have traditionally been successful in the predominant behaviorist paradigm of secondary and university science courses. The necessary change in emphasis needed to effect such changes is outlined in the NSES Professional Development Standards. What did this change in emphasis look like at Churchill?

When Jones came to Churchill 12 years ago, the department was staffed by a dedicated and proficient group of veterans who all but one retired within the next three years. The last one retired two years later. The method of instruction and assessment during those years could be characterized as predominantly behaviorist and traditional in its approach. Jones was conducting some inquiries, but in singular classes where the opportunity presented itself. For the most part this work was restricted to grades 11, 12, and OAC (Ontario Academic Credit—a fifth year that does not exist today).

An important first step to understand the changes that are needed to introduce and sustain inquiry in the classroom is to find where teachers have come from in terms of their own educational history. To do this, teachers and science educators at Lakehead University have begun investigating the beliefs about science and science education with which science teachers at Churchill began their careers. The results to date have been consistent. When asked to describe their own science education experiences and beliefs at the start of their teaching careers, three teachers described their own education as "traditional," heavily reliant on the memorization of facts and concepts. All had commenced their own classroom teaching using the strategies that had worked for them in their own educations. As one teacher said,

I was so used to the lectures, chalk-and-talk, and really focusing on the curriculum—that's basically what I did. And my labs were the usual "follow this, do these procedures, and here are a couple of questions." It was very traditional in terms of presenting science to the class and students. I taught the way I was taught.

Stories such as this are, we believe, common across science departments and serve to illustrate the challenges that teachers face when they seek to introduce inquiry.

New staff arrived to replace those who retired. These teachers were not rookies out of faculties of education but they were not grizzled veterans either. They had roughly five years of teaching experience, but in varied courses and schools, as it was difficult to find a full-time job in one school at the time. They knew each other, were friendly, and respected each other's work. Jones took the opportunity to start modeling some of his constructivist practices and showing exemplars of such work to this new group. Conversations about those practices began and eventually so did the first attempts by members of this group to try scientific inquiry themselves. Virtually all of these trials were being done in grades 11 and 12.

Over the next few years, several political decisions and one community-based decision had an impact on how science would get taught at Churchill. A new curriculum was brought into play; grade 9 classes were taught on a destreamed basis (at one common level no matter what the ability or intentioned destination of the student); and the fifth year of high school in Ontario (OAC) was dropped to bring the province in line with most other North American school systems. The community intervention was an application to the International Baccalaureate organization to award a school to Thunder Bay. This program became a reality and would operate out of Churchill.

While destreamed grade 9 classrooms are no longer a part of Ontario education, they did force our teachers to consider what kinds of teaching and assessment strategies could work in such an environment. The answer seemed to be constructivist strategies in which students did collegial, rather than group work. Although the old curriculum did contain some expectations and benchmarks requiring student exposure to scientific inquiry, few teachers understood how to apply them and even fewer did. The new curriculum contained many more expectations related to inquiry and the assessment landscape had begun to heave as a paradigm shift in the use and communication of assessment began to take place in response to the extensive wealth of research supporting such a shift. The loss of the OAC senior year and the requirement that International Baccalaureate science educators address scientific inquiry in a significant way led the department to the decision to expose all grade 9 students, regardless of level and destination, to a primer based on the ways and understandings of science researchers who incorporate scientific inquiry into their daily work.

The NSES Professional Development Standards emphasize the need for teachers to let go of the notion of "teacher as expert." In this paradigm, the teacher possesses the knowledge and skills that must be passed on to the students in class. It is also a very lonely paradigm. A pivotal decision made by Jones in 2000 has been instrumental in shaping the Churchill science department into how it appears today. This decision was to initiate conversations about the teaching and learning of science from an inquiry perspective. In making this decision, Jones was following the example set by his mentor and former science chair. These conversations were initiated by Jones, but increasingly over the years have been lead by other teachers, and are best summarized by Jones and Kaplanis (2006, pp. ii–ix):

> *Churchill's approach to science education is a program and not an approach. It is not one teacher, it is all of them. It is not one course or grade, it is all of them.... It can't be just knowledge. We must model the ways and understandings of scientific inquiry; we must teach those ways and understandings; we must practice those ways and understandings; we must provide an opportunity to experience those ways and understandings in novel and authentic contexts; and finally we must provide quality assessments in order to improve performance of those ways and understandings.*

These conversations have had three major impacts that mirror the NSES Professional Development Standards. The first has been the development of a science teacher community of practice. This means continuing their conversations and, increasingly, action research efforts with each other. As new teachers and student teachers arrive, they are mentored and coached along the inquiry continuum. As a department, they know that their motivation to continue stems from observing students become more successful at doing and understanding science. In order to get to this point in their teaching practices, these teachers have had to embrace a number of instructional and assessment strategies that support the use of inquiry in the classroom. The instructional strategies include the incorporation of different collaborative learning approaches (for example, jigsaw, think-pair-share, academic controversy); having students use analogy to show they understand a concept; using conferencing as a small-group instructional strategy; using authentic tasks, rich assessment tasks, and culminating performances to address curricular expectations; and ultimately, using scientific inquiry itself. The assessment strategies include the use of varied tools that do more than simply provide a grade; providing assessment criteria up front; using exemplars to establish how assessment criteria will be applied; developing assessment criteria with students; using exemplars to develop self and peer assessment competency with the assessment tool; using exemplars to "set the bar" to show students what quality work looks like; using assessment formatively to provide for improved performance; and using interviews and conferencing to provide assessment feedback.

The second major impact has been that biology, chemistry, physics, and general and environmental sciences were not taught as separate, specialized entities anymore. Since we are teaching, talking, and modeling the same approaches to inquiry and producing similar assessment products, we also realized that we needed cross-curricular (subject) knowledge to carry them out successfully, just like researchers in the real world. Students came to see such collegiality on inquiry assessments by staff as an important resource for themselves but also as a model for how science is done in the real world.

The third major impact has been in the negotiation of commonly held meanings to terms such as *scientific literacy* and *the scientific method*. The negotiation of common understandings is important, for the meanings that are applied to these terms influence how they are used, as Hurd et al. argued that the implementation of inquiry in the classroom required, among other things, that "teachers must understand precisely what scientific inquiry is" (1980, p. 158). For the teachers at Churchill, the work of Bybee (1997) has influenced the course of conversations around the meanings of scientific literacy. For teachers, scientific literacy means that students are able to construct, communicate, and use scientific knowledge, a goal that students of all ability levels can meet to some extent (Jones and Kaplanis 2006). To achieve this, students require practice in areas such as the grasping of meaning; the making of informed decisions; the communicating and defending of informed opinions; the ability to read and write in a science context; understanding the ways, abilities, and limitations of scientific inquiry; and the possession of, and therefore the understanding of, information necessary for survival and growth in the world we find ourselves in.

In seeking to develop the notion of scientific literacy, there are a number of factors to keep in mind. First, students will meet that goal with varying levels of success because, like much learning, it depends on age, developmental stage, intellectual health, life experiences, and quality of science education. Second, the type of literacy the teachers at Churchill are after is not the functional literacy that some refer to as the rote memorization of vocabulary, lists, and facts. Third, literacy should be inclusive of all students. The use of scientific inquiry, journaling, and collaborative learning strategies are a good way to do that. Fourth, using authentic tasks and problems in context with these strategies will go a long way to developing the kind of literacy the department is after. They also allow philosophical, historical, technological, and social dimensions to be integrated in some fashion.

The "scientific method" is another term the Churchill teachers have evolved a more inquiry-based understanding for. The use of quotation marks is deliberate; there is no one method that scientists use. In the words of Haas (2008, p. 43), science is, *not just a way of doing. It is a way of doing, a way of thinking. The scientist's curiosity is a way of life. All of the scientist's experiences are potential sources for observations. All of his observations are potential sources for progress and insight in the laboratory.*

For teachers, an understanding of the term is crucial, as "too many school curricula present scientific discovery as the inevitable outcome of the correct application of a rigorous, objective, disinterested, value free, and all-powerful scientific method" (Hodson 1999, p. 784). To move away from this position is hard work, as Jones and Kaplanis write,

it was one of those things I knew was wrong and it took me forever to figure out what it was and even more time to get it right. If you're like me and many of my colleagues, you teach the scientific method in about seven or so critical steps. It varies from teacher to teacher but the steps might include the following: curiosity—a question; background research; hypothesis formulation; experimental design; collection of data; manipulation/analysis of data; and summary/new questions. Sometimes a serendipitous event or intuitive hunch speeds the process, but oftentimes it can get downright tedious. You give them some examples and then have them write a test. (2006, pp. 8–9)

The Science as Inquiry Standard of the NSES has two features, "the ability to *do* inquiry and the development of understandings *about* scientific inquiry" (Bybee et al. 2008, p. 110). The standard (1996, chapter 6) describes how all students,

should have the opportunity to use scientific inquiry and develop the ability to think and act in ways associated with inquiry, including asking questions, planning and conducting investigations, using appropriate tools and techniques to gather data, thinking critically and logically about relationships between evidence and explanations, constructing and analyzing alternative explanations, and communicating scientific arguments.

For the teachers at Churchill, the meaning attached to the term *scientific method* is virtually identical. The scientific method, as it is introduced in grade 9, is something to be explored in terms of the Six Ps, which is adapted from the work of Thomas O'Brien of Binghamton University, New York:

Perceive: The first "P" heading is designed to practice making and recording of observations. Students need encouragement in two areas, to make as many observations as they can, and to make use of their senses. In addition, student observations can be shared with the class in order to give students practice in the presentation of their work. Teachers need to be prepared to have additional scientific equipment available for some requests that are relevant to the activity like hand lenses, dissecting microscopes, balances, and so on.

Ponder: Reflecting on what students already know is a good place to begin to ponder. To ponder is to start asking questions about the possible range of outcomes if something was done. Students should record each question, and not be satisfied with one possibility. Teachers need to be involved as a coach, asking "What if?" "Have you considered…?" and so on if students get stuck.

Predict: At this point students need to come to a consensus on which one or more of their outcomes is likely to occur. Students should include their reasons for thinking this way. The reasons may not be extensive or knowledgeable but this is an important step in learning how science works.

Plan and Perform: Poor planning results in the collection of unorganized and haphazard data. It must be reiterated to students that they need to plan and record each step they take. This will produce a short method, but it is the thinking about the process that is important. Teacher involvement and questioning is also critical at this stage. Teachers need to be available to prod, stimulate, encourage, and guide students to varying degrees. In terms of questioning, the questions should reflect the types of questions scientists ask: "Can you have confidence in a result (that may confirm or reject your prediction), on the basis of one trial? If more trials (say two or three) are conducted, how will you control the method (variables) so that each trial mimics the others?" After the plan is completed, students can then carry it out and record results of a qualitative and/or quantitative nature.

Postulate a Theory: The first attempts at this make for interesting class discussions until students begin to feel comfortable with the notion of putting forward ideas that may or may not be correct.

Publicize the Results: Remember the prediction about which the students came to consensus? Students should write a very short summary statement reminding the reader what they predicted would happen and then stating what actually happened. This section can also be used to complete a task that is integral to scientific inquiry and is also a great exercise to generate some critical thinking. Ask the students to come up with new research questions for study using the same basic premise that has been investigated. Sharing the new questions students offer is a good strategy. Constantly brainstorming independent variables helps students get better at it.

The key feature of the program is that students are not told that scientists design a method to gather data in order to answer their research question. Students learn by doing and so they undertake the process, not once but two or three times a semester. In addition to their other teaching strategies, this means that teachers need to spend time modeling, teaching, coaching, and practicing the process of inquiry. The context of the work is in actual inquiries with the use of exemplars. A vital consideration for improving student performance is the provision of appropriate formative feedback throughout each inquiry. Through engagement with each inquiry with their students, teachers also demonstrate their own expertise and worth. If the inquiries are authentic and relevant to the curriculum, then students and teachers begin to see success build on success. Success is cumulative: the learning that occurs in grade 9 is not left in grade 9; through grade 12 it is revisited, reviewed, extended, and repeated.

In concert with the focus on inquiry, teachers have also developed a range of assessment strategies that do more than simply provide a grade. These strategies include providing assessment criteria up front; using exemplars to establish how assessment criteria will be applied; developing assessment criteria with students; using exemplars to develop self and peer assessment competency with the assessment tool; using assessment formatively to provide for improved performance; and using interviews and conferencing to provide assessment feedback. These forms of assessment are discussed below. The department calls any evidence of the skills and understandings of inquiry "core evidence." The reason for this is that evidence is central to the doing and understanding of inquiry. Ideally, while students practice these skills consistently, teachers try to assess each of those skills and understanding two or three times during the semester.

The clear connection between the meanings that the teachers at Churchill have developed and the definitions of *scientific literacy* and the *scientific method* in chapter 2 of the NSES is clear. Two benefits of involving all teachers in these conversations are that the program is not one teacher, but every teacher. Further, all teachers practice inquiry and do so with a common philosophy. Two important points need to be made here: (1) The conversations were based on external expertise, but the meanings have become part of the fabric of the department. (2) These conversations are ongoing, as teachers join and leave the department. In 2001, two new staff members joined the department. One had two years of elementary science teaching experience and the other arrived directly out from the Lakehead University Faculty of Education. Both held tremendous promise to become great science teachers and they flourished in an environment where all senior members were accomplished mentors at providing the resources and supports necessary for these new members to use inquiry successfully as well. In 2005 two experienced, mid-career teachers arrived in the department. They deserve tremendous credit for both embracing the department philosophy and their willingness to be mentored themselves. It is the inquiry expertise, the all-inclusive collegiality, and the fun this department's teachers have that has made it easier for these teachers to integrate constructivist practices into their established routines. Both will be great mentors for the next teachers to join our staff.

While new teachers might arrive for a period here or there, it is unlikely that our department will change much in the next three or four years. However, mentoring still goes on, because we take up to six preservice teachers for practicum in every new semester. This is of great benefit to these new members of the profession, in that they get to observe such a workplace and are invited to take their first steps down that inquiry continuum in the comfort of such a supportive environment.

Program Description: Grade 9

The Ontario secondary science program, from Grade 9 through Grade 12, is designed to promote three goals:

- to understand the basic concepts of science;
- to develop the skills, strategies, and habits of mind required for scientific inquiry; and

- to relate science to technology, society, and the environment (Ontario Ministry of Education 2000a, p. 4).

So what does the program that emphasizes inquiry look like in practice? The introduction is the three-week-long Grade Nine Science—An Introduction to Inquiry unit, which teachers are free to develop individually to suit their own teaching styles and personalities. The unit begins with a few activities that get the students working together to do some of the things that scientists do, without the vocabulary and without an emphasis on retaining facts and concepts. The tasks require students to work together collaboratively, but the emphasis for the work will be to discuss the nature of that work, not assign a grade to it. The aim is to generate an enthusiasm to learn more. Teachers debrief their classes with conversations around specific activities to set the stage for the learning to come.

During these early days of the unit, teachers discuss safe operating procedures, hazardous materials handling, equipment, and so on. The unit has time scheduled for these discussions, but individual teachers use their own materials and expertise in leading these discussions. The belief is that individual teachers, working with their classes, are much better placed to make decisions regarding these particular lessons. The lessons that follow introduce students to the some of the vocabulary of science, in the context of the activities they have been doing. With the teacher, and among themselves, the class members discuss the ways in which scientists approach such activities. These lessons include using the scientific method, understanding variables, and planning controlled experiments. Students will be asked to create an analogy, using a poster, to show what they know and understand about the scientific method. It will be assessed with a rubric given out ahead of time. Students will also be shown exemplars to illustrate what each level of the rubric looks like.

Much of the data that are collected during inquiry are quantitative in nature. This necessitates that students understand how to estimate and measure using the SI system and the equipment available to them. Students need these skills as they move into the collection of their own data. Therefore, SI units of length, mass, area, and volume are introduced and used. Students should be able to convert between units on a scale and be able to carry out the skills of estimating and measuring for each of those systems.

Students also need to be able to manipulate data in some way. A common mistake is to push data manipulation before students are ready to learn these skills. Students need to be able to collect data from multiple trials or organize it from class data and then do simple things like calculate the mean. They should also be able to graph data and understand when to use a histogram and when a line graph is more useful. They should know what it means to extrapolate or interpolate from a graph and practice doing that. Producing lines of best fit from scatter plot data is also something they should be able to carry out. Advanced manipulative skills are best developed when students become ready for it. For example, teachers do not have students do correlation or t-test studies until grade 12.

Following from this series of lessons, students inquire into the concept of density. It is a concept that lends itself to inquiry-type activities because material can be handled and measured. The measurements of mass and volume have already been accomplished and the relationship between them is a fairly simple mathematical operation that qualifies as data manipulation. Mass and volume data points can easily be plotted on a graph, which is developed through classroom time teaching and practicing. Slopes can be calculated from the graphs, which allow comparison among different materials.

Finally, the materials used to study density lend themselves perfectly to student practice in making qualitative and quantitative observations. The real bonus occurs when students do some background research into those materials. Student research provides an opportunity to teach about citing such research in reports and about producing a references cited page with the bibliographic information. Students form groups and each group has a different material (wood, rubber, Styrofoam, water). Each group collects mass/volume data, produces a graph, calculates a slope, does background research, and considers the experimental error inherent in their methods.

The groups then attend a "density conference" to communicate their findings to other groups. Much is learned about materials, the concept of density, measuring, graphing, interpolating/extrapolating, and error analysis. Most importantly, students begin developing collaborative work skills and communication/presentation skills. The student products become the tools students use for the presentation.

Finally, each class pursues a messy problem that requires students to use indirect observation to collect data. Using Alka-Seltzer tablets, the students collect mass and volume data of the carbon dioxide gas given off. In order to do this they must be proficient at using electronic balances and graduated cylinders. Great care must be taken in the handling of materials and in measurement. Densities are calculated by each group and the results posted on the board. Finally, the actual density of carbon dioxide gas is put up on the board and a debriefing session is held to discuss why the group and class means vary from the actual value.

During the last few days of the unit, take-home inquiries are assigned. Students must pick one of three options and design an inquiry for it, which they will carry out at home. The safety considerations of all three inquiries are discussed in class before students start their work. A final report must be turned in for assessment that will be written based on the department inquiry template but modified to include only those components taught and practiced in class. A very interesting part of the task requires that students show their parents/guardians their work and explain the inquiry theory that it is based on (i.e., what their research question is, what their independent and dependent variables are, what variables have to be kept constant and what their control might be and so on). This task does wonders for both the students and the department. The department is fostering a discussion between student and parents; it is asking students to check their understanding by communicating with others; it connects the home to the school, while also demonstrating to parents what the department is doing. The report is due one week after the unit ends.

A key consideration is that the knowledge, skills, and attitudes toward inquiry are not isolated in this unit: They are developed across the Ontario curriculum units in biology, chemistry, and physics. In biology, the factors affecting mung bean germination has been developed as an inquiry, while in physics the factors affecting voltage across a wet cell has also been developed.

Program Description: Grade 10

When the department began to implement this program in 2000, the Ontario curriculum documents guided many of the decisions that needed to be made at the departmental level. The implementation needed to be made as a department for two reasons. The first is that if the introductory inquiry unit is going to take three weeks, then the teachers need to develop a consensus as to what is valued as essential curricular expectations from the four unit strands of chemistry, physics, biology, and Earth and space science. The second reason is that by undertaking an introductory unit in grade 9, every student is engaged with the notion of science as inquiry. Teachers will then be able to build on that introduction as the students move through their high school careers. If the skills and understandings of inquiry are dropped after grade 9, then a limited number of students will carry them forward. The skills and understandings developed in grade 9 are reinforced in grade 10 using a combination of structured, guided, and open inquiries (Colburn 2004). The grade 10 science course emphasizes development of understanding in biology, chemistry, Earth and space science, and physics. In chemistry, inquiries have been developed around the rates of reactions and factors influencing solubility. In physics, the work has concentrated on factors affecting the acceleration of a cart down a ramp.

In order to extend the learning that has occurred in grade 9, students in grade 10 are also provided with opportunities to work in conjunction with community groups and institutions. One example of this is the work that occurs with a local provincial historical park. The fur trade in the early 1800s was important in the establishment of settlements in the region and the historical park recreates this time period. Each winter, grade 10 students work with the staff at the historical park to investigate the insulating qualities of a range of furs such as beaver, moose, wolf, and wolverine. Another inquiry centers on the ecology of the convergence between the Laurentian and Boreal forests, including issues such as aspect, soil type, and drainage. Another example is the work of grade 10 students in the preparation of entries in the regional science fair competition, which is organized through the local university. The presentation of work and the capacity to speak to other individuals about the processes and products of inquiry are seen as important components of the science program. The science fair also provides students an opportunity to practice the presentation of their work before they present their culminating performance in an interview.

Assessment of Grades 9 and 10

One of the key aspects of assessment of the grade 10 science course is the increasing use of comprehensive culminating performances that involve students presenting their work to a panel of teachers, administrators, and community members with expertise in the area. This presentation involves both individual and group answers to ensure that all students are accountable for their learning. A template of the questions used for these culminating performances is reproduced here:

Grade 9/10 Culminating Performance

1. State the class Nature of the Problem and the Research Question your team decided on. What were some of the other questions debated ... why settle on this one?

2. Describe some of the background research related to how ...

3. What is an independent variable? What was the one used in this case? How did you go about changing it?

4. What is a dependent variable? What is your dependent variable in this case? How did you go about recording this? Were there other dependent variables considered?

5. What is a control set-up? What did your team use as a control in this situation? Why was this done?

6. What variables did the team decide were necessary to keep constant in order to maintain internal validity? Discuss how your method attempted to maintain these variables.

7. What is a hypothesis? How is it written? How is a prediction different? What was your prediction in this case?

8. Discuss the results relative to your hypothesis... what did you find out? What conclusions can you make about the work (why do you think it happened the way it did?).

9. Comment on the experimental error (tightness) of the investigation. If internal validity was compromised... what were those errors or difficulties? How could you modify the work to improve validity if you could repeat your work?

10. **Group Answer:** What future questions might be studied as extensions to the investigation you have discussed today? Other Comments?

Program Description: Grades 11 and 12

In grades 11 and 12, students are free to choose which science credits they will be studying in their final two years of secondary schooling. While the knowledge, skills, and attitudes that have been developed in grades 9 and 10 continue to be refined, a major emphasis of the program in these final years is a shift toward the quantitative analysis, and presentation of data. Having experience with inquiry as a way of knowing, students refine their skills in the areas of in-text citations and referencing, data manipulation, error analysis and the polishing of their introduction and discussion writing techniques. These are important skills, as they help to develop student confidence and proficiency in communicating and defending their work to peers, teachers, and others. Generally, at least two open inquiries are completed during each senior-level course.

For example, in grade 11 biology, one of the units of work is Internal Systems and Regulation. As part of this unit, students undertake a guided inquiry into the factors that impact the rate of enzyme reaction. The teacher notes and a student report for this unit are reproduced in Appendixes A and B. We have also included, as Appendix C, an open inquiry conducted in 2005 as an assessment task in grade 12 biology. Examples of inquiries developed through the senior year include the following types:

- Factors affecting bacterial growth
- Factors affecting transport through a membrane

- Factors affecting yeast populations
- Factors affecting photosynthesis
- Factors affecting homeostatic mechanisms

In physics, inquiries have been developed around the following topics:

- Acceleration and friction
- Conservation of momentum and kinetic energy in elastic collisions
- Centripetal forces
- Projectile motion
- Interference of light
- Specific heat capacity of various materials
- Bodies in equilibrium
- Conservation of mechanical energy

In chemistry, inquiries have been developed around the following topics:

- Variables involving polarity and mixing/dissolving
- Factors affecting reaction rates
- Biochemistry

In the new area of environmental science, students have begun working with local forestry companies to devise forestry plans that take into account a range of different, and often contradictory, demands.

Assessment of student inquiries is undertaken using exemplars of previous students' work, peer evaluation, and formative and summative assessments by the teacher. In Appendix D we have included a rubric for the assessment of inquiries that all grade 11 and 12 students work through before undertaking their work. One particularly effective method that has been used in the area of respiration and photosynthetic biochemistry has been the production of inquiry boards for the processes. This activity involves students combining their conceptual knowledge with their own background research to produce a visual presentation that reintegrates the discrete components of photosynthesis as a coherent whole. Upon the completion of the poster, the group must be prepared to defend their work in a feedback session with the teacher.

Evidence That the Program Is Exemplary

There are a number of ways in which we gauge the success of the science program at Churchill. These include the number of grade 10 students who elect to pursue science credits in grades 11 and 12; the postsecondary pathways chosen by students; evidence of success in postsecondary science courses at university or college; participation in regional, national, and international science competitions; and in the sharing of our experiences with other teachers within Canada, North America, and across the world.

Based on enrollment figures for the 2007–08 school year and projected student credit selections for the 2008–09 school year, three important points are obvious. The first is the slight decline in school-level student enrollments, a fact mentioned in our introduction. The second is that despite the reduction in enrollments, the number of students choosing science credits in grades 11 and 12 has increased by 2%. This increase ensures that the science department continues to occupy the position that it has held for the past few years, that of the largest number of student credits in grades 11 and 12. This preeminence has also contributed to fully 25% of Churchill's 2004–2007 graduating classes selecting a postsecondary destination that involves science.

Evidence from former students, one who has pursued science and another who has not, demonstrates the value of being taught using inquiry. We asked two students who we have kept in contact with for their answers to three questions about how the program has assisted them. Their answers are presented here:

Question 1: How has the way science is taught at Churchill helped you in your postsecondary studies?

Tracy: If we had any questions, most of the time we could answer them and everything seemed to make sense. When I took plant and animal biology in the university, I was very surprised at just how much I already knew from the year before. The same was true for chemistry. Some university students were confused about some of the concepts, but because everything was taught in such great detail in grades 11 and 12, it wasn't as difficult to learn or understand certain topics that others struggled with.

One thing I really liked about biology as well were the inquiry-boards we had to do on cellular respiration and photosynthesis. As much as we may have hated making those boards at the time, they were one of the main things that helped me to understand how both processes worked. I had no trouble when we went over those topics in biology the next year at university.

Briony: I will be continuing in International Relations in the fall at the university. While I will not be studying science, I feel that the pedagogy of the sciences at Churchill has encouraged critical thought and careful analysis in my postsecondary studies as well as the successful organization of written projects. Additionally, I feel that the interpersonal relationship between students and teachers at Churchill particularly in the sciences motivates the learner in any academic domain, promoting a much stronger desire to learn among students.

Question 2: Have you found yourself in a position to help or mentor other students in science by using conceptual knowledge/strategies you were first exposed to at Churchill?

Tracy: Throughout the year I have ended up helping a few students in a couple of my science courses. In biology, the inquiry boards helped quite a bit. Teaching the students how to grasp certain concepts was easier when it could be drawn out like it was on the photosynthesis and cellular respiration inquiry-boards showing each step of the processes.

Briony: [As this student is not continuing with science, the answer was no.]

Question 3: What does the term *science* mean to you?

Tracy: Science to me is exploring the unknown, and finding the answers of why and how. It is understanding the world around me and why things are the way they are. Science is very important to me and my area of study (biology major and eventually veterinary medicine). I have always loved my science courses in high school and the same is true for my courses at the university.

Briony: To me, the term *science* refers to experimentation in biological, chemical, and physical fields, and entails constant theoretical change, modification, and discover. Science combines language, mathematics, and precise observations of the world and its aspects and is founded upon an interpretive basis.

For the past seven years, the school has won the Most Extensive Participation award at the North-West Ontario Regional Science Fair, with seven divisional winners being invited to compete at the Canadian National Science Fair. In 2005, the Bi-National Forum on Lake Superior presented the school with the Stewardship Award in recognition of the environmental science course the school offers. Churchill also hosted 200 students and teachers at the Lake Superior Youth Symposium in May 2005 to learn about the Lake's environment and the management of environmental issues. The teacher of this course is now a key player in the development of environmental education courses by the Ontario Ministry of Education. In the annual National Biology Competition sponsored by the University of Toronto, Churchill's students have ranked as high as 43 out of 400 schools, and have always finished in the top half of the competing schools.

The ongoing work of promoting inquiry is another area in which the program is exemplary. Churchill's science teachers have shared their experiences with inquiry in a number of venues. These have included presentations to other school boards, the Science Teachers Association of Ontario, the National Science Teachers Association, and the Association for Science Teacher Education. Various insights into the program have also been published in professional and academic journals in North America and Australia. The department has also hosted visiting academics from Canadian and American universities. Using a grant from the Canadian Council on Learning, the department is currently video recording several of its inquiry-based classes for use as exemplars in preservice teacher education programs. One of the criteria for selection in this research was recognition by the council of exemplary practice.

Relation to the Visions of the U.S. National Science Education Standards

This inquiry program is now in its eighth year and has demonstrated how the U.S. National Science Education Standards can be met over an extended period of time. As a department, the science teachers at Sir Winston Churchill Collegiate and Vocational Institute share a common commitment to the ideals of teaching of science as inquiry. As individuals, they also have the flexibility to teach in ways that reflect their strengths as teachers. As a result, their students practice the skills and understandings of inquiry, have ownership of their learning, have a deeper understanding of the conceptual nature of the curriculum, and possess a strategy that will continue to produce solutions to both science and other problem-based scenarios throughout their lives.

References

American Association for the Advancement of Science (AAAS). 1993. *Science for all Americans*. New York: Oxford University Press.

Bybee, R. W. 1997. Towards an understanding of scientific literacy. In *Scientific literacy: An international symposium,* eds. W. Gräber and C. Bolte, 37–68. Kiel, Germany: Institut für die Pädagogik der Naturwissenschaften.

Bybee, R. W., J. Powell, and L. W. Trowbridge. 2008. *Teaching secondary school science: Strategies for developing scientific literacy*. 9th ed. Upper Saddle River, NJ: Pearson.

Colburn, A. 2004. Inquiring scientists want to know. *Educational Leadership* 62 (1): 63–66.

Haas, F. 2008. Data in search of a concept. In *Teaching secondary school science: Strategies for developing scientific literacy,* 9th ed., eds. R. W. Bybee, J. Powell, and L. W. Trowbridge, 42–43. Upper Saddle River, NJ: Pearson.

Hodson, D. 1999. Going beyond cultural pluralism: Science education for sociopolitical action. *Science Education* 83 (6): 775–796.

Hurd, P. D., R. W. Bybee, J. B. Kahle, and R. E. Yager. 1980. Biology education in secondary schools of the United States. *American Biology Teacher* 42 (7): 388–410.

Jones, D., and C. Kaplanis. 2006. *An introduction to scientific inquiry in grade nine*. Self-published.

National Research Council (NRC). 1996. *National science education standards*. Washington, DC: National Academy Press.

National Research Council (NRC). 2000. *Inquiry and the national science education standards*. Washington, DC: National Academy Press.

Ontario Ministry of Education. 2000a. *Curriculum document in science 9–10*. Toronto: Queen's Printer for Ontario.

Ontario Ministry of Education. 2000b. *Curriculum document in science 11–12*. Toronto: Queen's Printer for Ontario.

Note on Appendixes

In the interests of page control, we have provided curtailed versions of each of the Appendixes A, B, and C, while the rubrics used in these investigations are included complete as Appendix D. For the full version please visit *www.nsta.org/pdfs/InquiryAppendixes.pdf*.

Appendix A

Enzyme Investigation Teacher Notes

These teacher notes come from Doug Jones and are based upon several years' experience of using and refining this investigation.

Abstract

All of us teach biochemistry. A logical next step is to examine the structure and function on the molecules that allow and facilitate the reactions that occur in living things: enzymes. I did not write the original version of this. I believe I might have first seen a version in the old BSCS green version (this goes back to the early eighties). What's different is how I use the exercise and then assess the product to reach my objectives as they relate to scientific inquiry and deeper understanding. This investigation fits best for me in the grade 11 biology courses.

My objectives could be condensed to the following:

- Introduce and reinforce knowledge of enzyme action
- Review and practice writing hypothesis statements
- Collect and organize observations
- Conduct background research that supports the writing of summary statements

The approach itself is somewhat "messy" in the sense that I do not maintain a rigorous vigil over the method. The conceptual knowledge I want to shed light on becomes evident in spite of that and what I get instead is a chance to ask students to peer and self reflect on that "messiness" and then journal what they have noticed and how the method might be modified to tighten up the science (increase internal validity).

Another intentional "weakness" is that I have students conduct their research at the extremes or outside the normal limits of enzymatic reactions. I have a few reasons for doing this. One thing I can do is ask students to predict what enzymatic behavior might look like between the extremes. Teachers know that enzymes are extremely shape specific and that the conditions in which they can catalyze reactions is, generally, limited to narrow tolerance ranges. If I haven't given away the optimal conditions for this enzymatic reaction or drawn the normal curve that describes those conditions, then the field is open for future scientific inquiry by the students themselves to investigate those tolerance ranges and to do so in a much more rigorous fashion. For me, that happens in the first month of the grade 12 biology classes.

Finally, I do not hand out a "cookbook method" for students to follow as they work. Instead I use a series of sketches and verbal descriptions to uncover the task. The students' job is to record my instructions in their research journals in a manner that demonstrates they understand what must be done. Students are encouraged to ask any questions concerning the method they feel are necessary to fully understand what is required of them. With practice you will learn how to initiate and develop this conversation; what questions/concerns are valid and should be answered and which might be met with another question putting the onus back on the students. The benefit is that they begin to "own" the methodology.

One thing there can be no compromise on, however, is safety. Make sure that every student has heard your concerns about operating in a safe manner and is prepared to accept the responsibility to do so.

Finally, be aware that based on the size/maturity/thoroughness of your class, this investigation will probably need to take place over two days, even three initially, if you give the method like I do. For me the results are worth the investment.

Appendix B

Example of an Enzyme Investigation Student Report

Name ____Student X____

The nature of this experiment was to obtain a better understanding of the characteristics of an enzyme. The purpose of this investigation was to study the function of a catalase, and the factors that affect the reaction rates of the catalase.

Themes in this report:
1. Overview

2. Producing a Rating Scale

3. Reusing an Enzyme

4. Studying the Effects of Surface Area

5. Effect of Temperature on an Enzyme

6. Effect of pH on an Enzyme

7. Products of Reaction (enclosed)

It was predicted that the products of all the reactions done in this experiment were water and oxygen. To prove the presence of oxygen, a glowing splint was placed in a test tube full of gas. The splint reignited. Therefore, oxygen was present. To prove the presence of water, a strip of cobalt chloride paper was placed in the remaining clear solution. The paper turned pink in water. These results supported the hypothesis.

"Catalase has one of the highest turnover rates for all enzymes; one molecule of catalase can convert 6 million molecules of hydrogen peroxide to water and oxygen each minute" (Wikipedia, *Catalase*). The equation of this reaction is shown below:

$$2\ H_2O_2\ (l) \rightarrow 2\ H_2O\ (l) + O_2\ (g)$$

Appendix C

> ### Grade 12 Scientific Inquiry Student Exemplar

This report includes the framework that the student used to develop the experimental procedures, the actual procedures, and how the student made sense of the results.

The Effect of Diet on Blood Glucose (2005)

Name ___Student Y_____

The purpose or nature of the problem of this experiment was to determine the effect that diet or the consumption of carbohydrates had on the resulting concentration of glucose in the blood. In posing the research question, "What effect does diet and intake of carbohydrates have on the resulting blood glucose level?" it was hoped to determine an overall trend as well as to look at factors affecting this situation.

This report moves on to discuss the connections between blood glucose and homeostasis, leading to a paragraph that set up the experimental design:

In this experiment, diets needed to be chosen that would seem likely to have an effect on the blood glucose level, if homeostasis was not at work to maintain it. Therefore in conducting this experiment it was hoped to prove that homeostasis was at work within the body regardless of how much or little outside input there was of glucose through the diet. In order to do this, diets were chosen according to their glucose or carbohydrate content. One diet is very low in carbohydrates and instead, high in protein. The other is very high in carbohydrates, but low in both fat and protein content.

Two participants were used in the experiment with data collection over a two-day period:

The predicted outcome of this experiment was that homeostasis would continue to work and the blood glucose levels would remain fairly constant. The participant's blood glucose levels were monitored using a Fast Track device before, during, and after their two-day period of the diets listed above. The independent variable was the different diets and the dependent variable was the resulting blood glucose level.

The control used was a monitoring of each participant's regular eating habits and resulting blood glucose levels before the diets. Many aspects of the experiment were kept constant to reduce the risk of inaccuracy, such as both participants only drank water while on their diets, the diets were followed strictly, the times of meals and time of blood glucose monitoring remained constant, participants kept exercise levels to a minimum and pursued the same types of activities during both the control and days of the diets.

We conclude this brief tour through the account with the summary:

The purpose of this experiment was to determine the effect of diet on the resulting blood glucose level. After studying the effects of low and high carbohydrate diets, it was determined that homeostasis, the process that maintains levels in the body, continued to work even with the change in glucose input. The diet had little effect on the resulting blood glucose in this temporary change in diet.

Appendix D

Process and Product Rubrics for Peer/Instructor Assessment of Scientific Inquiry

Format

Level 1	Level 2	Level 3	Level 4
• The cover title is not appropriate • Graphs/Tables/Diagrams are not numbered or titled • In-text citations are not used. A references cited page is not used or poorly constructed • Formatting and organization have major errors and omissions • The report does not follow a logical line and requires some effort to read	• The cover title refers to the work but is poorly written • Graphs/Tables/Diagrams have titles/numbers but are formatted/used incorrectly • In-text citations are used to a limited extent. Citations and references cited pages are done incorrectly • Formatting and organization have some errors • The report is somewhat fragmented	• The cover title is satisfactory • Graphs/Tables/Diagrams numbering and titles are done with few errors • The number and level of in-text citations are appropriate. Most in-text citations and the references cited page are done correctly • Formatting and organization is satisfactory • The report is complete but somewhat sterile	• The cover title is eloquently stated • All graphs/tables are correctly numbered and titled • The use of in-text citations is thorough and relevant. They and the references cited page are done according to proper convention • Formatting and report organization is exemplary • The report has the feel of a well-told story

Introduction

Level 1	Level 2	Level 3	Level 4
• The nature of the problem and/or the research question are missing or incomplete • Background research is missing or not relevant to the problem and question at hand • The selection of independent, dependent, constants, and control variables is incomplete and/or has little regard for validity • The introduction does not conclude with a statement of predicted result or it does not relate to the research question	• There are inconsistencies with the nature of the problem and research question • Background research is not consistent with the problem and question at hand • The selection of independent, dependent, constants, and control variables is completed with some regard for validity • There is a prediction that concludes the introduction but it is incomplete or poorly framed	• The nature of the problem and research question are clear • Background research is provided that educates the reader about the nature of the researcher's inquiry work • The selection of independent, dependent, constants, and control variables are made with some consideration to the intended method of study • The introduction concludes with a prediction of outcome based on reflective prior knowledge	• The nature of the problem and research question are eloquently stated • Background research is provided in a way that elucidates the purpose/importance of the work and draws the reader into the inquiry • The selection of independent, dependent, constants, and control variables are justified and discussed in a cohesive approach to the intended method of study • The introduction concludes with a prediction of outcome based on reflective prior knowledge

Hypothesis/Materials/Method

Level 1	Level 2	Level 3	Level 4
• The hypothesis is missing; is not an if/then statement; or its length makes it cumbersome • The materials list is incomplete and little thought has been given to amounts/concentrations • The described method confuses the issues around collecting sufficient relevant data and does little to control variables and limit experimental error • The method is an itemized list stating each step to be taken; is not in past tense; and others would have difficulty repeating it • A diagram/photo is not supplied or has major problems with quality (clarity, detail, labels) • Safety considerations are not considered or are superficial	• The hypothesis is an if/then statement but is of an awkward, confusing, or lengthy nature • The materials list is complete but lacks information about amounts/concentrations • The described method has issues with the collection of sufficient, relevant data and controlling variables to reduce experimental error • The method is an itemized list describing each step of the process individually. It could be repeated by others to some degree • A diagram/photo is provided but may be lacking in clarity, accuracy, or labeling • Safety considerations are presented but not addressed	• The hypothesis is stated in a satisfactory, concise if/then statement • The materials list is complete and includes amounts/concentrations • The method follows principles of proficient experimental design to collect sufficient, relevant data and limit experimental error • The method is a narrative, written in past tense, and could be replicated by others with few issues • A clear and accurate diagram or photo with labels is provided • Safety considerations are identified and accounted for	• The hypothesis is stated in a clear, concise if/then statement that fits well with the research question • The materials list is complete and includes amounts/concentrations and preparatory instructions • The methods used to control internal validity and collect sufficient, relevant data are described clearly and accurately • The method is a well-written narrative of what was done to produce the inquiry and could be replicated by others • A clear and accurate diagram or photo with labels is provided • Safety considerations are identified and accounted for

Raw Data Display and Manipulation

Level 1	Level 2	Level 3	Level 4
• Data is presented in a haphazard manner at best without proper organization • Frequent errors are made concerning the use of labels and units • Frequent inconsistencies or inaccuracies in the error analysis exist • Calculations used are either of the wrong type or done incorrectly • A summary is not provided or is of little practical value	• Data has been presented but the format chosen is not the ideal one for the job • Some titles and/or units may be inappropriate or missing • There are some inconsistencies or inaccuracies in the error analysis • Some errors may be evident in the formula and/or method used for calculations • The summary does not clearly describe the trends/patterns in the data to the reader	• Data is clearly and logically organized using tables, charts, and/or graphs where appropriate • All appropriate labels and units have been included in the appropriate places • Calculations contain an error analysis reflecting the accuracy of the instruments used • Where calculations are necessary, the formula and method are accurately presented and explained • A summary statement points out to the reader any trends/patterns noticed in the data	• The criteria described at level three are presented with exceptional clarity and visual impact • The strategies chosen for data manipulation and the success using them indicate an aptitude for statistical analysis

Discussion and Summary

Level 1	Level 2	Level 3	Level 4
• The discussion does not arrive at an acceptable conclusion and does not use the data collected to formulate any interpretations • Background research was not used to augment the discussion and knowledge of scientific concepts was limited • No reference is made to the hypothesis or is trivial at best • Virtually no weaknesses in the investigation are identified … those that are tend to be of a trivial nature • A summary statement is not used or is poorly conceived	• The discussion arrives at a conclusion but the interpretation of the results is not based on the data collected or is somewhat superficial • There is little evidence that background research or knowledge of scientific concepts was used to augment the discussion • Reference is made to the hypothesis • Some of the weaknesses in the investigation are identified but little is done in the way of modification for improvement • There is a summary statement but it is not focused	• The discussion arrives at a conclusion based on a valid interpretation of the results that includes data collected for this purpose • A synopsis of background research and scientific concepts relevant to the discussion at hand is included • Reference is made to the hypothesis and the ability of the researcher(s) to support it • Weaknesses in the investigation are identified and appropriate modifications are suggested to overcome such problems if the inquiry was to be repeated • The summary statement identifies the key learning	• The discussion is a well-thought-out, finely crafted work that takes the reader through an interpretation of the data • Background research is congruent to the research question, hypothesis, and work at hand • An identification is made of weaknesses in the investigation along with modifications for improvement • Suggestions made of new questions/ directions the work might take in the future • A summary statement highlights the major findings

Erasing Lecture-Laboratory Boundaries: An Inquiry-Based Course Design

Bonnie S. Wood
University of Maine at Presque Isle

Setting

The University of Maine at Presque Isle (UMPI) is one of seven autonomous campuses within the University of Maine System. UMPI combines liberal arts and selected professional programs for 1,400 undergraduates and also serves as a cultural and educational resource for the entire community. Traditional students (24 years old or younger) make up 62% of the student population, while nontraditional students make up 38%. The University has adopted an adventurous learning focus that permeates the curriculum, student life, and even the classrooms themselves. My pedagogy supports the theme of adventurous learning.

The campus sits on 150 acres surrounded by the rolling hills and potato fields of northern Maine; it is 14 miles west of the Canadian border and 400 miles north of Boston. The city of Presque Isle, population 9,500, is the primary commercial center of the region. Aroostook County (the largest U.S. county east of the Mississippi) covers an area larger than Connecticut and Rhode Island combined, but has a population of only 74,000 people, half of whom reside within a 25-mile radius of Presque Isle. Both Presque Isle and Aroostook County have steadily lost population since 1960, while the state of Maine has gained. In 1999 the median household income in Presque Isle was $29,325. According to the 2000 census, among city residents 25 years of age or older, 14.8% have a bachelor's degree and 6.2% have a graduate or professional degree. The majority of UMPI students are poised to be first-generation college graduates.

Aspects of NSES Visions the Program Addresses

The program described in this chapter supports several National Science Education Standards and their visions for needed changes in Teaching Standards, Assessment Standards, and Content and Inquiry Standards.

For Teaching Standards, the course design

- focuses on student understanding and use of scientific knowledge, ideas, and inquiry processes;

- guides students in active and extended scientific inquiries;
- provides opportunities for scientific discussion and debate among students;
- continuously assesses student understanding and involves students in the process;
- shares responsibility for learning with students; and
- supports a classroom community with cooperation, shared responsibility, and respect.

For Assessment Standards, the course design

- assesses scientific understanding and reasoning; and
- assesses to learn what students do understand.

For Content and Inquiry Standards, the course design emphasizes

- understanding scientific concepts and developing abilities of inquiry;
- learning subject matter disciplines in the context of inquiry;
- integrating all aspects of science content;
- studying a few fundamental science concepts;
- implementing inquiry as strategies, abilities, and ideas to be learned;
- activities that investigate and analyze science questions;
- investigations over extended periods of time;
- using evidence and strategies for developing or revising an explanation;
- communicating science explanations;
- groups of students often analyzing and synthesizing data after defending conclusions;
- doing more investigations in order to develop understanding, ability, values of inquiry, and knowledge of science content;
- applying the results of experiments to scientific arguments and explanations; and
- public communication of student ideas and work to classmates.

Introduction

A decade ago, my original goal for reforming my teaching methods was simply to lead some sort of active learning exercise during every class meeting. I began by adapting ideas from books and journal articles. As I became more comfortable with my new teaching style, I designed some of my own activities. Within a couple of years I completely abandoned my lectures and began to use what I termed "lecture-free teaching," a comprehensive pedagogy that I will describe in detail in the NSTA Press book *Lecture-Free Teaching: A Learning Partnership of Science Educators and Their Students* (Wood, forthcoming).

During the next reform phase, I increased the length of time of each class meeting. With the inclusion of in-class activities, students began to complain that traditional 50-minute class periods were not long enough. Both my students and I felt rushed and the topics lacked coherence when activities ended abruptly without appropriate closure or had to be completed at home or at the next class. In response I changed "lecture" sessions from 50 minutes three times per week to 75 minutes two times per week.

Ultimately, I erased the arbitrary boundary between lecture and laboratory. In contrast to the traditional weekly schedule of three 50-minute lectures plus a three-hour laboratory at a different time of the week, and often with a different instructor, my classes now meet with me in the laboratory, twice a week, for three-hour sessions. I have gradually replaced instructor demonstrations and cookbook-style laboratory exercises with inquiry-based activities: Students, in their cooperative learning teams, employ the scientific process to develop their own hypotheses and then design and perform experiments to support their hypotheses.

I've learned that the teaching strategy I select for a course must be much more than a collection of active learning exercises that relates to the course content: Coherence is vital, both within each class meeting and also from week to week throughout the semester.

Building Cooperative Learning Teams

Within the first 15 minutes of the first day of class for every course I teach, students are randomly organized into heterogeneous learning teams with whom they will work for the entire semester. These teams of four or five students work together on in-class and laboratory activities, as well as occasional homework projects.

On Day 1 of the semester, soon after building the learning teams, students work together to complete an in-class activity that helps bond the group. When choosing this first exercise, I consider that it should be more than an ice-breaker. The first activity should demonstrate the coherence for which I strive by introducing skills that students will apply later in the semester. Because my course designs are constantly evolving, I am always trying new ideas.

Introduction to Inquiry-Based Learning

Because I make liberal use of case studies, the first class meeting is an ideal time to introduce this teaching method that often involves students working in their learning teams on a case requiring small-group discussion. In General Biology I, I choose an introductory case study that is not only inherently interesting to students, but also acquaints them with the scientific process and to the structure of a scientific report. This first activity of the semester provides connections to the inquiry-based laboratory exercises in which they will participate throughout the semester.

"Cell Phone Use and Cancer: A Case Study to Explore the Scientific Method" (Parilla 2006) is among the hundreds of case studies published by the State University of New York at Buffalo on the peer-reviewed website of the National Center for Case Study Teaching in Science (*http:// ublib.buffalo.edu/libraries/projects/cases/case.html*). I first hand each learning team copies of five different news articles from the lay press about research on cell phone use and cancer. Each team member reads at least one of the short articles and summarizes it for his or her learning team. The group discusses differences among the headlines of the five articles, and then analyzes each article for scientific methodology described and results and conclusions stated. Based on these short articles in the lay press, the learning team offers suggestions for improvement of the scientific study. At the end of the exercise, I give every student the original research article (Lönn et al. 2004) on which each of the shorter articles was based so they can compare information presented by lay press to what the scientists who did the study conveyed in their original journal article. For many students, this is the first time they have read an article in the primary literature. At the completion of the activity, I explain to them that the original article is a model for the scientific report each of them will write during the semester.

The course syllabus I distribute at that first class meeting describes the several writing assignments for the semester, including the "Scientific Report of a Laboratory Investigation." I intentionally avoid the term *lab report* to differentiate what I expect in this first year of college class from what they may have produced as high school students after completing a cookbook-style laboratory exercise.

Implementation of Inquiry-Based Learning

In Week 2 of the semester, learning team members examine the General Biology I topic schedule for the titles and dates of the four or five inquiry-based lab exercises scheduled throughout the term, and each student in the team chooses a different exercise for which she or he will write the scientific report. During a recent semester, students investigated diffusion and osmosis, enzyme activity, photosynthesis versus cellular respiration in plants, fermentation in yeast, and eutrophication. Before the day scheduled for each content topic, students are expected to have completed assigned textbook reading. Guided by my written and verbal instructions, they first practice some relevant laboratory procedures. Then each group chooses from a selection of subtopics to investigate. Each team then decides on and states their hypothesis, after which they design and perform an experiment to test their hypothesis. The experiment must be something that can be accomplished using supplies and equipment available in the laboratory or on the campus land. In one case (a laboratory exercise on eutrophication) I drove the students in a university van to nearby ponds and lakes to collect water samples. Although students complete each investigation as a team and all team members are responsible for participating in the laboratory procedures and understanding the related concepts, only one student from each team writes the scientific report for a specific investigation and he or she is graded individually on this report.

For investigations scheduled near the beginning of the semester, I give more specific instructions and suggestions. Students take more responsibility for choosing materials and methods as they gain laboratory experience and competence later in the semester. Figure 1 (p. 184) is an example of instructions for a laboratory exercise scheduled for one-third of the way through the semester. They are included in the content outline titled "Cellular Energy and Enzymes." Figure 2 (p. 186) is an example of instructions for a laboratory exercise scheduled for the final class meetings of the semester that is preceded by a visit by a guest speaker who was doing research on the effects on local bodies of water of chemical fertilizers applied to surrounding farmlands. These instructions are included in the content outline titled "Humans Impacting the Environment."

I instruct students to follow carefully the "Scientific Report of Laboratory Investigation Grading Criteria" (Figure 3, p. 187). An important component of the process of writing the scientific report is taking a draft report to the campus writing center for a consultation with a peer tutor. Although some of the peer tutors are excellent, the greatest benefit of this requirement is teaching students to write a first draft and then revise it after someone unfamiliar with the topic reads and critiques the draft.

At the University of Maine at Presque Isle, professors teach and grade everything ourselves. We have no teaching assistants or lab managers. An advantage of students taking turns writing the entire scientific report is that when the class performs a laboratory investigation, I do not receive a multipage report from every student in the class, but just one from each learning team. Because the scientific report is a one-per-semester assignment for an individual student, he or she has about 10 days to complete it (including the visit to the writing center) and the report counts for a considerable number of points. As I observe the learning teams, I see they are very engaged in the processes of correctly stating a hypothesis, designing an experiment with appropriate controls, examining the data to determine whether they support their hypothesis, and discussing how future experiments could be conducted to improve the collection of data or to consider new hypotheses. The individual scientific reports are generally a more polished, higher quality product than the smaller scale lab reports I assigned in the past.

An unexpected and important consequence is the allocation of responsibility that occurs among the team members. I do not need to formally assign roles to each student within a team to ensure equal participation: The student who is responsible for writing the scientific report spontaneously assumes the role of principal investigator and oversees all aspects of the investigation. Furthermore, with a clear and specific list of grading criteria (Figure 3, p. 187) a student understands my expectations before performing the investigation and can work relatively independently to write the scientific report.

Because each team uses different sets of equipment and supplies, students are, for the most part, responsible for collecting their own materials from the laboratory shelves and cabinets, for correctly washing the glassware and putting supplies and equipment away afterward, and for cleaning their lab table for the next class. Although I am always in the laboratory, closely supervising experimental procedures with a strong emphasis on safety, I have observed another unexpected benefit of this independence and responsibility: A marked decrease in passivity among the students. All the students become very comfortable in the laboratory setting and their competence in setting up and conducting experiments, both safely and efficiently, visibly increases as we progress through the semester.

A concept that is at first difficult but becomes a valuable lesson when students perform inquiry-based as opposed to cookbook-style laboratory exercises is that their experiments do not have to "work." Although I urge them to state a hypothesis that they believe will be supported by the resulting data, I reassure them that discovering an incorrect hypothesis or a flawed experimental design can produce even more significant learning than having the results be as expected. Students soon realize they can still write a meaningful scientific report and may, in fact, create a more interesting discussion section about unanticipated results.

Evidence of Impact of the Program

In addition to my observations in the previous section, two studies recently published in the *Journal of College Science Teaching* corroborate the effectiveness of my methods. The first (Moore 2008) reported that lab attendance is strongly correlated with students' academic performance in introductory science courses and concludes that higher rates of laboratory attendance may be due to the fact that labs are often more interactive than lectures. I have observed that student attendance has greatly improved since I combined "lectures" and laboratories.

A second article (Burrowes and Nazario 2008) described the results of a three-way comparison of the effectiveness of a big lecture course (110 students) with a separate lab taught by a teaching assistant; a small lecture course (32 students) with a separate lab taught by a teaching assistant; and what the authors call a "Seamless course: Integrated lab-lecture in a lab setting" (32 students) that is similar to my setting. They analyzed student learning, students' attitude toward biology, and students' perceptions of both the botany and the zoology courses they investigated. Their results strongly support my hypothesis that a combined lecture and laboratory course more effectively engages students in the process of science, and improves learning while developing scientific process skills.

Voluntary comments made on the end-of-semester evaluations by my own students are almost unanimously supportive of the combined lecture–laboratory. Students often suggest that all science classes at the university should be taught this way. A sample of written comments from students in my General Biology I course (a class for both majors and nonmajors that also fulfils part of the General Education Curriculum science requirement) include the following:

"I really enjoyed this class. I found the discovery-based learning model of this class to be a very good form of teaching. I found that I was able to retain more and made the material covered easier to relate to. I would welcome other classes structured in a similar fashion, especially science courses."

"I've never had a science class that I have been able to feel like I knew what was going on. This teaching style has helped me to understand the concepts being studied. I wish that I could have had this kind of exposure to science at an earlier age. It might have made a difference in my chosen career."

"Overall I learned a lot this semester. I stress learned over memorized."

"I learn better through hands-on work."

"I was worried about the different teaching style, but I have found that I have a better understanding of the material and can apply it to different situations. This has been my most challenging class, but also my most rewarding."

"I enjoy the unique style of teaching. Having a variety of ways to learn keeps me interested."

"I am completely impressed with how you applied the new teaching method to this class. It is inspiring as a future teacher."

References

Burrowes, P., and G. Nazario. 2008. Promoting student learning through the integration of lab and lecture: The seamless biology curriculum. *Journal of College Science Teaching* 37 (4): 18–23.

Lönn, S., A. Ahlbom, P. Hall, and M. Feychting. 2004. Mobile phone use and the risk of acoustic neuroma. *Epidemiology* 15 (6): 653–659.

Moore, R. 2008. Research and teaching: Are students' performances in labs related to their performances in lecture portions of introductory science courses? *Journal of College Science Teaching* 37 (3): 66–70.

National Center for Case Study Teaching in Science Case Collection. *http://ublib.buffalo.edu/libraries/projects/cases/ubcase.htm.*

Parilla, W. V. C. 2006. Cell phone use and cancer: A case study to explore the scientific method. National center for case study teaching in science case collection. Available from *www.sciencecases.org/cell_phone/cell_phone.asp.*

Wood, B. S. Forthcoming. *Lecture-free teaching: A learning partnership of science educators and their students.* Arlington, VA: NSTA Press.

Figure 1. Laboratory Activity

In Vitro Gas Suppression: Beano—Enzymes to the Rescue

[Adapted from Frame, K. (2002) *In vitro* gas suppression: Beano—enzymes to the rescue. In *Shoestring Biotechnology. Budget-Oriented, High-Quality Biotechnology Laboratories for Two-Year College and High School* (pp. 125–138). Reston, VA: National Association of Biology Teachers.]

Homework Activity: Reports on Enzyme Dietary Supplements by Learning Teams
- Summary of what these products have in common.
- Do concerns about flatus exist in all cultures?
- What sorts of traditional herbal remedies for flatus exist in families and ethnic groups?

Introduction to the Laboratory Protocol
Preparation of bean solution (for entire class) by two students
1. Place 100 grams (~ one-half can) cooked canned beans and 200 ml water into a blender and blend for 5 minutes or until the mixture appears smooth. If it's too viscous, add some more water.
2. Filter mixture through two layers of cheesecloth.

Setup of test tubes (by each learning group)
1. Grind up one Beano tablet in a mortar and pestle and dissolve in 2 ml distilled water.
2. Label test tubes #1 (bean solution + Beano) and #2 (control).
3. Add 4 ml of filtered bean solution to each test tube.
4. Take a baseline reading of glucose concentration in Tubes 1 and 2 at Time "0" by adding a drop of liquid from each tube to a glucose detection strip. Wait 30 seconds and make a reading by comparing the color of the strip to the chart for the glucose detection kit. Record your readings in mg/dl (*be sure to read at exactly the time specified by the manufacturer).
5. After 30 seconds take a second measurement.
6. Tape your glucose detection strips to your data page and record which test tube and time it represents and the glucose reading.
7. Use a clean pipette to add one Beano tablet dissolved in 2 ml water (accomplished in "A" above) to Tube 1. Pipette the mixture up and down to make sure it is mixed well. Use another clean pipette to add 2 ml of water to Tube 2 and pipette the mixture up and down to ensure that it is mixed well.
8. Take glucose measurements every 5 minutes for another 15 minutes and record your data.
9. Explain why you observed your results.

Design an *In Vitro* Experiment for Your Learning Group
1. The following supplies will be available for your experiment:

- can of cooked beans
- ½ bag of same kind of beans soaked in water overnight
- milk
- Beano and Lactaid tablets
- glucose detection sticks
- safety glasses (wear when using acids and bases!)
- vinegar
- dropper bottles of hydrochloric acid (HCl)
- dropper bottles of sodium hydroxide (NaOH)
- wax pencils

- thermometers
- 10 ml graduated cylinders
- disposable pipettes or washable droppers
- 500-ml beakers
- water baths
- hot plates
- ice
- pH meters/paper, pH buffers
- mortar and pestle to grind up tablets
- blender
- balance

2. Read the instructions for use of Beano on the package and discuss them in terms of what you know about factors affecting enzyme activity (review your notes on Outline 5, IV, D on page 44).

3. You may use the canned, cooked beans or the soaked, uncooked beans or both.

4. After considering what you know about enzymes, form a hypothesis and design an experiment with your learning group.

    a. Your hypothesis must be something quantifiable.

    b. Frame your hypothesis statement using an "if . . . then" format.

5. Get approval for your experiment from the teacher.

6. Perform your experiment (use safety glasses when working with acids and bases).

7. Graph your results.

Presentation of Experimental Designs, Results, and Conclusions

1. Each learning group will present their experimental design, results, and conclusions to the rest of the class.

2. Students will critique the experiments of each learning group.

Discussion

1. What conclusions can we draw from the results of all the experiments?

2. What part of a plant is a bean? Why does gas form in the human colon when beans are consumed?

3. What would be the effect of leaving all your test tubes intact and testing again in 24 hours? Why?

Design an *In Vitro* Experiment

(Include this design in your laboratory report.)

Design an Analogous Experiment Using Lactaid and Milk

(If there is time, perform this experiment.)

Figure 2. Laboratory Activity

Eutrophication

[Adapted from McComas, W. F. Ed. 2002. *Investigating Ecology in the Laboratory,* pp.145–146. Jefferson City, MO: National Association of Biology Teachers]

"Eutrophication (the increase in the nutrient status of water with sometimes disastrous consequences to the organisms living in it) is a serious problem associated with the overuse of fertilizer in areas of intensive agriculture. It may also occur as a result of high levels of nutrient-rich effluent (for example from treated domestic sewage) entering water courses that cannot provide adequate dilution (e.g., when summer flow rates are low)."

—*McComas, 2002*

Available to you are the following supplies and equipment:
- pond/river/creek water
- distilled water
- glass beakers
- chemical fertilizers used in gardening (Miracle-Gro)
- wax pencils to mark water levels
- grow lights
- thermometers
- microscopes (light and dissecting)
- pH paper

1. With your learning group, design and conduct an investigation of the effects of chemical fertilizers on eutrophication of water. (Have the teacher approve your experiment before you proceed.)

2. Your scientific report should include data collected, graphs, and drawings of organisms, along with a discussion of the following questions:
   - What is eutrophication and why does it have a negative effect on the organisms that live in ponds or rivers? (A detailed explanation of this is required.)
   - Why do ponds and lakes in northern Maine experience eutrophication?
   - What chemical elements are most likely to contribute to eutrophication?
   - Should the citizens of northern Maine be concerned about this?

Figure 3. Scientific Report of Laboratory Investigation

Grading Criteria
(Distribution of points as described below)

First Author's Name: _____

Topic of Laboratory Exercise: _____

Signature of Writing Center Tutor: _____

Date of Writing Center Consultation: _____

TOTAL POINTS OUT OF 30 = _____

Title and Authors

2 Title is written at the top of the report (not on a cover sheet) and is descriptive, concise, and appropriate in tone and structure for a scientific journal. Title allows reader to anticipate the experiment design. You are listed as the first author with contributing learning group members listed as second, third, and fourth authors.

1 Title is descriptive but does not allow the reader to anticipate the experiment design. Names of authors are incomplete or misspelled.

0 Title and authors are on a separate cover sheet; title is the same as the general topic of the laboratory exercise (as given in the coursepack).

General Considerations

2 All material is placed in the correct sections as described below and organized logically within each section; the organization runs parallel among the different sections. The report is neatly typed, single-spaced, with correct spelling and grammar. Pages are numbered in the upper right corners. The entire report is in paragraph form. All measurements are in SI units with proper abbreviations; genus and species are underlined or italicized with genus capitalized. Underlining in the text is not done for any other purposes (as for emphasis).

1 The materials are placed in the correct sections all of which are written in paragraph form, but the report does not have a neat appearance or contains frequent errors of spelling and grammar or does not use SI units or correctly write genus and species of organisms.

0 As for 1 but the materials are incorrectly located in the sections or the sections are missing.

Abstract

3 Is 100 words or less and contains the purpose of the experiment, a brief description of methods, results, and conclusions.

2 Is lacking one of the elements listed for 3 and/or is too long or too short.

1 Is lacking more than one of the elements listed for 3 and/or is too long or too short.

0 Abstract missing or does not contain the elements listed for 3.

Introduction

5 Contains background information from the literature (primary references) that directly relate to the experiment. The in-text citation form is correct and citations are paraphrased (quotation marks are not used). Purpose of the experiment and your hypothesis are clearly stated. Information from the coursepack is not copied but rather the topic is described in your own words, using information you have learned in Biology 112 both in class and from your own reading.

4 As for 5, but background information from the literature is lacking, along with citations.

3 As for 4, but purpose OR the hypothesis are lacking.

2 As for 3, but both purpose and hypothesis are lacking.

1 Information in the Introduction belongs in another section of the report.

0 Introduction is missing or is not written in your own words.

Materials and Methods

5 The materials are described in paragraph form (not listed like ingredients in a recipe). Section is written in past tense and contains all relevant information, in an appropriate chronology, to enable a reader to repeat the experiment. The exact procedure you actually followed is described, not necessarily what was written in the coursepack. Information is complete enough so everything in the rest of the report can be related back to "Materials and Methods," but the section avoids unnecessary, wordy descriptions of procedures. Precise measurements are given using SI units.

4 As for 5, but contains unnecessary or wordy descriptions.

3 As for 5, but gives sequential information in a disorganized, confusing way.

2 Describes an experiment that is marginally replicable, so that the reader must infer parts of the basic design. The procedures are not quantitatively described.

1 Describes the experiment so poorly or in such a nonscientific way that it cannot be replicated. Contains information that belongs in a different section.

0 Materials and Methods section is missing or is not written in your own words.

Results

5 Contains quantifiable experimental data with the units clearly defined and labeled in both text and graphics. Drawings, graphs and tables are included where appropriate. Figure captions are placed below the figure; table captions above the table. Figure and table captions are informative and can be understood independently of the text. Results are described in paragraph form in the text and the text refers to each table and figure. Your actual results are described, rather than extrapolations or what you should have gotten (save this for Discussion). No explanation is given for the results.

4 As for 5, but figure and table captions cannot be understood without reading the text.

3 As for 4, but the data reported in the text, the graphs, or the tables include information that is irrelevant to the purpose of the experiment or the hypothesis.

2 Quantifiable experimental data are present, but the quantities or intervals are inappropriate or information is not displayed graphically when appropriate.

1 The section does not contain or communicate quantifiable results. The information belongs in another section of the report.

0 The Results section is missing.

Discussion

5 Both observed and expected results are summarized including a statement of why you think you got the results presented in the "Results" section. Errors and inconsistencies in procedure are pointed out. Possible explanations of unexpected results are given as well as suggestions for further and/or improved experimentation. A statement of whether the hypothesis is accepted or rejected is made by comparing your hypothesis with the data.

4 As for 5, but accepting or rejecting the hypothesis is lacking.

3 As for 4, but suggestions for further and/or improved experimentation are lacking.

2 As for 3, but unexpected results are ignored.

1 The results are summarized, but are not interpreted.

0 The Discussion section is missing.

References

3 References are primary journal articles, textbooks or peer-reviewed internet sources (i.e., from a journal, not from a source like Wikipedia). References, listed using in American Psychological Association (APA) style, are correct, complete, and consistent. All references have been cited in the text (authors' name and date) and all citations in the text have been included in the references section. The reference list is arranged in alphabetical order according to the first author's surname. First names are given as initials. (For examples of reference style, see any issue of *The American Biology Teacher,* a journal located in the UMPI library.)

2 As for 3, but consistent APA style is not used.

1 As for 2, but some references are inappropriate (i.e., are not from primary journal articles, textbooks, or peer-reviewed internet sources) or are not cited in the text or citations in the text are not included in the references section.

0 The references section is missing.

Ecological Monitoring Provides a Thematic Foundation for Student Inquiry

Erin Baumgartner
Western Oregon University

Chela Zabin
Smithsonian Environmental Research Center and University of California, Davis

Joanna Philippoff, Erin Cox, and Matthew Knope
University of Hawaii–Manoa

Setting: What Is OPIHI?

Our Project in Hawaii's Intertidal (OPIHI) is a network of schools and scientist volunteers engaged in the widespread, systematic monitoring of Hawaii's rocky intertidal zones. OPIHI originated through a partnership funded by the National Science Foundation's Graduate Fellowships in K–12 Teaching program. The original OPIHI model was a joint project between University of Hawaii–Manoa (UHM) zoology graduate student Chela Zabin and University Laboratory School (ULS) marine science instructor Erin Baumgartner (Baumgartner and Zabin 2008). Dr. Zabin's research focused on invasive intertidal invertebrates, and she felt that involving students in biodiversity monitoring would improve their scientific skills, while providing much needed assistance in gathering much needed data. This initial partnership developed a thematic framework to allow students to conduct investigations about intertidal organisms and ecology while collecting useful scientific data. This framework became OPIHI. As more fellows, teachers, schools, and funding organizations have adopted OPIHI, they have modified the project to suit their needs. In this chapter, we summarize the ideas behind OPIHI, describe the original model of investigation, and examine how OPIHI has been used by different groups to answer a range of student questions, all while maintaining the original thematic focus on intertidal ecology and authentic scientific investigation.

Opihi (*Cellana* spp.) are large gastropod mollusks, also known as limpets, found only in the rocky intertidal zone in Hawaii. These animals are representative of the many reasons for our interest in Hawaii's intertidal zone. They inhabit a unique habitat, are of ecological and cultural importance, and their numbers are decreasing due to urbanization and overharvesting. In the OPIHI teaching and research model, students conduct a range of scientific investigations. These investigations are connected to the monitoring of species richness and abundance in the intertidal habitats throughout the Hawaiian islands. Among the most accessible marine ecosystems, intertidal zones are especially susceptible to human impacts but also ideal for school or community research projects.

The OPIHI model was based in part on the Long-Range Monitoring and Experimental Training for Students (LiMPETS) program in California. LiMPETS is a volunteer-based program that involves students and teachers in environmental monitoring of California's rocky and sandy coastlines (Osborn, Pearse, and Roe 2001). We used the LiMPETS model as the foundation for the OPIHI effort, making the needed adjustments to accommodate for our own scientific and educational goals, as well as for the unique characteristics of Hawaii's intertidal zone.

Intertidal coastlines have been well studied in temperate regions (the focus of LiMPETS), but until recently, very nearly ignored in Hawaii. Regular monitoring is informative about many phenomena of importance to conservation efforts. In Hawaii, where few descriptive studies have been carried out, the recognized need to describe and explore patterns of community structure in relation to environmental characteristics has been in large part answered by OPIHI students.

Goals of OPIHI

The primary goals of OPIHI are (1) to establish baselines of information about intertidal species richness and abundance of organisms, (2) to increase monitoring of intertidal regions around Oahu and Hawaii by providing students to monitor different types of intertidal organisms, and (3) to build scientific literacy as outlined by the American Academy for the Advancement of Science (1990). These goals are also aligned with the science education reforms recommended by the National Science Education Standards, henceforth referred to as the NSES (NRC 1996).

Field ecology is a great introduction to scientific methodology, as well as to concepts such as biodiversity, zonation, and invasion biology. OPIHI's scientific goals provide the context for the scientific inquiry undertaken by students. These goals are built around the NSES and the corresponding Hawaii Content and Performance Standards (HIDOE 2005) and Ocean Literacy Essential Principles (Schoedinger, Cava, and Jewell 2006) as outlined in Table 1. These standards focus on scientific habits of mind and require problem-solving and critical-thinking skills while supporting particular content knowledge through the thematic emphasis on the ecology of the intertidal zone. The knowledge outlined in all these standards arises through student investigations. These investigations involve gathering data on patterns of diversity and abundance and testing hypotheses about ecological interactions (including those involving humans) to explain those patterns. In these ways, students are prepared to meet the goals for school science established by the NSES, especially gaining direct experience with the natural world and using scientific processes and principles in decision making.

Table 1. NSES Met by OPIHI With Corresponding Hawaii Content and Performance Standards and Ocean Literacy Essential Principles

National Science Education Standards	Hawaii Content and Performance Standards—Science	Ocean Literacy Essential Principles
Science as Inquiry	Standard 1: The Scientific Process: Scientific Investigation: Discover, invent, and investigate using the skills necessary to engage in the scientific process	Principle 7: The ocean is largely unexplored
History and Nature of Science	Standard 2: The Scientific Process: Nature of Science: Understand that science, technology, and society are interrelated	Principle 6: The ocean and humans are inextricably interconnected
Life Science (Interdependence of Organisms)	Standard 3: Life and Environmental Sciences: Organisms and the Environment: Understand the unity, diversity, and interrelationships of organisms	Principle 5: The ocean supports a great diversity of life and ecosystems

OPIHI, as a project-based program, is in keeping with NSES *More Emphasis* recommendations for teaching. We know that to truly learn science, students need to participate in the full and total practice of science (Barab and Luehmann 2003). OPIHI students build scientific knowledge through an extended scientific inquiry. Student understanding of scientific processes is as significant as content acquisition, and all knowledge is built through active inquiry. Students gain as much, if not more, content knowledge from a project-based unit than from a lecture approach, and develop the skills they need to find and evaluate additional information on their own (Baumgartner and Zabin 2008; Passmore and Stewart 2000).

Research has shown that without explicitly addressing how scientific knowledge arises from scientific practice, hands-on inquiry activities have little impact on student understanding of the nature of science (Sandoval and Morrison 2003; Windschitl et al. 2007). The real-world experience of science involves interaction through discussion, argument, and collaboration (Barab et al. 2001). Discussion and reflection is essential to conceptual change and lasting knowledge (Tytler 2002). OPIHI students form learning communities both within the classroom and with other OPIHI schools as they work together to gain new knowledge about the Hawaiian intertidal zone. Project-based learning has real-world relevance if it is flexible enough to provide for diverse experiences in different settings and contexts (Payne 2006). While there are thematic foundations that are shared by all engaged in the project, the curriculum is adaptable to school and classroom learning goals and to individual student needs and interests.

The Hawaiian Intertidal Zone: A Unique Learning Facility

The intertidal zone is a unique marine environment covered with water during high tide and exposed to air during low tide. The intertidal community is comprised primarily of marine algae, invertebrates, and fish that are often uniquely adapted to this environment. Some of the most important scientific theories of both the 19th and 20th centuries originated from ecological experiments conducted in intertidal zones. The concept of keystone species, for example, originated from studies of intertidal species' diversity and trophic dynamics (Paine 1966, 1969). Due in part to a low-tidal amplitude, the nearby presence of a well-studied subtidal coral reef ecosystem and season period of high swell activity, Hawaii's intertidal zone has received little scientific study as an ecosystem and even less conservation attention. However, Hawaii's ecosystem provides exciting potential for research, and questions about the diversity and abundance of intertidal organisms are the foundation for inquiry conducted by OPIHI students.

Students who have participated in OPIHI projects represent schools from across the state of Hawaii. To date, 12 schools have participated in OPIHI. These include eight public schools (including three charter schools) and four private schools. Eight participating schools are high schools and four are middle schools. One OPIHI school is parochial, another is a Hawaiian immersion school, and a third serves students with special learning needs. In addition, at least two informal education organizations have adopted OPIHI as part of their educational programs. This broad spectrum of schools served by OPIHI demonstrates the wide adaptability of the intertidal zone as a learning environment and focus of study.

OPIHI in Practice

The OPIHI instructional model develops scientific content and skills through direct experience. Students become specialists, not just in intertidal ecology and diversity, but also in the species that they are monitoring. They form a community of learners as they work together to develop expert knowledge and share questions and ideas with one another. This learning strategy does not require that the instructor have large amounts of background knowledge, because the focus is on making observations, asking questions, and determining how to answer those questions. Students are thus responsible for building their own knowledge.

At the core of the OPIHI model is an image of learning and teaching based on the discipline of science. Linn and Songer (1993) found that students could more effectively gain conceptual knowledge about their everyday experiences when they had formulated a dynamic view of science. The *Teaching Science as Inquiry* (CRDG 2005) instructional cycle (Table 2) reflects the flexible and collaborative nature of scientific inquiry and supports the development of scientifically literate students who recognize the dynamic nature of science (Pottenger and Berg 2006).

The original OPIHI framework as developed at University Laboratory School was a semester-long project. The students involved in the original development of OPIHI were a heterogeneous group of high school freshmen enrolled in a marine science course at ULS, an urban Honolulu charter school. ULS is a small (approximately 500 students total) K–12 school with only 50 students per grade level in grades 6–12, all of whom experience the same curriculum every year. Students are selected by stratified lottery to represent a cross-section of Hawaii's education population, one of the most diverse in the United States. In subsequent years, OPIHI teachers at other schools have modified the program to suit their individual needs. Lesson plans and ideas for all of the activities described are available on the OPIHI website, *www.hawaii.edu/gk-12/opihi*. Let's examine the components of the program.

Table 2. The *Teaching Science as Inquiry* Learning Cycle

Phase	Description	
Initiation	• *Originate Interest* that results in a problematic focus • *Develop a Focus* for the inquiry: a question, problem or need	**Instruction (embedded in all phases)** • *Communicate* new concepts, methods, and connection within student community • *Communicate* new concepts, methods, and connections through pedagogic and other means of reaching the larger public
Invention	• *Create a Testable Resolution (hypothesis)* of the question, problem, or need • *Create a Test Design (experiment)* or way to determine the workability or the degree of success of the resolution	
Investigation	• *Carry Out a Test* according to the design in the invention phase • *Carry Out an Analysis* according to the design in the invention phase	
Interpretation	• *Evaluate Results:* researchers draw conclusions about the workability or success of testing • *Evaluate Conclusions:* community evaluates the research conclusions, discussing validity, alternative explanations, and additional information	

Initiation

As in scientific investigations, our inquiry learning is initiated when the asking of a question identifies a problem to be solved. The teacher can initiate an investigation through a question or presentation of a phenomenon, but it is best stimulated through student curiosity. We initiate the project while building scientific inquiry skills to prepare for the larger research project. The first OPIHI lesson initiates student curiosity about intertidal organisms and takes students through a small-scale version of the complete scientific inquiry cycle.

Students are organized into research teams responsible for studying specific taxonomic groups of intertidal organisms, such as fish, echinoderms, or mollusks. The first OPIHI class sessions allow students to be creative and examine the organisms (both living and preserved specimens) with a few guidelines provided to ensure the safety of the students and the organisms. The only other required part of the assignment is for each student group to record a set of observations and questions about the organisms.

These observations and questions are then used as the foundation for a small research study when students choose one of their initial questions to develop into a testable hypothesis. We found that a good guiding question to ask the students is "What is a question that you could answer in this classroom with available materials over the next two to three days that poses little harm to you or your organisms?" Questions like "Do anemones eat algae?" are answerable within this context.

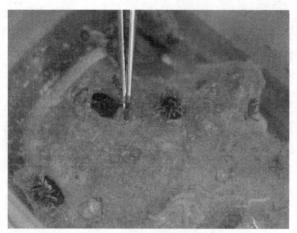

Figure 1. Offering Algae to an Anemone

The mini-investigations built by students to answer their questions help them learn more about their focus organisms and gain experience in using scientific practices to answer questions. The group of students that asked about anemones' feeding habits conducted an experiment to answer their question. The students offered the anemones small bits of algae, brine shrimp, and chocolate, and then recorded the animals' reactions to each food item.

Students also use books and the internet to supplement and verify the information collected during their mini-investigations. One of the aspects of authentic scientific practice emphasized in OPIHI is the use of multiple sources of information. Students gather new information directly through their own research, but they also have access to field guides and scientific books and papers. They also gain information from other scientists by working with one another and with scientific experts in the field. All this information is used by each group of students to prepare a lesson they will present to the class on the general biology of their taxonomic group. These presentations provide all students with a basic familiarity of the intertidal organisms they will encounter and build expertise among the groups that will specialize in each taxonomic group.

Invention

The process of building taxonomic expertise both encapsulates the phases of scientific inquiry and initiates an OPIHI field investigation. The curiosity developed by students during the mini-investigations about their organisms and the environment in which they live leads to the invention phase of the learning cycle. Invention includes the development of a hypothesis to guide an investigation, as well as the design of the method to answer the question or solve the problem. This phase of OPIHI focuses on trip planning, and includes hands-on activities to familiarize students with tools and techniques they can use to find out more about their organisms. This part of the sequence is the heart of the project, and the main activity engaged in by most OPIHI schools.

OPIHI relies heavily on the power of sampling. Sampling is an important tool because it allows students to gain information about a population, community, or environment without counting every single sea urchin, algal clump, or grain of sand. The data students use to answer their questions are almost always sampling data, so it is important that they understand how to use these techniques to conduct fieldwork.

A complete summary of the OPIHI sampling strategies has been previously published (Baumgartner and Zabin 2006). These strategies include introductory activities to demonstrate the power of sampling by determining the proportion of jellybeans in a jar or M&Ms in a bag. We also introduce students to the primary field-sampling techniques of transects and quadrats. Students learn how to conduct point-intercept transects by counting organisms or substrate directly under predetermined points along a transect line. They also learn how to place quadrats along transect points to estimate the percentage of different kinds of cover contained within the quadrat or to count cover directly beneath intersecting points formed by a grid of lines strung within the quadrat.

Figure 2. Student Using a Quadrat

Students are not simply told which methods to use. The professional practice of science involves learning about, testing, and evaluating methods of investigation. Students have this same opportunity by trying different sampling methods and evaluating the pros and cons of each for different purposes. Finally, they may conduct a small investigation of a schoolyard (or other convenient area) as a trial to more effectively plan their intertidal study. Even if they are not planning to conduct an extensive field study, it is important for students to think about how they might employ the techniques in a real-word research situation.

The development of the field methodology is one part of the planning students must do to prepare for their investigation. They also gather information about potential hazards from their own research into the organisms and from state-provided water safety materials to prepare an intertidal first-aid kit and develop a set of safety rules. We have found that when students are involved in this planning process, discipline issues are minimal. Students are also responsible for planning and compiling their own field collecting kits. Using tide tables to plan for optimal times for fieldwork is an important part of planning and has the added benefit of introducing or reinforcing the concept of tides and skills in reading tide tables.

Investigation

After planning their field study, the students are ready to begin their investigation. The investigation is the part of the learning cycle that most involves the actual gathering of new information. During investigations, observations are made and recorded, hypotheses are tested, and data are collected and analyzed. Investigation frequently leads to initiation of new questions that can be incorporated into the current investigative framework or later used to stimulate new investigations.

OPIHI students use sampling techniques to find out about the diversity and abundance of intertidal organisms. On field trips, students record information about site conditions, quantify substrate cover including algae and benthic organisms using transects and quadrats, and conduct searches for different organisms, identifying as many as possible *in situ*. Organisms

Figure 3. Students identify and record intertidal organisms along a transect line.

that cannot be identified in the field may be returned to the classroom if covered by the collecting permits issued by the Hawaii Department of Land and Natural Resources. Organisms not covered by permits or from protected sites can be photographed or sketched. Students are assisted in the field by scientific volunteers from various research organizations.

Upon returning to the classroom, students use scientific keys to complete organism identification, sometimes contacting volunteer scientific experts at UHM and the Bernice P. Bishop Museum for assistance. Once identifications are made, students compile their field data and gather biogeographic and ecological information on each species. They record the most current information about each organism in data notebooks. This additional data includes taxonomic affiliation; whether it is endemic, indigenous, or introduced; and the geographic and depth ranges.

Interpretation

By recording all information gathered during the course of a project in their data notebooks, the students learn how to effectively record observations and organize information in preparation for interpretation. Interpretation is both a reflective, internal process and an objective, external process. The student researchers must take the time to evaluate for themselves the information they have gathered, make conclusions, and consider alternative explanations. This information is then presented within the classroom community and ideally beyond to the larger scientific community for peer evaluation and review.

Students interpret their data by examining the patterns found between different sites, at the same site over space and time, and within taxonomic groups. Students are then able to hypothesize possible reasons, including human impacts, for those patterns. In the first year of the project, of the six sites visited, the greatest diversity of introduced species was collected from Kaneohe Bay, Oahu. One student hypothesis was that the presence of a marine lab in Kaneohe Bay might be contributing the incidental release of nonnative study organisms. An alternate hypothesis was that the Kaneohe Marine Corps Base could be introducing species via ship transport. As OPIHI projects have continued over multiple years, students have had the option to compare data from different years and different sites.

Instruction

Doing science includes the communication of findings to other scientists and to the public. Students aren't only responsible for interpreting their data but for sharing what they have learned with others. Instruction is integrated into each part of this learning cycle and emphasizes the flow of information from student to student. The instruction process is embedded throughout the entire learning cycle, ongoing even while students are engaged in other aspects of the process. As students

Figure 4. Demonstrating Use of a Quadrat During the OPIHI Teacher Workshop

gain new knowledge through investigation, the process of sharing it both within and beyond their community constitutes instruction.

An essential element of the project-based learning used in OPIHI is that the final products developed by students (which are also used for assessment of learning) are performance-based and tied into the authenticity of the project. ULS students, for example, have developed final projects that included scientific poster sessions (Baumgartner 2003). Students' final projects should summarize what they did as the public record of their work and document gains in both content and skills knowledge. Student posters, for example, include an overview of the project goals, the methods used and the rationale for those methods, a description of the data patterns with an analysis of those patterns, and an overall evaluation of their success with the project. In short, the poster itself should reflect the complete scientific inquiry cycle in which the students have immersed themselves to answer their questions. By planning a public exhibition to share their projects with a larger community, including their families, scientific experts, and students in other science classes, the students also have an opportunity to answer questions about their work and to provide feedback on the other projects conducted by their peers.

Student peer review emphasizes the importance of clear communication and instruction and also underscores the role of the scientific community. Students should have the opportunity to provide peer reviews of all final projects, with justification of their reviews. This requires all students to think critically about their own work in addition to that of their colleagues. While reviewing the work of others, students also think about how their own work compares, what they did well, and where they could improve.

This portion of the project can also help increase community awareness, as the student products are used to disseminate information on the intertidal zone in the community. An audience beyond the classroom also increases the authenticity of the experience and augments student engagement. When students know their work is being shared before a larger audience, they tend to be more engaged in performing at a high level. The willingness of the instructors to share the students' work with a larger audience also demonstrates belief in the students' abilities to conduct scientific investigations.

The Flexibility of OPIHI

OPIHI is designed to be flexible and fit within the goals of the class or school. The primary educational objective of the project is to build scientific literacy by getting students to develop and conduct a scientific study, but that study is not prescribed. Because the field data collection does require a particular set of skills, the one commonality of OPIHI projects is that students need to participate in a series of lessons to prepare them for fieldwork. Although all OPIHI participants have access to the same resources and strategies, and all participants engage in some form of monitoring, individual schools have used the program to span a wide variety of questions.

Conducting a project is an extremely rich experience for students and teachers, but is of necessity a time-consuming instructional method. The flexibility of the OPIHI program has also been necessary because of the time required and because individual classrooms need to tailor the project to their curricular schedules. The long-term aspect of the project is advantageous when OPIHI projects serve as platforms for study of other topics. When content-specific lesson plans are tied into the project, students share a common experience and foundation for constructing new knowledge. For example, students at one OPIHI school built model food webs of their intertidal organisms on the classroom wall as a way to examine food webs and trophic dynamics within the system they had come to know very well.

Incorporating Other Disciplines

One way in which OPIHI can be adapted for use in different formats is that a project can be made integrative and incorporate elements from other disciplines such as mathematics, language arts, the fine arts, and social studies. Sampling techniques and statistical analysis of biodiversity provide opportunities to integrate mathematics curricula within the project. Additionally, when students participate in the dissemination of their results, they must exercise their spoken communication skills, as well as their writing, graphic, and fine motor skills to develop reports, presentations, posters, or brochures. Lastly, when examining human pressures on the intertidal system, students must consider a wide variety of sociological factors.

During the second year of the project at ULS, the school received a small grant from the Hawaii Invasive Species Committee to monitor invasive algae. The students wanted to find out more about how the intertidal zone had changed over a longer period of time than the single year in which they had been monitoring. They asked their social studies teacher to help them develop a sociological survey about intertidal use practices. The survey contained questions for community members, including elders. They were asked about the intertidal community when they were young, what kinds of resources they used from the intertidal zone, and how they perceived the current status of those resources as well as other intertidal changes. The students found that there had been, over a span of about 60 years (according to the oldest person surveyed), some reductions in both abundance and diversity of intertidal algae and edible mollusks in the intertidal zone. The students' monitoring data showed large populations of certain kinds of invasive algae throughout the sites they sampled. This combination of the natural and social sciences enabled the students to put their data into a more human perspective.

Site Adoption and Site-Specific Problems

When Farrington High School, a large urban public school, joined the OPIHI effort in 2004, they developed a new model of investigation by adopting a site to monitor through repeated visits during the year, in contrast to the visits to multiple sites made by ULS. The school is in an area with a strong community identity, and their teacher wanted to capitalize on that sense of identity to engage them in a site-based project grounded in their local community. The most easily visited site was also one near the school, which required a five-minute bus ride. Following their first trip to the site, the area was affected by a large sewage spill. By a serendipitous coincidence, the students had collected data on the benthic community of algae and invertebrates prior to this spill. Following reopening of the site by the State Department of Health, they were able to return and gather data to assess the impact of the spill on the area's intertidal organisms.

As more schools from different geographic areas (including neighbor islands) have joined OPIHI, it has enabled the collection of data to examine patterns of intertidal diversity and abundance across space and time. Some schools have undertaken projects to develop field guides and identification cards that are specific to their island or even to a particular site. Other schools have focused on monitoring particular species at individual sites. Overall, the site adoption model has been engaging for students who identify with sites in their communities and through the network of other OPIHI schools. Students have gained the opportunity to learn how their site compares to others in the state, beginning the process of local to global connection.

Science Clubs and Alternative Programs

Some OPIHI schools have used the project as a way to structure alternative activities for students. Some schools may not be able to work the OPIHI activities into the regular curriculum, but have taken the option of making it the focus of a club or free-choice learning opportunity. Kahuku Intermediate School, a rural public school that joined OPIHI in 2005, used OPIHI as a basis for science club activities. The science club conducted the OPIHI activities after school, investigating intertidal organisms, learning sampling techniques, and monitoring a nearby intertidal site. The teacher advising the club wanted to use OPIHI to provide a means for the students to develop science fair projects. Each individual or pair of students identified a question about the intertidal zone for their project. The students received additional lessons from scientific volunteers on tagging, sampling, and experimental design. The students then spent several weeks collecting data and analyzing the results.

One of the benefits of having multiple schools involved in projects with a common theme through OPIHI is that it provides for the formation of a scientific community beyond the school. In recent years, we have been able to host multischool field trips on Saturdays late in the school year as extension activities for students who work together to sample Shark's Cove, a large protected site on Oahu's north shore. In 2006, three schools worked together to sample the site and in 2007, four schools visited the site together. As different schools focus on different aspects of OPIHI and ask different questions, this activity provides an opportunity for these students from different backgrounds and with different expertise to share what they have been learning about intertidal ecology with one another.

Meeting Diverse Learning Needs

The OPIHI project has also been adopted by ASSETS School in Honolulu. ASSETS is a private school that specializes in serving a population of students that is primarily gifted and dyslexic. However, many ASSETS students also work with a wide range of learning differences such as dysgraphia, auditory and visual processing challenges, attention-deficit disorder, and attention-deficit/hyperactivity disorder. By utilizing many of the diverse teaching approaches encompassed by OPIHI lessons, the various types of auditory, visual, and kinesthetic learning styles of students with special needs can be met. A full learning cycle of an OPIHI project allows all students to achieve success in at least one focal area. Heterogeneous groupings for work, conducted both in the science laboratory and in the field, provide each student the opportunity to become a teacher to their peers, regardless of their unique learning style.

Impact of OPIHI on Students and Science

OPIHI emphasizes the use of multidimensional assessment of student learning. Quantitative assessment of student learning at ULS, where the project has been most carefully documented, indicates both content and skill gains by students (Baumgartner and Zabin 2008). Concept inventories distributed to ULS students have shown significant gains in student content knowledge about intertidal ecology. Likewise, assessment of writing samples via a rubric has also shown significant gains in skills knowledge, pertaining to both general scientific investigation skills and sampling skills. Concept inventories completed by students at other schools have shown gains in content knowledge similar to those of the ULS students, although different concepts show different degrees of gain depending on the goals and emphasis of the project. ULS students have demonstrated increases in knowledge sophistication and correcting of misconceptions following independent study of taxonomic groups through OPIHI. Their performance on unit exams of concepts taught through the OPIHI thematic unit was no lower than on those taught through more traditional instruction (Baumgartner and Zabin 2008). This assessment data, summarized in Table 3, indicates that students can learn very effectively through the OPIHI model.

In spring 2007, project volunteers distributed surveys to 200 students participating in OPIHI projects at five schools. Using a scale of 1 (not at all) to 5 (very well), students rated their ability to identify invertebrates (mean rating = 3.85) and algae (mean rating = 3.60) with the help of ID cards and books and to use sampling techniques (mean rating = 3.92). Students were generally confident of their sampling abilities and felt that they would be able to monitor any new intertidal area they might encounter (mean rating = 3.81).

Much of the OPIHI data on student achievement are qualitative and related to student products. But, the scientific results of the projects are considered to be one element of their achievement. OPIHI students have presented their data or other products related to their projects in different venues. Students at ULS, for example, have presented data from their projects in several venues outside of school, including presenting to students beginning OPIHI at other schools, at a graduate seminar series at UHM, and even as a peer-reviewed poster in a regional

Table 3. Summary of Student Assessment at ULS (Baumgartner and Zabin 2008)

Assessment	Statistical test	Result
Concept inventory: 50 concepts self-reported on Likert scale of 1 (Never heard of concept) to 5 (could teach another)	2-sample unpaired t-test comparing pre-post project using pooled aggregate 2003 and 2004 classes (n = 104)	t = 17.7; df = 105; p ≤ 0.0001
Writing Sample: "How would you conduct a thorough study of the intertidal zone?" assessed via rubric for awareness of safe practices, scientific methods, and sampling methods	Chi-square comparing pre-post project in 2003 (n = 51) and 2004 (n = 48)	2003 awareness: p ≤ 0.0001 2003 science: p = 0.0026 2003 sampling: p ≤ 0.0001 2004 awareness: p ≤ 0.0001 2004 science: p = 0.0003 2004 sampling: p = 0.0003
Content knowledge: Lists about taxonomic groups to compare number of concepts listed, misconceptions and corrections listed, and number of concepts gaining sophistication	2-sample paired t-test comparing pre-project, post-book research, and post-field research	<u>Concepts listed</u> Pre/post book research t = 12.80; df = 93; p ≤ 0.0001 Pre-post field research t = 14.00; df = 95; p ≤ 0.0001 <u>Misconceptions corrected</u> Pre/post book research t = 4.90; df = 93; p = 0.0002 <u>Book-field research</u> t = 1.09; df = 92; p = 0.1389 <u>Sophistication gains</u> Book-field research t = 5.02; df = 94; p ≤ 0.0001
Exam scores: Project-based unit exam comparison to traditional unit	2-sample paired t-test comparing exam scores of lecture-based unit versus project-based unit	t = 0.919, df = 207, p = 0.179

scientific conference (Baumgartner and Zabin 2008). A group of Maui students wrote up their OPIHI activities for a feature article in their school paper.

OPIHI students at ASSETS School have also created scientific posters for a research symposium to demonstrate what they have learned about intertidal ecology to their peers in the fourth, fifth, and sixth grades. Each middle-school student involved in the OPIHI project used the preliminary data he or she generated on an initial field trip to generate specific questions that each was interested in answering on subsequent field trips to the same intertidal site. This process encouraged "ownership" of the project and fueled the curiosity that lead to the development of the research symposium. The symposium was designed as an opportunity for students to share the results of their projects in a semiformal setting with peers of their own grade level and to slightly younger students. By presenting and receiving feedback on the knowledge they had gained throughout the program, students were able to reinforce the concepts learned in a constructivist framework. The symposium also gave students the opportunity to act as science instructors. Further, this process cultivated curiosity about the OPIHI program in the younger students, who will have the opportunity to participate in OPIHI in the coming years. Lastly, the posters and presentations in the symposium served as a direct assessment tool for teachers to evaluate the depth of each student's learning.

OPIHI also has the potential to impact student attitudes. The 200 students taking the 2007 survey responded to the statement "I have become more interested in the intertidal zone as a result of learning about it and going on field trips" with a mean rating of 4.05 on a scale of 1 (strongly disagree) to 5 (strongly agree). Student responses to the open-ended question, "What do you know now about the intertidal zone that you didn't know before?" demonstrate the types of learning that took place:

"That it wasn't really just a dead place but it a beautiful place with a lot of creature [sic] and marine animals, and algae living there. I never thought it would have been that interesting."

"Before I thought that the intertidal area didn't have a lot of organisms, now from what I learned I know I can identify and relate with the organisms that lives [sic] there."

"I mostly learned about marine animals. I didn't know there were any dangerous creatures except wana [sea urchins] and jellyfish. I learned to be much more careful about which animals I choose to hold or touch. I also discovered transects and quadrats, which were really cool, too!"

"It is hard work being accurate about the information you record."

In an attitude survey given to OPIHI students at ULS in 2003 and 2004, when students were asked the question, "What do you know now that you didn't know before?" Nearly one-third (31%) of the students commented on the interconnectedness of ecological systems like the intertidal zone, demonstrating that participation in a biodiversity monitoring project linked to instruction in ecology can help bridge the growing gap between humans and the environment. One of the major learning outcomes cited by students is also a major scientific goal of the project. Students noted the pride they took in adding to the body of knowledge about Hawaii's intertidal diversity. As the project originated partially to fill a gap in intertidal research in Hawaii, the students' ownership of that goal confirms that we have managed to successfully align the scientific and educational goals of the program.

Indeed, the scientific impact of OPIHI, and the outcomes produced by the students and the scientists with whom they have partnered are substantial. In what is to our knowledge the first broadscale study of intertidal species richness in Hawaii, more than 500 taxa of fish, invertebrates, and macroalgae have been collected and identified by the students and verified by scientific volunteers. The species lists have high rates of endemism, particularly among the invertebrate species. Further, a considerable proportion of species (about 9% of algae and 11% of invertebrates) are nonnative or cryptogenic. While many of the invaders have distributions limited to one site, several species of algae and a species of barnacle have become widespread and are frequently among the most abundant organisms at many sites.

Questions about the validity and reliability of data collected by students are one of the primary challenges of conducting a program like OPIHI that seeks to gather scientifically useful data through student projects (Harnik and Ross 2003; Lawless and Rock 1998). Projects like OPIHI need to ensure that the data collected is valuable to the researchers, while the experience of gathering it is still meaningful to the students (Penuel and Means 2004; Lawless and Rock 1998). Moreover, part of the power of such a project is the empowerment of students when they realize they can do real science. This power can be lost when student data is not used in an authentic capacity (Harnik and Ross 2003).

In 2007, researchers Erin Cox and Joanna Philippoff designed a study to examine the validity of the data collected by OPIHI students (2008). Working independently, students and two researcher teams simultaneously collected data on diversity and abundance of intertidal organisms using the same standard OPIHI sampling techniques. The study used variation between researcher teams as a benchmark to compare students' abundance and diversity values. This comparison indicated that abundance estimates did not differ significantly between researchers and students (paired t-test, n = 7, p = 0.45). Researchers tend to estimate greater diversity than students but these differences were not statistically significant (paired t-test, n = 8, p = 0.18). These results indicate that student data is accurate for dominant species with high abundances.

In a detailed examination of 233 student data sheets from multiple years, including different schools and sites, to determine what kinds of errors students were most likely to make, we found that the majority of errors were related to sloppy data collection rather than errors in identification or methodology (Philippoff, Banngartner, and Cox 2008). These sloppy errors, like neglecting to record site conditions or failing to record scientific names, are easily addressed and corrected through instruction. Moreover, student errors were tied to a few specific aspects of instruction or student experience, such as having more opportunity to practice sampling techniques, and provide us with ways to improve instruction for better data collection in the future.

OPIHI: Looking Ahead

Over the past six years, OPIHI has grown from a class project to a statewide program and has expanded to over a dozen schools on four islands. While early OPIHI projects relied heavily on project volunteers, primarily GK–12 fellows, recent efforts have been implemented to increase the use and sustainability of the OPIHI effort in Hawaii.

The original OPIHI Website (*www.hawaiiintertidal.org*) introduced the project and provided background information on intertidal research. The current site (*www.hawaii. edu/gk-12/opihi*), hosted long-term by UHM, includes the background and rationale for the project, tips for starting a project, lesson plans to connect OPIHI projects to content outlined by national and state standards, and data sheets that are aligned to different geographic sites throughout the Hawaiian islands. This site has enabled teachers to conduct OPIHI projects with less on-site support from project volunteers. As the project continues to grow, with more teachers independently taking on OPIHI activities, we have recognized the need for an online database to allow students to input their data directly and to download and compare with other schools' data.

The website also provides information for OPIHI science volunteers who are willing and available to assist on field trips. These science volunteers have been an essential part of many OPIHI projects and their involvement has made this project possible. One of the necessary goals of OPIHI is to continue to connect teachers with science volunteers if they desire the help. The website is one venue that has enabled us to make volunteering easier for these scientists. Teachers can also contact project volunteers who will send e-mail notices to the list of science volunteers about upcoming field trips. We find that as teachers continue to use OPIHI activities with their students, they require less assistance from the volunteers. However, the volunteers are still valuable, especially in providing assistance to start-up projects.

In 2007, funded by the Bernice P. Bishop Museum Education Through Cultural and Historic Organizations program, the first OPIHI Workshop for teachers introduced 25 teachers and informal educators to the OPIHI project. Organized and conducted by Joanna Philippoff, the workshop provided background on the OPIHI goals and rationale; taught teachers how to use and facilitate the OPIHI sampling methods; and provided experience in collecting, handling, and identifying invertebrates and algae.

Participants completing pre- and postworkshop surveys demonstrated significant gains in confidence using OPIHI strategies (Table 4, below). When asked on an evaluation survey to respond on a scale from 1 (strongly disagree) to 5 (strongly agree), "How useful was the workshop?" the average participant response (n = 19) was 4.89. We have learned that at least five participants (20%) have been using OPIHI as a theme for their own scientific inquiry projects. These include adaptation of the OPIHI strategies for microbial sampling and connections to Hawaiian ethnobotany and traditional uses of intertidal *limu* (algae). One of the OPIHI projects developed by a teacher in the workshop was recently featured in the *Envision Community Connections* publicity video produced by Hawaii Coral Reef Initiative and Mililani High School.

Table 4. Gains in Confidence Using OPIHI Methods Reported by Workshop Participants

| Statements
I am confident in my ability to:	N	Sign Test for Median
teach science as inquiry	15	p = 0.0195
teach project-based learning	15	p = 0.0625
teach sampling techniques	14	p = 0.002
monitor (survey) a newly discovered area	15	p = 0.0017

In addition to the OPIHI workshop held at Bishop Museum, the Curriculum Research and Development Group has also incorporated OPIHI activities into the *Fluid Earth/Living Ocean* and *Teaching Science as Inquiry: Aquatic Science* professional development series. The use of

OPIHI activities in these venues have helped increase the emphasis on sampling as a way to learn ecology and highlight the importance and availability of the intertidal zone as a model site for ecological study. As part of this effort, OPIHI activities were recently featured through the Hawaii Interactive Television Series, *Teaching Science Through Inquiry*.

While OPIHI projects emphasize the use of inexpensive, easily acquired materials, there are still some costs associated with field activities, including busses and substitute teachers. As the GK–12 program previously paid many of these costs, this has been one of our biggest concerns for sustaining OPIHI. To address these issues, we have established a "lending library" of equipment and field guides available for requested use by teachers, and the OPIHI website also includes resources to help teachers construct their own equipment. In 2007, ReefCheck Hawaii generously adopted OPIHI as one of its outreach efforts, and has budgeted funds to support the costs of teachers using OPIHI in their classes. With our partners in ReefCheck Hawaii, we are also engaged in an ongoing search for funding to continue the support of the OPIHI project. We anticipate that as the program continues to grow that a full-time project coordinator position will be needed to provide information for teachers, connect them to science volunteers, manage data entry, coordinate assessment data, and disseminate information about the project, which are all roles now filled by volunteers.

Summary

Contrary to the opening chapters of many science textbooks, true scientific investigation rarely proceeds in a step-by-step fashion. The OPIHI framework and the learning cycle in which it is grounded represent the often nonlinear process of science. During an investigation, new questions are often initiated and the interpretation of data leads to the invention of new hypotheses or study. The flexibility of the OPIHI project allows for this aspect of the scientific process, while still providing a real research context that is meaningful and relevant. This aspect of the project has led to changes in the various OPIHI projects in different venues over the years while still allowing for widespread monitoring of Hawaii's intertidal zone. Most importantly, instruction in both process and content of science is embedded throughout the OPIHI project and is ongoing and multidirectional. OPIHI students teach one another as they learn about and take ownership of intertidal organisms and sites. The power of OPIHI as a thematic foundation for answering different kinds of questions while still contributing to the larger body of scientific knowledge about Hawaii's intertidal zones is highlighted by several examples from different schools' use of OPIHI to meet their own learning goals.

We close this chapter with a passage from *The Log from the Sea of Cortez* by John Steinbeck (1951, p. 92) that eloquently summarizes the power of scientific inquiry we have seen through the OPIHI project:

> *It is easy to remember when we were small and lay on our stomachs beside a tide pool and our minds and eyes went so deeply into it that size and identity were lost, and the creeping hermit crab was our size and the tiny octopus a monster. Then the waving algae covered us and we hid under a rock at the bottom and leaped out as fish. It is very possible that we, and even those who probe space with equations, simply extend this wonder.*

Acknowledgments

OPIHI has been funded by NSF training grant #0232016, the Hawaii Community Foundation, the Hawaii Invasive Species Committee, the Bernice P. Bishop Museum Education through Cultural & Historic Organizations program, and ReefCheck Hawaii. We wish to thank the many OPIHI teachers and students for their energy, enthusiasm, and feedback. Many thanks go to the generosity of the science volunteers from the UHM Ecology, Evolution & Conservation Biology Program, the UHM Marine Option Program, the Bishop Museum Natural Science Division, the Kohala Center, the Hawaii Institute of Marine Biology, Mokupapapa Discovery Center, and the Hawaiian Islands Humpback Whale National Marine Sanctuary. The authors particularly wish to thank Ken Kaneshiro for his gracious support of our activities, Ken Longenecker for supporting and assisting with coordination of the OPIHI workshop, and Blu Forman and Norine Yeung for design and support of the OPIHI websites.

References

American Association for the Advancement of Science (AAAS). 1990. *Science for all Americans*. New York: Oxford University Press.

Barab, S. A., K. E. Hay, M. G. Barnett, and K. Squire. 2001. Constructing virtual worlds: Tracing the historical development of learner practices/understandings. *Cognition and Instruction* 19 (1): 47–94.

Barab S. A., and A. L. Luehmann. 2003. Building sustainable science curriculum: Acknowledging and accommodating local adaptation. *Science Education* 87 (4): 454–467.

Baumgartner, E. 2003. Student poster sessions. *The Science Teacher* 71 (3): 39–41.

Baumgartner, E., and C. J. Zabin. 2006. Visualizing zonation patterns. *The Science Teacher* 73 (6): 60–64.

Baumgartner, E., and C. J. Zabin. 2008. A case study of project-based instruction in the ninth grade: A semester-long study of intertidal biodiversity. *Environmental Education Research* 14 (2): 97–114.

Cox, T. E., and J. K. Philippoff. 2008. Evaluation of the accuracy of student-generated data from a Hawaiian intertidal monitoring project. Paper presented at the Hawaii Educational Research Association Annual Meeting, Honolulu.

Curriculum Research and Development Group (CRDG). 2005. *Teaching science as inquiry: Astronomy inquiry guide*. Honolulu: CRDG.

Harnik, P.G., and R. M. Ross. 2003. Assessing data accuracy when involving students in authentic paleontological research. *Journal of Geoscience Education* 51 (1): 76–84.

Hawaii Department of Education (HIDDE). 2005. *Hawaii state content and performance standards for science III*. Honolulu: Hawaii Department of Education.

Lawless, J. G., and B. N. Rock. 1998. Student scientist partnerships and data quality. *Journal of Science Education and Technology* 7 (1): 5–13.

Linn, M. C., and N. B. Songer. 1993. How do students make sense of science? *Merrill-Palmer Quarterly* 39: 47–73.

National Research Council (NRC). 1996. *National science education standards*. Washington, DC: National Academy Press.

Paine, R. T. 1966. Food web complexity and species diversity. *American Naturalist* 100: 65–75.

Paine, R. T. 1969. A note on trophic complexity and species diversity. *American Naturalist* 103: 91–93.

Passmore, C., and J. Stewart. 2000. *A course in evolutionary biology: Engaging students in the "practice" of evolution*. Madison, WI: Wisconsin University National Center for Improving Student Learning and Achievement in Math and Science.

Payne, P. G. 2006. Environmental education and curriculum theory. *The Journal of Environmental Education* 37 (2): 25–35.

Penuel, W. R., and B. Means. 2004. Implementation variation and fidelity in an inquiry science program: Analysis of *GLOBE* Data Reporting Patterns. *Journal of Science Education & Technology* 41 (3): 294–315.

Philippoff, J. K., E. Baumgartner, and T. E. Cox. 2008. An analysis of common student technical errors in field data collection. Paper presented at the Hawaii Educational Research Association Annual Meeting, Honolulu.

Pottenger, F. M., and K. Berg. 2006. Inservice training in science inquiry. Paper presented at the Pacific Circle Consortium Conference, Mexico City.

Osborn, D. A., J. S. Pearse, and C. Roe. 2001. Monitoring the rocky intertidal with high school students and other volunteer groups. Paper presented at the Society for Conservation Biology annual meeting,Hilo, Hawaii.

Sandoval, W. A., and K. Morrison. 2003. High School students' ideas about theories and theory change after a biological inquiry unit. *Journal of Research in Science Teaching* 40 (4): 369–392.

Schoedinger, S., F. Cava, and B. Jewell. 2006. The need for ocean literacy in the classroom. *The Science Teacher* 73 (6): 44–47.

Steinbeck, J. 1951. *The log from the sea of Cortez*. New York: Penguin.

Tytler, R. 2002. Teaching for understanding in science: Constructivist/conceptual change teaching approaches. *Australian Science Teachers' Journal* 48 (4): 30–35.

Windschitl, M., K. Dvornich, A. E. Ryken, M. Tudor, and G. Koehler. 2007. A comparative model of field investigations: Aligning school science inquiry with the practices of contemporary science. *School Science and Mathematics* 107 (1): 382–390.

Enhancing the Inquiry Experience: Authentic Research in the Classroom

Karen E. Johnson
Niver Creek Middle School

Michael P. Marlow
University of Colorado

nquiry in science classrooms involves the ability to pose a question, explore phenomena relating to the question, acquire new understandings, communicate new ideas, and relate or compare ideas with what other scientists have found (NRC 2000). The Endangered Lake Fish (ELF) project is a collaborative, authentic inquiry that integrates science, mathematics, social studies, language arts, and technology through engaging students in breeding and investigations of Lake Victoria cichlids. Cichlids are freshwater fish found throughout the world. The cichlids used in the ELF project included species of yellow scrappers, hippo point salmon and blue glint, originally found in Lake Victoria, Africa. Students participated in a variety of authentic inquiry activities during the school year, and at the culminating celebration the student-developed inquiries were presented at Inquiry Day held at the university.

Endangered Lake Fish Project (ELF): Essential Features of Inquiry

The ELF project has incorporated the *More Emphasis* conditions (NRC 1996) in a variety of ways. The strength in the ELF project fostered individual student's interests and experiences. Student-generated research questions related to the cichlids promote scientific knowledge and understanding. Doing authentic research in the classroom enriched student understanding about the natural world. Students used scientific processes to make decisions and extend their own understanding through scientific inquiries. The ELF project provided a variety of opportunities for students to debate scientific concerns through the use of case studies. These case studies were designed as detailed narrative accounts of a dilemma or experience that was sufficiently substantive and complex to allow for multiple levels of analysis and interpretation. Furthermore, these case studies were designed to engage students in authentic science inquiries that allowed them to better explore the social complexities of this topic.

The ELF project continuously assessed student understanding and involved students throughout the process through the use of scoring rubrics and peer reviews. The community of learners consisted of a shared responsibility of learning among teachers, students from across the country via e-mail, and the scientific community at the university level.

Teachers worked collaboratively to enhance their science programs at their schools and within their classrooms. At the beginning of the program, the primary goal for many teachers was to set up the aquarium and keep the cichlids alive. As teachers communicated collaboratively, they learned about cichlid care. Also, their goals became more complex and inquiry-based as well. The most successful classrooms were those in which teachers were learning along with their students and in situations in which teachers provided support and encouragement to student questions and inquiries.

ELF Participants

The ELF project community consisted of approximately 60 classrooms, from grades 1 to 12, throughout Colorado and Michigan. Classrooms in the Denver area represented schools from five area school districts. Students participating in this project represented broad ethnic diversity and included native and nonnative English learners from a wide range of socioeconomic levels. Teachers participating in the ELF project included veteran teachers and novice teachers with various experiences with providing open inquiry in their classrooms. The project provided teacher workshops, background informational manuals, project-specific case studies, aquaria and associated equipment, and endangered Lake Victoria cichlids for each classroom.

Many of the classrooms used this project throughout the year from the first weeks of school to teach students about scientific processes, and ending the year with a culmination of student developed inquiry projects. The following two scenarios are examples of a day in a Michigan and a Colorado classroom. They represent many similar days in other ELF classrooms.

Classroom Scenario 1

What an exciting day at Montcalm Elementary fifth grade! All homework and lesson plans went "right out the window" related Paul Cook, the teacher. His students, along with students in 60 other Michigan and Colorado classrooms were part of a project investigating a number of species of endangered Lake Victoria cichlids. Each classroom had at least one aquarium with the endangered fish. The species of Lake Victorian cichlids in the Montcalm classroom was called the blue glint. These had not reproduced for anyone in the project up to that exciting day.

On this day, one of the students noticed that the male blue glint was being very territorial with the rock in the tank. He had all the females over to the other side of the tank with the exception of one. He was jerking and convulsing all around her—doing his "dance" thing! The students recognized that this action was very typical of the breeding behavior of the other types of cichlids. They quickly set up the camcorder in order to tape any breeding that took place. As the class reported, "The video we got was super! We actually caught the female laying her eggs on the rock and then picking them up in her mouth! The eggs were clearly seen!" As part of the student's research agenda, the class had been providing eggs from the Lake Victoria cichlids to a University of California research study. One student summarized,

We discussed as a class what we should do with these eggs. It was decided by an overwhelming majority that we would attempt to raise these fish (since no one in schools had ever done that before) instead of sending them to Dr. Coleman for his egg research. We did feel a little bad

however, that he still did not have any samples of Blue Glint cichlid eggs for his research. We watched the video (awesome close-ups!) over and over again all morning long. Suddenly one of the students noticed what no one else had. The female missed some of the eggs! We watched the video even closer. Just as the student had pointed out, at one point, the female laid about five eggs on the rock but before she could pick them up in her mouth, they were caught in the current and swept off the rock. The female never chased them down. Instead we watched as a couple of the eggs were sucked up the filter tube. Students all over the room immediately scrambled to the tank to see if any of the other eggs were loose on the aquarium floor. We found one egg on the tank bottom and two in the filter, stuck to the sponge. We discussed whether or not these eggs would hatch. The class determined that since we saw no visible sign that these eggs were fertilized by the male (remember they were just laid by the female) that they were "duds," as useless as chicken eggs. Suddenly, another student had a brilliant thought. Why not send these eggs to Dr. Coleman! It was great! Students began cheering so loudly that we had to close our room door! We could raise our babies and still contribute to Dr. Coleman's egg research! We packed the three eggs into the alcohol vials and labeled them "unfertilized" and sent them out to Dr. Coleman.

Classroom Scenario 2

The Mountain View Elementary students were the first Colorado students to have baby hippo point cichlids born in their classroom. When Judy Kelly, the first-grade teacher, entered the room early that morning she noticed small, almost clear objects swimming in a circle at the bottom of her aquarium. What were they, she wondered? She realized that they were baby cichlids. Her first thought was how exciting it will be to show the students when they arrive. She then decided that it might be better to let them discover the new babies themselves. Standing by the door as her students trooped into the room, with many stopping to peer into the aquarium to greet the fish, she anxiously waited for one to discover the new babies. No one said anything as they settled into their desks. Judy wondered if she should tell the class, but the decision was not needed on her part as a late-arriving student stopped at the tank and exclaimed, "We have babies!" That was not to be the last decision taken away from her that morning. The students rushed to the tank, talking excitedly to each other. "The rest of the school has to be told. We have to get messages to the other classrooms about our babies. We have to send Dr. Mike a message right away, and he needs to know that there are baby cichlids in a Colorado aquarium." Students began suggesting that some send the messages and some would draw what the baby fish looked like. A number of students returned to their desks and began writing in their journals. A group decision was made to record an announcement with the video cam to be sent over the schoolwide system. Finally Mrs. Kelly was needed. "Where is the class video cam?" The students discussed who would be in front of the camera making the report and what would be included in the report. The teacher decided to let things continue. All the students were excitedly involved in various aspects of reporting, gathering data, and drawing pictures. "So much for the morning plans," Mrs. Kelly thought to herself. After a number of "takes" the group decided that the video was a good report and sent it to the office for the rest of the school to find out about the great event. Finally, internet messages were sent and observational data recorded and the class was ready to go on with the day.

Unique Features of the ELF Project
1. *Scientifically Oriented Questions*

One of the strongest aspects of the ELF project is the ability to engage students in scientifically oriented questions. Each classroom participating in the ELF project received a 29-gallon aquarium, heater, filter, and thermometer. Once the classroom aquarium was established, teachers arranged to have the fish brought in. The day the fish arrived was always filled with excitement and anticipation. Students would ask questions regarding the cichlids and teachers would record student questions to use as a guide for student investigations. In order to foster this engagement, students became acquainted with the issues surrounding the community of Lake Victoria, Africa. The primary method of fostering this engagement consisted of the use of case studies written on a student level and focusing on some of the pertinent issues surrounding Lake Victoria and the endangerment of the African cichlids.

Teachers used case studies as a means for engaging students in the issues surrounding the endangerment of the cichlids. The case studies helped students identify potential problems found throughout the case and helped students make connections among the issues. For example, in a sixth-grade classroom, students brainstormed the list of potential problems and created concept maps regarding how the issues are related to one another.

The use of case studies with diverse language learners requires additional supports. In one classroom the teacher restructured the case study into a two-column format, allowing space on each page for concept development. The case studies were further chunked into numbered paragraphs, allowing students an easy means to refer to their source of ideas and inferences. First modeled and then guided by the teacher, students learned to highlight key words and phrases, write summary statements, sketch summary pictures, define new vocabulary, write questions, and pose possible solutions to the unfolding problem. As one student expressed,

> "When you read a book, kids get bored and seem less involved and kind of quit on it. When you are doing it as a group (case study), it's so exciting because these are real, live creatures you're working with and that makes it more fun."

Another student in a different class that did not use the supports used by the diverse language teacher expressed a similar idea saying,

> "The stories are different from the book. You see different things, and maybe you imagine something different"

One lesson learned from this example is the importance of using a case study, within the context of an inquiry. In this case, real endangered fish engaged the students. The support of a case study allowed the diverse language learners to reach the same conclusions and understandings regarding the situation in Lake Victoria.

In some of the classrooms, after students preliminarily created their own connections with the case study characters, students were given roles to play in a town meeting forum. The main actors of the town meeting included the native fisherman, the Nile perch, the cichlids, a tourist, a commercial fisherman, a scientist and the government. Students played their roles and discussed solutions to the problem of cichlids dying in Lake Victoria.

In all classrooms, after the cases were processed and students had displayed an understanding of the endangered lake fish dilemma, students brainstormed their own scientific questions that potentially could be investigated through the cichlids in their classroom. This process started with observations of the cichlids' behavior. Observations included behavior characteristics such as the area of the tank that the cichlids would stay most often, what food they liked to eat, and whether or not the cichlids could see or hear. Table 1 illustrates the depth of student questions regarding the endangered lake fish.

Table 1. Sample of Student Questions

Sample of Third-Grade Student Questions
I wonder why do they turn white?
How can we know if our fish is a female or male?
How do we weigh fish?
How do we take care of fish?
Sample of Sixth-Grade Student Questions
Drums and whistles: What sounds and how long do fish hear?
Fake fish and sharks: How do fish act when they see something?
How do fish act at night in the dark and when they wake up in the light?
Do cichlids see color?

2. *Priority Given to Evidence in Responding to Questions*

One powerful aspect of the ELF project included the use of student questions to investigate the cichlids and the ability to allow students to write testable questions and to determine how to collect data in order to answer the questions posed. The most challenging part of this step included the importance of allowing time for students to develop their question and determine how they would carry out their designs. The teachers' role consisted of assisting and supporting students in creating testable questions and providing support and materials in order for students to carry out their investigations. Students were also able to communicate with other students involved in the ELF project to create questions and to design investigations. An e-mail system was used to foster student conversations and promote dialogue among students from different schools and across states.

Student questions were categorized into research-based questions and scientifically designed questions. Students choose one question to investigate and designed their own procedures for collecting data. For example, one group of students wanted to determine how fish react to a house in the tank. Students had to determine the best method for answering their question and for keeping track of the number of fish inside the house and outside the house every minute for 17 minutes. Table 2 illustrates student data collected for this experiment.

Table 2. How Will Fish React to a House in the Tank?

	Minutes																
	1	2	3	4	5	6	7	8	9	10	11	12	13	14	15	16	17
In	1	2	4	3	1	0	1	0	2	3	4	2	1	3	2	0	1
Out	3	2	0	1	3	4	3	4	2	1	0	2	3	1	2	4	3

Another group of students wanted to answer the question, "How will the fish react to fruits and vegetables?" Students had to determine how to collect evidence related to this question; they decided on the following procedures:

"We will put in chunks of fruits and vegetables in the tank and then time the cichlids. We will determine how fast they are going to eat the chunks of fruits and vegetables and time them for two different things, a cucumber and an apple."

As students made decisions regarding how to collect evidence related to their questions, they made decisions that improved their designs. This high level of thinking did not take place at the onset, and teachers' roles consisted primarily of asking questions to students in order for students to improve their data collection strategies and techniques.

3. *Explanations Formulated From Evidence*

Students formulate explanations based on the evidence they collected. This aspect of the project often included a presentation of the results in the form of a poster or PowerPoint presentation. Through presentation of material, students would continue to ask additional questions and facilitate classroom discussions to achieve scientific understanding. This provided a rich dialogue among students and deepened understanding of authentic scientific knowledge.

One topic that many students wanted to explore was how female and male fish interact with each other, in particular mating behaviors. One group of students wanted to introduce a cichlid from one tank into a new tank of cichlids. The following dialogue took place:

"Our prior knowledge is that the fish in our classroom have been trying to mate. The fish in Ms. C's classroom is the only one in the tank. We predict that our fish and Ms. C's fish will mate. We are going to take one of our female fish and put it up in Ms. C's tank with her male fish. We will watch them for a week."

Students observed the fish for 15 minutes, collecting observational data regarding how each fish acted toward one another. Students observed that within five minutes of placing the female fish in the tank with the male, the male fish began chasing the female fish and nipping at it. The students immediately removed the female fish. After a discussion of what to do next, students decided to take a larger fish to place it into the tank with the male. The following dialogue took place at then end of the second experiment:

"First our fish was being harassed by Ms. C's fish. So we got another fish and it started to harass her fish. Ms. C's fish had cuts on it. Our fish was bigger than Ms. C's fish. Then both of the fish started to clean the rock. Ms. C's fish started to get red on its side. We think our fish is a male because male fish turn red to show they are dominant."

The students created explanations based on the evidence and observations.

4. Explanations Connected to Scientific Knowledge

After collecting and discussing evidence with their peers, students typically headed to the computer and prepared e-mail conversations with other students in the project. The primary goal was to share the experiences and results, but it also provided a forum for connecting their understanding to other resources and knowledge. For example, a situation arose in which students were making observations and measurements of the length, volume, and mass of each cichlid, when one group of students noticed that there were small seeds at the bottom of the container with the fish. Students began asking questions and formulating explanations as to what they had discovered. Students decided that these "seeds" must be eggs and immediately began formulating a plan of action. A couple of students went directly to the computer to e-mail other classrooms and asked others about their experiences and successes raising eggs. Other students went to the library and collected information regarding cichlid eggs. Another group of students began brainstorming a course of action regarding the mother and the eggs. The class decided that they should place the eggs in a separate tank away from the other cichlids and discussed what the tank needed to be like to best simulate the environment inside a mother cichlid's mouth. They made decisions regarding the temperature of the water, how long the mother would remain in the tank with the eggs before they took her out, and the essential needs of the tank such as a heater and filter. They immediately went to work setting up a 10 gallon tank and transferred water from the original tank in order to create the same environmental conditions.

Each day, students would go to the tank and watch the eggs lying at the bottom. After day five, one student noticed the eggs seemed to be moving. As we watched closely, students realized that the eggs were spinning. Excitement arose throughout the classroom and students decided they needed to videotape their observations. Each day, they videotaped a 15-minute period of time and as the days passed, students realized they had documented the egg development of cichlids. Four of the eleven eggs hatched into tiny fry. This sparked a new series of questions for students, which they researched in the library, on the web, and with other students in other classrooms in the project.

5. Explanations Communicated and Justified

Students participating in the ELF project also had an opportunity to present and communicate their research on campus at Inquiry Day. Students refined their research and presented their projects to other students also involved in cichlid research. Inquiry Day was held during the month of May, at the University of Colorado, Denver. Students were arranged as audience members and as presenters. Students were provided with Inquiry Day T-shirts and poster boards and came to the day as experts on their project. A schedule was created for each student to present his or her project and time was allocated for each student to be an audience member for other projects. When students were not presenting or listening to presentations, they could participate in a variety of activities that tied art concepts, math, social studies, and literacy to the ELF project. Each school also received a banner to hang at their school, depicting the accomplishments of Inquiry Day and student learning.

Evidence of Student Learning

As described previously, student learning is evidenced in each aspect of the project. From the beginning stages of the inquiry, student questions provided evidence of scientific thinking. Beginning questions such as "How do we take care of cichlids?" to scientifically based questions such as, "Do cichlids see color?" guided the project. Students learned how to ask questions that would also lead to a scientific investigation. As evidenced earlier, students show higher levels of thinking through the use of case studies related to the endangered fish. For example, one sixth-grade student's explanation regarding how to solve the problems associated with Lake Victoria described the issue as follows:

> *"A lot of problems are happening at Lake Victoria right now, but I think that the biggest problem is the introduction of the Nile perch. The Nile perch eats most of the smaller fish that the village people eat, so that was one of the problems the Nile perch caused. Another problem was that the Nile perch were too big. When the village people tried to dry them out, they would get rotten because there was too much fat. The village people had to smoke the perch. The village ended up cutting down part of the forest in order to smoke the perch. The problem of the Nile perch needs to be fixed."*

This example shows higher-level thinking and the complexities of problem solving into a real issue.

As described previously, student assessment associated with the various investigation decisions was accomplished while conducting experiments with the fish. Poster presentations, PowerPoint presentations, and evaluation of other experiments lead to higher-level thinking and discussions among student groups. Students were able to effectively discuss their own research and in turn were able to question other research in a more effective manner, as compared to students who did not participate in the ELF project. For example, one middle school had six science teachers, two that participated in the ELF project and four who did not. Students participating in the ELF project scored higher on district performance-based assessments that were given to each student. The performance-based assessment evaluated the effectiveness of students in two areas: (1) conducting an investigation and (2) communicating about the investigation. Figure 1 compares the student scores of ELF classrooms and non-ELF classrooms for two years.

Additional evidence of student learning was collected throughout Inquiry Day. Approximately 50 students were interviewed regarding their attitudes about inquiry science and participation in the ELF project. Student questionnaires indicated that students were much more motivated to learn, and they learn more with the hands-on experiences and discussions regarding the ELF project as compared to lecture and textbook-format classes. Interviews with students found that more than three-quarters of the students questioned indicated that this excitement and motivation extended beyond the ELF project into other science topics. These findings have

Figure 1. Inquiry Performance Assessment

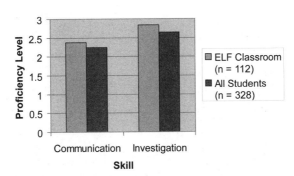

led to strong evidence indicating that authentic open-ended inquiries lead to stronger investigation and communication skills and positive attitudes toward science. These are major goals for all science teachers today and for all their students.

Summary

The ELF project incorporated many aspects of student-led inquiry research and scientific learning. This does not happen without the support of effective facilitation from the teacher. The placement of equipment and suggestion of a research topic alone will not generally result in a successful project. This is especially true in an elementary classroom (Marlow and Marlow 1996). A professional development plan must accompany the new project. This plan must contain ongoing support for the teacher both in the form of a series of planned meetings and workshops, as well as continuous assessment and a resource/information system relating to the project. The system developed for the Lake Victoria Project involved a series of meetings prior to the placement of the fish in the classrooms. Sessions were presented on general aquarium management, water chemistry in an aquarium, history of the research topic, research techniques in general and the specific research protocol for this project. E-mail connections were established for teachers and their students to communicate with the researchers and other classrooms in the project. Teacher collaboration across grade levels, socioeconomic areas, and across state boundaries encouraged all teachers involved in the ELF project.

Conclusion

Based on the implementation of the Lake Victoria experience, we have identified a number of areas that we feel should be considered in any student research project.

- All research emphasizes active, hands-on involvement of students utilizing real-world issues or materials that are meaningful to them.
- The methods used to initially engage the students and at the same time provide needed content information must actively involve the students. Passive lectures or readings will not necessarily engage the students to the degree necessary for a successful inquiry.

- In order for teachers to successfully facilitate a meaningful inquiry, they need the necessary resources, background information, and access to experts.
- If an inquiry can be connected to a number of other classrooms, student learning will be enriched and teachers will have access to "group thinking" with the other teachers in the project.
- Finally, projects should, when appropriate, contain "encourage integration across the curriculum" components to deepen understanding and offer various outcomes concerning the topic with the total school program.

References

Marlow, M. P., and S. E. Marlow. 1996. Research in the classroom. In *Issues in Science Education,* eds. J. Rhoton and P. Bowers, 88–95. Arlington, VA: National Science Teachers Association.

National Research Council. (1996). *National science education standards* Washington, DC: National Academy Press.

National Research Council. (2000). *Inquiry and the national science education standards: A guide for teaching and learning*. Washington, DC: National Academy Press.

"If We Are Supposed to Understand Science, Shouldn't We Be Doing It?"

Tina Harris
Anderson Community School Corporation

My teaching career, like many others, began with me teaching high school in a basic science classroom where the students asked this chapter's title question. The only answer I could truthfully give them was "Yes, we should be doing it," and then proceeded to do science the way I had been taught, using cookbook labs. Although I had completed a major in science at a top science and engineering university, I had never done an open inquiry activity and it did not occur to me to ask that of students, especially in a basic class. As a matter of fact, I was considered a bit of an idealist for doing any labs with my classes, but we set up ground rules and things went fairly well. My students knew the other science teachers were watching to see if we would damage their equipment so they could stop loaning it to us. We did not break anything and the students enjoyed the respect and responsibility that went with doing the lab activities.

A few years later I was transferred to a middle school. At that time the school was at the beginning of a transformation to a "Middle School Concept" and provided professional development (PD) in teaching areas I had not been previously exposed to like cooperative learning, new ideas in classroom management, alternative assessments, and thematic unit development with interdisciplinary units. Even though the PD was not science focused, it was pedagogy focused and provided tools I could immediately integrate with my hands-on science lessons for a greater emphasis on major concepts. My lessons became more like directed inquiry rather than direct instruction (NRC 2000), but my lessons were still teacher-centered.

Shortly after my school adopted teaming I attended my first of several NSF-funded professional development programs[1] that introduced me to inquiry teaching. From the beginning, we were required to assess our teaching styles using the ESTEEM protocol (Burry-Stock and Oxford 1995) before the workshop, again at the end of the following school year, and each year for three years after completion of the summer program. At first the idea of giving students complete control over their learning seemed far-fetched to me and many other teachers because

---

[1] NSF-funded workshops attended were EPIC Center (1996), INSITE (1997), and ENVISION (2001). All were conducted by researchers at Purdue University.

I initially understood it as all student-driven all the time. And of course, thinking of my more "challenging" students first, there was no way my nerves could deal with that! But, I could see my classes meeting some of the intermediate or guided inquiry goals (NRC 2000); so I decided my ultimate teaching goal would be at the intermediate level. I also decided to start with just one step at a time, be it a chapter or an entire unit, and grow from there. Each summer I chose a PD program based on the unit I wanted to improve. In this way my personal PD was a long-term plan that emphasized learning science through investigation and inquiry (NRC 1996, p. 43). The benefits of the NSF programs were that each emphasized a community of practice approach, which provided support not only during the workshop but in follow-up sessions and through e-mail collaborations.

In the process, I found I enjoyed teaching more and my students exceeded my initial expectations. I learned more from the collaborations provided than I could have ever learned through my own reading. I discovered how the use of inquiry allowed me to meet the needs of students with different learning styles or abilities in REI classes (Harris and Rowlen 2003; NRC 1996, p. 30). I also found ways to integrate aspects of some inquiry units with teachers who were members of my interdisciplinary team. I shared what I had learned and tried with other science teachers in my district and through professional meetings.

I discovered that for students to be successful I needed to introduce these new ways of thinking and doing science gradually. Students were not accustomed to being responsible for their own learning; they had always been "spoon-fed" textbook information. Students not only needed instruction as to how to do inquiry, but also in social skills that accompany inquiry types of lessons. To help them transition to a point where they and I were comfortable in a student-driven lesson, I began introducing directed and guided-inquiry activities that were as short as 30-minute lessons over a few periods. Many of these began with a direct instruction (teacher-directed) activities to introduce the concept. Based on the students, we would work our way up to activities that were close to open inquiry for some students and genuine open inquiry for those who were comfortable with that level of responsibility as a final assessment for the unit. The following sections describe how I used a short, one-class lesson to introduce a physics topic, a one-week activity on erosion, and a final unit assessment on force and motion, which lasted approximately three weeks. These are followed by some reflections and final thoughts on my use of inquiry in my middle level classroom.

A Short Lesson: Newton's Second Law

This activity was developed by a team of teachers in the late 1990s as part of an inquiry unit on force and motion during an NSF workshop on integrating technology. Students were given directions on how to construct a marble ramp using a ruler with a groove down the center and rolling a marble down it into a small paper cup with a "door" to catch it. It was based on the activity found in *Janice VanCleave's Physics for Every Kid* (VanCleave 1991). The students worked in small groups of two or three and measured the distance the cup moved as the marble rolled into it. Students ran the activity three times and averaged the results. We shared the results as a class and discussed why different groups found different results and what factors might have influenced the data. After brainstorming the factors, we reviewed which of them were manipulated and which were dependent and independent variables. Then student groups were asked to learn more about the dependent variable by choosing from the list an independent variable to change, test, and report the results to the class. Although the dependent variable was chosen by the teacher, the means of testing it, the choice of what to measure and how, and the way the group reported results to the class were chosen by the group (NRC 2000). The role of the teacher was facilitator, moving between groups suggesting ways to interpret the data, helping with equipment or set-up when needed, and answering questions or suggesting places to look for more information for the class presentations (NRC 1996, p. 32).

Assessment was based on participation and the class presentation. Class presentations were simply posters on which students listed the question they chose to investigate, the method they used, the data they collected, and how they interpreted the results. These were formative assessments based on the correct use of science-process skills we had considered, the choice of data collected, and whether or not their interpretation was based on the data presented (NRC 1996, p. 87).

The concept of acceleration was not something that eighth-grade students innately understood. Because it is not a property that can be directly measured, it must be solved for using mathematical models. Student presentations provided comments like "With a higher ramp the marble was moving faster so it had more force when it hit the cup," and "With two marbles, the cup moved farther so there must have been more force; but it was not twice as much like we thought it would be," and "The cup moved farther with a larger marble than a smaller one. Even though we didn't measure the speed of the marbles, we released them from the same height; the one used in demo last week; everything fell at almost the same time so we thought they were probably moving at the same speed; the only thing that could have caused a difference was the different weights."

Because the students were comfortable with the concept of speed, the next step of this lesson was to introduce the relationship between speed and acceleration and encourage students to think about and explain why Newton chose acceleration for his second law of motion (NRC 1996, p. 36). This inquiry lesson provided more student interest in the topic than simply reading about it in the book and provides a personal experience and a mental model for students to draw from in later lessons (Gilbert and Ireton 2003).

A Medium Length Lesson: Erosion Using Stream Tables

Sometimes an introduction activity could not be fit into a single class period and had to be spaced out over the course of the week. One example was the unit on weathering and erosion (NRC 1996, p. 158). After reading the section of the text on stream characteristics, we created stream tables to determine what factors might lead to those characteristics. During my first NSF workshop, another teacher had explained that stream tables could be improvised in the absence of funds for the "real thing" by using a variety of containers. I chose to use plastic shoeboxes for their versatility in other labs and ease of storage. I mixed a 3:1 mixture of white sand and diatomaceous earth (Figure 1), and we used cups and straws for the water source (Sneider and Barrett 1999). On the first day, students simply played with the models to learn how to use the siphon and set up the equipment successfully on their own. They were assessed for the quality of their participation. Students were intrigued with the idea of a siphon and of being able to look at stream processes at such a different scale (Harris 2006).

Figure 1. Basic Model of Stream Table in Plastic Shoebox

On the second day, I asked them to set up their stream table box, but did not give them specific instructions on how to do so, and asked them to let it run for the class period, describing the stream "as an ant would see it" every 5 minutes for 30 minutes. At the end of that time, the class discussed how their streams had changed and why they thought the changes had occurred. The assessment for this part was formative based on the detail of their group description and how they designed their stream. The quality of the observations made and analysis of student ideas of what they thought caused those changes also made the assessment formative (NRC 1996, p. 84). Students were asked to use terminology from the text to describe features they observed using their "ant vision." Because there were no specific guidelines on how to construct the stream, group results differed in the angle of the box or the volume of the water that flowed, which provided a starting point to list the factors that affected the stream development. All ideas were recorded on a poster.

The next day we reviewed the list from the day before. Students were then asked to draw from personal experiences with flowing water in local streams, streams or rivers they had visited, or simply water flowing down the street in their neighborhoods for additional factors that might affect the rates of erosion (NRC 1996, p. 220). Student groups were asked to choose a factor they felt affected the rate of erosion from the list we had developed and then to develop an experiment using the equipment provided or by bringing in additional materials. Groups used an investigation planning sheet[2] to develop their experiment or plan of action and assigned roles to group members. The goal for the plan sheet was to provide prompts for inquiry skills (NRC 2000, p. 19–22). Because of the student-developed nature of the topic (chosen from a class-developed list), students developed procedures but were also guided by worksheet prompts. Because of student choice regarding the data collection and analysis, I considered this activity to be more of a guided inquiry than the shorter activity (NRC 2000, p. 29). The only requirement provided by the instructor was that the experiment took at least 30 minutes. They could consider the data from the first day as a control if they wished. But they were told that they would have to collect data in such a way that they could compare it to whatever control they chose and use it to support their analysis and conclusions for the whole class.

Each group took photos of their "stream" and used these to create posters for their class presentation. They also had access to the computer if they wished to use a spreadsheet or graphs. They also had an option of creating an accompanying report. Figures 2–6 show the variety in the student hypotheses. Students varied the rate of flow of the water, the angle of the stream (slope), the materials through which the stream had to navigate, and the sources of flow, all of which actually affect stream flow. Some students were interested in how man-made obstacles like dams might be constructed; in the process they discovered several factors that can lead to dam failure.

---

[2] For additional information on inquiry units and inquiry planning guides mentioned in the article see references at *www.wetheteachers.com*.

Figure 2. Students compare the effects of gravel vs. only soils on stream erosion.

Figure 3. Students compare the effects of different types of paper on the flight distance of various paper airplane designs.

Figure 4. These students were interested in whether or not sunglasses advertised to block UV radiation actually did so. They designed a box with the lenses of the glasses covering a gap and a UV light above and UV sensitive beads inside that would change color if the glasses did not, in fact, block UV radiation. They tested several brands that did and did not claim to block UV.

Many groups chose to work on setting up their presentations while they ran their experiments because the class discussed using the same five-minute intervals as a control between the initial activity and their experiment. Groups were encouraged to use the textbook and other reference books to look up names for features that appeared in their streams, such as meanders, terraces, cut-banks, sandbars, deltas, and alluvial fans. Some used the class computers to find real-world examples of features to use as visual aids with their definitions. As students worked, they were reminded that they would have to teach these terms to their classmates, who may not have observed the same features in their streams.

Most groups found time to wander around the room during the activity to see what everyone else was doing and to ask questions at that time. As they visited other groups, they had the opportunity to practice with terminology (NRC 2000, pp. 22–23). Presentations were done at the conclusion of the activity. The purpose of the presentations was to provide opportunities for students to practice organizing their thoughts and speaking to groups about their experiences and for other students to ask critical questions concerning the results. The students also came up with a rubric to evaluate classmates on presentation skills such as "covering the topic" (actually telling what they would be discussing, why they explored it, and how), providing clear explanations, talking loud enough to be heard, and answering questions (NRC 1996, pp. 36–37). The presentations therefore provided students with opportunities to practice communicating results, defending explanations, and providing peer reviews. Students took so much pride in their work that they chose to take their posters home instead of leaving them with the teacher's files.

Student responses to the essay questions for this unit used terminology about stream development accurately and demonstrated much better understanding than previous lessons had. Previously, test questions where students were asked to label parts of streams would frequently go unanswered. Students who constructed streams in class and actually saw what the pictures referred to with their own eyes were better able to label stream features correctly, and some added additional features to the illustrations that were present but not labeled for response. Student evaluations of the unit indicated that students felt that the experiences with the stream tables, as well as a later field trip to a local tributary, helped them to have a better understanding and appreciation of how streams erode their environment. During that field trip some were able to point out the cut-bank and sandbar in the location selected for water monitoring.

A Long Inquiry: Force and Motion Final Project

The final project for the unit on force and motion was mirrored after the unit previously described in the short inquiry. Student groups had to develop and carry out their own inquiry investigations. First, we brainstormed the question "What makes things stop and go?" on the chalkboard. This list included references to either the forces that change motion or the devices that actually change their motion. We used sticky-notes for this step and when we were done, we went back and classified the responses as objects or forces. Student groups were then asked to look at the list created and choose one area that interested them, like planes, cars, bicycles, or falling objects, and to develop a question about that area that could be answered in ways that could be tested for validity (NRC 1996, p. 32).

Groups had to present their questions to the instructor before they were allowed to proceed to the next step, because this was the first time that each group would be undertaking unique investigations. For some groups the development of a testable question took the longest time of any part of the process except for the data collection itself. The task asked students to think in ways that they had never done on their own. Students found that although they ask questions all the time, they had never taken the time to think about how to use measurement to define an original topic. Some groups managed to develop their question in a single class period. For groups that appeared to be getting frustrated, after the first few tries they were reminded that in class we always started with identifying the variables we wanted to look at and those we wanted to control and developed our questions from those, so they should look at their own topic and do this process themselves. If they still needed assistance, the teacher was there to facilitate. Students were reminded of past successes and of the processes that worked well. Sample paragraphs showing some of the questions in the student final forms are shown in Box 1.

Box 1. Sample Student Inquiry Questions

How does mass affect the pull of gravity?
We are going to do experiments like weighting things with different masses and then dropping them to see how fast they fall. This has to do with making things stop and go because if you drop something, gravity pulls it to the Earth. When it hits the ground, the gravity is not strong enough to pull it though the Earth so it stops.

How do different designs of paper planes affect how far they fly?
We will first make many paper planes and fly them. Then we will choose three or four planes and do experiments on them. First we will add weight to the back of the plane. Then we will add weight to the front of the plane. Then we will throw the planes harder and softer to see if it changes the distance. The reason we are doing this is to see how friction can pull down the planes.

How does the shape of the boat affect the way it moves through the water?
Our question has to do with stop and go because the shape of the boat may affect the way it stops and goes and the way it moves. We are going to make different shapes of boats and see how the shape affects the way they move through water. (see below)

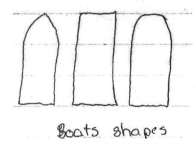

Boats shapes

One of the more interesting questions dealt with the force of water from a large "soaker" water rifle. After considering all the factors that might make the water gun work, and a discussion of why it might be difficult with the equipment available to measure the force of the water directly, the group decided on measuring the force of the water indirectly based on the distance it moved a golf ball down a track with 3 pumps, 5 pumps, and 10 pumps of air and a full tank of water. Another group discussed how they wanted to do something with their bicycles that they rode to school daily. One member brought in a story about how they had skidded on gravel earlier in the week and the group decided to determine how different surfaces affected braking distances of the bike (NRC 1996, p. 30).

Once the groups had their questions, they proceeded through the investigation planning sheet, getting teacher approval at certain points before continuing to the next step. This allowed the teacher to identify sources of difficulty before the groups had begun. The investigation planning sheet acted as a prompt to consider steps necessary to design a successful investigation (NRC 1996, p. 32).

After recording the question, the second checkpoint for the student groups was after they had completed their research to make sure the information they found was applicable to the question they developed (NRC 1996, p. 82). For the group working on the water gun problem, it was decided that they would design the experiment similar to the marble experiment discussed earlier, where measuring the velocity of the moving golf ball would give its acceleration and, knowing its mass, they could then determine the force to reach that acceleration. The students themselves recognized a means of transferring a previous class activity to solve a new problem (NRC 1996, p. 37).

The group working on the bicycle braking distance submitted several drafts, because initial drafts failed to determine all the variables they would need to control (e.g., speed prior to braking, force of braking, etc.). Because the equipment needed for measuring the force of braking directly was not available, the students decided that they would use a bike with coaster brakes (to eliminate any problems with hand grips) and apply the brake from the top of the rotation to as far as it would go downward. They also had to determine a means of using a constant speed. The group decided this would be done using a predetermined distance to speed up in a set amount of time so they would always know the speed.

Other group projects ranged from testing how sports balls of different shapes flew differently through the air when launched by a slingshot to determining how different diameter skateboard wheels affected the speed and distance it would travel after a certain amount of force. Still others stuck to more basic labs like the speed of falling objects of different shapes, and the height of a water rocket with different amounts of water added.

In the final checkpoint in the process, after the development of hypotheses and prior to the actual experiment, the student groups created lists of variables, equipment lists, and lists of responsibilities (see Box 2, p. 230). The inclusion of a responsibilities list allowed for individual participation assessment (from both teachers and other students).

Groups then began their investigations and collected the data they had decided would be most useful. The role of the teacher during this process was as facilitator. The teacher moved from group to group watching the experimentation and data collection, took photos for groups to use in their final report or for records, helped with equipment difficulties, and assisted with

Figure 5.

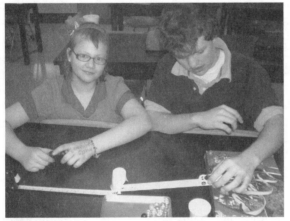

Figure 6.

Figures 5 and 6. Students first did the directed inquiry activity with a marble to see how far it moved the cup and how long it took from start to finish (Figure 5). They then decided to see if toys they brought from home, like this car, also moved the same distance in the same time. After reviewing the chapter, they decided that perhaps they should find the mass of each toy and marble and make them similar. They used larger marbles and added clay in the car until they were the same mass.

Figure 7.

Figure 7. At the end of each project, students shared their results with classmates. This student's group created a 6-page poster report. Each page covered a specific aspect of the project. Students determined the grading rubric prior to the project and how to peer-review the presentations prior to giving them.

Box 2. The Steps of Our Investigation and What Materials We Will Need

Steps	Materials
1. Measure the balls and compare sizes	• Balance • Two different-sized balls
2. Hold the balls side by side to center them	• Meterstick (for height)
3. Drop the balls at the same time	• Stopwatch
4. See which drops first	• Eyes
5. Record results	• Paper and pencil

Drawing of what our experiment will look like

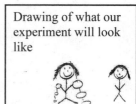

Who is responsible for which jobs?

Team member	Responsibility (in order of completion)
Ashley	Bring objects to drop
Mary	Measuring mass of objects
Cari	Measuring distance objects dropped
Natalie	Data recorder
Ashley and Cari	Make table of data and graph for report
Mary	Write report
Natalie	Make poster for presentation
Everyone	Cleanup during lab

---

general problem-solving questions. As a facilitator, one role was to ask open-ended questions concerning how the experimental data was related to the group hypotheses, how it tied in with the research the group had done prior to starting, and how it tied in with various preliminary activities or readings that had been done in class (NRC 1996, p. 32). Sometimes, if more than one group had similar projects or projects with similar hypotheses, they were asked to observe each other's activities and refer to other group projects in their final reports to the class if they thought it would help their arguments (NRC 1996, p. 46).

Assessment during the project was based on participation and peer assessment. Each group member would fill out a card assessing his or her own learning—often in comparison to other groups—using the rubric the class had developed on whether or not they successfully participated in group activities, listened, and contributed to the success of the project (NRC 1996, p. 84). Project groups were formed by the students, so many worked with friends, but that did not affect their candor in evaluation of each other. Students were amazingly honest and sometimes reported things the teacher missed while interacting with other groups. The students used the daily rubric to "fill the teacher in" on things not previously noted. One example would be "Ashley's" comment: "I would like to acknowledge [Mary]. She was the main person to help me, although [Natalie] helped too, but not as much. [Cari] didn't do hardly anything, but she did do a little bit the first day or two. After that she just sat and watched."

A final report was turned in by each individual. In it, each student used the information from the research and data collected to make conclusions concerning the investigation the group had completed. Student groups also made presentations to the whole class where many chose to model their experiments as well as getting more data for analyses. The presentations were evaluated using the same rubrics described previously.

Students really enjoyed the project overall, although final comments indicated that many felt there was too much writing involved. Student comments ranged from "I really liked not having to read the science book, but the reports were too long," "We had fun working outside of the classroom for a change," "You should do this again next year," and "This was great. Why don't we do every science unit this way?"

Reflections

During each science unit and after longer inquiry activities, students were asked to review the science processes used as a part of the final evaluation. A journal was also kept during the unit describing daily activities. Students were asked to list what helped them to learn about the topic studied, what was confusing, and what should be changed for whatever reason, to evaluate their own lessons and performances (NRC 1996, p. 68). The list and definitions of the processes we emphasized were found in the book *Rising to the Challenge of the National Science Education Standards: The Processes of Science Inquiry (5–8)* (Ostlund and Mercier 1996). When pressed to think about it, students were amazed at the number of process skills and the number of times they used each of these in the simplest investigation when they developed it themselves. And the reflections helped them to better remember the skills and use the terminology correctly in essays and class conversations (NRC 1996, pp. 82–84).

It is interesting that students from previous years still talk about their excitement at creating and following through on these inquiry activities. One of my previous students was back in middle school recently, this time as a student teacher. He made a point of stopping by my classroom to talk to the students about his experiences doing science in my class and how he had few additional opportunities in secondary school choosing and doing his own research. I believe that the creativity and ownership provided by inquiry lessons motivate students to do things that they (and to be honest, myself as a teacher as well) had not imagined they could do on their own. I felt the applied science provided students with experiences they were otherwise lacking to build new science knowledge (Bransford, Brown, and Cocking 2000) while also experiencing the richness and excitement of achieving a better understanding of the world around them (NRC 1996, pp. 145–148).

This was also evident in student evaluations at the end of the school year when students completed a final evaluation using a Likert survey. Of the 100 students who completed the year-end survey after completing several inquiry lessons, 70% felt that choosing and answering their own question helped them to better understand the purpose of the readings; 73% liked being able to create their own investigation instead of doing an activity with a known answer and liked the fact that their investigation was different from what others in the class did. When asked if they would take another science class, 75% said inquiry activities made science more interesting and 70% indicate that they would sign up for more science courses if taught like this one. In comparison, in answers to similar questions from a year without inquiry activities 68% said science was interesting and only 52% said they would consider signing up for an additional science class.

These student-led inquiry activities also provided a means for my curriculum to be dynamic. Other teachers taught the "same year" over and over again, but each year is different in my classes, with student-initiated projects exploring the same content, but in new, refreshing ways. As the curriculum was modified over the years, I lost the unit on force and motion and added a new unit on light and sound. Students investigated the nature of color mixing, the effectiveness of UV sunglasses, and the principles of solar energy, among other topics (NRC 1996, p. 155). With my interdisciplinary team, we initiated a review of the 20th century and students chose areas of technology and looked at how they had changed over time (NRC 1996, pp. 212 and 220). During the astronomy unit, teams investigated different planets and the end result was a CD-ROM on the solar system we shared with the feeder elementary schools, adding a project-based learning component to our inquiry (NRC 2000, p. 22).

Conclusion

This all began with the NSF programs. The workshops I attended provided me with a sense of community and achievement. The workshops required participation at the state level in group presentations, but since then I have authored sessions where I presented or copresented at state and national science teacher conferences. Attending the workshops helped make teaching more enjoyable and make me feel less isolated, because there were few others in my building who understood not only the science but this new vision of how to teach it. I finally felt like I was doing something worthy of applying for grant money to support my lessons, so I applied and was awarded several small grants for my school.

Some workshops required that I offer professional development in my building, district, and at professional meetings, which further expanded my community of practice. In the process I became more of a producer of knowledge and a facilitator, and I developed a sense of actually being a Master Teaching Professional (NRC 1996, pp. 68–70). It provided me with confidence as I worked as a mentor to preservice and new teachers and served on curriculum commit-tees within my district. This sense of professionalism led to increased involvement in both state and national science teacher organizations in committees and elected positions (NRC 1996, p. 223). I would never have considered being eligible for these positions before I attended these programs. And because of this involvement, I had the opportunity to work on the development and improvement of state science standards over the years (NRC 1996, p. 239).

These were the positive consequences of my wanting to become a better science teacher. But in recent years, it has become more difficult to do the inquiry assessments; in the past few years I have not been able to do them at all. A combination of two factors has led to this outcome. First, time taken from instruction by standardized testing as a result of the No Child Left Behind (NCLB) law has made it difficult to find the time it takes to work through the inquiry process. Second, funding cuts to the district from the state and local levels have led to our district abandoning the "Middle School Concept" and moving toward the original Junior High School; at the time of this writing, we are only a middle school in name, not ideology or ontology.

But time always exists in the schedule for shorter inquiry activities. And for students who are interested in learning more about science, there is an after-school science club, so they can experience inquiry in a more informal environment (NRC 1996, p. 220). Sadly, this does not allow students who have not yet achieved success in science the experience of personal discovery. Those students who have not discovered a love for *this* style of science do not attend. As a result, we lose potential scientists and science advocates. As the pendulum seems to be losing its momentum in focusing on only the basic skills and teacher-led learning, I look forward to the swing back to student-centered instruction that is inevitable in this new age of communication.

References

Bransford, J. D., A. L. Brown, and R. R. Cocking. 2000. *How people learn: Brain, mind, experience, and school*. Washington, DC: National Academy Press.

Burry-Stock, J. A., and R. L. Oxford. 1995. Expert science teaching educational evaluation model (ES-TEEM): Measuring excellence in science teaching for professional development. *Journal of Personnel Evaluation in Education* 8 (3): 267–297.

Gilbert, S. W., and S. W. Ireton. 2003. *Understanding models in Earth and space science*. Arlington, VA: National Science Teachers Association.

Harris, T. 2006. The gift of interpretation in a science classroom. *The Hoosier Science Teacher* 32 (2): 50–56.

Harris, T., and P. Rowlen. 2003. Student learning styles met through inquiry learning. *The Hoosier Science Teacher* 29 (1): 23–26.

National Research Council (NRC). 1996. *National science education standards*. Washington, DC: National Academy Press.

National Research Council (NRC). 2000. *Inquiry and the national science education standards: A guide for teaching and learning*. Washington, DC: National Academy Press.

Ostlund, K. L., and S. Mercier. 1996. *Rising to the challenge of the national science education standards: The processes of science inquiry (5–8)*. Arlington, VA: National Science Teachers Association.

Sneider, C., and K. Barrett. 1999. *River cutters*. 4th ed. Berkeley, CA: Lawrence Hall of Science.

VanCleave, J. P. 1991. *Janice VanCleave's physics for every kid: 101 easy experiments in motion, heat, light, machines, and sound*. New York: Wiley and Sons.

Inquiry: A Challenge for Changing the Teaching of Science in Connecticut

Holly Harrick
Connecticut Science Center

Introduction

Reading, writing, and arithmetic served as the basics of public education in Connecticut schools through the 20th century. Science, although considered a core subject that all students should take or at least be exposed to, was most often a second-tier concern in the K–12 learning experience.

As we entered the new millennium, Connecticut began to look upon the basics in a new way, focusing on literacy, numeracy, and inquiry. A catalyst for inquiry gaining its rightful place of importance in Connecticut education was the State Board of Education's 2004 adoption of the *Core Science Curriculum Framework* (CSDE 2004). The framework includes a set of inquiry standards that are based on the *National Science Education Standards* and the subsequent addendum to the standards, *Inquiry and the National Science Education Standards*. The science framework clearly established that Connecticut recognized the increasing importance of science, technology, and mathematics—process skills as well as content—in preparing students for their futures in the 21st century and for the continuing economic success of the state.

As evidence of this newly recognized importance of science and inquiry, the State Board of Education committed to adding science testing to the Connecticut Mastery Testing (CMT) for grades 5 and 8 in 2008. Approximately 40% of the test will assess inquiry skills, and 60% of the test will assess science content.

However, it seemed clear that most elementary teachers in the state were not adequately prepared to teach science with the depth of content and with the instructional focus on inquiry that the framework demanded. Fortunately at this same time, the Connecticut Science Center (CSC) moved from idea to reality. Ground was broken for the center in 2005, with an opening date of 2009. But the center did not wait for a building to exist before it began to respond to this daunting challenge of preparing elementary teachers to use inquiry-based learning in their schools. The CSC recognized that one of its most important contributions to preparing Connecticut's students for their futures in the new millennium would be to serve as a major resource for helping the state's teachers become comfortable with the inquiry process as well as to increase their science content knowledge. In early 2005, the center was awarded a major grant from the GE Foundation to run a teacher professional development program to focus on this challenge.

The CSC professional development program was predicated on the belief that the center could provide a model of excellence for professional development in science for "providers of [professional development] at any given stage of the continuum that would offer high quality opportunities grounded in best-practices and current theories of learning science" (Harkins, Moss, and Harrick 2007, p. 4). Ultimately, the challenge was to change the teaching of science in Connecticut's schools, which meant changing the view of science as a subject you simply read about to a subject focused on inquiry skills that required "identification of assumptions, use of critical and logical thinking, and consideration of alternative explanations" (NRC 1996, p. 23).

The Foundation for Change

From the very beginning, the Connecticut Science Center (CSC) was committed to developing its Introduction to Inquiry Professional Development Program consistent with the Professional Development Standards of the NSES. The center believed that in order to effect a systemic change in the teaching of science in the state, it would have to design a professional development program that recognized "the developmental nature of teacher professional growth and individual and group interests" (NSES Professional Development Standard D). Key to the center's design was the belief that it would "be nearly impossible to convey the experience of inquiry to students in schools if the teachers themselves have never experienced it" (NRC 1996, p. 60).

Thus the center designed its professional development program to mirror the way that students should be learning science. This led the center to focus its design work on the findings of the NRC report *How People Learn*, which synthesized research findings on science learning as follows:

- Understanding science is more than knowing facts.
- Students build new knowledge and understanding on what they already know and believe.
- Students formulate new knowledge by modifying and refining their current concepts and by adding new concepts to what they already know.
- Effective learning requires that students take control of their own learning.
- The ability to apply knowledge to novel situations, that is, transfer of learning, is affected by the degree to which students learn with understanding.

The CSC focused its first-year institutes on having teachers "actively investigating phenomena that can be studied scientifically, interpreting results, and making sense of findings consistent with currently accepted scientific understanding" (NSES Professional Development Standard A). In effect, the participants in these institutes experience inquiry in the same manner that their students will. It is also important to note that most of the facilitators of the first-year institutes are practicing teachers. This adds much creditability in the minds of the participants.

Another critical component of the center's professional development model is found in Standard A: "Science learning experiences for teachers must encourage and support teachers in efforts to collaborate" (NRC 1996, p. 59). Most participants work in teams of teachers from the same school, which results in collaborative learning not only during the institutes but also back in their schools. Teaching can be a very isolating profession, and collaborative professional development increases the likelihood of teachers changing their approach to teaching science and helps them to embrace the importance of science literacy for all students, not just the academically gifted.

NSES Professional Development Standard A also emphasizes that teachers of science must "understand the fundamental facts and concepts in major science disciplines" (NRC 1996, p. 59). The CSC understands that "Teachers of grades K–4 are generalists who teach most, if not all school subjects." Thus, "elementary teachers of science need to have the opportunity to develop a broad knowledge of science content" (NRC 1996, p. 69). This has resulted in the center developing additional workshops for elementary teachers focused on science content such as electricity and magnetism, properties of matter, light and sound, weather, erosion and river formation, and force and motion. These workshops are, of course, approached using the inquiry model.

A key tenet of NSES Professional Development Standard B is that "Learning experiences for teachers of science must use inquiry, reflection, interpretation of research, modeling, and guided practice to build understanding and skill in science teaching" (NRC 1996, p. 62). All of these experiences are woven throughout the fabric of the CSC's institutes, as can be seen in the overview of the institutes presented later in this chapter.

Standard B also emphasizes that "The development of pedagogical content knowledge by teachers mirrors what we know about learning by students; it can be fully developed only through continuous experience" (NRC 1996, p. 63). Thus the center's institute model encourages participant involvement over three periods—in the summer, during the school year, and following the school year. All participants are provided with the opportunity for ongoing support from the center during the school year.

NSES Professional Development Standard D stresses the need for professional development program coherence and integration (NRC 1996, p. 70). Coherence of the teachers' learning experience has been a primary goal of the center's program. Standard C emphasizes that "Professional development activities must extend over long periods and include a range of strategies to provide opportunities for teachers to refine their knowledge, understanding, and abilities continually" (NRC 1996, p. 68). That is why the CSC's program has such diversity in its workshops and follow-up sessions.

Standard D also indicates that quality professional development should include a variety of stakeholders: teachers, administrators, teacher educators, members of professional organizations, etc. (NRC 1996, p. 70). The collaborative integration of those with a vested interest in improving the teaching of science will increase the likelihood that change will occur. The center thus encourages teams from school districts to participate together in the institutes.

This standard also states that "Individual teachers of science should have the opportunity to put together programs of professional development, as should groups of teachers" (NRC 1996, p. 71). This is clearly reflected in the "three hat model" of participation in the institutes. The participants are asked to view their experiences in the institutes through the lens of themselves as learners, then as teachers, and finally as workshop facilitators. The Connecticut Science Center is totally committed to affecting a systemic change in the teaching of science in Connecticut, and it firmly believes that ongoing professional development for current teachers will be necessary for this to occur. The center's Introduction to Inquiry Professional Development Program is predicated on this belief and has been designed to respond to "the developmental nature of teacher professional growth and individual and group interests" (NRC 1996, p. 72). Thus, the center's professional program is intended to be responsive to individual teacher needs and district needs while pursuing an overarching goal of improving the teaching of science for all children in the state.

Blueprint for Change

When the Connecticut Science Center's professional development team began planning for its Inquiry Professional Development Program, four recurring findings from research guided its work. These findings reinforced the professional experiences of the members of the planning team and have been further reinforced by many research studies.

First, research has established that if you truly wish to change classroom instruction, professional development must be "extended in time, with time built in for practice, coaching, and follow-ups" (Snow-Renner and Lauer 2005). One study focused specifically on science teachers and inquiry-based instruction. Supovitz and Turner (2000) found that at least 80 hours of professional development were necessary before most teachers changed their instructional practices. However, research has also shown that most teacher professional development is in the form of one-day workshops with no follow-up (NSDC 2001 and NRC 2001). Thus, the CSC designed a program of professional development that is ongoing, with intensive, multiday workshops, follow-up sessions, and in-school support during the year.

Second, effective professional development engages teachers as adult learners and does so using the approaches and activities in which their students will be engaged (Mundry 2005). Many other studies have reached similar conclusions, finding that when professional development involves teachers in the practices their students might use, the teachers are more likely to adopt those practices (Desimone et al. 2002; Supovitz and Christman 2003).

Third, effective professional development "must provide teachers with a way to directly apply what they learn to their teaching" (AERA 2005, p. 3). A study of professional development effectiveness for science and mathematics teachers concluded that when professional development activities were directly related to the teachers' curriculum responsibilities, the teachers were more likely to adopt the practices suggested to them (Garet et al. 2001). School administrators responsible for the professional development program for their teachers can attest that most teachers want to walk away from professional development activities with something they can implement in their classrooms the next day.

Fourth, professional development is more likely to affect change in teachers' instruction if it is designed so that a team of teachers from the same school or same grade level participate together in the professional development (Snow-Renner and Lauer 2005). The Eisenhower Mathematics and Science Consortia and Clearinghouse Network also emphasized that "Effective professional development experiences provide opportunities for teachers to work with colleagues and other experts in professional learning communities to improve their practice" (Mundry, Spector, and Horsley 1999, p. 8).

With this research base as a foundation, the CSC's Introduction to Inquiry Professional Development Program was launched in the summer of 2005 with a series of inquiry-based professional development institutes. Based on workshop models of the Exploratorium Institute for Inquiry in San Francisco, the center's professional development program is a three-year immersion experience in inquiry-based learning and teaching.

Like the Exploratorium's program, the CSC's professional development series is designed to provide powerful, transformative experiences by immersing participants in the process of inquiry. A primary goal is to develop in participants, through hands-on investigations as well as reflection and group discussion, an understanding of inquiry that can be taken back to school districts and shared with colleagues. Emphasis is placed on the development of the professional practitioner.

The program is rigorous and demanding of all participants. In order to implement inquiry-based learning successfully in the classroom, superintendents and principals are asked to support their teachers both financially and with release time for professional development activities. The goal is to provide an in-depth professional development experience with additional support provided over a three-year period that enables teachers to become comfortable with the inquiry process and to develop their science content knowledge. Note, however, that individuals or teams may also participate in just the first year of the program if full participation is not possible.

Taught as a "train the trainer" model, participants are encouraged to provide professional development for other teachers in their district. Enrollment in the CSC's professional development program is selective and dependent on the district's desire for and support for inquiry-based learning and teaching. As part of the three-year commitment, teachers are asked to participate in the evaluation of the program.

Overview of the CSC Inquiry Professional Development Program

The program is organized with three major institutes, each five days in length, plus a two-day follow-up after the completion of the school year. Institutes are offered in the summer and during school vacations so teachers do not have to be away from their classrooms. This is important in a time when qualified substitutes are in short supply. In addition, the CSC also provides additional support during the school year including coaching, modeling, and planning with participants.

Participants are encouraged to be part of the program for all three institutes; however, this is not a requirement. On average, 25–30% of the first-year participants (Cohort One) have returned for the second institute and approximately 35–40% from Cohorts One and Two returned for the second and/or third institute. Attendance in the two-day follow-up workshop has increased as well, approximately 25% in the first summer and increasing to approximately 35% in the second summer.

Year One

The Center provides a five-day "Introduction to Inquiry" workshop that is based on the Exploratorium's many years of professional development experience. The workshop introduces participants to the inquiry process of teaching and learning, guides participants in strategic planning for incorporating inquiry into the classroom, and assists participants in building capacity to incorporate inquiry in their entire school or district.

During the school year, the center offers a variety of supports for the participants. This includes opportunities to observe other teachers using inquiry-based instruction, to be observed and coached by program staff members, and to be assisted by program staff members in developing or revising inquiry-based lessons.

Following the school year, the two-day follow-up session provides the opportunity for participants to share their successes and to identify areas of needed improvement. Participants bring samples of lessons (written and videotaped) and samples of student work. In addition, the participants begin to plan for providing inquiry-based professional development for teachers back in their school(s) or district.

Year Two

Participants from the previous year attend the second five-day "Classroom Applications" workshop. This workshop deepens participants' understanding of inquiry, provides an opportunity to further develop inquiry-based lessons, and also provides experience with an instructional coaching model so that they can better assist the teachers in their schools in making the transition to teaching science using an inquiry-based approach. At the end of the school year, there is another two days of follow-up for all previous workshop participants. In this session, participants share inquiry-based revisions included in their district curricula and review and analyze samples of student work. Participants also share and critique the inquiry-based professional development they have developed for teachers in their schools or district.

Year Three

Those participants who previously attended both the Introduction to Inquiry and the Classroom Applications workshops are eligible to participate in the third "Formative Assessment" workshop. This workshop provides practice in creating and using assessments in the science classroom and furthers the understanding and practice of instructional coaching methods. Once again, at the end of the school year, participants from all previous inquiry workshops are invited to another two-day follow-up session for revision of and reflection on their continuing inquiry work.

Descriptions of the Core Workshops

The Connecticut Science Center's Introduction to Inquiry Professional Development Program's three core institutes is the foundation for the professional development program. The institutes are offered during the summer or during school vacations so that teachers do not have to be out of their classrooms in order to participate.

All three of the institutes are designed so that the participants as learners are provided with multiple opportunities to engage in inquiry activities that will allow them to construct their own meaning and further their own understanding of science and learning. A major goal is to have the participants experience the inquiry-based learning just as their students will and as described in the chart of "Essential Features of Classroom Inquiry" in the National Science Education Standards. We believe this will lead to the participants implementing what they have learned in their own classrooms with their students.

We strongly believe that it is a long journey from procedural knowledge to conceptual understanding. It has been our experience that very few professional development opportunities exist that focus on providing educators with opportunities for metacognition. It is one thing to construct an inquiry lesson and identify the features that move the lesson further toward being "student-centered" and away from "teacher-directed." It is quite another to actually implement that lesson in the classroom and reflect on its efficacy in promoting student understanding of science concepts.

Introduction to Inquiry Workshop

This is the first workshop in the professional development program, and it is offered during the summer and during some school vacations. It is an intensive five-day workshop focused on inquiry-based science learning and teaching. The focus of the workshop is on understanding the structure of inquiry and using that structure to develop an inquiry lesson to take back to the classroom.

Goals: Participants will understand

- the meaning of inquiry-based learning;
- the importance of inquiry-based learning in science;
- that different approaches to hands-on science work for differing learning objectives;
- that hands-on science activities do not in and of themselves equate to an inquiry experience;
- the importance of questioning skills in the inquiry process;
- that science content can be learned through inquiry;
- that inquiry has a definite structure and using that structure, a model inquiry lesson can be prepared;
- how to redesign existing lessons to be more inquiry based; and
- how reading, writing, and mathematics can be incorporated into inquiry-based science learning.

Learning Activities: Participants will

- learn as students in inquiry-based lessons (e.g., Stream Table Investigation and Motion and Design lesson);
- view videos of actual inquiry-based lessons in classrooms;
- reflect on their learning in journals;
- reflect on their learning in small- and large-group discussions;
- review inquiry-based science kits;
- develop inquiry-based lesson plans; and
- plan implementation strategies for sharing the learning in their schools.

Sample Inquiry-Based Activity: Stream Table Investigation
The Stream Table Investigation takes participants through a full inquiry process. They begin with an exploration of stream flow and erosion and then complete a focused inves-

tigation on a question of their choice. Next, participants have a chance to share what they have found during their investigations. The process culminates in a discussion that allows them to reflect on and analyze their inquiry experiences. This is based on an activity created by the Exploratorium.

Classroom Applications Workshop

The second workshop in the professional development program is an intensive five-day, summer workshop that reviews the inquiry process and shows direct application to the classroom. This workshop comes a year after participants have learned the structure of inquiry and what it looks like in a lesson. During the school year previous to their attendance in this workshop, they have had opportunities to try out their newly created lessons using inquiry with their students. The applications workshop gives participants the opportunity to begin to focus on the individual components of inquiry and conceptualize how teaching through inquiry engages students and furthers their students' understanding of science concepts. Participants are immersed in a full inquiry in which they deconstruct the experiences one activity at a time. They then apply their new learning to the refinement of their own lessons. Templates, assessments, and rudimentary coaching models are also presented. After year two, most participants can begin to construct some conceptual knowledge about how this inquiry process works with students and how it increases their learning.

Goals: Participants will understand

- how students construct meaning through the inquiry process;
- the importance and purpose of "thinking tools;"
- how nonfiction and fiction may be used in science inquiry lessons;
- the importance of teacher synthesis and student reflection in an inquiry lesson as they relate to student learning;
- the role of performance assessments in determining student understanding of science concepts and the difference between formative and summative assessment;
- the role of teacher leadership and its application to teachers and to their school or district; and
- the role teachers can play in coaching other teachers in inquiry-based instruction.

Learning Activities: Participants will

- participate as students in an inquiry-based lesson (e.g., Shadows Investigation);
- deconstruct strategies in inquiry lessons;
- develop science lessons with inquiry-based strategies embedded in them;
- analyze state standards and identify essential questions;
- develop appropriate formative and summative performance assessments for their inquiry lessons;
- view videotapes of actual inquiry-based lessons in classrooms and identify inquiry strategies used;

- role-play various situations they may experience as they begin to share their new learning with others in their schools or districts;
- practice various "coaching" strategies they may employ as they return to their schools or districts;
- reflect on their individual learning in journals; and
- reflect on their learning in small- and large-group discussions.

Sample Inquiry-Based Activity: Shadows Investigation

The Shadows Investigation takes participants through a full inquiry process. They begin with an exploration of various light sources and shadows cast by various objects, and then they conduct a focused investigation on a question they choose. Next, participants have a chance to share what they have found during their investigations. The process culminates in a discussion that allows them to reflect on and analyze their inquiry experiences. This is adapted from an Exploratorium activity.

Formative Assessment Workshop

The third workshop in the professional development program is an intensive five-day workshop focused on the formative assessment of inquiry in the classroom. It also provides additional training in modeling and coaching of science educators. It is offered during the summer.

Goals: Participants will understand

- how to observe and interpret students' use of the process skills of science;
- the importance of process skills and how to assist their students' development of these skills;
- how to create indicators of development for specific scientific ideas and the nature of feedback that helps student learning;
- the value of students assessing their own and their peers' work and ways to communicate goals and criteria to students; and
- effective strategies for modeling and coaching teaching colleagues in inquiry-based instruction.

Learning Activities: Participants will

- experience and develop strategies for differentiation of inquiry-based lessons;
- examine the use of formative assessment in an inquiry-based classroom;
- develop formative assessments for an inquiry-based unit of their choice;
- discuss the integration of formative assessment across the curriculum;
- analyze sample student work (e.g., science notebooks, assessments, etc.);
- share instructional techniques with each other;
- create rubrics and checklists to assess inquiry-based work;
- develop open-ended questions; and
- experience a variety of assessment tools for use in their classroom.

Participants

Districts that wish to be part of the CSC Inquiry Professional Development Program are encouraged to send a team that includes three to five teachers, a school-level administrator or a district-wide administrator, and a scientist, who can either be a university professor or corporate scientist. The team may also include a museum educator or science center educator. Additional individuals may participate in the workshops even if they are not part of a school or district team.

Participants have come from districts throughout the state, including urban, suburban, and rural areas. There are 167 school districts in Connecticut and so far participants in the program have come from more than 40 districts. There are approximately 50 informal science education institutions in the state, and participants in the program have come from more than 20 of them.

Although the program was designed for K–12 teachers, the majority of the participants so far have been elementary teachers. However, the number of middle and high school participants has increased each year. The vast majority of the participants have five or more years of teaching experience and the average age of the participants has been approximately 40.

Commitments of the Teacher Participants
Year One

- Observe a master teacher facilitating inquiry-based instruction at least once during the school year.
- Receive coaching from a master teacher for an agreed upon inquiry-based lesson.
- Collaborate with a school administrator on at least one inquiry-based unit.
- Observe and collaborate with fellow participants in planning and delivering inquiry-based instruction at least twice during the school year lessons and units.
- Participate in two days of follow-up that include analysis of student work and teaching experiences.

Year Two

- Participate in groups to discuss and rewrite lessons/units to be more inquiry-based.
- Lead inquiry-based professional development for colleagues in their schools.
- Participate in two days of follow-up that include analysis of student work and teaching experiences as well as professional development experiences.

Year Three

- Continue revising lessons/units to be more inquiry-based.
- Provide inquiry-based professional development to fellow colleagues in their school.
- Participate in two days of follow-up that includes analysis of student work and unit/lesson modifications to reflect inquiry-based instruction as well as analyses of professional development implementation.

Commitments of the District

- Pay for their team's registration fees for the institutes.
- Provide stipends for the teachers when they participate in sessions during the summer or during school vacations.
- Provide engaging materials for the students in their schools to use in science inquiry, for example, purchasing science kits and replenishing them.

Commitments of the Connecticut Science Center

- Provide highly trained professionals to deliver inquiry-based training.
- Provide the "Introduction to Inquiry" training manual to each participant.
- Provide participants with support during the school year.

Ongoing Support by the Connecticut Science Center

The CSC recognizes that the best professional development is that which provides ongoing support for teachers. To that end, the center offers the following support for three years:

- Arranging for a teacher or a small team of teachers to visit a teacher(s) in another district while he/she is delivering an inquiry-based lesson
- Coaching a teacher(s) as they deliver an inquiry lesson
- Assistance for principals or science administrators in observing and evaluating learning through the inquiry process
- Assistance for science coordinators and/or administrators in developing a strategic plan for implementing inquiry in a building or across the district
- Planning and/or critique of inquiry lessons a teacher(s) has developed

The Resulting Change

This is the third year of the Connecticut Science Center's Introduction to Inquiry Professional Development Program. There have been more than 500 participants in the program thus far, and we have perceived that the program has been very successful in building a solid core of teachers in the state who are now committed to transforming science teaching to inquiry-based instruction.

To assess the impact of the program in changing teaching practices, The University of Connecticut Neag School of Education was hired in 2005 to conduct a program evaluation. The data collected thus far has been the result of pre- and post-surveys from the 2005, 2006, and 2007 Introduction to Inquiry workshops, a one-year follow-up assessment for Cohort One (2005) and Cohort Two (2006) participants, a follow-up workshop assessment for the participants in the two-day follow-up workshops in 2006 and 2007, and a postsurvey for those who attended the Classroom Applications or Formative Assessment workshops.

The survey instrument used was a modified version of an instrument developed during the first year of the program. The survey instrument was the same for the cohorts in both 2006 and

2007, thus allowing direct comparisons between the cohorts. Comparisons to the first cohort (2005) were made when deemed appropriate.

In an effort to create a better picture of the results from the surveys, questions were grouped into categories based on content. These categories were created through the revision of the year one assessment and a reflection on the areas of emphasis. Survey questions were grouped based on these categories and analyzed for their reliability using Cronbach's alpha (UCLA's Academic Technology Services). This design allowed for a systematic view of the participant's results.

Based on the study, the university evaluation team drew the following statistically valid conclusions from the data they had collected.

- **Participant awareness of the importance of inquiry teaching increased.** As one respondent said, "I experienced learning science as I wish I had done when I was in school. Actually doing inquiry science really was meaningful, and students deserve it too."
- **Participants perceived a significant increase in their ability to teach science through inquiry.** In 2006 the increase in this measure was 16.3% and the increase in 2007 was 19.2%.
- **Participants increased their level of understanding about inquiry-based instruction as a result of participating in one or more of the institutes.** The results of the 2006 and 2007 surveys were very similar. Statistics from 2007 exemplify this perceived level of understanding. The following presents a list of the percentage of participants who indicated that they had good or excellent understanding of the topic that was being surveyed:

  - The strategies needed to implement inquiry learning: 79%
  - The skills needed to engage students in inquiry: 81%
  - How to modify lessons to become more inquiry-based: 69%
  - How to teach science from an inquiry perspective: 80%
  - Participants were convinced that inquiry would benefit their students and thus increased their use of inquiry-based instruction in their classrooms. The postprogram survey data clearly demonstrated that almost all participants intended to use inquiry-based instruction after completing the program. The "one year later" surveys from the 2005 and 2006 cohorts indicate that the participants did use inquiry-based strategies in their science instruction.

We also learned from the university study that some aspects of the program need to be reconsidered. For example, only 47% of the survey respondents who attended the Introduction to Inquiry workshop felt they had a good or excellent understanding of appropriate assessment strategies to help students achieve science standards. Also, 56% of the respondents indicated that they wanted somewhat more or much more application of their learning to their classrooms. As a result, we adjusted some portions of our workshops.

Our evaluations thus far have focused on the extent to which our participants understand inquiry-based instruction in science and the extent to which they change their instructional practices. This was a primary goal in establishing our program. However, we believe that inquiry-based science instruction will significantly improve student skills and knowledge and research seems to support this conclusion. For example, the Southwest Regional Education Laboratory (2007) did a review of 1,300 studies on the effect of teacher professional development on student achievement. Although they found very few studies that they considered rigorous, they concluded that "teachers who receive substantial professional development—an average of 49 hours in the nine studies—can boost their students' achievement by about 21 percentile points." Another study, one focusing on science specifically, conducted by Educational Testing Service (Wenglinsky 2000) found that teacher professional development in hands-on laboratory skills resulted in a jump in students' science test scores.

Connecticut will be adding science testing as part of the Connecticut Mastery Test program beginning in the spring of 2008. The tests are being constructed with a strong inquiry focus, and therefore the test results over a period of time should provide us with valuable data relative to our program's impact on student achievement. We should be able to analyze the scores of students whose teachers have participated in our program and compare their results to students whose teachers have not participated.

Nevertheless, the success of our professional development program will continue to lie first and foremost in our ability to change the teaching of science to promote inquiry-based learning teacher-by-teacher and school-by-school. That is why we have volunteered to participate in a field test of an Inquiry Science Instruction Observation Protocol (ISIOP) developed by EDC's Center for Science Education (Minnie 2007). This instrument should allow us to measure more precisely how teachers are using inquiry with their students.

What We Have Learned in Developing and Implementing Our Program

We believe the following points will be most helpful to people considering or already planning for a professional development program to increase the inquiry-based focus of science teaching in their buildings or districts:

- **Promoting an inquiry environment does not happen in a short period of time.** It is not realistic to expect an overnight change in a teacher's pedagogy. The CSC's program staff has been firmly convinced of and immersed in inquiry-based science teaching for some time, and we needed to realize just how much time other educators would need to truly buy into changing their practices. For example, our expectations for participants in Cohort One were that they would prepare an inquiry-based unit to implement in their classrooms the following year, as well as provide inquiry training for their peers in their schools/districts. We were quickly confronted with the reality that participants only had time during the workshop to begin to develop an inquiry lesson, not complete an entire unit. We also found they needed time during the school year to try out their lesson, reflect on its strengths, and identify areas needing improvement in order to internalize the concepts of inquiry-based teaching and learning. Only after they had adequate opportunities to try inquiry in their own classrooms did they achieve a level of comfort enough to begin to explore the possibility of sharing their lessons or delivering professional development in some way in their schools and districts. As a result, we quickly adjusted our expectations and theirs.

- **Inquiry-based professional development should not be dependent on the science education of the participants.** Participants bring a wide variety of science backgrounds. In 2007, about 20% of the participants had only one or two science courses in their undergraduate programs but another 20% had 10 or more science courses. Over half had taken 0–2 graduate science courses, but 10% had 10 or more graduate science courses. Thus, accommodations must be in place to be certain those with little science education are not overwhelmed while concurrently accommodating those with degrees in science. This is a very large challenge. One of our responses has been to develop grade-level, content-specific workshops that give teachers experiences with learning content directly related to the Connecticut Science Frameworks in addition to the Introduction to Inquiry workshop program. Other workshops we have developed as a result of the differing needs of our participants include "Integrating Language Arts and Science" and "Science Notebooking." These workshops are in direct response to requests from our participants as noted in their workshop evaluations.

- **To provide exemplary workshops, you must have exemplary workshop facilitators.** We spend a lot of time "growing" our facilitators. Even with conceptual understanding of inquiry-based instruction and practical experiences as a teacher using inquiry-based instruction, it is no guarantee that the teacher can be an exemplary workshop presenter. Exemplary facilitators understand how adult learners learn and can develop appropriate workshop activities that will further participants' understanding of inquiry. They also have to be able to facilitate the workshop so that it actively engages the participants.

  We were extremely fortunate to have a core group of educators who attended the Exploratorium's Institute for Inquiry workshops. From this core group in 2005, we solicited additional participants who were exemplary educators and had successfully incorporated inquiry into their professional practice and were interested in becoming future workshop facilitators. As part of their training, they attended all three workshops in our Introduction to Inquiry program as learners, then apprenticed for a week in the Introduction to Inquiry workshop and participated in each of the two-day follow-up workshops and various additional training sessions and meetings held throughout each successive school year.

  Their success as exemplary workshop facilitators is clearly evidenced in our workshop evaluations. The following are sample responses from participants when asked about the one thing they liked best about the Introduction to Inquiry workshop.

  The best aspect of the Institute was the opportunity to experience inquiry in the presence of so many enthusiastic learners, teachers, facilitators, and practitioners.

  The team of presenters and their expertise in guiding our learning was the best thing.

  It has been extremely important to the success of our program that the majority of our facilitators are classroom teachers who are inquiry practitioners. Classroom teachers teaching classroom teachers always adds credibility to professional development.

- **Success must be measured in a variety of ways because no single evaluation instrument can capture multiple, diverse goals.** While we are pleased with the results of our evaluations thus far, we are always searching for ways to broaden our evaluation process. To that end, as we complete our final year of the GE Education Foundation grant funding cycle, we are looking at ways to expand the ways we measure the impact of our program.

  We are investigating the ideas of "Empowerment Evaluation" to help us to better examine our measures of success through the eyes of our participants. This evaluation model is based on the idea that evaluation is most meaningful when planned, administered and reflected on by the individuals actually engaged in the learning activity (Fetterman 2000). After all, if the function of assessments is to inform instruction, then we need to be fully vested in the information we wish to receive in order to inform and improve our own practice.

  We are also looking at additional ways to work with outside evaluators to measure the degree of implementation of inquiry in the actual classrooms of program participants and also to assess student attitudes, skills, and content knowledge as a result of their teachers' attendance in our workshops. As mentioned earlier in this chapter, we have volunteered to participate in a field test of an Inquiry Science Instruction Observation Protocol (ISIOP) developed by EDC's Center for Science Education (Minnie 2007), which should help us to measure more precisely how teachers are using inquiry with their students.

- **Full participation is ideal, but teachers can benefit from participating in just the introductory institute.** We believe in our three-year model. It is consistent with what we know about the length of time it takes to change a teacher's practice. However, the reality is that not all districts can afford and not all teachers are ready to make a three-year commitment. We have learned that there is significant value in including those participants who can only be part of the introductory workshop. That participation lays a strong foundation for inquiry-based science instruction, and hopefully the teachers will take advantage of other opportunities to expand their inquiry knowledge.

Into the Future

An ancient Chinese proverb says, "The journey of a thousand miles begins with one step." At the Connecticut Science Center, we recognize that our journey has really just begun, but we believe we have already taken giant steps in helping transform the teaching and learning of science in Connecticut to an inquiry-based approach.

As we continue on our inquiry journey, we will celebrate our successes and always be looking for ways to respond to our challenges even more effectively. We are learners, too, and most especially we are inquirers.

References

American Educational Research Association (AERA). 2005. Teaching teachers: Professional development to improve student achievement. *Research Points* 3 (1): 1–4.

Connecticut State Department of Education (CSDE). 2004. *Core science curriculum framework: An invitation for students and teachers to explore science and its role in society.* Available online at *www.sde.ct.gov/sde/lib/sde/word_docs/curriculum/science/framework/sciencecoreframework2005v2.doc.*

Desimone, L. M., A. C. Porter, M. S. Garet, K. S. Yoon, and B. F. Birman. 2002. Effects of professional development on teachers' instruction: Results from a three-year longitudinal study. *Educational Evaluation and Policy Analysis* 24 (2): 81–111.

Exploratorium Institute for Inquiry: Exploring the Art of Science Education. *www.exploratorium.edu/ifi/index.html.*

Fetterman, D. 2000. *The foundations of empowerment evaluation.* Thousand Oaks, CA: Sage Publications.

Garet, M. S., A. C. Porter, L. Desimone, B. F. Birman, and K. S. Yoon. 2001. What makes professional development effective? Results from a national sample of teachers. *American Educational Research Journal* 38 (4): 915–945.

Harkins, H., D. Moss, and H. Harrick, 2007. Exploring the connections between in-service professional development and pre-service science methods. *Connecticut Journal of Science Education* (Fall/Winter) 45.

Minnie, D. 2007. The inquiry science instructional observation protocol (ISIOP) development project. Education Development Center Inc: Center for Science Education. *http://cse.edc.org/projects/projectview.asp?pid=3719*

Mundry, S., B. Spector, and S. Loucks-Horsley. 1999. Working toward a continuum of professional development learning experiences for teachers. *NISE Research Monograph* 17: 1–46.

National Center for Educational Statistics (NCES). 2001. Teacher preparation and professional development: 2000. *http://nces.ed.gov/pubs2001/2001088.pdf.*

National Research Council (NRC). 2000. *How people learn: Bridging research and practice.* J. Bransford, A. Brown, R. Cocking, eds. Washington, DC: National Academy Press.

National Research Council (NRC). 2000. *Inquiry and the national science education standards: A guide for teaching and learning.* Washington, DC: National Academy Press.

National Research Council (NRC) 1996. *National science education standards.* Washington, DC: National Academy Press.

National Staff Development Council (NSDC). 2001. *Standards for staff development.* Oxford, OH: NSDC.

Snow-Renner, R., and P. Lauer. 2005. McRel insights: Professional development analysis. McRel (Mid-continent Research for Education and Learning). *www.mcrel.org/PDF/ProfessionalDevelopment/5051IR_Prof_dvlpmt_analysis.pdf.*

Southwest Regional Education Laboratory. 2007. *Reviewing the evidence on how teacher professional development affects student achievement.* Available online at *http://ies.ed.gov/ncee/edlabs/regions/southwest/pdf/REL_2007033.pdf.*

Supovitz, J., and J. Christman. 2003. Developing communities of instructional practice: Lessons from Cincinnati and Philadelphia. *CPRE Policy Briefs. A report from the Consortium for Policy Research in Education.* 1–10.

Supovitz, J., and H. Turner. 2000. The effects of professional development on science teaching practices and classroom culture. *Journal of Research in Science Teaching* 19 (2): 189–211.

Wenglinsky, H. 2000. *How teaching matters: Bringing the classroom back into discussions of teacher quality.* Princeton, NJ: Educational Testing Service.

UCLA's Academic Technology Services. What does Cronbach's alpha mean? *www.ats.ucla.edu/stat/spss/faq/alpha.html.*

Learning Science With Inquiry in the Clark County School District

Ellen K. Ebert
Clark County School District, Las Vegas

Kent J. Crippen
University of Nevada

Cindy Kern
Green Valley High School, Henderson

Rebecca Reichenbach
Western High School, Las Vegas

Cheryl Waldman
Palo Verde High School, Las Vegas

Setting

I n 2005, Project PASS (Proficiency And Success in Science) was funded as a Mathematics and Science Partnership by the Nevada Department of Education. The partnership consisted of the Curriculum and Professional Development Division of the Clark County School District, the Center for Mathematics and Science Education at the University of Nevada, Las Vegas, and the Southern Nevada Regional Professional Development Program. This three-year collaborative project was initiated with the goals of improved quality of instruction and subsequent student achievement on the Nevada high school science proficiency exam. It also sought to support the implementation of a recently revised, integrated, freshman science course emphasizing scientific inquiry. For many of the teacher participants, Project PASS helped to bring about important changes in their teaching practices. Using vignettes written by three participating teacher teams, this chapter describes use of authentic classroom inquiry, its impact on student learning, and the potential of professional development for scaffolding the PASS experience. To understand the classroom inquiry described in the vignettes, it is helpful to first understand our setting and the context of our professional development project.

The Clark County School District (CCSD) in Southern Nevada was the setting for Project PASS. As of 2006, CCSD served a K–12 student population numbering more than 300,000 and ranked fifth largest in the United States. CCSD covers nearly 8,000 square miles and includes the greater Las Vegas metropolitan area. Due to its broad geographical expanse, CCSD includes rural, suburban, and urban schools. In 2007, the number of Hispanic students enrolled in CCSD reached majority status at 40%.

Project PASS had an ambitious vision for teacher development, one that recognized the power of educated, capable professionals for effecting change. The professional development model for Project PASS included a comprehensive, integrated system of education and professional development with four major annual activities: (1) a two-week summer institute focusing on science content knowledge, (2) graduate coursework, (3) professional learning communities of participants, and (4) site-based action research. The ideas of the summer institutes and graduate coursework were intended to serve as initiators of reformed classroom practice. Support was provided via the professional learning community, and action research was the vehicle for establishing and documenting the impact of the reform. The evidentiary results presented here were captured through this action research process.

The summer institutes were framed with broad, integrated questions written from the perspective of local students. Within each institute, participating teachers engaged as science learners, shared ideas, developed a collective sense of responsibility for student learning, and experienced a nontraditional way of teaching and learning science. These are documented elements for creating leaders and sustaining change in instructional methods (Bryk et al. 1998; Fullan 2001). The institutes concluded with a capstone project where participants collaborated within an integrated perspective to synthesize and apply the science content. In her vignette, Rebecca Reichenbach describes how her team used one of the big questions from a summer institute to build an authentic inquiry for students related to urban heat island effects in the reconstruction of their inner city school.

Conceptual change, self-regulated learning, and accommodating special populations were the three main theoretical ideas addressed in the graduate coursework, and each became an annual theme. Conceptual change theory recognizes the importance of prior student knowledge and systematizes the process of developing those ideas into a scientific understanding (Duit 2003; Posner et al. 1982). Self-regulated learning emphasizes individual control of motivation, cognition, and metacognition in a science learning environment (Nolen 2003; Schraw, Crippen, and Hartley 2006). Accommodating special populations addresses the challenges of science learning for students with unique abilities and English language learners, two well-represented populations in urban areas. In their vignettes, Cindy Kern and Cheryl Waldman describe two unique approaches to using inquiry to develop these three theoretical ideas for their students.

Vignettes

The National Science Education Standards (NSES) describe five essential features of inquiry and their variations (NRC 1996). Our goal in preparing this chapter was to describe the implementation of inquiry instruction along a continuum, illustrated through a range of strategies, conducted in three unique school contexts. The schools described in the vignettes include a high-risk, inner-city high school, and two suburban high schools each with enrollments of approximately 3,000 students. In each of the three classrooms highlighted in this chapter, inquiry is designed to promote science learning among a diverse group of learners.

Vignette 1 describes *inquiry along a continuum* in a biology class at Palo Verde High School. Students pose questions about observations made as a result of a scaffolded inquiry. Scaffolded inquiry implies an instructional design that includes elements that highlight and accentuate the key elements of the process (e.g., writing prompts, modeling exercises). The students study evidence obtained in their investigations to develop a scientific understanding from their data. Throughout the process, they continue to formulate evidence-based explanations that are carefully recorded in their interactive notebooks. Ms. Waldman guides them to independently examine resources beyond their texts and classroom while maintaining their notebooks as the medium for creating plausible explanations. The end result is a scientific question proposed to address observations gleaned through an investigation.

The second vignette describes a more *open inquiry* envisioned by students at Western High School. The impetus for the inquiry is the broad question of "Why is it so hot in Las Vegas?" Using the phenomenon of urban heat-island effect, students at Western took advantage of a construction program at their school and designed experiments to determine whether their school contributes to urban heat-island effect. As a result of their study, students found new confidence as budding scientists and began asking deeper questions for research. Their teachers, Ms. Reichenbach, Ms. Holt, and Mr. Smith, discovered that students took a greater interest in reading and being able to communicate their findings through written text as well as in oral presentations. They also found a growing interest in science, as evidenced by increased enrollment in higher-level science classes.

The third and final vignette takes place in a suburban high school in Henderson, Nevada. Students in Ms. Kern's biology classes explore the ideas of osmosis and diffusion by *designing their own investigations* to address the broad question of "What happens to eggs when placed in solutions that are hypotonic, isotonic, and hypertonic?" Using the guidelines established by the NSES, these students experienced less direction from their teacher and had a greater opportunity to direct their own inquiries. Each day, students evaluated their inquiry questions by making observations and collecting data. They decided which observations were meaningful for their scientific understanding and could be justified when presented to their peers.

In preparing the vignettes, we asked the teacher authors to focus their writing around the following structure: (a) how the professional development experience served as a springboard to implementing inquiry in the classroom, (b) the setting and specific inquiry activities, (c) the connection to the state and national standards, and (d) the evidence for student learning. These stories speak to the potential of professional development with dedicated teachers for reforming classroom practices and positively impacting student learning and enjoyment of science.

Vignette 1: Scaffolding Inquiry With an Interactive Notebook

(Cheryl Waldman, Palo Verde High School, Las Vegas, Nevada)

Entering the teaching profession after 10 years as a research scientist in the biotechnology industry might suggest that I would be skilled at an inquiry-based approach to science education with high school students. However, the shift from science researcher to science educator was slow until recently, with participation in Project PASS. My teaching has been transformed and improved. My confidence to instruct other teachers has increased greatly, and research involving my own students has provided rewarding insights into strategies for their academic success. In this vignette I express how the experience with Project PASS changed my views of inquiry, describe how an interactive notebook can be used to scaffold the inquiry process, provide classroom and personal examples, and supply evidence for the impact of scaffolded inquiry with an interactive notebook on student learning.

For many science teachers, incorporating inquiry into classroom instruction can be a challenging and often misunderstood practice. It certainly was for me. Even as a former scientist skilled in investigation and the *how* and *why* of science, my use of inquiry in teaching was lacking. The inclusion of inquiry in our newly adopted state science standards only served to increase the challenge. Three years of internalizing educational theory about the conceptual change process and self-regulated learning pointed repeatedly to the importance of inquiry in the science classroom. It became apparent that I needed to put the theory into practice in order to transform my classroom into a place where students feel energized and motivated to experience and engage in science. Project PASS provided the motivation for me to step outside my comfort zone as controller of the body of knowledge to become more of a facilitator and coach of the investigative nature of science. In the process of "letting go" as a teacher (*inquiry along a continuum*), my students used their own thinking, actions, feelings and strategies to accomplish the tasks required of them through open and guided-inquiry laboratory experiences.

As a teacher engaged in the inquiry process, I was encouraged by the leadership team of Project PASS to facilitate breakout sessions that complemented the specific theme of the Summer Institute. In year two that theme was based on astronomy, guided by the question, "What is my unique place in the universe?" As a biochemist and cell biologist, my confidence to lead peers in activities involving unfamiliar content was quite low. Once again, it was necessary to move outside my comfort zone, examine the data generated by the activities in the sessions, research the topics, and then communicate explanations to my peers. Surprisingly, the process resulted in the collaboration of ideas among teachers and a deeper understanding of the activities and how they might be implemented with students. In the third summer, there was less ambivalence on my part because of these positive experiences.

My personal growth as a student, teacher, and leader is clearly a result of participation in Project PASS. Most importantly, including inquiry in my classroom has generated benefits for my students. There is a heightened sense of engagement and motivation. Now, students in lab groups must share their ideas to make sense of the experimental design, collectively interpret data, and negotiate any disagreements about process or conclusions (NRC 2000). At first, there was frustration and resistance to my refusal to answer all their questions, but students began to see that their success depended on their ability to be more self-directed. As their competence and confidence increased in subsequent inquiry-based activities, their enthusiasm became decidedly more noticeable. Repeatedly, students now ask, "Are we doing another lab today?" This is a typical question from any science student, but now I see it as an opportunity for active learning where they are involved in the ownership of their thinking. In my experience, interactive notebooks were the key to fulfilling the NSES vision for inquiry.

An interactive notebook is a powerful tool for scaffolding the inquiry process. The basic idea has roots in a number of programs (AVID 2007: Teachers' Curriculum Institute 2000), but its essence is a varied set of strategies for creating a personal learning tool that supports students through the inquiry process and empowers them for achievement (Waldman and Crippen 2009). Most current, high-level strategies for inquiry science like Vee maps (Coffman and Riggs 2006; Gowin and Alvarez 2005; Roehrig, Luft, and Edwards 2001) or the Science Writing Heuristic (Hand and Keys 1999) are easily adapted to the scheme of the notebook. Because of its multiple components and its integration into the inquiry process, an interactive notebook becomes a powerful learning aid.

Teaching science as inquiry involves getting the elements of the process to flow as information through an interactive notebook. An interactive notebook-supported activity involves a three-part flow of information. Instruction starts with an "in" activity, the work of the day constitutes a "through" activity, and an "out" activity draws important connections among the big ideas. The entire process is mapped and recorded onto the pages of a traditional bound paper notebook and students quickly come to expect this process as the mechanism for learning science.

Students now engage in a variety of laboratory experiences that require them to ask questions, design experiments, examine evidence to formulate explanations, and respond to questions. Typical, prescriptive laboratory experiences have been reconfigured so students must collaborate to interpret and negotiate understanding from their results and use their notebooks to make meaning of the process. The following examples are intended to illustrate how traditional activities have been transformed into inquiry learning experiences.

A typical osmosis experiment using dialysis tubing and solutions of various concentrations was transformed by focusing students on using the results of their own experiment to propose explanations, rather than confirming predetermined conclusions. After graphical analysis, student groups formulated explanations and used their data to answer questions related to their observations. Accustomed to a shift in teacher's role in facilitating only parts of the laboratory experience, students have become more dependent on discourse with their peers (NRC 2000).

A second example involved the enzymatic reaction of hydrogen peroxide decomposition with catalase. Comparing experimental results among all members of the class and arguing for their conclusions was a strategy used to establish factors affecting the rate of catalysis. Students started by designing and diagramming experiments to test the effects of temperature and pH. They decided how to rate bubble production and constructed graphs as a class with the understanding that they would be required to use them in support of their explanations. This activity correlates with Teaching Standard B of the NSES that encourages teachers to model the processes of inquiry, including openness to new ideas and data while maintaining the skepticism characteristic of science (NRC 2000).

Conducting action research in my classroom serves as a final example of inquiry and represents the most intriguing part of the PASS experience. Developing a research question about interactive notebooks allowed a critical and more reflective examination of the notebook's impact on students. The process of generating a question; deciding on instruments to use; researching the topics related to learning in this modality; and collecting, analyzing, and sharing data are the essence of inquiry learning (NRC 2000).

Evidence of Learning

Action research has afforded a personal opportunity to use inquiry to provide a window into my practice (NRC 2000). A group of science teachers at our school designed an action research project to investigate the impact of interactive notebooks as an inquiry scaffold on student achievement and attitudes about science. Our investigation involved three different academic levels of students who had an established negative belief in their ability to perform science.

Our findings indicate that students perceive interactive notebooks to impact their ability to learn science positively and that the notebook significantly increases their ability to organize the materials associated with learning (Figure 1). These results establish the important relationship between the interactive notebook and student achievement. As information flows through the interactive notebook to support the conclusions of an inquiry, so flows understanding.

Figure 1. The relationship between student grades and evaluation scores of their interactive notebooks for a group of students over one quarter of instruction (n = 156)

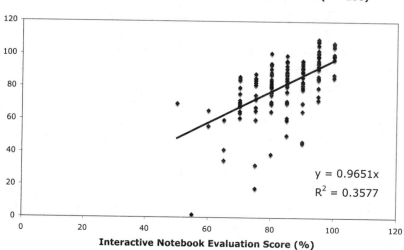

Overall Grade as a Function of Interactive Notebook Score (n = 156)

$y = 0.9651x$

$R^2 = 0.3577$

Interactive Notebook Evaluation Score (%)

As a result of inquiry science scaffolded with interactive notebooks, students demonstrated more favorable attitudes toward science and a willingness to engage in the process of scientific inquiry (Figure 2). Although a subjective indicator, such positive perceptions result in students being more willing to engage in the process of science, more aware of the relevance of science to their lives, and encouraged to enroll in more science classes in the future. With interactive notebooks, students come to understand the role of evidence gathering and sense-making in scientific inquiry. Using the notebook as a canvas to formulate plausible explanations and develop hypotheses for study fosters the inquiry process.

Ultimately, Project PASS has helped refocus my practice to a more specific path. Through inquiry with an interactive notebook, students have opportunities to manage their own

Figure 2. A comparison of survey responses about confidence related to thinking about science from students of three teachers using an interactive notebook to scaffold scientific inquiry in the classroom

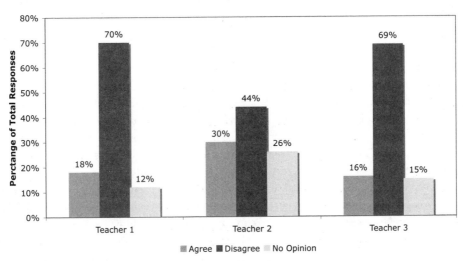

"During science activities, I prefer to ask other people for the answer rather than think for myself."

cognitive, metacognitive, and motivational strategies. Learning from this process, students make more effective choices in their path of lifelong learning by improving techniques for managing their motivation, incorporating new learning strategies, and practicing sense-making and reflection.

Vignette 2: Addressing Misconceptions About Heat Through a Real-World Inquiry Application

(Rebecca Reichenbach, Shelly Holt, and Christopher Smith, Western High School, Las Vegas)
Western High School is a "grand old dame" in the rapidly expanding urban center of Clark County School District. The original building was constructed in 1961 when its attendance area was on the edge of town surrounded by a relatively prosperous population. Over the years it rose to the heights of an elite school, but based on state testing it has now plunged to take a place as the district high school consistently posting some of the lowest passing rates and scores in reading, writing, and mathematics. In a district that serves over 300,000 students and builds a new high school every 12 months, we have held our bottom position for several years now and face the current year knowing we are perhaps the only Clark County High School facing the fifth year of failure to make acceptable Annual Yearly Progress.

When we started with Project PASS in the summer of 2005, we were dealing with a high transiency rate, high dropout rate, low graduation rate, low attendance, and an incredibly high apathy level in our students. We had a facility where little worked and much was falling apart. In other words, it had become a fairly typical urban high school.

Project PASS was advertised to Clark County science teachers in the spring of 2005 as a program designed to enhance our teaching skills and familiarity with new state standards, so we three teachers signed up to take advantage of the program. Our goal was to increase our personal content knowledge and maybe see something new that would give us a better grip on student attention. We found the materials and concepts presented to us that summer to be highly intriguing. If these methods could capture our attention so effectively, how well would they work with our students?

We entered the fall semester of 2005 with a new outlook on approaching students that could bring us to a higher level of engagement. We would encourage them to investigate the world around them instead of just turning to us for all the answers (NRC 2000). Project PASS had allowed us to experience inquiry methods ourselves as students and to start designing our own new inquiry projects in a setting where we received supportive and valuable feedback. We had opportunities to try inquiry practices and gain skill in their presentation. When the 2005 fall semester began, we knew we would have a network of people on which to fall back if we struggled with the implementation of inquiry teaching.

We also entered knowing we had a unique opportunity because Western High was being rebuilt. After 40 years, our facility had reached a point where it could no longer be repaired and the decision had been made to rebuild the entire campus. We would be holding classes for the next few years in the middle of a construction zone as portions were torn down, rubble removed, and new buildings constructed. Because we were landlocked in a heavily urban zone and did not have enough land to build one of the newer, standard high school buildings, we were told that our campus would have a unique design. Our design would be a green design, incorporating many features included to reduce heat gain and save power.

Our teacher group set out to incorporate the new building construction into a series of lessons for our students to learn not only about heat transfer, but also how science is applied in and affects our everyday lives. To assess student understanding, we developed surveys based on common heat- and science-related misconceptions as pre- and posttests. Students gave responses using a standard Likert-type scale.

Our first lesson took place as a two-day series. Day one was lecture-based to give students a background about heat transfer. We discussed radiation, convection, and conduction, including several examples. Students were informed that they would have to apply this knowledge to a lab challenge during the following class. Day two was themed "The Can Challenge."

At the beginning of day two, students were introduced to the idea that designing material that would not lose heat quickly could be a lucrative career; for example, Starbucks coffee cups are unique. Students explored the initial question "How much money do you think Starbucks spends each year to buy those coffee cups?" They were then posed the problem: Given the particular set of materials here, your group must design a container that will retain the heat in a cup of hot water better than any other group. We provided them with the following materials: Styrofoam cups in two different sizes, aluminum foil, empty soup cans, spongy shelf liner, plastic wrap, toilet paper, paper bags, and tape. The class discussed and compared successful designs with the not-so-successful.

Our second lesson was an investigation of the effects of color on heat gain and radiation. We found inexpensive model town puzzles that we constructed and glued to foam board in different colors: white, yellow, and black. We placed these under shop lamps and asked students to predict which would be hottest by the end of class. The class then went outside to walk around campus and record temperatures of materials of different colors, using handheld infrared thermometers. Upon return to the classroom, these data were compared and discussed (NRC 2000).

Our third and final lesson involved a comparison of different materials and design. Students were again asked to walk around campus and compare temperatures recorded from different building materials. During year one (2005–06) they were able to compare our new theater building to the old classroom wing, but during year two (2006–07) the old wing was torn down midyear and we took readings from the new three-story classroom building. Students in year two compared not only building materials, but also aspects of the design from different faces of the building to see how the architects reduced heat gain on the south side versus the north. After collecting temperature data outside, we returned to the classroom and students discussed their findings and why they thought the design worked to reduce heat gain. It is important to note that we did not tell them which features of the building were designed to reduce heat gain. We simply told them that there were some odd features visible on our building and they were to discover why the architects would have put them in place.

We have much anecdotal evidence that leads us to believe that we have reached our students at a level that was lacking before the implementation of inquiry in our classrooms. We observed that apathy in our students greatly decreased, attendance increased, dropouts in our classes decreased, and students were genuinely unhappy if they had to leave our classes for any reason. It is not uncommon to hear students express genuine regret when they transfer to other schools. One said, "This is the first science class I ever really got." The students also expressed and followed through on interest in taking more science classes. To quote our students, "The science classes got it goin' on. We wanna be here."

Evidence of Learning

In year one, individual teacher differences likely had a larger effect on student learning than did inquiry instruction due to the large group of participating teachers (n = 10). However, we did see a significant increase in scores among those students who completed more of the series of activities than others (Table 1). The mean raw scores were generated by adding correct responses on our survey after they had experienced our inquiry lessons. Unfortunately, not all our teachers were able to implement the entire series of labs but their scores do serve to provide us with a snapshot showing the increase found by doing our simple inquiry walks around campus versus the in-classroom activities alone.

Table 1. A comparison of posttest scores (%) for students completing one vs. two inquiry lab experiences

	One Inquiry Lab Experience	Two Inquiry Lab Experiences
Students	82	102
Mean	63.2	73.0
SD	12.9	11.7
Range	38–93	42–102

In year two we reduced the number of teachers implementing the lessons to the three core investigators involved with Project PASS. This time, our results were much clearer. Our freshman students who learned about heat using our inquiry lab series scored a full standard deviation higher on heat-related concepts than those who were in a traditionally taught classroom (Table 2). Unfortunately, the shift is not as visible among our upper-class students, but we note that the biggest gains were found in the lowest-scoring quartiles. It is also significant to note that in year two we did not administer the final survey until a full month after our final inquiry lesson, so our gains show true long-term learning.

Table 2. Comparison of posttest scores (%) for freshman and upper-class students who completed a series of inquiry laboratory activities with students taught in a traditional fashion

Freshman Students

	Inquiry Group	Comparison Group
Number of Students	144	27
Mean	71.8	64.9
SD	11.6	13.1
Range	40–94	42–93
Median	73	69
Quartile 1	64.5	58
Quartile 3	80	75
Mode	76	69

Upper-class Students

	Inquiry Group	Comparison Group
Number of Students	37	28
Mean	65.24	60.96
SD	9.44	12.97
Range	45–81	37–84
Median	66	59.5
Quartile 1	59	54
Quartile 3	73	69.25
Mode	76	54

We also collected anecdotal evidence of learning. There was a marked increase in "AHA!" moments by our students through the series of lessons. It is exciting seeing students arguing about their own investigation about the false benefits of putting white rock near their homes ("It increases the reflected energy, so the house increases in heat!") as well as knowing they are seeing the applications of science to their lives ("We're remodeling and my dad is really interested in what we've been learning.").

We have seen an increase in attendance in our classes. Dropout rates in our classes have decreased significantly. One of the teachers (Reichenbach) has gone from year one with classes starting at 40 in September and having only 12 in attendance in May to starting with 40 and ending with 35. Overall, our rate of students enrolling in additional science classes has also increased. Our science program had been suffering for several years. We had offered two Advanced Placement (AP) courses and several honors-level courses in the past, but by 2001–2002 interest in our high-level classes had dropped to where we could only offer these courses in alternating years. By 2003–2004 no AP courses were offered. In 2004–2005 just six honors sections appeared in our master teacher schedule.

While only 3 of our 11 science teachers have been intimately involved with Project PASS, we enlisted the entire department to try our "heat island" lessons in the 2005–2006 school year. That year, every science student experienced some form of our inquiry lessons. The very next year, we were able to not only offer, but actually had enough students sign up to add AP Biology, Zoology Honors, and Forensic Science to our master teaching schedule. We jumped to nine total honors sections. In 2007–2008 we also added AP Physics and now have 10 honors sections. Next year we will also be offering AP Chemistry. In three years we have rebuilt our program to a point where it is stronger than ever before.

Vignette 3: One Egg of a Problem–Osmosis Through Inquiry

(Cindy Kern, Green Valley High School, Henderson, Nevada)

When I started my career, I was initiated into teaching at a school that expected nothing but the best from everyone—administrators, teachers, support staff, and students. The school's motto is "Commitment to Excellence," and few within our halls accepted anything less. This environment was great for my practice, but I felt that I was missing something and had no name for it. Prior to my involvement with Project PASS, I was a very raw teacher who worked primarily from instinct and collaboration with my colleagues. PASS provided three years of theory-to-practice professional development focused on inquiry, conceptual change, and fostering students as self-regulated learners. These ideas have transformed my teaching and, more importantly, the educational experience I provide to students. The following lab, completed by 10th-grade Biology students and 9th-grade Biology Honors students, is an inquiry activity that serves as an example of the fundamental change in my instructional methods. Following the first PASS summer institute, where we focused on the idea of inquiry-based instruction, I adapted the lab from a teacher-directed lab to a student-centered one. In each subsequent year, as my knowledge of conceptual change and teaching to develop self-regulated learners increased (NRS 2000), I found a connection to using full inquiry and the lab evolved into an experience that is not easily forgotten by students.

The inquiry lab "One Egg of a Problem" is embedded in a unit on cells. Prior to the start of the cell unit, I spend two days working through analogies of passive transport, active transport, and the cell membrane. To develop an understanding of a concentration gradient, students are asked to stand in one corner of the room as closely together as possible. They are asked to identify themselves in terms of concentration. Then students spread throughout the room until they are most comfortable. Inevitably, students space themselves reasonably close to equilibrium. Again they are asked to identify themselves in terms of concentration. When they return to the corner, I emphasize how much energy is required in coaching and insisting to get them to move to a higher concentration. By contrast, when they are allowed to go wherever they choose, the word "Go!" is enough for them to move to areas of low concentration. Following this activity, students draw an annotated illustration identifying a concentration gradient and the energy requirements when moving along and against a concentration gradient.

Next, a balloon activity is used to develop a conceptual model for the cell membrane. I prepare about 40 balloons with a variety of extracts (e.g., vanilla, lemon, and peppermint) that are contained within 40-gallon trash bags. I remind students to identify the balloons in terms of concentration and predict what will happen when the trash bags are opened and put on the floor. Each student chooses a balloon, which they smell and pass around. Eventually, a student will pose the question, "How can we smell the extracts while the balloon stays inflated?" Through a class discussion, an analogy develops for the balloon as similar to a chain-link fence, where some objects are small enough to move through the holes while others are not. We then walk down to the baseball field and throw baseballs, softballs, soccer balls, golf balls, marbles, and ping-pong balls at the chain-link fence. Students draw an annotated illustration comparing the balloon skin with the chain-link fence and the molecules contained within the balloon to the different balls we threw at the fence. Finally, an analogy is made between the balloon and a cell membrane. The similarities and differences between the balloon containing the extract and a cell containing water are discussed. This is done to set up the one-week-long student-directed inquiry lab.

"One Egg of a Problem" presents students with the following problem statement: "You have one week to make your egg bigger, make the same egg smaller, and then return it to its original size without breaking the cell membrane." Students are given a raw egg and must first dissolve the shell with vinegar, leaving the cell membrane intact. They then have one week to work through a problem that illustrates the process of osmosis. To explore and test prior to starting the development of their procedures, students are provided with a couple of broken eggs. Working in pairs, students have a class period to develop procedures and identify two qualitative and three quantitative data points to collect as evidence that their egg has changed in volume. A variety of supplies are available, including beakers, graduated cylinders, string, rulers, distilled water, baking soda, Karo syrup, vinegar, tap water, salt, an electronic balance, and a host of other odd items. I encourage them to ask for other supplies and after getting approval, to bring materials from home. Students are excited, but are *really* outside their comfort zone. Having previously participated in a student-directed lab, they know that there will be some trial and error, but the uncertainty can be a bit unsettling. I require a written procedure for the next day and an explanation of what they predict will happen and why (*inquiry along a continuum*).

This is a fun-filled week of triumph and defeat, elation, and frustration. Students eagerly enter class with anticipation in their eyes and questions on their lips. Students are given 25–50 minutes each day to collect their data and subject their eggs to their next set of procedures. This time is also used to compare results and collaborate on successful procedures, as well as for inferring why some procedures worked and others did not. The informal conversations are used as a springboard to generate small- and large-group discussions. Typically, several groups will identify the movement of water from an area of high concentration to an area of low concentration, and this helps to guide the remaining groups in developing their experiment. Again, in terms of concentration gradient, water, and the cell membrane, students make a labeled drawing of what is happening with their eggs. By the end of the activity, students have developed a definition of osmosis and are encouraged to review and revise their procedures based on these discussions.

All further discussions are held within the context of cellular transport. When working in small and whole groups, students are asked to speak *osmotically* using the scientific terms. Take just a moment to imagine a class with 41 students, of which as many as two-thirds are simultaneously speaking osmotically while the other third is listening osmotically. It is a powerful venue for students to work through their scientific understanding.

Throughout the cell unit, students are continuously representing their understanding of cells and cellular processes with a concept map as a metacognitive tool (Vanides et al. 2005). Students are given a bank of concepts at the beginning of the unit and are asked to revise their concept maps continually to reflect their most current understanding of the topic. With terms like *hypertonic, hypotonic,* and *isotonic*, the concept bank helps to direct students toward adopting a scientific understanding. As students work through their growing understanding of cellular transport, they examine these concepts within the context of the "One Egg of a Problem" lab and with collaboration among peers; they begin to classify solutions using scientific terms.

At the end of the week (seven days), the majority of students have successfully solved "One Egg of a Problem." More importantly, they have applied the concepts of passive transport and osmosis to a scientifically oriented question. The final step involves students using their data as evidence while communicating their explanations (NRC 2000).

The Curriculum and Professional Development Division of our school district has developed Friday Symposia as a medium for students throughout our district to communicate and justify the results of their inquiries to a broad audience of their peers. Friday Symposia are online videoconferences where students use classroom webcams to talk to anyone signed on to a symposium. Since this lab was implemented with collaboration and discussion as an integral component, it seemed fitting to participate in a symposium by doing a whole-class presentation. The only directions provided to students for their presentation was to use the "RECALL" conclusion format: R = reason (purpose), E = experiment (brief synopsis), C = call back (review of data), A = analysis, L = lapses, and L = learned (what was learned and new questions). Students divided themselves into five groups, each responsible for a section of the RECALL conclusions. The presentation included student-created analogies for describing the permeability of a cell membrane; a skit, "Osmosis: The Musical," that visually reenacted osmosis with a narration explaining the science; data tables and graphs created in a spreadsheet and presented with presentation software; and concept maps demonstrating an overall understanding of osmosis. It was an incredible experience that properly brought the inquiry cycle full circle.

Evidence of Learning

Throughout the cell unit, students were continuously working on personal concept maps. A total of four are assigned at specific times during the unit of instruction (Kern and Crippen 2008). The first three maps serve as formative assessments and are used to identify existing ideas, including misconceptions and persistent misconceptions from one concept map to another, and as well as any changes in student scientific understanding. These maps also encourage metacognition, intended to facilitate the development of a scientific understanding.

To illustrate student learning within the inquiry experience, a series of concept maps will be presented for a real student with the pseudonym of John Doe. John worked on his map continuously throughout the unit, but maps are collected at four points within the inquiry unit. As a temporal collection, the maps demonstrate the development of one student's scientific understanding while learning through inquiry in the cell unit.

The first concept mapping activity is meant to identify John's prior knowledge of the concepts to be covered in the pending cell unit (Figure 3). Students are provided a list of the major concepts for the upcoming unit as a concept bank. The concepts in the concept bank are chosen from a combination of the curriculum materials and the national and state standards. The student concept map presented as Figure 3 indicates that John lacks a scientific understanding of cellular transport. The relationships among the concepts are limited and, for the most part are incorrect. By associating active transport, osmosis, and diffusion, John demonstrates a significant misconception. For the teacher, the understanding presented on this map provides critical insight for facilitating John toward a more scientific understanding throughout the inquiry process.

Figure 3. John Doe's first concept map produced prior to instruction in an activity to identify prior knowledge

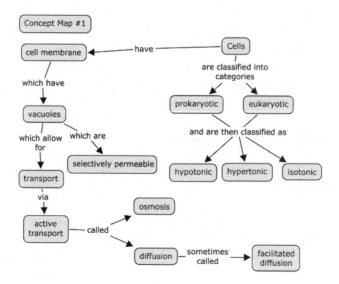

The second concept mapping activity occurred after the analogies for passive and active transport were introduced (Figure 4). Learning is evident in the relationship John makes between cell membrane and selectively permeable. The connection here is weak, with little demonstration of scientific understanding. However, this is to be expected at this early stage of the unit. A persistent misconception is apparent in the association between active transport and osmosis. The structure of the concept map indicates linear thinking with no interconnections. From the teacher's perspective, John's learning is limited and more than likely will result in nonlearning.

John's third concept map was due at to the end of the "One Egg of a Problem" inquiry, prior to developing the Friday Symposia presentation (Figure 5). Evidence of learning is found primarily in the phrases he uses to link the concepts. John is demonstrating a scientific understanding of the relationship among cells and transport. Furthermore, the persistent misconception associated with active transport and osmosis has been overcome. The incorporation of the concepts *isotonic, hypotonic,* and *hypertonic* indicates a higher level of understanding, though he does not fully understand the relationship among the three concepts. The structure of the concept map is still linear and the lack of interconnectedness indicates that the scientific understanding has not yet translated into meaningful learning.

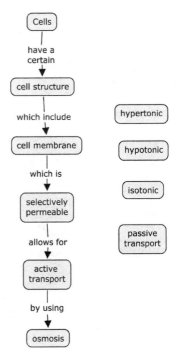

Figure 4. John Doe's second concept map produced at the first natural break in instruction

Figure 5. John Doe's third concept map produced at the second natural break in instruction, following the "One Egg of a Kind" inquiry investigation

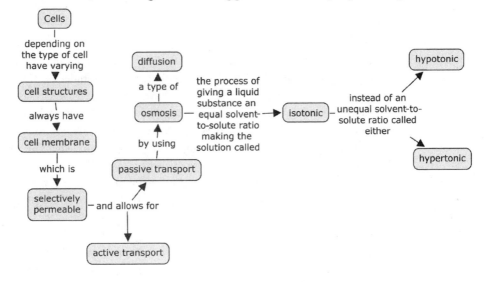

The fourth and final concept map is due on the last day of the unit (Figure 6). The map suggests that the final two elements of inquiry are effective tools for scaffolding his learning. The third concept map helped to identify his understanding of cellular transport and the fourth represents his understanding after comparing his ideas with scientific understanding and communicating his ideas to his peers. John's learning is evident in both the quality of the linking phrases and the structure of the concept map. The linking phrases he uses suggest that a scientific understanding has been assimilated into his conceptual framework. The interconnectedness of the concepts, although limited, indicates that his learning has been meaningful.

Figure 6. John Doe's fourth and final concept map produced on the last day of the inquiry unit

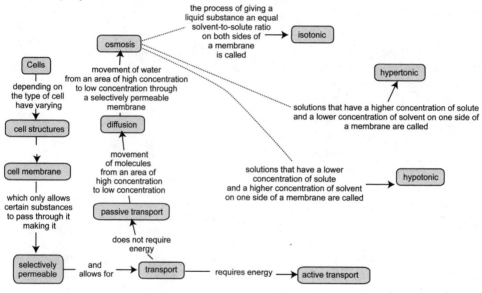

Project PASS intertwined inquiry, conceptual change, and students as self-regulated learners into a professional development experience that has and will continue to impact student learning for years to come. For students in my classes, their experiences have been directly affected as a result of my participation in Project PASS and through my work to translate educational theory into practice. Through PASS, I found the missing piece to my teaching: strong educational theory and action research as a process to understand its impact on students. Implementing all the NSES elements of inquiry is essential for students to experience meaningful learning. Individuals in a class of 40 have the opportunity to address their prior conceptions, compare their idea with scientific understanding, and communicate their assimilated idea while investigating a scientifically oriented question. These key elements scaffold meaningful learning in the form of conceptual change. Engaging students in a metacognitive activity such as concept mapping throughout an inquiry provides a strategy for monitoring student learning as well as a tool for students to restructure their conceptual framework. Inquiry's impact on student learning is evident in the series of concept mapping activities that show students moving from a naïve perspective of science to a deeper, scientifically literate conceptual understanding.

Conclusion

The vignettes of this chapter highlight the work of three teacher teams who participated in a long-term professional development program, accepted the challenge for change, and worked diligently to implement the inquiry vision of the National Science Education Standards. According to the NSES, classroom inquiry can take many forms, but it includes five essential features. As illustrated by the projects described in this chapter, implementation of these features can occur along a continuum, but collectively, inquiry-based instruction can have a powerful impact on students.

The interactive notebooks described by Cheryl Waldman in the first vignette serve as a powerful personal learning scaffold for the inquiry process that empowers students for achievement. Using inquiry along a continuum, Ms. Waldman guides students toward evidence and sources of knowledge while maintaining their notebooks as the medium for creating explanations. Plausible explanations are generated, communicated, and justified within the classroom environment. The end result is a scientific question proposed to address observations gleaned through an investigation. With this technique, students come to value the sense-making process of scientific inquiry and become aware of the knowledge and skills required to control their learning. Control of learning is empowering, and empowered science students are confident and focused on improving their achievement. Results in the form of surveys and notebook assessment scores show increases in students' attitudes toward science, use of scientific inquiry, and achievement.

In the second vignette, Rebecca Reichenbach described how a group of teachers at a traditionally underperforming inner-city school capitalized on a school construction project to create an open inquiry rooted in the lives of their students. This authentic project engaged students in understanding how the construction of their new school contributed to the temperature they experience daily through the urban heat-island effect. The teacher team worked hard to personalize the science of the construction process for students and it paid big dividends for student motivation for engaging in science and learning. Students asked deeper questions and took a greater interest in reading, writing, and talking about science. In comparison to other students who did not learn with the inquiry approach, the students who used the inquiry materials scored higher on measures of learning. The teacher team at Western High School is excited to find a growing student interest in science and larger enrollments in higher-level science classes.

In the final vignette, Cindy Kern described an inquiry where students designed their own investigations to address a series of questions pertaining to the movement of materials within and among cells. These students evaluated their inquiry questions by making observations, collecting data, and rationalizing their results. The interpretation of results included the need for successful justification by presentations to their peers, which contributed significantly to their scientific understanding. In an authentic twist, the students presented and defended their results to an audience from across the school district at the online Friday Symposia videoconference.

Throughout the inquiry, students used concept mapping to scaffold their developing understanding and these maps served as a powerful piece of evidence for learning.

The results of the projects described here speak to the potential of long-term professional development with dedicated teachers for reforming classroom practices and positively impacting student learning and enjoyment of science. In our follow-up surveys with participating teachers, the most often cited successes of Project PASS were a better understanding of student learning and the process of action research. In our context, teachers who understand and accept a robust model of student learning are attuned to evaluate the products of student thinking continuously, are conscious of the important role of motivation in the classroom, are encouraged to examine their practice using the tools of science, and are indeed a powerful enterprise. The legacy of Project PASS is written in the successful science inquiry experiences of students across Clark County Nevada.

References

American Association for the Advancement of Science (AAAS). 1989. *Science for all Americans*. Washington, DC: American Association for the Advancement of Science.

AVID. 2007. Advancement Via Individual Determination. Available online at *www.avidcenter.org*.

Bryk, A. S., P. B. Sebring, D. Kerbow, S. Rollow, and J. Q. Easton. 1998. *Charting Chicago school reform: Democratic localism as a lever for change*. Boulder, CO: Westview Press.

Coffman, C., and L. Riggs. 2006. The virtual vee map: A template for Internet inquiry. *Journal of College Science Teaching* 36 (1): 32–39.

Duit, R. 2003. Conceptual change: A powerful framework for improving science teaching and learning. *International Journal of Science Education* 25 (6): 671–688.

Fullan, M. G. 2001. *The new meaning of educational change,* third ed. New York: Teachers College Press.

Gowin, B. D., and M. C. Alvarez. 2005. *The art of educating with V diagrams*. Cambridge: Cambridge University Press.

Hand, B., and C. Keys. 1999. Inquiry investigation. *The Science Teacher* 66 (4): 27–29.

Kern, C., and K. J. Crippen. 2008. Mapping for conceptual change. *The Science Teacher* 75 (6): 32–38.

National Research Council (NRC). 1996. *National science education standards*. Washington, DC: National Academy Press.

National Research Council (NRC). 2000. *Inquiry and the national science education standards*. Washington, DC: National Academy Press.

Nolen, S. B. 2003. Learning environment, motivation, and achievement in high school science. *Journal of Research in Science Teaching* 40 (4): 347–368.

Posner, G. J., K. A. Strike, P. W. Hewson, and W. A. Gertzog. 1982. Accommodation of a scientific conception: Toward a theory of conceptual change. *Science Education* 66: 211–227.

Roehrig, G. H., J. A. Luft, and M. Edwards. 2001. Versatile vee maps. *The Science Teacher* 68 (1): 28–31.

Schraw, G., K. J. Crippen, and K. D. Hartley. 2006. Promoting self-regulation in science education: Meta-cognition as part of a broader perspective on learning. *Research in Science Education* 36 (1): 111–139.

Teachers' Curriculum Institute. 2000. History alive! Interactive student notebook. Available online at *www.teachtci.com/forum/isn.aspx*.

Vanides, J., Y. Yin, M. Tomita, and M. A. Ruiz-Primo. 2005. Using concept maps in the science classroom. *Science Scope* 28 (8): 27–31.

Waldman, C. A., and K. J. Crippen. 2009. Integrating interactive notebooks. *The Science Teacher* 76 (1): 51–55.

Inquiry Produces Changes: What We Have Learned

Robert E. Yager
University of Iowa

W hat a fascinating year! What a joy to learn about creative teachers who have helped develop inquiry-centered programs. This latest ESP volume consists of 18 chapters—all with unique stories of success and ideas for seeing inquiry in action for students, teachers, parents, and other educational leaders.

One of the most interesting results of the yearlong effort has been the realization from many "would-be" contributors that they were not actually "doing" inquiry. The kits, texts, activity guides, the stated curriculum, the teaching approaches all professed to be inquiry-oriented. But, as the stories about programs unfolded, there was realization that there was little real evidence of success in terms of student learning. Often, the teacher observations and scores on typical assessments were the only indicators of success. Success was related to grades and teacher observations. It seemed that all that was needed were conscientious students and a desire on their part to repeat what the lessons sought to illustrate.

Real inquiry demands investigations, questioning, multiple evidences of success, and preparation for unexpected results. The best indicators for success are what students do with their learning when not in the classroom with their given teacher. Instead too many students are merely trying to figure out answers to textbook or teacher-constructed test questions, often with multiple-choice options.

Many of the 49 authors contributing to this monograph have specifically mentioned their continued learning with students and their dependence on individual students for engagement and experience with all five of the Essential Features of Inquiry. This is opposed to teachers being in control, preparing the lesson plans, getting materials ready, and providing assessments to be sure students were attentive and that they could repeat the definitions and skills that they had been taught. When inquiry is a focus, teachers are freed from making all the instructional decisions, such as,

- what criteria is evidence of success;
- what activities students must do;
- how to grade student success;
- what to use as criteria for real learning;
- how to share student learning with others in the school and community, including the outside world (which occurs with the publication of this monograph).

Certainly all 18 chapters provide unique glimpses of inquiry in action—in elementary, middle, and high school classes; with teacher preparation; with research participation in collaboration with professionals; with a variety of unique areas of expertise and situations where K–16 students actually experience science as inquiry.

The 49 authors share their own growth, experience, and ideas; they invite more collaboration, always enlarging and expanding their own learning and defining more appropriate roles as inquiry teachers. With inquiry, teachers assume very different roles: as learners, as helpers, as stimulators, as cheerleaders, and as building and community leaders. All the teacher authors try to make learning and thinking possible and foremost as the purpose of education and schooling. Indeed, teaching itself becomes inquiry.

It is not surprising to see evidence in each chapter that students' attitudes are more positive, that learning extends beyond the class period and schools, and that results of inquiry can be observed and marveled with greater satisfaction than from doing cookbook labs. The chapters are exciting and diverse while exhibiting the full meaning of inquiry and indicating how it exemplifies the real meaning of science itself. The variety in terms of geography, teaching level, and institutions and agencies involved adds richness while indicating the fundamental problems with state or district curriculum structures, textbooks, prescribed laboratories, and the use of inquiry and science in classes with all students doing the same things. There is power in diversity and an opportunity for students to learn from and with each other.

The chapters illustrate well the nature of real inquiry. Some chapters focus on students of all ages learning with accomplished and enthusiastic scientists as a part of the learning team. Others deal with the preservice experiences of teachers as well as with the continued development of inservice teachers. The chapters focus on a variety of assessment efforts—seldom dependent on repetition of skills, recitation of text materials, following directions carefully, or always getting the right answers to all responses for teacher-directed assessments.

The examples in these chapters as a set can be used to illustrate the "doing" of science and the use of science as a vehicle for learning (the five Essential Features of Inquiry) rather than reviewing the "products" of science, which actually represent but the mass of information found in typical textbooks. Rarely are the textbooks in use free of errors; few include the results of new discoveries that are constantly being amassed.

All authors join me in asking readers to question us further, to continue following our emerging stories, to help determine the accuracy of some of our ideas. Members of our National Advisory Board were quick in requesting additional information indicating when information was lacking to validate some of the generalized conclusions. Many were shocked at the limitations that seem to result from the No Child Left Behind legislation, and for the lack of agreement among administrators, parents, and all teachers about the visions of the National Standards and how these were ignored as State Standards were developed (often with much more specificity and more information that is found in typical texts). Several noted that textbook adoption states present problems with doing inquiry because content is "prescribed" while merely hoping that graduates can think and use it in making personal and societal decisions.

Again, readers are invited to correspond with authors regarding questions the chapters stimulate, about support materials that could not be included, and about information regarding students and modules that have been developed since copy was provided for the printing of this monograph. Appendix 2 provides a list of all authors and their affiliations. We hope the ESP monograph can also invite even more collaboration and more active research efforts. We do not look upon the 18 chapters to be "end-of-stories." Instead we hope they can be starting points for more discussion, sharing of ideas, ways of trying new approaches, and also assessing successes as evidence and reasons for making inquiry even more central to our science teaching. Indeed, inquiry provides the basis for more and better student thinking and more reasons for real science learning. When personal experiences result in real learning for all students, it can be used effectively the rest of their lives. This is not the case for the typical content in textbooks and state standards.

Appendixes

Less Emphasis/More Emphasis
Conditions of the National Science Education Standards

The *National Science Education Standards* envision change throughout the system. The **teaching standards** encompass the following changes in emphases:

LESS EMPHASIS ON	MORE EMPHASIS ON
Treating all students alike and responding to the group as a whole	Understanding and responding to individual student's interests, strengths, experiences, and needs
Rigidly following curriculum	Selecting and adapting curriculum
Focusing on student acquisition of information	Focusing on student understanding and use of scientific knowledge, ideas, and inquiry processes
Presenting scientific knowledge through lecture, text, and demonstration	Guiding students in active and extended scientific inquiry
Asking for recitation of acquired knowledge	Providing opportunities for scientific discussion and debate among students
Testing students for factual information at the end of the unit or chapter	Continuously assessing student understanding
Maintaining responsibility and authority	Sharing responsibility for learning with students
Supporting competition	Supporting a classroom community with cooperation, shared responsibility, and respect
Working alone	Working with other teachers to enhance the science program

Source: National Research Council (NRC). 1996. *National science education standards.* Washington, DC: National Academy Press, p. 52. Reprinted with permission.

The *National Science Education Standards* envision change throughout the system. The **professional development standards** encompass the following changes in emphases:

LESS EMPHASIS ON	MORE EMPHASIS ON
Transmission of teaching knowledge and skills by lectures	Inquiry into teaching and learning
Learning science by lecture and reading	Learning science through investigation and inquiry
Separation of science and teaching knowledge	Integration of science and teaching knowledge
Separation of theory and practice	Integration of theory and practice in school settings
Individual learning	Collegial and collaborative learning
Fragmented, one-shot sessions	Long-term coherent plans
Courses and workshops	A variety of professional development activities
Reliance on external expertise	Mix of internal and external expertise
Staff developers as educators	Staff developers as facilitators, consultants, and planners
Teacher as technician	Teacher as intellectual, reflective practitioner
Teacher as consumer of knowledge about teaching	Teacher as producer of knowledge about teaching
Teacher as follower	Teacher as leader
Teacher as an individual based in a classroom	Teacher as a member of a collegial professional community
Teacher as target of change	Teacher as source and facilitator of change

The *National Science Education Standards* envision change throughout the system. The **assessment standards** encompass the following changes in emphases:

LESS EMPHASIS ON	MORE EMPHASIS ON
Assessing what is easily measured	Assessing what is most highly valued
Assessing discrete knowledge	Assessing rich, well-structured knowledge
Assessing scientific knowledge	Assessing scientific understanding and reasoning
Assessing to learn what students do not know	Assessing to learn what students do understand
Assessing only achievement	Assessing achievement and opportunity to learn
End of term assessments by teachers	Students engaged in ongoing assessment of their work and that of others
Development of external assessments by measurement experts alone	Teachers involved in the development of external assessments

The *National Science Education Standards* envision change throughout the system. The science **content and inquiry standards** encompass the following changes in emphases:

LESS EMPHASIS ON	MORE EMPHASIS ON
Knowing scientific facts and information	Understanding scientific concepts and developing abilities of inquiry
Studying subject matter disciplines (physical, life, Earth sciences) for their own sake	Learning subject matter disciplines in the context of inquiry, technology, science in personal and social perspectives, and history and nature of science
Separating science knowledge and science process	Integrating all aspects of science content
Covering many science topics	Studying a few fundamental science concepts
Implementing inquiry as a set of processes	Implementing inquiry as instructional strategies, abilities, and ideas to be learned

CHANGING EMPHASES TO PROMOTE INQUIRY

LESS EMPHASIS ON	MORE EMPHASIS ON
Activities that demonstrate and verify science content	Activities that investigate and analyze science questions
Investigations confined to one class period	Investigations over extended periods of time
Process skills out of context	Process skills in context
Individual process skills such as observation or inference	Using multiple process skills—manipulation, cognitive, procedural
Getting an answer	Using evidence and strategies for developing or revising an explanation
Science as exploration and experiment	Science as argument and explanation
Providing answers to questions about science content	Communicating science explanations
Individuals and groups of students analyzing and synthesizing data without defending a conclusion	Groups of students often analyzing and synthesizing data after defending conclusions
Doing few investigations in order to leave time to cover large amounts of content	Doing more investigations in order to develop understanding, ability, values of inquiry and knowledge of science content
Concluding inquiries with the result of the experiment	Applying the results of experiments to scientific arguments and explanations

Management of materials and equipment

Private communication of student ideas
and conclusions to teacher

Management of ideas and information

Public communication of student ideas
and work to classmates

The *National Science Education Standards* envision change throughout the system. The **program standards** encompass the following changes in emphases:

LESS EMPHASIS ON	MORE EMPHASIS ON
Developing science programs at different grade levels independently of one another	Coordinating the development of the K–12 science program across grade levels
Using assessments unrelated to curriculum and teaching	Aligning curriculum, teaching, and assessment
Maintaining current resource allocations for books	Allocating resources necessary for hands-on inquiry teaching aligned with the *Standards*
Textbook- and lecture-driven curriculum	Curriculum that supports the *Standards*, and includes a variety of components, such as laboratories emphasizing inquiry and field trips
Broad coverage of unconnected factual information	Curriculum that includes natural phenomena and science-related social issues that students encounter in everyday life
Treating science as a subject isolated from other school subjects	Connecting science to other school subjects, such as mathematics and social studies
Science learning opportunities that favor one group of students	Providing challenging opportunities for all students to learn science
Limiting hiring decisions to the administration	Involving successful teachers of science in the hiring process
Maintaining the isolation of teachers	Treating teachers as professionals whose work requires opportunities for continual learning and networking
Supporting competition	Promoting collegiality among teachers as a team to improve the school
Teachers as followers	Teachers as decision makers

The emphasis charts for **system standards** are organized around shifting the emphases at three levels of organization within the education system—district, state, and federal. The three levels of the system selected for these charts are only representative of the many components of the science education system that need to change to promote the vision of science education described in the *National Science Education Standards.*

FEDERAL SYSTEM

LESS EMPHASIS ON	MORE EMPHASIS ON
Financial support for developing new curriculum materials not aligned with the *Standards*	Financial support for developing new curriculum materials aligned with the *Standards*
Support by federal agencies for professional development activities that affect only a few teachers	Support for professional development activities that are aligned with the *Standards* and promote systemwide changes
Agencies working independently on various components of science education	Coordination among agencies responsible for science education
Support for activities and programs that are unrelated to *Standards*-based reform	Support for activities and programs that successfully implement the *Standards* at state and district levels
Federal efforts that are independent of state and local levels	Coordination of reform efforts at federal, state, and local levels
Short-term projects	Long-term commitment of resources to improving science education

STATE SYSTEM

LESS EMPHASIS ON	MORE EMPHASIS ON
Independent initiatives to reform components of science education	Partnerships and coordination of reform efforts
Funds for workshops and programs having little connection to the *Standards*	Funds to improve curriculum and instruction based on the *Standards*
Frameworks, textbooks, and materials based on activities only marginally related to the *Standards*	Frameworks, textbooks, and materials adoption criteria aligned with national and state standards
Assessments aligned with the traditional content of science	Assessments aligned with the *Standards* and the expanded education view of science content

Current approaches to teacher education	University/college reform of teacher education to include science-specific pedagogy aligned with the *Standards*
Teacher certification based on formal, historically based requirements	Teacher certification that is based on understanding and abilities in science and science teaching

DISTRICT SYSTEM

LESS EMPHASIS ON	**MORE EMPHASIS ON**
Technical, short-term, inservice workshops	Ongoing professional development to support teachers
Policies unrelated to *Standards*-based reform	Policies designed to support changes called for in the *Standards*
Purchase of textbooks based on traditional topics	Purchase or adoption of curriculum aligned with the *Standards* and on a conceptual approach to science teaching, including support for hands-on science materials
Standardized tests and assessments unrelated to *Standards*-based program and practices	Assessments aligned with the *Standards*
Administration determining what will be involved in improving science education	Teacher leadership in improvement of science education
Authority at upper levels of educational system	Authority for decisions at level of implementation
School board ignorance of science education program	School board support of improvements aligned with the *Standards*
Local union contracts that ignore changes in curriculum, instruction, and assessment	Local union contracts that support improvements indicated by the *Standards*

Contributors

Natalie S. Barman, coauthor of *Developing a Relationship With Science Through Authentic Inquiry,* is a trustee clinical lecturer at Indiana University Purdue University at Indianapolis.

Anthony Bartley, coauthor of *Science as Inquiry at Sir Winston Churchill Collegiate and Vocational Institute,* is associate professor at Lakehead University in Thunder Bay, Ontario, Canada.

Erin Baumgartner, coauthor of *Ecological Monitoring Provides a Thematic Foundation for Student Inquiry,* is assistant professor of biology at Western Oregon University in Monmouth, Oregon.

Shari L. Britner, coauthor of *Developing Inquiry Skills Along a Teacher Professional Continuum,* is an associate professor of science education at Bradley University in Peoria, Illinois.

Erin Cox, coauthor of *Ecological Monitoring Provides a Thematic Foundation for Student Inquiry,* is a graduate researcher at University of Hawaii–Manoa in Honolulu, Hawaii.

Kent J. Crippen, coauthor of *Learning Science With Inquiry in the Clark County School District,* is associate professor at University of Nevada in Las Vegas, Nevada.

Donald Dosch, coauthor of *Student Inquiry and Research: Developing Students' Authentic Inquiry Skills,* is a teacher at Illinois Mathematics and Science Academy in Aurora, Illinois.

Ellen K. Ebert, coauthor of *Learning Science With Inquiry in the Clark County School District,* is project facilitator for the Clark County School District in Las Vegas, Nevada.

Michelle Edgcomb, coauthor of *Developing Inquiry Skills Along a Teacher Professional Continuum,* is a laboratory coordinator and instructor at Bradley University in Peoria, Illinois.

Kevin Finson, coauthor of *Developing Inquiry Skills Along a Teacher Professional Continuum,* is a professor of science education at Bradley University in Peoria, Illinois.

Holly Harrick, author of *Inquiry: A Challenge for Changing the Teaching of Science in Connecticut,* is a professional development project manager at Connecticut Science Center in Hartford, Connecticut.

Tina Harris, author of *"If We Are Supposed to Understand Science, Shouldn't We Be Doing It?"* is a science teacher at Anderson Community School Corporation.

Richard Hudson, coauthor of *Science Is Not a Spectator Sport: Three Principles From 15 years of Project Dragonfly,* is director of science production at Twin Cities Public Television in St. Paul, Minnesota.

Lauren I. Inouye, coauthor of *Natural Scientists: Children in Charge*, is a teacher at Hanahau'oli School in Honolulu, Hawaii.

Karen E. Johnson, coauthor of *Enhancing the Inquiry Experience: Authentic Research in the Classroom*, is a science teacher at Niver Creek Middle School in Thorton, Colorado.

Doug Jones, coauthor of *Science as Inquiry at Sir Winston Churchill Collegiate and Vocational Institute*, is science department chair at Sir Winston Churchill Collegiate and Vocational Institute in Thunder Bay, Ontario, Canada.

Cynthia Kaplanis, coauthor of *Science as Inquiry at Sir Winston Churchill Collegiate and Vocational Institute*, is a teacher at Sir Winston Churchill Collegiate and Vocational Institute in Thunder Bay, Ontario, Canada.

Cindy Kern, coauthor of *Learning Science With Inquiry in the Clark County School District*, is a teacher at Green Valley High School in Henderson, Nevada.

Matthew Knope, coauthor of *Ecological Monitoring Provides a Thematic Foundation for Student Inquiry*, is a graduate researcher at University of Hawaii–Manoa in Honolulu, Hawaii.

Christopher Kolar, coauthor of *Student Inquiry and Research: Developing Students' Authentic Inquiry Skills*, is coordinator of research and evaluation at Illinois Mathematics and Science Academy in Aurora, Illinois.

Ardi Kveven, author of *Inquiry at the Ocean Research College Academy (ORCA)*, is executive director of Inquiry at the Ocean Research College Academy at Everett Community College in Everett, Washington.

Thomas R. Lord, coauthor of *Promoting Inquiry With Preservice Elementary Teachers Through a Science Content Course*, is a professor of biological sciences at Indiana University of Pennsylvania in Indiana, Pennsylvania.

Paula A. Magee, coauthor of *Developing a Relationship With Science Through Authentic Inquiry*, is a clinical assistant professor at Indiana University Purdue University at Indianapolis.

Michael P. Marlow, coauthor of *Enhancing the Inquiry Experience: Authentic Research in the Classroom*, is assistant professor of science education at University of Colorado, Denver in Denver, Colorado.

Kelly McConnaughay, coauthor of *Developing Inquiry Skills Along a Teacher Professional Continuum*, is a biology professor and associate dean of liberal arts and science at Bradley University in Peoria, Illinois.

Wayne Melville, coauthor of *Science as Inquiry at Sir Winston Churchill Collegiate and Vocational Institute*, is assistant professor at Lakehead University in Thunder Bay, Ontario, Canada.

Chris Myers, coauthor of *Science Is Not a Spectator Sport: Three Principles From 15 Years of Project Dragonfly,* is the director of Project Dragonfly at Miami University in Oxford, Ohio.

Lynne Born Myers, coauthor of *Science Is Not a Spectator Sport: Three Principles From 15 Years of Project Dragonfly*, is director of learning media for Project Dragonfly at Miami University in Oxford, Ohio.

Douglas Paulson, coauthor of *Inquiry Is Elementary: Differing Approaches to Inquiry Within Two Elementary Schools*, is a curriculum integrator at Monroe Elementary School in Brooklyn Park, Minnesota.

Patricia C. Paulson, coauthor of *Inquiry Is Elementary: Differing Approaches to Inquiry Within Two Elementary Schools*, is a professor of science education at Bethel University in St. Paul, Minnesota.

Joanna Philippoff, coauthor of *Ecological Monitoring Provides a Thematic Foundation for Student Inquiry*, is a graduate researcher at University of Hawaii–Manoa in Honolulu, Hawaii.

Pascale Creek Pinner, author of *Science Projects: Successful Inquiries in Eighth-Grade Science*, is 2008 Hawaii State Teacher of the Year, teacher in residence at Hilo Intermediate School in Hilo, Hawaii.

Rebecca Reichenbach, coauthor of *Learning Science With Inquiry in the Clark County School District*, is a teacher at Western High School in Las Vegas, Nevada.

Steve Ross, coauthor of *Natural Scientists: Children in Charge*, is a teacher at Hanahau`oli School in Honolulu, Hawaii.

Susan Roth, coauthor of *Inquiry Is Elementary: Differing Approaches to Inquiry Within Two Elementary Schools*, is a curriculum and technology integrator at Riverview Specialty School for Math & Environmental Science in Brooklyn Park, Minnesota.

Judith A. Scheppler, coauthor of *Student Inquiry and Research: Developing Students' Authentic Inquiry Skills*, is coordinator of student inquiry and research at Illinois Mathematics and Science Academy in Aurora, Illinois.

Diane L. Schmidt, coauthor of *From Wyoming to Florida, They Ask, "Why Wasn't I Taught This Way?"* is associate professor at Florida Gulf Coast University in Fort Myers, Florida.

Timothy Scott, coauthor of *Student Outreach Initiative: Sowing the Seeds of Future Success*, is associate dean of the College of Science at Texas A&M University in College Station, Texas.

Joseph I. Stepans, coauthor of *From Wyoming to Florida, They Ask, "Why Wasn't I Taught This Way?"* is professor emeritus of science and mathematics education at University of Wyoming in Laramie, Wyoming.

Susan Styer, coauthor of *Student Inquiry and Research: Developing Students' Authentic Inquiry Skills,* is a teacher at Illinois Mathematics and Science Academy in Aurora, Illinois.

Joseph Traina, coauthor of *Student Inquiry and Research: Developing Students' Authentic Inquiry Skills,* is a biology teacher at Illinois Mathematics and Science Academy in Aurora, Illinois.

Holly J. Travis, coauthor of *Promoting Inquiry With Preservice Elementary Teachers Through a Science Content Course,* is an assistant professor of biological sciences at Indiana University of Pennsylvania in Indiana, Pennsylvania.

Cheryl Waldman, coauthor of *Learning Science With Inquiry in the Clark County School District,* is a teacher at Palo Verde High School in Las Vegas, Nevada.

Linda Williams-Tuenge, coauthor of *Inquiry Is Elementary: Differing Approaches to Inquiry Within Two Elementary Schools,* is an elementary principal at Riverview Specialty School for Math & Environmental Science in Brooklyn Park, Minnesota.

Craig Wilson, coauthor of *Student Outreach Initiative: Sowing the Seeds of Future Success,* is director of the future scientists program at Texas A&M University's Center for Mathematics and Science Education (CMSE) in College Station, Texas.

Rose Wippler, coauthor of *Inquiry Is Elementary: Differing Approaches to Inquiry Within Two Elementary Schools,* is principal of Monroe Elementary School in Brooklyn Park, Minnesota.

Robert Wolffe, coauthor of *Developing Inquiry Skills Along a Teacher Professional Continuum,* is a professor at Bradley University in Peoria, Illinois.

Bonnie S. Wood, author of *Erasing Lecture-Laboratory Boundaries: An Inquiry-Based Course Design,* is a biology professor at University of Maine at Presque Isle in Presque Isle, Maine.

Chela Zabin, coauthor of *Ecological Monitoring Provides a Thematic Foundation for Student Inquiry,* is a research scientist at Smithsonian Environmental Research Center and University of California, Davis in Davis, California.

Index